P9-CDL-021

Pascal

Adam Dylewski

WHERE THE TAILOR WAS A POET...

Polish Jews and Their Culture

an illustrated guide

translated by
Wojciech Graniczewski and Ramon Shindler

Originally published in Polish as
"Śladami Żydów polskich"

Photographers
Anna Olej/Krzysztof Kobus and others

Translators
Wojciech Graniczewski and Ramon Shindler

Proofreaders
Robin Gill and Ann Cardwell

Practicalities (pp 275–310)
translated by Arkadiusz Belczyk

Consultant (Hebrew and Yiddish terms)
Eleonora Bergman

Specialist adviser
Joachim S. Russek

Graphic layout and cover design
Witold Siemaszkiewicz

Cover photographs
main photo: Bogdan Krężel
additional photos: Anna Olej/Krzysztof Kobus

Cartographers
Michał Kucharski, Wojciech Kowalski, Katarzyna Bischoff – Carta Blanca

Supervising editor
Agnieszka Hetnał

Project manager
Mariusz Dyduch

Edited and typeset by
Magdalena Pieczka, Ryszard Bryzek, ASTRA Kraków

First published, 2002 (Updated 2003)

The author and the publisher of this guidebook made every effort to ensure that its content is accurate. They cannot accept any responsibility for consequences arising from the use of information provided herein.

Onet.pl SA, Oddział Wydawnictwo Pascal
43-300 Bielsko-Biała
ul. Kazimierza Wielkiego 26
pascal@pascal.pl
www.pascal.pl

ISBN 83-7304-113-3

CONTENTS

During the seven centuries of the presence of Jews in Poland, an extraordinary Jewish culture was formed. It was made up of literature, theatre, music, sculpture, painting, press and architecture. It was created by all members of society: scholars, artists, politicians, merchants, craftsmen and ordinary people by the sheer wealth of their customs and traditions. This culture, in the broad sense of the word, has had a great impact upon Jews dispersed to the four corners of the world. I am sure that millions of these people feel some emotional ties with Poland.

In the seven centuries of the co-existence of these two nations on the same Polish land there have been many attempts to both erect and demolish the walls separating them from each other. The extermination of Jews planned by the Nazis and carried out in occupied Poland awoke in many people an overwhelming desire to destroy these walls once and for all.

The examples of attempts by many noble individuals, both Jews and Poles, to build peace between the two nations despite the difficulties, represent a commitment and a challenge for each new generation.

Among such initiatives I also include this practical guide to the culture of Polish Jews. It contains a vast amount of interesting information of great value to tourists. It is also an excellent source of knowledge about the history, culture and religion of Polish Jews. There is a growing interest in Jewish tradition and culture in Poland. This guidebook is a tiny bridge over the chasm, supported on the pillars of historical facts and presented in a simple and comprehensible way. May its interesting form and content help us not only to fill the gaps in our awareness of the history of Polish Jews, which is at the same time a part of our own history, but also to remove animosity. May it promote all attempts to make a lasting and just peace with those people living beneath the same sky. I am convinced that the desire to do exactly this inspired all the people involved in the creation of this most useful work. I encourage all those in the priesthood and those charged with the education of the younger generation of Poles to make use of this book in whatever way they can.

Archbishop Stanisław Gądecki
Chairmen of the Polish Episcopate
Council for Religious Dialogue

Gniezno, 25 March 2002

"There are no little Jewish towns in Poland any more". These words written by Antoni Słonimski, a Polish poet of Jewish descent, were ringing in my ears when in January 1985 for the first time in many years I came back to the country of my childhood. I was then a member of an Israeli parliamentary delegation which came to Poland to commemorate the 40th anniversary of the liberation of Auschwitz-Birkenau.

In a very peculiar way these words were still with me when I came here ten years later as the chairman of the Knesset, and yet again when after another six or seven years I found myself travelling the length and breadth of Poland, this time as Israeli ambassador.

There are hardly any Jews in Poland today, just a handful. The deserted synagogues, the wrecked cemeteries; these are but misty memories of the magnificence that used to be. Strolling along the streets of Warsaw, Łódź, Lublin, Białystok or Cracow, it is hard to believe that just 60 years ago these cities were wonderful, vibrant centres of Jewish culture.

Tykocin, Izbica, Szczebrzeszyn, Kock, Leżajsk, Lelów, Przysucha; all of these towns were once symbols of the Jewish presence in this land. As the poet wrote, "there are no more those little towns where the shoemaker was a poet, the watchmaker a philosopher and the barber a troubadour". When we travel in Poland today we can only imagine what a beautiful, colourful and fascinating world it must have been here before 1939, a world where Yiddish could be heard almost as often as Polish.

There are hardly any Jews in Poland any more, but still, in a paradoxical and almost obsessive way, they are present in the Polish collective consciousness. What other explanation can there be for the bewildering success of the books by Isaac Bashevis Singer and other Jewish authors? On my travels I meet people, mostly very young, thirsting for knowledge and persistently searching for traces of the Jewish presence in Poland, a presence which stretches back almost a thousand years. Above all, these are the people to whom this book by Adam Dylewski is addressed.

Prof. Shewach Weiss
Ambassador of Israel to Poland

S. Weiss

And the stones will cry out...

"Where the Tailor Was a Poet; Polish Jews and Their Culture" is a special guidebook. We can still meet some of the people with intimate knowledge of that lost world, who walked along that beaten track where only footprints now remain. The younger generation will have the opportunity to get to know about the special phenomenon of the co-existence in one land of two peoples of great ethnic and religious differences. They will also learn that in this period lasting for centuries much good was created in many different spheres. That world was destroyed not by a natural cataclysm but by people blind with hate. But hatred will never be victorious. This is why the Nazis were unsuccessful in their attempts to destroy the Jewish people and raze their material, spiritual and religious culture to the ground. Neither did Communism manage to make that destruction complete. Each remaining part of a wrecked synagogue, each lonely grave overgrown with weeds, all of these today bear testimony to the truth. "And the sun shone and was not ashamed!" These are the prophetic words of Chaim Nahman Bialik from his poem *In the City of Slaughter*, about the pogrom in Kishinev in 1903.

Although places and monuments are the main subject matter of this guidebook, it is also a rich source of information about the history of Jews in Poland in particular, as well as Judaism in general. It is not very often the case that such a difficult subject, dealing with man's cruelty towards his fellow man, has been approached with so much earnestness, respect and even reverence. Those who follow in the footsteps of this book will not only become aware of the mark left by Jews on the Polish landscape but also of the entire social, religious and Christian context in which Jewish culture in Poland developed. Although this process was not free of problems, it took place systematically over a period of many centuries, with Jewish culture becoming an integral part of Polish national heritage.

It is worth returning to these experiences from the common path of Poles of the Christian and Mosaic faiths. Not only is it a good history lesson but also an excellent example for a world embroiled today in so much conflict.

Bishop Tadeusz Pieronek
Rector of the Papal Theological Academy in Cracow

Cracow, 10 April 2002

Thank you so much for asking me to write a few words about the book *Where the Tailor Was a Poet; Polish Jews and Their Culture.*

I am very grateful to you for providing all of us with so much information concerning the glorious and rich past of Polish Jews and all that remains of it. Your guidebook is well presented and easy to read.

We cannot bring back what has been destroyed. At least through your work we have the chance to remember. Thank you.

Michael Schudrich
Rabbi
Jewish Communities of Warsaw and Łódź

Warsaw, 10 April 2002

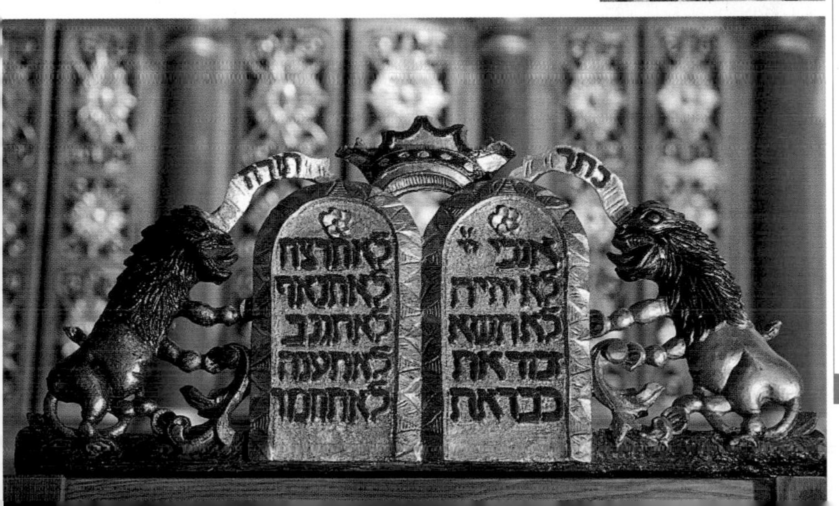

From the Author

Jews were part of the creation of a great commonwealth of nations and languages which for many centuries was referred to as the Republic of Poland. Apart from a wealth of literature, they left behind countless buildings and cemeteries which bear testimony to the glory of their history and culture. Despite decades of neglect, something else has remained, something that may be of even greater importance: our consciousness of the Jewish presence in Poland.

This guidebook describes from the point of view of a tourist the remnants of Poland's Jewish past as they are at the beginning of the 21st century. It was necessary to accept some limitations. Some of the less important monuments have been omitted, especially those which have fallen into decay or have been remodelled. I also excluded those which are situated in places not easily accessible to tourists or without appropriate infrastructure. Wrocław aside, I did not focus much on the monuments of Jewish culture which belong to the legacy of German Jews. Much attention has been given, however, to those places which have been restored and now house museums and exhibitions. Basing the guidebook on the remaining monuments of Jewish culture also limited discussion of the issues connected with the Holocaust and the fates of Jews during the Second World War, although I am completely aware of the importance of this subject. This book does not claim to be an authoritative piece of academic research, nor is it a voice in a learned discussion aimed at estimating the age of particular monuments. Due to limitations of space it does not deal in depth with each and every local Jewish community that once existed in Poland. Despite all the shortcomings typical of a pioneering work of this kind and dealing with such a delicate topic I hope that this book will help to rekindle the memory of the Jews of Poland.

I am deeply indebted to Jan Jagielski from the Jewish Historical Institute for his patient advice and for supplementing and verifying certain sections of the book. I would like to thank Leszek Hońdo for his remarks regarding the chapter on the Małopolska region. I am also grateful to the marvellous photographers Anna Olej and Krzysztof Kobus who, visiting those places described in the text, were the first to read and comment on this guidebook. Thanks also go to Ninel Kameraz-Kos and Yale Reisner for all their support and help. This book could not have been written without the gracious help of all those people who regularly devote time and energy to the care of the monuments of Jewish culture. I would like to take this opportunity to express my gratitude to Krzysztof Czyżewski and Wojciech Szroeder from Sejny, Mr Chruściel from Kraśnik, Maria Gajda and Jan Werenc from Przysucha, Monika Polit from Stryków, Józef Honig from Lublin, Krystyna Kiersnowska from Leżajsk, Anna Kuk and Tomasz Nowak from Bobowa, Maria Martyna from Brzesko, Roman Stasiak from Kock, Sara and Beniamin Sonnenschein from Oświęcim, Mirosław Szulewski from the Polish-Israeli Friendship Society in Lublin, Ewa Wroczyńska from the Museum in Tykocin, Grzegorz Zamoyski from Rzeszów, Jerzy Znojek from the District Museum of Pińczów, the employees of the "Wersal Podlaski" company in Białystok, the staff of the Art Exhibitions Bureau in Rzeszów, as well as the many other people who so kindly helped me while I was writing this book.

I dedicate this book to my friend
Jakub Duszyński,

Adam Dylewski

INTRODUCTION

A Culture Salvaged

Polin, the Jewish word for Poland, may be translated as "a good place to relax", (from the Hebrew: *po*, meaning "here", and *lanuach*, meaning "to take a rest"). Everyone in this shared homeland was affected by Poland's fate. Both Jews and Poles suffered great losses as the story of the relationship between these two nations was so brutally interrupted by Nazi genocide. The memory of this relationship still exists, however, in the form of culture and historic monuments.

One can observe today a renaissance in the Jewish way of life in Poland. Schools are being opened, *oholot* are being rebuilt, exhibitions of Judaica are being created and some synagogues are being brought back to life. More and more people are becoming interested in Jewish music and cuisine. One can only hope that the symbol of Polish-Jewish relations in the 21st century will be the crowd of thousands fascinated by Jewish culture, dancing in the street at the festival in the Cracow district of Kazimierz.

As they search for their own identity, many young Poles are attracted towards a culture which once thrived in their country.

THE HISTORY OF THE JEWISH PEOPLE

In its semi-legendary version, the history of the Jewish people is part of the cultural legacy of mankind. Written as it is in the pages of the Bible, it belongs to a common heritage with familiar names and a collective understanding of symbols such as paradise, Noah's Ark, and the burning bush.

Before 2000 Before Common Era – Jewish nomads wander across the land of Egypt and Mesopotamia.

2000–1400 B.C.E. – Conquest of the land of Canaan, which from around the 10th century B.C.E is known as Israel.

600 B.C.E. – Slavery in Babylon: settlement in Mesopotamia.

600–100 B.C.E. – Formation of the kingdom of Judea and other states; Jews are one of the peoples of the eastern coast of the Mediterranean Sea.

100 B.C.E. – Conquest of Palestine by the Romans.

70 Common Era – The emperor Titus conquers and destroys Jerusalem, stifling aspirations to independence in Judea and causing the exodus of its peoples.

Until 1000 C.E. Exiles settle in Asia Minor and North Africa, and then in Europe, in the territories spread from what later became Ruthenia to as far as the Iberian Peninsula.

800–900 C.E. – First Jews in Poland (referred to as Radhanites, the Jews from the towns on the River Rhone) trade with Slavonic tribes, mainly in fabrics, furs, silk and slaves. Proof of this may be the Polish word *Żyd* (Jew), coming from Old French and taken from Judeu, the Roman version of the geographical term Judea.

960–965 C.E. – The first instance on Polish soil of a Jew known by name is Ibrahim ibn Jacob

The Generations of Israel
A relic of nomadic times when Jews formed kin tribes is reflected in their traditional division into 12 generations: Asher, Benjamin, Dan, Gad, Issachar, Yosef, Yuda, Levi, Naftali, Ruben, Symeon, Zebulon.

The *Haggadah*, recounting the story of enslavement of Jews and the Exodus from Egypt, is read during the *Seder* meal (below: an illuminated 15th-century manuscript of the *Haggadah*).

In the first millennium the division of Jews into two groups, **Ashkenazim** and **Sephardim**, took place. The main differences between them are in the order of prayers, the approach to studying the *Talmud* and the pronunciation of Hebrew. The roots of *Ashkenazim* are in Germany. They adopted one of the dialects of this country as their own language, and this is how the Yiddish language came into being. *Sephardim*, or Spanish Jews, came from the diaspora which settled in the Iberian Peninsula and also from the countries of North Africa. Their culture (they communicated in Ladino) reached its zenith between the 11th to the 15th century only to die out when they were banished from Spain. *Sephardim* constituted no more than 10% of the total number of Jews in Europe, but they belonged to the elite, as they were well educated and spoke foreign languages. Figures such as Moses Maimonides, Yehuda ha-Levi, Salomon ibn Gabirol, and Benedict (Baruch) Spinoza all came from Sephardic families. Poland was one of the countries that took them in after they were driven out of the Iberian Peninsula. Together with *Sephardim* brought over to Zamość by Jan Zamoyski, came the Peretz family, the forefathers of Yitzchak Leibush Peretz.

Travelling Jews
by Wincenty Smokowski

(Abraham son of Jacob), a trader-diplomat from Tortosa in Spain. He is part of a delegation of the Khalif to Germany and Bohemia. In his diary he talks about the land of Mshko (referring to Mieszko I, Prince of Poland).

From 1100 C.E. – Large influx of Jews into Poland, mostly from Bohemia by way of Silesia.

1264 – Prince Bolesław the Pious signs the Statute of Kalisz setting legal foundations for the presence of Jews in the Wielkopolska region and subjecting them to the prince's judiciary, more lenient than the municipal and castellan courts. They are also given freedom to trade and to conduct their own financial operations. From then on they are able to travel throughout the whole country. Jews are referred to as "slaves of the treasury", as they are often collectors of taxes or customs duties. The penalty for killing one of these collectors is even more stringent than that for causing the death of a knight.

1350–1400 – The reign of King Casimir the Great, regarded in Jewish tradition as a period of great happiness. Numerous legends circulate about the love affair between the king and the beautiful Esther from Opoczno.

At the turn of the 13th century Jews worked in mints belonging to princes. This is when the bracteates, Polish silver coins with Hebrew inscriptions, were made.

Self-government was a major achievement of Polish Jewry. Its basic unit was the *kahal*. They were gathered in provinces called "lands", which sent their delegates to the central body of Jewish self-government called Vaad Arba Aratzot (The Diet of the Four Lands). From 1581 it was convened twice a year, usually in the towns of Lublin or Jarosław.

1400–1500 – Ethnic tension, riots, removal of Jews from certain areas, including, in 1495, their being driven out of Cracow and into Kazimierz.

1500–1600 – Jews slowly isolated from the rest of society: the granting of the *privilegia de non tolerandis Judaeis*, a law forbidding Jews to settle in some 20 towns or more. An equal and opposite law is also passed and the majority of large Jewish communities, living in their own clearly defined quarter surrounded by a wall, are given the *privilegia de non tolerandis Christianis*. Two examples of this are the Kazimierz district in Cracow (1568) and Poznań (1633). Some of these laws forbidding settlement remain in force until the 1860s.

1559 – King Sigismund August allows the *kahalim* complete freedom to organise themselves internally and to choose their own rabbi.

1581 Ultimate form of Jewish self-government as King Stefan Batory grants Jews autonomy on a scale unprecedented in Europe.

1648–1658 – Period in which several pogroms take place and manifestation of particularly bloody anti-Jewish sentiment in Ukraine. Cossacks consider Jews to be tools in the hands of Polish lords. Thousands of Jews are killed. Many decide to emigrate.

End of 18th century – The number of Jews living in the Republic of Poland reaches 900,000 (10% of the entire population).

1794 – The Kościuszko Insurrection. Berek Joselewicz from Kretynga in Lithuania, the most famous Jewish fighter for freedom of Poland, becomes the commander of the Jewish legion, and later of the entire cavalry. He fights until 1809, before finally succumbing at the Battle of Kock.

Turn of 19th century – The emergence of two great intellectual movements within Jewish society: the *Haskalah* and Chasidism.

1830–1831 – Jews participate in the November Uprising against Russia. In Warsaw, from February 1831, the units of the Orthodox Jews' City Guard stand out from the others by retaining their traditional beards. They achieve fame by their defence of the Czerniakowski and Mokatowski tollgates.

At the time of decline of the Commonwealth of Poland Jews worked in 50 different handicraft professions and in trade. They were also active in medicine, chemistry, money lending and tavern leasing. Contacts between Jewish communities from various towns proved to be helpful in international commerce. They created a very competitive pan European network of trade connections. Very few Jews, however, held lucrative positions, the majority leading very modest lives as travelling tailors, shoemakers, tinkers and barber-surgeons. There were also those suffering from real poverty, often crippled or ill, who were reduced to begging (above: *A Jew Mending a Carpet* by Wacław Kościuszko).

THE HASKALAH AND CHASIDISM

The *Haskalah* (enlightenment) was a cultural movement initiated by Berlin Jews from the followers of Moses Mendelssohn. The supporters of the *Haskalah*, called *Maskilim* (the enlightened), stipulated equality of rights, secular education and changes in the accepted way of life (such as the abandoning of traditional costumes and the Yiddish language). They also proposed that Jews should broaden the scope of their professional skills and become involved in new activities, such as agriculture. *Chasidim*, sometimes referred to as ultra-Orthodox Jews, took the opposite standpoint. Apart from its religious character, this mystical movement from the Podole region also aimed at preserving the traditional customs, language and attire. Some Chasidic groups, among them the followers of the Halberstam dynasty of Nowy Sącz, implemented a radical social programme which prohibited Jewish children from attending Polish schools and learning the Polish language.

The newspapers report that the "holy spark of citizenship" has suddenly appeared in Jewish souls.
1862 – Jews are granted equal rights within the Kingdom of Poland as one of Wielopolski's reforms. Following this, however, anti-Jewish legislation is introduced in Russia, restricting, among other things, the areas in which Jews may live and the professions they may join. These anti-Semitic bans are not lifted in Russia until 1917.
1863 – Jews take part in the January Uprising. The Rabbi of Warsaw, Dov-Ber Meisels, is imprisoned in the Citadel. Henryk Wohl and Leopold Kronenberg become financial advisors to the National Government.
1867 – Equal rights are granted in those parts annexed by Austria.
1869 – Equal rights are granted in those parts annexed by Prussia.
1881 – *Litvaks*, Jews from the former Grand Duchy of Lithuania, which after annexation became part of the Russian Empire, are forced to move to the Kingdom of Poland under the May laws introduced after the assassination of Alexander II in 1881. They are greeted with a hostile reception from Poles

The patriotic-religious demonstration of 1861 was bloodily suppressed. Among the victims there were also Jews, including a student Michael Landy (below: *Funeral of Five Victims in Warsaw in 1861* by Aleksander Lesser).

and Polish Jews; the former fearing changes in relations between the two nations, the latter worrying about economic competition. *Litvaks* find themselves isolated. They have their own synagogues, schools and press. Polish Jews consider them to be inaccessible and conceited. Mixed marriages are a rarity and the *Litvaks* waste no time in moving to America or Palestine.

Although Jews were not notorious for breaking the law, criminal circles favoured some Yiddish or even Hebrew expressions, which are part of criminal jargon, even in Polish, to this very day: *melina* (shelter), *trefny* (unclean), *ferayna* (company), *moyra* (respect) and *dintoyra* (revenge), the last one deriving from *din Tora* – the religious court of law.

"In front of Tony all felt *moyra*
But there was one set in his ways
So he soon learnt about *dintoyra*
And he was finished off in days"

From a song *A Party in Gnojna Street*

End of 19th century – Mass emigration caused by state sponsored anti-Semitism in the part annexed by Russia and abject poverty in the Austrian part. In the final decade of the century a quarter of a million Jews leave the Kingdom of Poland, with an equal number departing from Galicia between 1890 and 1910. Initially, their principal destination is the United States. Later more of them make their way to Palestine.

After 1896 – The emergence of Zionism, a political and cultural programme based on Theodore Hertzl's thesis entitled *The Jewish State*, in which he postulates the creation of a Jewish homeland. In 1897 the first world congress takes place under the auspices of the World Zionist Organisation. Between 1910 and 1920, Zionists resolve once and for all to return to Palestine. The Po'alei Zion is the last Jewish political party in Poland, finally being dissolved on 1 February 1950.

1917 –1918 – Poland regains independence. Many Jews prove their patriotism and within the ranks of the Legions at least 80 of them are killed. 190 are awarded the Cross and Medal of Independence.

1919 – Along with all other citizens Jews are given equal political rights. The new state signs a treaty regarding minority groups, ensuring respect for their customs and religious practices as well as guaranteeing freedom and equality in everyday life. Despite this, Jews do not hold high office. Jewish Members of Parliament are sometimes seen by Poles as anti-state elements.

1934 – The treaty guaranteeing minority rights is suspended. Regulations striking at the very heart of Jewish autonomy become commonplace, including, in 1936, the law restricting ritual slaughter. Openly anti-Semitic acts follow, among them the segregation of Jews in lectures at university and the principle of *numerus clausus* in the law profession.

1939 – At the outbreak of war the Jewish population of Poland totals 3,460,000. Most Jews live in the towns and cities of the

At the turn of the 20th century the Jewish press was regularly published in Yiddish, Polish and Hebrew.

The anti-socialist and anti-Zionist right-wing **Agudas Isroel** (The Israel Union) was the dominant Jewish Party in the pre-war Polish Republic. Established in 1912 in Katowice as a representation of the Orthodoxy, it followed a programme based on religious guidelines. It considered Jews as a religious and not national community. Orthodox Jews dominated the rabbinical councils and had many representatives in the Polish parliament and senate. Tzaddik Alter from Góra Kalwaria was one of their leaders. Agudas Isroel operated in Poland until 1949.

The socialist **Bund** was the main Jewish party on the left of the political scene, its full name being Algemayner Yidisher Arbeter Bund in Lite, Rusland un Poyln (The General Jewish Workers Union in Lithuania, Russia and Poland). It was established in 1897 in Vilna. Initially it was linked with the Russian Socialist Revolutionary Party. In 1919 it became a separate legal political assembly in Poland and the Baltic states. The leaders of the Bund maintained that Jews were a separate nation living in a diaspora and possessing their own culture. They differed from Agudas Isroel in their attitude towards religion and from the Zionists in their questioning attitude towards the programme of migration to Palestine. The Bund had the largest number of Jewish supporters among the left-wing parties and strong representations in religious communities, but before the Second World War it was not represented in the parliament by its own members. There were many other organisations affiliated to the Bund such as: Cukunft for youth, Skif for the children, JAF (Jewish Working Woman) and Morgenshtern, a sporting association. The Bund resumed its activity after the war. It had one representative in parliament, winning a seat in 1947 in coalition with the Polish Socialist Party. It was formally dissolved in Poland on 16th January 1949. It still exists abroad through the activities of institutions such as the Medem Library in Paris and the central archive office in New York City.

central and southern parts of the country or in the borderlands. As many as 42.4% make their living as craftsmen; the majority of them tailors. Some 36.6% are involved in commerce, 4.5% in transport, 4.3% in agriculture and horticulture, over 2% in health care, with about the same number in education. About 1.8% are in free professions, such as law.

Details of the Holocaust during the Second World War may be obtained from many reliable sources. Therefore this introduction is limited to dates and events only.

1939–1942 – The so-called "policy of annihilation", involving *Einsatzgruppen* supporting the operations of Wehrmacht.

3 September 1941 – In the camp at Auschwitz, the first use of a gas chamber as an instrument of death.

December 1941 – Creation of the first death camp in Chełmno on the River Ner.

20 January 1942 – The Wannsee conference ending with the decision to pursue a policy of genocide, referred to as *Endloesung* ("the final solution to the Jewish problem").

1942–1943 – The *Aktion Reinhard* involving the confiscation of property and funds belonging to Jews and mass murder. To this end the SS open special accounts at the Reichsbank.

1942–1945 – The continent of Europe witnesses the death of six million Jews. In Poland approximately 90% of the Jewish community is murdered.

In October 1939 the Nazis began imprisoning Jews in ghettoes.

19 April 1943 – The Warsaw Ghetto Uprising. A group of insurgents fight among the rubble until 16 May, with some resisting until October 1943.

October 1944 – The CKŻP (The Central Committee of Jews in Poland) representing the Jewish minority is formed in the territories liberated by the Soviet Army.

1945 – The March of Death, in which concentration camp prisoners are herded into the depths of the Third Reich.

1945–1949 – The final years in the existence of a closely-knit Jewish community in Poland. Spontaneously created Jewish committees take responsibility for organisational matters in a similar fashion to the pre-war religious communities. In 1947 there are 80 congregations, 38 synagogues presided over by 25 rabbis, 36 religious schools and, until 1949, even the *Netzach Isroel Yeshivah* in Łódź.

1945–1968 – Jewish settlement in Lower Silesia. For a few years after the war and with the approval of the CKŻP, attempts are made to establish a culturally autonomous Jewish enclave. 30 separate communities are created (including those in Dzierżoniów, Bielawa, Wałbrzych, Kłodzko, Legnica, Świdnica, and Nowa Ruda). 60,000 people repatriated from Soviet territory live here. The Polish State, however, does not accept the existence of the enclave. Every time the country's borders are opened, Jews leave for Palestine and the West. Jewish settlement in Lower Silesia comes to an end in 1968, the only remaining evidence of it being the religious community in Legnica and a number of branches of the community in Wrocław.

1947–1950 – Mass emigration.

After 1950 – The totalitarian system places restrictions on the religious activities of Jews, but the ZRWM (the Religious Union of Members of the Mosaic Faith) is allowed to exist and in 1956 assumes a representative function, only to lose it after the events of 1968. There is also the secular TSKŻ (the Social-Cultural Association of the Jews in Poland), which practically disappears during the period of Stalinist repression. From 1956 to 1968 the association stages a revival but soon withers again. Today, the TSKŻ publishes a weekly newspaper in Yiddish and Polish entitled "Dos Yidishe

Mordechai Anielewicz (1919–1943) was one of the leaders of the Jewish Combat Organisation.

Janusz Korczak (1878–1942), whose real name was Henryk Goldszmit, is known world-wide. The old doctor died in the death camp at Treblinka together with children from his orphanage.

The number of Jews in Poland

14th c	1,000
16th c	20,000
17th c	100,000
ca 1750	200,000
1800	900,000
1900	2.5 million
1921	2.8 million
1939	3.46 million
1946	192,000
1956	15,000
1968	6,000
2000	3,500

Vort – Słowo Żydowskie" (The Yiddish Word). The younger generation starts to show more and more interest in the activities of religious Jewish communities.

8 March 1968 – A student rally takes place at Warsaw University. As a result of internal party wrangling, people of Jewish origin are accused of inciting anti-state activity. A thorough purge based on race and nationality is begun. It even affects Poles married to Jews. Deprived of the wherewithal to live, many Jews are forced to emigrate, among them the film director Aleksander Ford, who made "Krzyżacy" (The Teutonic Knights) based on the book by Henryk Sienkiewicz. Several writers are not allowed to publish. A number of university faculties allegedly dominated by Jews are dissolved, including the Department of Philosophy in Warsaw. In all, some 30,000 people are made to leave the country in what was known as the "March Emigration".

1970–1980 – Jewish life in Poland almost non-existent.

1983 – The synagogue in Warsaw is renovated.

1989 – After an absence of many years, a rabbi is once again appointed in Poland.

1997 – The attitude of the Polish state towards the Jewish community returns to normal. In parliament a bill is passed recognising the Union of Jewish Communities as the representative of members of the Mosaic faith. In keeping with centuries-old tradition the community is the fundamental unit of Jewish life and, apart from its religious duties, it is also responsible for education and charitable activities. Dialogue begins on the rather complicated subject of the history of Polish-Jewish relations, the most serious example being the controversy surrounding *Neighbours: the Destruction of the Jewish Community in Jedwabne*, a book by Jan Tomasz Gross, published in 2001.

Young people have once again started attending synagogues (below: celebrations of the festival of *Purim* in Warsaw).

RELIGION

Jews are followers of Judaism, also known as Mosaism or the Mosaic faith. The principal feature of the Jewish religion is a belief in a single God. The main figures from the very beginning of Judaism are the patriarchs Abraham, Isaac and Jacob, and Moses leading the Chosen People to the Promised Land. The fundamental text is *Tanach*, Hebrew for the Bible, consisting of the Five Books of Moses (in Hebrew known as *Torah*) the 21 books of prophecies

Jewish Communities in Poland (as of 2001)

The Union of Jewish Religious Communities
Warsaw, ul. Twarda 6, ☎ +22 6200667
Gdańsk branch, ul. Partyzantów 7
Poznań branch, ul. Kosińskiego 28
The Bielsko-Biała Jewish Community, ul. Trzeciego Maja 7
The Katowice Jewish Community, ul. Młyńska 13
Bytom branch, ul. Piekarska 56
Częstochowa branch (correspondence to be addressed to the Katowice community)
The Cracow Jewish Community, ul. Skawińska 2
The Legnica Jewish Community, ul. Chojnowska 12
The Łódź Jewish Community, ul. Pomorska 28
The Szczecin Jewish Community, ul. Niemcewicza 2
The Warsaw Jewish Community, ul. Twarda 6
Lublin branch, ul. Lubartowska 84
The Wrocław Jewish Community, ul. Włodkowica 2
Dzierżoniów branch, ul. Krasickiego 24
Wałbrzych branch, ul. Mickiewicza 18
Żary branch, ul. Zaułek Klasztorny 3

(*Neviim* in Hebrew) and the 13 books of scriptures (*Ketuvim*). It differs from the version used by Christians in the absence of the books of Tobias, Judith, Baruch as well as the Book of Wisdom and both Books of the Maccabees and the Wisdom of Sirach. The Bible is accompanied by a commentary, the *Talmud*, which is divided into the *Mishnah* or main normative text and the *Gemara* or printed commentary on the *Mishnah*. The *Talmud* comes in two versions: *Talmud Jerushalmi* (the Jerusalem Talmud) from the fourth century and *Talmud Bavli* (the Babylonian Talmud) from the sixth century. The religious rules and regulations contained in the *Talmud* are collectively referred to as *Halacha*, while the parables and legends are called *Agada*.

Of great significance are two treatises based on the *Talmud*. One is *More Nebuchim* (A Guide for Wanderers, 1192) by Moses Maimonides, also known as RaMBaM, 1135–1204), the other is the *Shulchan Aruch* (A Set Table, from the 16th century), a ritual code drawn up in Palestine by Joseph Caro. An oral tradition also exists, usually in story form and fulfilling a similar function to the Christian Apochrypha. It remains outside the basic books of the law but is, nevertheless, the source of many beliefs, folk demonology among them.

Daily prayers take place in the morning, afternoon and evening, and Sabbath prayers in the morning. On holidays prayer times are dictated by tradition, for example on *Yom Kippur* they last from morning until dusk. Friday evening and the eve of festivals are

The main duty of a follower of Judaism is prayer to be offered on weekdays, on *Shabbat* and during other religious festivals (below: *A Praying Jew* by Szymon Buchbinder, the late 19th century).

Jews with the Torah by Fryderyk (Fryc) Kleinman (1933).

particularly important for prayer. Also on awakening a Jew should say *Mode ani*, a thanksgiving for the return of the soul, as it is thought that while one is asleep the soul is with God. Each day an adult believer should participate in three services: *Shacharit* in the morning, *Mincha* in the afternoon and *Maariv* in the evening. Each of these services has its own special set of prayers, among them being *Shema*, a profession of faith, *Kaddish*, the prayer for the departed, and *Shmone esre*, the eighteen blessings. Other important parts of the liturgy include *Aliyah*, the reading of the *Torah* by members of the community, and *Haftorah*, readings from the book of the prophets.

The head and shoulders are covered with a *tallit*, symbolising a fear of God and worn in the synagogue traditionally by men only (among *Chasidim* exclusively by married men). *Tefillin* (phylacteries) are two small boxes containing the *Shema* as well as extracts from the *Torah*, written on tiny rolls of parchment. *Tefillin* are bound by leather straps to the forehead and the left forearm to symbolise the giving of heart and mind to God. Constant bowing while praying is a familiar custom and the reason for this, as you can see for yourself, is that it helps concentration.

Jewish attire worn at the time of prayer: *tallit*, a white cotton (or woolen) shawl adorned with *tzitzith* (fringes) at the corners.

The Kabbalah

The *Kabbalah* is closely linked to the Jewish religion, although it is not canonical in character. Supernatural signs are sought not only in texts but also in the meaning of texts and even in the symbolic interpretations which can be ascribed to individual letters. In the Middle Ages, *Kabbalah* developed as a reaction to the teachings of Maimonides.

The exploration of *Kabbalah* is meant to be a sequence of revelations, one after another. A kabbalist of the highest level of cognition is known as *Baal Shem* or lord of the name, meaning the one who knows the secret names of the Almighty. The Polish *Baal Shem* was the 16th century figure Elijahu of Chelm, who was probably the creator of the *golem*. The fundamental work of the *Kabbalah* is *Sefer Yetzirah* (the Book of Creation), presumed to have been written by the ancient Judaic sage Shimon bar Yochai. This book appeared

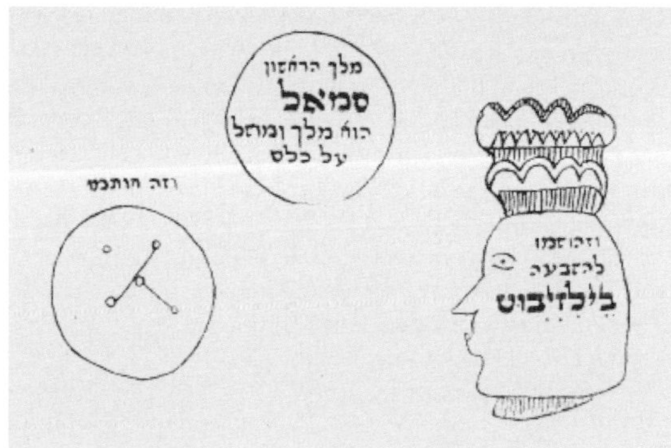

Contemplation of the essence and role of the divine being in relation to the creation and existence of the world is the subject matter of the *Kabbalah*. A combination of the letters of the Lord's name is the source of this mystical science preoccupied with exorcisms, fasts, repentance and ascetic practices.

in a new version in the 13th century, edited by Moses ben-Shem Tov of Leon. It was also given a new title *Sefer ha-Zohar* (the Book of Splendour). *Zohar* was never on the curriculum in Jewish religious schools. It was passed down from generation to generation as a secret form of study. *Kabbalah* made its way to Poland in the 16th century along with the disciples of Izaak Luria Ashkenazi, who was also called *Ari ha-kodesh* (the Holy Lion).

Sabbataism and Frankism

The Polish Republic was a place rich in spiritual life, blossoming with mystic and messianic movements, which in turn influenced the spirituality of the Jews. One of the very first of these was Sabbataism, originating in the Turkish lands. Sabbatai Tzvi never set foot in Poland but his teachings gained recognition here. The Sabbataists claimed that the start of history was heralded by the creation of the world, but, at the same time a fundamental division occurred: *sefirot* (singular: *sefira*), male emanations of God, including *Binah* or intelligence, *Hesed* or mercy, *Gevurah* or punishment, *Tiferet* or beauty, all of which kept the world in existence somewhere between mercy and punishment, separated from *Shechina* (the female element of divinity). *Shechina* was imprisoned in the material world in the shell of evil. The whole object of existence is the continual joining of *Shechina* with *sefira tiferet*. The role of the Jews is to extract from the material prison the greatest number of elements of *Shechina*, in other words divine sparks. This may be achieved thanks to a life without sin. However, those leading a spotless existence do not have access to the most sinful spheres and so *Shechina* remains imprisoned. This is why chosen individuals, such as the *Messiah*, have to reach the very bottom of sin in order to free *Shechina* and redeem the world. From this point of view the conversion of Sabbatai Tzvi to Islam was the act which liberated *Shechina*.

The mystic Sabbatai Tzvi (1626–1676) lived in the Ottoman Empire and was considered by many to be the Messiah. Alarmed by the scale of the phenomenon, the Turkish authorities forced him to accept Islam and exiled him to Albania. This act only reinforced the myth and the movement around it.

Jacob Frank, a kabbalist from the Podole Region, often referred to the teachings of Sabbatai Tzvi.

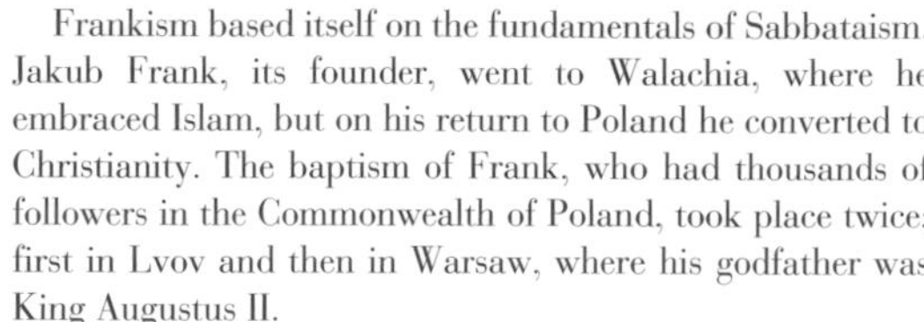

Frankism based itself on the fundamentals of Sabbataism. Jakub Frank, its founder, went to Walachia, where he embraced Islam, but on his return to Poland he converted to Christianity. The baptism of Frank, who had thousands of followers in the Commonwealth of Poland, took place twice; first in Lvov and then in Warsaw, where his godfather was King Augustus II.

Frankism has a crucial significance for social conscience, as it is possible to say that this movement set the process of assimilation in motion, allowing thousands of Jews to become instantly polonised.

Chasidism

To a large extent, this quite exceptional movement shaped the entire face of Polish Jewry. It was created by Izrael ben Eliezer of Międzybóż in Podole, who was born in Okopy św. Trójcy, and lived from 1700 until 1760. He was known as the *Baal Shem Tov* (Lord of the Good Name). He began his work at the age of 36, travelling around the borderland towns, where he performed faith healing, exorcisms and indulged in prayer. In the words of Majer Bałaban, "His most impassioned prayer was capable of moving a rock and setting the forest alight. With this prayer he could move the heavens and hold back sentences passed by God". The movement which formed around Izrael ben Eliezer was called Chasidism, from the Hebrew *Chasidim* meaning "the pious ones".

There is no one single doctrine which identifies Chasidism. Each *tzaddik* held his own views and this sometimes led to heated disputes. It is, however, possible to talk of shared characteristics of *Chasidim*: the use of ecstatic practices, emphasis on the role of enthusiasm during prayer, merging of the secular and religious worlds and the conviction of the existence here on Earth of *nitzotzot* (holy sparks) which piety releases from the "shell of evil", so that they can return to their divine source.

Tzaddikism was created by Elimelech from Leżajsk, who preached that the person who adores God most of all becomes *tzaddik* (the righteous one) and, thanks to spiritual virtues, may become a link between the Lord and those who believe in Him (below: the pilgrims in the *ohel* of *tzaddik* Elimelech from Leżajsk).

Tzaddikim most often settled in small towns. With their disciples gathered around them, they dispensed advice and in some cases their homes would become a centre for pilgrimages. They attached great importance to songs and so the concept of tzaddikism accompanied the development of Jewish folk music played by what are known as *klezmer* bands. The dignity of the *tzaddik* was often inherited. Dynasties were conducive to

THE MOST IMPORTANT CHASIDIC DYNASTIES AND GROUPS

Dynasty	Historical centres (countries outside Poland in accordance with contemporary borders)	Present places of residence
Aleksander	Aleksandrów Łódzki, Łódź	Israel, USA, London, Antwerp
Amshinov (continuation of Wurke)	Warka, Mszczonów, Otwock	Israel, USA (New York)
Belz	Bełz (Ukraine)	Israel
Biala (continuation of Paszische)	Przysucha, Biała Rawska	Israel, Switzerland, Lucerne
Dobow	Bobowa	Israel, London, Antwerp, Toronto, Montreal
Dynow	Dynów, Błażowa – Blużew dynasty Bukowsko – Bukowsk dynasty, Munkacz Munkaczevo (Ukraine)	Israel, USA (New York)
Ger	Góra Kalwaria	Israel, USA
Kaliw	Nagykálló (Hungary), Rozdol (Ukraine)	Israel, USA
Karlin-Stolin	Karolin (suburb of Pinsk, Belarus), Stolin (Belarus)	Israel, USA
Kock	Kock	united with the group Góra Kalwaria
Kosów-Wyżnic	Vyzhnitsia in Bukovina (Ukraine), Oradea (Romania)	Israel, Usa (Monsoy, New York)
Koznic	Kozienice	Israel, South America
Lelow	Lelów	USA, Israel
Lubawicz	Lubavichi and Lida (both in Belarus)	USA, ISrael
Modżyc	Dęblin, Kazimierz Dolny, Zwoleń	Israel
Ożarów	Ożarów	Israel
Radomsk	Radomsko	united with the group from Góra Kalwaria
Rożyn-Sadagora	Rozhan, Sadagora (suburb of Chernivtsi) Boyany, Chortkov, Husiatyn (all in Ukraine) and Przemyśl (Poland)	Israel
Satmar	Satu Mare (Romania) – Satmer dynasty Sighetu Marmasiei (Romania) – Siget dynasty	Israel, USA
Slonim	Slonim, Belarus	Israel, USA (Detroit)
Wasluj	Vaslui, Bukarest (Romania)	Israel
The Bratslav group without a dynasty	Bratslav (Ukraine)	Israel

permanence and also enabled the movement to develop. The places where *Chasidim* gave thanks to God on a daily basis were known as *shtiblech* (rooms). They also used very simple and modest houses of prayer called *kloyzn*.

Chasidim, at that time, associated themselves almost exclusively with the lands of the Commonwealth of Poland. The Chasidic movement in the Podole region was the driving force behind the establishment of centres in Bukowina (Sadagora near Chernivtsi, now in Ukraine), Hungary, or in present day Romania (Satu Mare or Satmar). The only *Chasidim* to be found in Western Europe, where the *Haskalah* reform movement was predominant, were those who emigrated.

THE JEWISH QUARTER

Jews generally lived together in one street or created their own quarter. This was determined not only by the need to have constant access to *kosher* products or places of worship, but also by decrees passed by the administrative authorities. In each district one could always find the following: a synagogue, the seat of the *kahal* (usually next to the synagogue), a *cheder* (school), a *mikvah* (ritual bath), a slaughter-house, a hospital, a wedding hall and a cemetery.

The houses were tightly packed together and any gaps in a building were quickly filled with annexes and other additions as, despite growth in the population, the authorities did not extend the boundaries of the Jewish districts. You can see a typical compact structure of this kind around the Market Square II in Łęczna.

From the 16th century the term ghetto was used to describe any district or town officially divided up for Jews to inhabit. Here they governed using their own laws, their own authorities and having a separate cultural identity, which was sometimes reinforced by the *privilegia de non tolerandis Christianis*. In Poland the only ghetto was in fact Kazimierz, just outside Cracow. Generally speaking, Jews and Poles existed together in a sort of symbiosis, even to the point of living in houses on the same market square. However, for

A *mezzuzah* is a small oblong case containing a parchment scroll on which the words of *Shema*, one of the most important Jewish prayers, are written. It is a characteristic marker of a Jewish home, placed on the right side of the doorframe. A person entering the house should touch the *mezzuzah* with two fingers, and then raise them to his lips. Indentations where *mezzuzot* once were can still be seen on the walls of houses in eastern and southern parts of Poland.

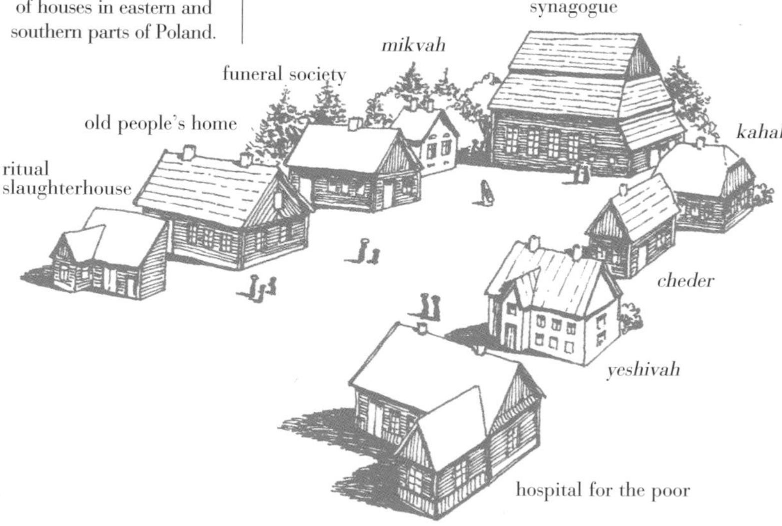

Streets brimmed with everyday life (above: the Jewish street in Mława, photo from 1916).

various economic reasons, the *shtetl* (small local Jewish town) peculiar to Poland, began to take shape. Here everyone followed their own customs. If someone wished to settle or set up their own workshop, they first had to meet with everyone's approval. After the Holocaust these strong regional communities were reborn outside Poland in what are known as *Landsmanshaftn*. The probable swansong of these associations is the creation of aproximately 500 *Yizker bicher* (Memorial Books), perpetuating for posterity the life of each *shtetl*.

The Synagogue

The synagogue is the place for religious worship and for the interpretation of teachings (a house of learning, in Yiddish *shul*).

In everyday Polish, until around the 17th century, the dual concepts of 'synagogue' and 'house of prayer' were synonymous. From then on, the term 'synagogue' was sometimes reserved for large, richly decorated buildings. The expression 'house of prayer' was used to describe a more modest place of worship, sometimes merely occupying one room or floor of an ordinary house, a good example of which is the Chevrat Nossim synagogue in Lublin, still standing to this day. After the Second World War the distinction between the two concepts became somewhat blurred. One also comes across the expression *beit ha-midrash* or *beit midrash*, which alternates in meaning with those mentioned above or is reserved for houses of study where the *Talmud* is studied and discussed all day long.

The Reform synagogue served the followers of the *Haskalah*. It was referred to as *Tempel* (below: The Tempel Synagogue in Cracow.

The *tas* is a richly adorned shield hung on the *Torah*.

Plan of a Synagogue
Based on the Remuh Synagogue in Cracow

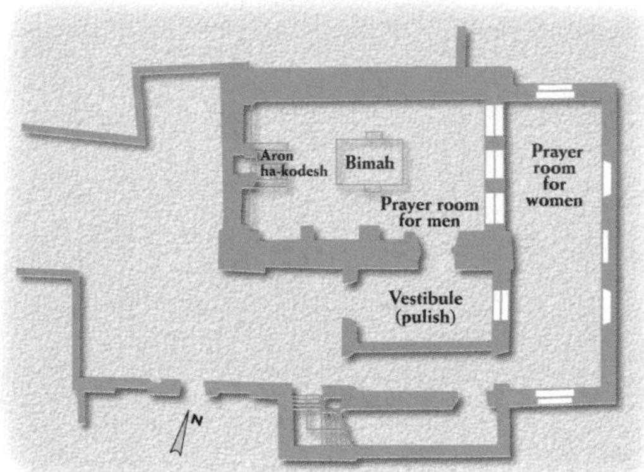

The most important place in the synagogue is the *aron ha-kodesh* (Holy Ark) and it is here that the *Torah* scrolls are kept. You can see examples of a magnificent *aron ha-kodesh* in the synagogues in Tykocin, Włodawa and Bobowa. The ark is often in the shape of a cabinet, positioned against a wall facing Jerusalem (in Poland the eastern wall). Characteristic features of the ark are the following: *parochet* (an embroidered curtain covering the doors), *kaporet* (the upper part of the curtain) and *ner tamid* (the eternal light in the form of a lamp). In the recess there are the parchment scrolls of the *Torah* wrapped in *meil* (a cover, literally: a mantle). In the Askhenazic tradition it is all finished off with a silver adornment shaped like a crown and called *Keter Torah* (the crown of the *Torah*). One may not touch the *Torah* scrolls directly when reading from them and so, for this purpose, one uses a *yad* (decorative pointer) the end of which is usually in the shape of a tiny hand.

The most immediately visible part of the synagogue is the *bimah*, a raised platform with a pulpit, usually situated in the middle. It is from here that blessings are said and texts from the *Torah* read. To enter the synagogue one goes through a spacious vestibule known as a *pulish*.

The *menorah* is one of the best known symbols of Judaism. Its flame signifies unity with the Lord.

Synagogue services are conducted by a rabbi, who also is responsible for the correct order of prayers on any given day. On display in the museum in Tykocin you will find a rabbi's room as well as all those things without which he could not perform his duties. The *chazan* (cantor), whose presence emphasises the significance of music in Judaism, sings certain parts of the service. In poorer communities in Poland the cantor very often had other responsibilities, such as

The Books of the Torah

The five books of the *Torah* bear the names of their first words:
Be-reshit – "In the beginning" – The Book of Genesis
Shemot – "These are the names" – The Book of Exodus
Va-ikra – "The Lord called" – The Book of Leviticus
Be-midbar – "In the wilderness" – The Book of Numbers
Dvarim – "These are the words" – The Book of Deuteronomy

that of butcher. Community funds and the fees of synagogue members were used to support the positions of rabbi and cantor, who were required to wear a special outfit called a *mantel*.

Ordinary members would also take part in the running of the service. They would be called up to say a blessing over the *Torah* or read from it. To be granted such an honour it was sometimes necessary to pledge a sum of money in aid of the synagogue, the highest bidder being chosen. The following members were exempt from bidding: the groom a week before his wedding, the father of a new-born child, a boy just before his *bar mitzvah* or a person saying *Kaddish* on the anniversary of the death of a loved one. If the highest bid was entered by several members, then lots would be drawn to decide the winner.

Another important figure was the *shammus* (caretaker of the synagogue). It was his job to summon the faithful to prayer, which he did by banging on the shutters with a small wooden hammer. He also made sure that shops closed at the appointed hour. The *sofer* (calligrapher) was responsible for transcribing the texts of the *Torah* and those to be put inside *mezzuzim*, as well as writing out marriage certificates and other similar documents. This post was only ever held by men.

Torah scrolls are wound onto two wooden reels and in the Sephardic culture finished off with adornments in the shape of pomegranates or *rimmonim* (bells).

On the eastern wall of a synagogue, a *mizrach* (decorated tablet), often bearing an image of Jerusalem or the Temple, is placed to indicate the direction of prayer.

Most Jewish communities contained three social strata: *ashirim* (the wealthy), *beynonim* (the middle class) and *aniyim* (the poor). The richest members had the greatest influence upon how the *kahal* was run, but also paid the highest taxes. The Talmudists were not part of this structure and were often exempted from both *hazakah* and the poll tax. The characters who stood out were the beggars. While a *shnorer* was a "stationary" beggar, a *rayzer* would wander from town to town. People held them in respect, for, according to folk tales, the Prophet Elijah whose arrival would precede that of the Messiah was to come in the guise of a beggar (above: *A Jewish Water-Carrier in the Market Square in Kazimierz Dolny* by Adolf Behrman).

A service may take place anywhere and not just in a synagogue, but only when there is a *minyan* (number), that is to say ten adult males who have been *bar mitzvah*.

The Jewish Community

The basic unit charged with organisational matters was the *kahal* or community council. Its scope was so wide that some writers even refer to it as "the control centre of the Jewish way of life". The *kahal* was similar in some respects to the Christian parish, but had much greater powers in the areas of taxation, law, schooling, charitable aid and welfare care. It arranged funerals, maintained cemeteries, schools and ritual baths, as well as supervising the slaughter of animals and the sale of meat. In closed Jewish districts it also kept up a police force and a health service.

A traditional *kahal* house was characteristic of Poland, as it was here that the Jewish community enjoyed its greatest independence and, as a consequence, employed more officials than anywhere else. The *kahal* house was usually to be found close to the synagogue. It was only slightly less grand in appearance. There is a good example of one in Sandomierz.

At the head of the community were the elders, who were called *parnasim* or *roshim*. They were the community's representatives to the state authorities. They were also in charge of financial matters. Funds allocated for the functioning of the *kahal* were collected by a fiscal clerk or, when performing slightly different duties, a *gabai* (treasurer). Funds flowing into the public purse came mainly from two sources: a poll-tax and *hazakah*, fees in respect of living and staying on the territory of the Jewish community.

Papers documenting the life of the community formed a special book known as a *pinchas*. Although very few of these still remain, they are a fundamental source of knowledge about the workings of the *kahal* and of the members of the community.

Schools

When his son was three years old, a Jewish father would begin to teach him the Hebrew alphabet. At the age of four a child would start to attend *cheder* (a primary religious school). *Cheder* buildings are among the most widely-found monuments of Jewish culture in Poland. In Warsaw alone there were as many as three hundred *chadarim*.

The teaching programme in *cheder* covered reading and interpretation of the Bible, as well as arithmetic and moral principles. Lessons took place throughout the whole year without a break, apart from Saturdays and holidays. A *cheder* teacher, known as *melamed* or sometimes *rebe*, is often the main childhood character in Jewish autobiographies. Physical punishment is a noticeable feature in the pedagogical practices of these teachers. In theory it was meant at the very most, to consist of a "gentle whack with a thong or belt" (M. Fuks), but, according to many accounts, including those of Bernard Singer, the penalties were sometimes harsh and administered with a cane. The teacher's assistant was a *belfer* or *bahelfer*.

Graduates of a *cheder* could continue their studies in two different kinds of school. A *Talmud-Torah* was something akin to a religious school for poor children and was very much a continuation of the subjects taken in *cheder*. In a *yeshivah*, where a male would study until he married, the curriculum was devoted entirely to the *Talmud*. The aim of a *yeshivah k'tana* (small *yeshivah*) was to perfect a student's knowledge of the *Talmud* and *Torah*. A *yeshivah g'dola* (large *yeshivah*) trained rabbis, *dayanim* and Talmudists.

A number of Polish *yeshivot* achieved international recognition (Mira, Radun near Vilna and the Lublin Academy of Sages which has been operating since 1925). Those training to be rabbis were educated in pairs, stemming from a requirement which demanded knowledge of two schools of commentary on the *Talmud*: *Beth Hillel* and *Beth Shammai*. The former always gave simple solutions

Schooling and education have always been central to Jewish life and culture (above: a *cheder* in an 18th-century print).

Jewish Schools in Poland (as of 2001)

Kindergarten: Warsaw, ul. Wawelberga 10, ☎ +22 8626331

Primary Schools: Warsaw – Lauder Morasha, ul. Wawelberga 10, ☎ +22 862633; Wrocław – Lauder Etz Chaim, ul. Włodkowica 5, ☎ +71 3746117.

Educational centres: Gdańsk, ul. Partyzantów 9, ☎ +58 3483018; Cracow, ul. Kupa 18, ☎ +12 4293657; Łódź, ul. Narutowicza 24, ☎ +42 6301450; Warsaw, ul. Twarda 6, ☎ +22 6203496; Wrocław, ul. Włodkowica 9, ☎ +71 7817110.

All these centres are run by the Ronald S. Lauder Foundation, which has also revived Jewish schooling in other areas inhabited by Polish Jews (in cities such as Lviv, Minsk and Vilnius). The curriculum is not different from other schools except for the teaching of Hebrew and a different holiday calendar. Students are accepted regardless of their descent.

In a museum in Włodawa you can see the restored room of a *melamed* (teacher). It is the only one of its kind in Poland.

to problems, the latter decidedly more intricate ones. Tradition states that while here on Earth we function according to *Beth Hillel* and in heaven, according to *Beth Shammai*.

Secondary education was provided by brotherhood schools (*Chevrat Talmud-Torah*), but there were fewer of these than there were *yeshivot*. The most outstanding authorities on the *Talmud* could be awarded the title of *gaon*, meaning genius, and this was recognised by Jews everywhere. This honour was given extremely rarely. During the period of the Commonwealth of Poland it was received by one person only, Elijahu ben Shlomo of Vilna, also known as the Gaon of Vilna (18th century).

The above-mentioned educational system applied only to *bachur* (male youth). Until as recently as the beginning of the 20th century young girls were educated at home. During the inter-war period there were 2,560 Jewish religious schools operating in Poland and in all they educated some 171,000 pupils.

After the Second World War *chadarim* continued to function, as did *yeshivot* in Cracow, Szczecin and Wrocław. There was even the *Netzach Israel* (Eternal Israel) Rabbinical College in Łódź. Altogether there were 34 schools and

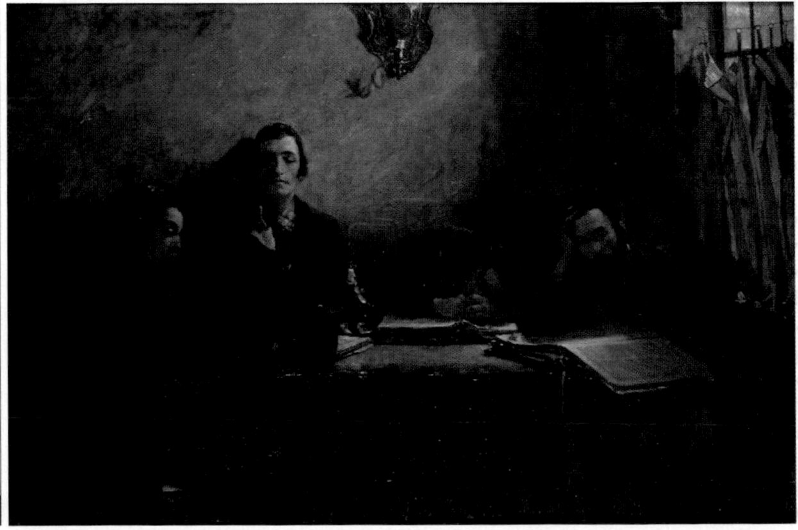

The Teaching of the Talmud by Samuel Hirszenberg.

some three thousand students and pupils. The Communist regime, however, found it impossible to tolerate the existence of religious schools. In 1948 the all *yeshivot* were closed down, in 1950 the remaining schools were nationalised and, in 1954 the use of Yiddish during lessons was forbidden, although this was rescinded in 1956. All Jewish schools were finally closed in 1968, making a comeback only after the changes of 1989. The first one was opened in 1993.

The purification ritual in the *mikvah* takes the form of total immersion in water of a person wearing a long white shirt. It is similar to the ritual of baptism in some Protestant churches.

The Mikvah

Another fundamental community institution was the *mikvah* or ritual bath. In theory there should be a separate and appropriately equipped *mikvah* for either sex. In practice, however, for reasons of poverty in some communities, there was only one *mikvah*, with different bathing times for men and women. The source of the water used in a *mikvah* is of great importance and it must be natural, for example rainwater or water drawn from a spring. Bathing is obligatory before *Yom Kippur* and other holidays, and for women this applies also after menstruation and childbirth.

The Ritual Slaughterhouse

Every Jewish community was obliged to have its own slaughterhouse and it was here that *shechita*, the ritual killing of animals, was performed by the *shochet* (butcher) and the *bodek* (assistant). Cattle and poultry were slaughtered using a special knife, employing no more than three strokes, the object being to drain out all of the blood. The *bodek* was also charged with the task of what would now be referred to as veterinary inspection of meat.

A rational explanation of this procedure derives from the fact that the custom arose when Jews were wandering in the wilderness, where strict rules regarding the keeping of food had to be observed, particularly as meat containing blood perished quite quickly. A more popular interpretation suggests that the whole point of ritual slaughter is to release the soul from *gilgul*, the sphere of incarnation. In Poland many of these slaughterhouse buildings still exist but they now serve completely different purposes. Be sure to visit the "roundhouse" in the Kazimierz district in Cracow.

The only form of funeral acceptable in Judaism is burial. Traditionally graves should face Jerusalem and the cemetery should be divided into separate sections for women and men (below: the picturesque Jewish cemetery in Bobowa).

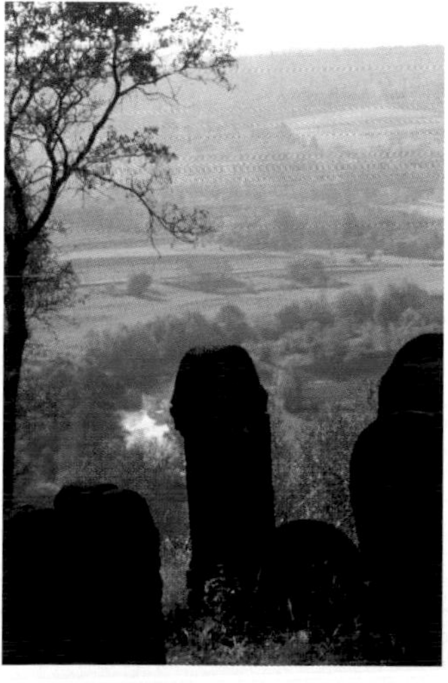

Explanations of Gravestone Symbols

Hands in a gesture of blessing (1) – descendants of Aaron, the High Priest
Jug (also with a bowl) (2) – descendants of Levi
Dove – peace
Star of David (3) – the national symbol
Crown (4) – piety, knowledge of the Torah
Book (5) – wisdom, the study of the Talmud and the Torah
Lion – belonging to the tribe of Yuda; the names Ari, Arie, Leib
Deer (6) – when the deceased belonged to the tribe of Naftali; the names Tzvi, Naftali, Hersh, Hirsh
Money-box (7) – a benefactor
Butterfly – the wandering of the spirit
Eagle – the protective power of the Lord
Palm – abundance; redemption of the Jews
Menorah (8) – the symbol of Judaism
Candelabrum (Sabbath candles) – a woman (one of her main duties is to light the Sabbath flame)
Snake swallowing its tail – the symbol of Leviathan, at a cemetery it denotes Messianic times

An *ohel* (tent) is a special kind of tomb, resembling a closed chapel and containing the remains of a great rabbi or *tzaddik*. Several *oholot* have been renovated or reconstructed since 1989, and can be seen in Leżajsk (below), Bobowa, Przysucha and Kock.

The Jewish Cemetery

Not every Jewish community had its own cemetery in Hebrew called *beit kvarot* (the house of graves) or *beit olam* (the house of eternity) and referred to by Poles as *kirkut* (deriving from German *Kirkhof*) except in the Małopolska and Lublin regions where they were known as the "burial grounds". Sometimes the representatives of a *kahal* without a cemetery negotiated with other Jewish communities in order to be allowed to bury their dead. This applied mainly to places where Jews were officially forbidden to live.

Judaism states that a cemetery is an unclean place and restrictions apply particularly to representatives of *cohanim*, (ministers). A related warning addressed to them can be seen by the gate of the Remuh synagogue in the Kazimierz district of Cracow.

On a *matzevah* (gravestone) the name of the deceased is inscribed and also the date according to the Hebrew calendar, on which he or she passed away. One will also find certain time-honoured phrases such as: "in blessed memory" or "may she be admitted to eternal life". It is worth looking closely at the way *matzevot* are adorned, as Jewish sepulchral art is very special indeed.

The oldest Jewish cemetery in Poland still in existence is, by all accounts, the one in Lublin, dating from 1540, but the oldest tomb, from 1203, was uncovered during archaeological excavations at the former site of the cemetery in Wrocław. Hundreds of cemeteries have been destroyed and the majority of those that remain suffer from neglect, yet their existence serves as a solemn reminder of the fate of Polish Jews. Of greatest interest to visitors are the following: the Remuh cemetery in Cracow, the cemetery in ul. Ślężna in Wrocław, the Old Cemetery in Lublin and the cemeteries in Warsaw (ul. Okopowa), Łódź, Tarnów and Lesko.

In Jewish tradition marriage is considered to be a entirely new stage in a person's life, in fact, almost like starting it again from the very beginning.

FAMILY

A rich family life was a defining feature of the Jewish community in Poland. Establishing a family and having children is a prescription of Judaism, and, apart from widows and widowers, it was unusual to find people living on their own.

A Wedding

Spinsterhood was considered contrary to human nature and celibacy was held in contempt. When a girl was almost fifteen and a boy a little older (with the passing of time these age limits were revised upwards) their parents would call on the services of a professional matchmaker known as a *shadchan*. Students at a Talmudic college were always

Jewish Surnames

Polish Jews had no surnames until the end of the 18th century. In their relations with the outside world they used patronymics instead, usually with the conjunction *ben* (son), for example: Shmuel ben Nachman. Matronymics were used in synagogue liturgy, for instance: Shloyme dem Rivke (Shlomo, son of Rebecca). Western style regulations regarding surnames were introduced at the time of the partition of Poland by the authorities of the occupying countries. In 1806, in the part of the country annexed to Prussia Jews were given surnames combining names of jewels and plants with affixes such as -man, -baum, -berg, -stein etc., examples being Goldbaum, Rosenberg, Silberman, Rubinstein. In the part of the Polish territory annexed to Russia, Jewish surnames were created without any specific rules and therefore they sound Slavonic (Petersburski, Brodski), although some of them retained traditional Jewish elements (Rabinovich, Lewicki, Kaganovich – the last one being derived from Cohen).

The young couple came in separately and stood together under the *chupah* (wedding canopy).

regarded favourably when it came to choosing a husband for a girl from a wealthy family.

When the *shadchan* brought a suitable couple together, the parents would sign a *tnaim achronim* (marriage contract) guaranteed by a sum equal to 50% of the dowry. A *ketuba*, an additional contract, assured the fiancee that in the event of divorce part of the dowry would be returned to her. The dowry, paid by the father of the bride, was a condition of concluding a marriage. In some cases the *kahal* or, perhaps a *ha-chnasat kala* (special dowry brotherhood for poor girls) would pay the necessary amount, so that daughters from impoverished families could get married.

A rabbi could issue a divorce ruling. A *get* (divorce letter) presented to a wife had the same effect.

Until the end of the 19th century a wedding would usually be held in the open air, often in front of the synagogue. The ceremony was divided into two halves: *kidushin* (the sanctification; the sacrament) and *nisuin* (marriage; act of consummation). A rabbi conducting the ceremony, along with a cantor and a *shammes*, had to be present. The couple would receive a *ketubah* (decorative marriage certificate). The fiance would also receive a *tallit* and a *kitel* (white shirt) from the girl's parents.

After showering the newly-weds with seeds, rice and nuts and wishing them *mazel tov* (good luck) everyone would make their way from the synagogue to the wedding house or to a rented hall. The part of leader of the dance was played by a *badchen* or wedding clown, a figure very characteristic in Polish-Jewish culture. He would start proceedings by delivering an improvised morality story on the subject of married life. Then he would slip into the role of director of entertainment, which usually included making lewd comments. The most famous *badchen* of all was Herszele from Ostropol. The rabbis fought against the presence of *badchen*, but the last ones were still going strong up to the Second World War. The newly-weds would be presented with *drasha* (gifts). After the feast the dancing would start, the tunes being played by *klezmerim*, who, alongside the leader of the dance, were an integral part of a Jewish wedding.

Marriage

In a traditional Jewish family roles were very clearly defined. The husband made the decisions, while it was up to the wife to prevent arguments from taking place, show understanding and take care of all domestic matters. If a couple had a serious altercation, then they would go to the rabbi and ask him to settle the matter. The rabbi would deliver his verdict in writing. The party whose version of events was inconsistent with the truth would be punished with a flogging. Passing such verdicts was one of the basic duties of all rabbis, including such authoritative figures as Moses Isserles or Shlomo Luria. If the situation was beyond repair, the rabbis would issue a divorce statement. The clauses in the pre-marriage contract, agreed by the spouses' parents, would then come into effect.

Children

A pregnant woman was treated with extraordinary care and very often was not even allowed to get out of bed. A child born to a Jewish mother is considered a Jew.

The best possible news was always the birth of a boy and in such an event a procedure strictly dictated by tradition, as

The main duty of a Jewish family was to have and raise children and this was strictly adhered to. Tradition dictated that a childless marriage lasting over ten years was grounds for divorce (photo from 1930).

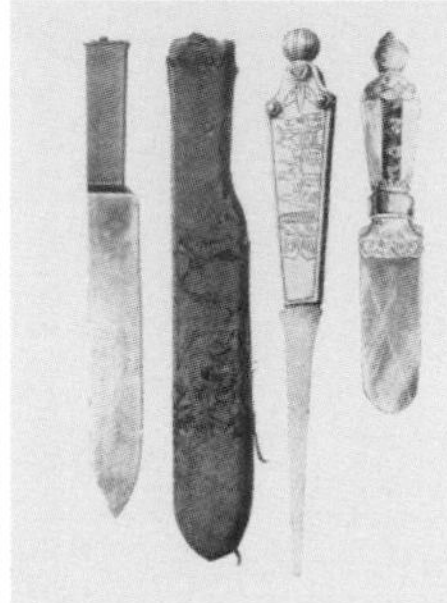

Ritual circumcision is performed by a *mohel*. The male whose task it is to hold the child during the ritual is called a *sandak*. In Poland these two were also assisted by *kvater* and *kvaterin* (godfather and godmother). Their duty was to pass the child to the *mohel* (above: knives used for circumcision).

well as the *kahal*, would come into effect. Between the birth and the circumcision ceremony the child would be carefully guarded and it was the women's job to watch over his cot. The *mohel* (circumciser) would lay out cards with kabbalistic signs around the boy and also place a knife under a cushion, the purpose of this being to foil any kidnap attempts by Lilith, the first wife of Adam and the enemy of every family since the world began.

The ritual of *B'rit milah* (circumcision) was then performed, during which the removal of the foreskin took place (in accordance with Genesis 17:10 "Every male among you shall be circumcised").

After the ceremony there would be a feast to celebrate receiving another child into the community of followers of Judaism. Here too, certain rules had to be followed. Those present could only be family members, the rabbi, the cantor, the *mohel* and the *sandek* (the community's representative to the town authorities). Neighbours were also sometimes allowed to attend, as were members of the poor. Guests were served by special waiters, called *sarverim*. The circumcision was also the opportunity to give the boy his name, whereas in the case of girls, this was done in the synagogue when the father was called up to read from the *Torah*.

Death

Polish Jews would never talk about death and, as a rule, they would never write a will. Only the wealthiest chose to have their personal fortunes settled posthumously and they would have to adhere to certain conditions, which included giving contributions to the needy and various institutions belonging to the *kahal*. It was commonly thought that as a person breathed

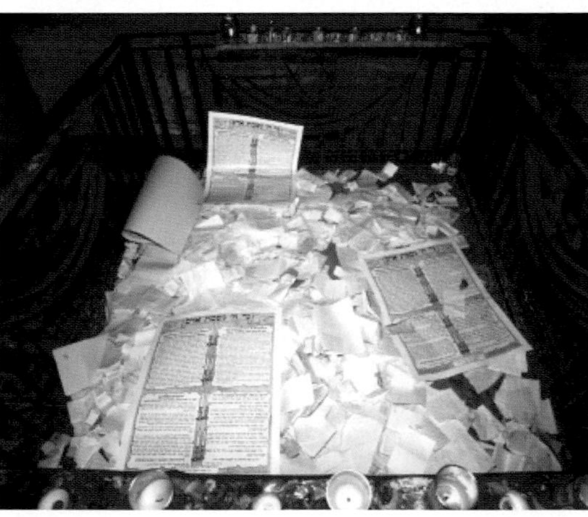

Pilgrims to the graves of great rabbis leave behind *kvitlech* (little notes containing requests) which the deceased is then supposed to forward to the Lord.

his last, he was visited by the Angel of Death. At the very sight of him the terrified individual opened his mouth, whereupon a drop of poison fell into it, bringing life to an end. It is for this reason that after a death all the water in the house was poured away, as the poison may have found its way there as well. The body would be then placed on the floor on a bundle of straw and candles lit and positioned next to the head.

The funeral would be held as soon as possible after the person had passed away, preferably on the same day late in the evening. Members of the *Chevrat Kaddisha* (Funeral Brotherhood) would participate in the ceremony. The body was ritually washed (special spoons were used to pour water over the body of the deceased), and the beard was tidied. The corpse was then wrapped in a linen sheet, and in the case of a married man in a *tallit* as well. It was the custom of Ashkenazi Jews to dress the deceased in a *kitel*, a long white shirt worn previously at his wedding. The bottom of the grave was laid out with a wooden board. Two other boards supported the walls. After positioning the corpse with the head in the direction of Jerusalem (to the east), the fourth board was placed on top and the grave covered in earth. The eldest son would recite the prayer *Kaddish Yatom* (*Kaddish* for the orphan). *Shiva*, the period of mourning for the whole family, lasted seven days. During this time they would eat simple meals, walk around the home without shoes on and sit on very low chairs. In addition men would not shave their beards for thirty days (*shloshim*) and ripped the edge of an article of clothing they were wearing, which symbolised the tearing up of the attire in an act in of despair.

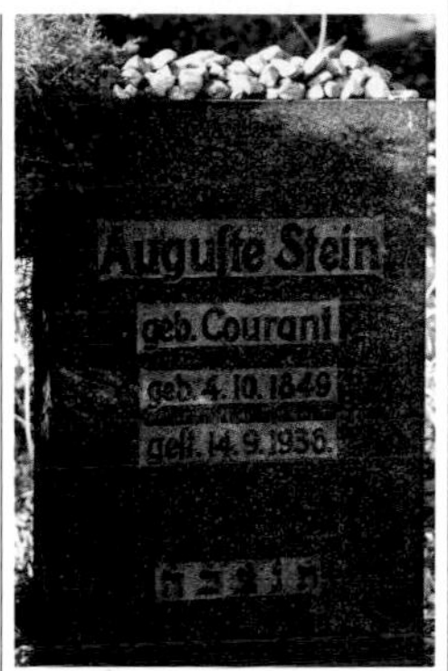

When visiting a grave, the tradition is to leave a small stone, not flowers.

Dates of Commencement of Months in the Jewish Calendar

Months	5765	5766	5767
	2004/2005	2005/2006	2006/2007
Tishri (IX/X)	16 IX 2004	4 X 2005	23 IX 2006
Cheshvan (X/XI)	16 X 2004	3 XI 2005	23 X 2006
Kislev (XI/XII)	14 XI 2004	2 XII 2005	22 XI 2006
Tevet (XII/I)	13 XII 2004	1 I 2006	22 XII 2006
Shevat (I/II)	11 I 2005	30 I 2006	20 I 2007
Adar (II/III)	10 II 2005	1 III 2006	19 II 2007
Adar sheni (additional)	12 III 2005	not in 2006	not in 2007
Nisan (III/IV)	10 IV 2005	30 III 2006	20 III 2007
Iyar (IV/V)	10 V 2005	29 IV 2006	19 IV 2007
Sivan (V/VI)	8 VI 2005	28 V 2006	18 V 2007
Tammuz (VI/VII)	8 VII 2005	27 VI 2006	17 VI 2007
Av (VII/VIII)	6 VIII 2005	26 VII 2006	16 VII 2007
Elul (VIII/IX)	5 IX 2005	25 VIII 2006	15 VIII 2007

At the beginning of a *Sabbath* feast *kiddush* is said over a glass of wine (above: *kiddush* cups). If there is no wine, *kiddush* is said over two pieces of *challah* (white bread), to commemorate the double portion of manna, which Jews received on Fridays, during their journey through the wilderness.

Memory of the deceased was kept alive in many ways. During *yortsait* (the anniversary of the death) *Kaddish* was recited, along with *El male rachamim* (Oh Lord, full of mercy). Another form of remembrance was the *Yizkor* service, in which a prayer for the departed was said in the synagogue on *Yom Kippur*, the last day of *Pesach* and the second day of *Shavuot*. In Poland, in connection with *Yizkor*, special notices remembering the dead were put up on the walls of synagogues.

THE JEWISH CALENDAR

The traditional Jewish system for measuring time is based on the lunar calendar but is verified according to the solar one. The year is made up of twelve months containing 29 or 30 days and beginning with each new moon, making a total of 354 days. *Adar sheni* is an extra month added each leap year. Days are also added and subtracted to the months of *Cheshvan* and *Kislev* in a somewhat similar fashion to 29 February. The liturgical year runs from the festival of *Pesach* in the month of *Nisan*, and the numbered, calendar year from the festival of *Rosh Hashanah* on the first day of the month of *Tishri*. The week begins on *Yom alef*, Hebrew for "the first day", corresponding to Sunday, and the remaining days of the week do not have names as such but numbers instead. As with all ancient calendars, dusk marks the point where a day begins and this is why *Shabbat* and holidays begin on *erev* (the eve) of the day in question.

In a calendar year Jews celebrate five major festivals, each of which is referred to as *yom tov* (good day). Three of these *Pesach*, *Shavuot* and *Sukkot* are holidays associated with the

The Beginning of Sabbath

In Warsaw, Sabbath candles are lit 20 minutes before the time of sunset given in an ordinary calendar. For other Polish towns, the time adjustment in relation to Warsaw time is given in minutes, for instance: in Warsaw on 4th Tishri 5762 / 21st September 2001, the sun sets at 6.39 pm, and so the time for the lighting of candles is 6.19 pm – which means that in Białystok candles are to be lit at 6.10 pm and in Bielsko-Biała at 6.27 pm, and so on as below:

Białystok: –9	Dzierżoniów: +17	Cracow: +4	Olsztyn: +2	Tarnów: 0
Bielsko-Biała: +8	Gdańsk: +9	Legnica: +19	Poznań: +16	Wałbrzych: +19
Bydgoszcz: +12	Gliwice +9	Lublin: –6	Przemyśl: –7	Wrocław: +16
Bytom: +8	Katowice: +8	Łódź: +6	Rzeszów: –4	Zgorzelec +24
Częstochowa: +8	Kielce: +1	Nowy Sącz: +1	Szczecin: +26	Żary: +23

Exodus from Egypt, while the other two, *Rosh Hashanah* and *Yom Kippur* are penitential. The other important festivals are *Purim* and *Chanukah*.

Shabbat

Shabbat, a day of peace and quiet after a week's work, recalls how the Lord rested after labouring to create the Universe. Polish Jews celebrated the Sabbath in accordance with very strict rules. On Friday evening, just before the sun set, and while the men were in the synagogue, a female member of the household would light two candles (symbolising divine light and the human spirit) and recite the appropriate blessing. When the men returned, everyone sat down to a celebratory meal and *Shabbat* songs were sung.

The Friday night meal was to be plentiful (families in need were helped by the *kahal*), marking as it did the beginning of three important meals known as *scuda*. The second was lunch on Saturday, when *chulent* was eaten, and the third on Saturday evening, when fish and *challah* were served. The Sabbath menu also included *gefilte fish*, chopped liver, stuffed chickens' necks, *kishkes* and *kugel*.

Work was not permitted, especially that which would in any way change the natural environment (ploughing, sowing, construction) and activities such as writing and lighting a fire, as well as those resembling them (like printing or switching on a light) were also prohibited. There were two ways round the *Shabbat* restrictions. One could employ a *Shabbes goy* (a non-Jew to do all those forbidden little chores) or take advantage of an exception to the rules. Jews were allowed to perform certain activities, feeding animals and serving food being a couple of examples, as long as they took place in a carefully demarcated and enclosed area, known as an *eruv*. This was done by stretching a symbolic piece of string around the part of town in question, thus creating a closed space. On *Shabbat* in Poland one could always see these lines of string around almost every *shtetl*, leading to lots of jokes from Christian neighbours about the Jewish telegraph service. So as not to break the rule about cooking and then eating a hot meal, chulent was served for Saturday lunch. As it is cooked slowly in an oven for several hours, it was put there before *Shabbat* began and was ready to be eaten the following day.

Rosh Chodesh

Although somewhat less significant in religious terms, *Rosh Chodesh*, the monthly celebration of a New Moon and a new month, is a popular holiday lasting one or two evenings. The celebrations lead to *Kiddush Levana* (the Sanctification of

The Sabbath ends with the *seuda shlishit* (a Saturday evening meal) and the *havdalah* celebration. This is when besamin herbs are placed in a specially decorated spice-box which is often in the shape of a turret. The aim of burning herbs is to soothe *neshama yetera* (the other soul) which leaves a pious Jew at the end of the Sabbath.

In Poland the festival of *Rosh Hashanah* is called Trumpet Day (above: *The Trumpet Festival* by Aleksander Gierymski).

the Moon) which takes place three days after the appearance of the New Moon. In a *shtetl* of old, this meant the men conducting a colourful evening prayer service under the stars. Afterwards they would greet anyone they met in the dark with the customary *shalom aleichem* (peace be with you).

Rosh Hashanah

The Jewish New Year falls in autumn on the first day of the month of *Tishri*. The celebrations last two days. On the eve of *Rosh Hashanah* one is required to cut one's hair, bathe and put on new clothing. The ritual known as *Tashlich* involves shaking out the contents of one's pockets into water in a symbolic act of cleansing. In the synagogue a *shofar* (ram's horn) is blown. In the evening everyone partakes of a celebratory meal consisting of round loaves of *challah*, honey, pomegranates, dates and fish. Only sweet dishes are served, in the hope that the whole year will be that way. Some Jews also believe that whatever happens to a person on the very first day of the New Year will have a bearing on his or her fortunes in the following twelve months. Many rabbis refuse to accept such customs and beliefs as they are not found anywhere in the Books of the Law.

Rosh Hashanah is followed by *Yamim Noraim* (The Days of Awe), ten days of penitence preceding *Yom Kippur*.

Yom Kippur

The holiest day in the Jewish calendar is *Yom Kippur* (Day of Atonement). It falls on the 10th day of *Tishri* and commemorates Moses descending from Mount Sinai and delivering the tablets with the Ten Commandments to the Chosen People. On this day God forgives all sins, the gates of heaven open and understanding prevails. *Yom Kippur* begins with the *Kol Nidre* service, in which the congregation prays for forgiveness for all those obligations that they have failed to fulfil in the past year. *Yizkor*, a special prayer for the departed, is also recited. The *aron ha-kodesh* is covered with a special ark curtain. A 25-hour fast is strictly observed, beginning before dusk on *Erev Yom Kippur* and ending at sunset on the following day. All work is forbidden and one is not even allowed to wash.

In Poland, celebrations contained one or two local characteristics, including the custom of *kapores*, which involved the sacrifice of a white cock or hen. The bird would be spun in the air for a moment while the following was said: "This is in place of me, this is instead of me, this is my penitence". Many rabbis condemned this custom and these days no sacrifices are made.

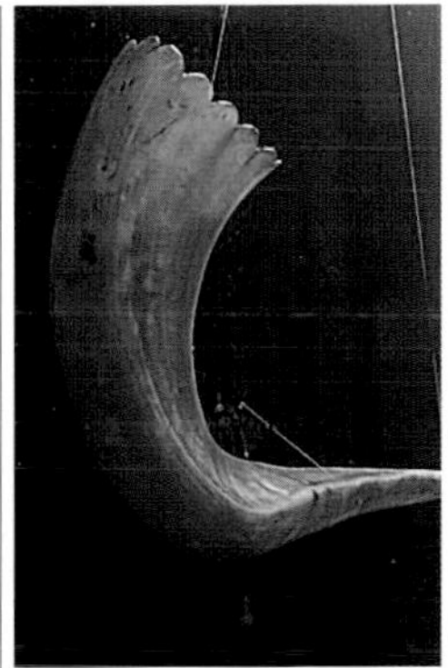

Blowing a ram's horn called a *shofar* marks the end of the celebration of *Yom Kippur*. This ancient tradition follows the imperative of the Scriptures: "In the day of atonement shall ye make the trumpet sound throughout all your land". (Leviticus 25:9) The horn is blown in such a way as to produce a specific sequence: one long sound followed by three staccato sounds and then three short ones.

Sukkot

Sukkot, the Feast of Tabernacles, in Poland known as *Kuczki*, commemorates the years the Jews spent wandering in the wilderness before they reached the Promised Land. It also denotes the end of the harvest season. It begins on the fifteenth of *Tishri*, just four days after *Yom Kippur*. *Sukkot*, referred to in texts as "the time of our great joy" lasts eight days, the four days in the middle being working days or "half-holidays". In the *Sukkah* (tabernacle) each of the first seven days is devoted to a symbolic guest, in turn, Abraham, Isaac, Jacob, Joseph, Moses, Aaron and David. Meals are eaten in the *Sukkah*, which is usually put up in the yard or on the balcony. This festival is celebrated according to these verses taken from the Bible: "Ye shall dwell in booths seven days; all that are Israelites born shall dwell in booths: That your generations may know that I made the children of Israel to dwell in booths when I brought them out of the land of Egypt" (Leviticus 23:42). In many houses before the war it was possible to come across rollers able to lift part of the roof over the attic in such a way that it looked like a *Sukkah*. All of the constructions erected for the feast of

Etrog, a citrus fruit was kept in a special richly decorated receptacle.

Simchat Torah (The Day of the Celebration of the *Torah*), sometimes referred to as the Holiday of the *Torah*, takes place one day after the end of *Sukkot* and closes the annual cycle of the reading of the *Torah* (above: *The Holiday of the Torah* by Tadeusz Popiel).

During the festival of *Chanukah* the lights are put in a *chanukiya* (special candelabrum).

Sukkot had at least one thing in common: an opening in the roof through which the sky was visible. During *Sukkot* Jews had an obligation to eat sweet dishes and to avoid sour ones.

The seventh day, called *Hoshana Raba* (Great Rejoicing), is the most important day of the festival. A morning service took place, in which worshippers, holding an *etrog* (citrus fruit) and a *lulav* (bunch of palm branches), waved them up and down in the direction of the four points of the compass. During the service the *Torah* was carried round the synagogue seven times with the congregation following. Sometimes one could also see the custom of beating the ground with a willow twig, which was supposed to ensure fertility. It was also a good day for fortune telling and there was a belief that if you did not see your shadow on *Hoshana Raba*, you would not survive the year. *Shmini Atzeret*, the eighth day, brought the holiday to an end and with it the requirement to spend time in the *Sukkah*. In Israel, *Simchat Torah* is celebrated on this day. In Poland it was a separate festival.

Simchat Torah

During an evening service, all of the scrolls of the *Torah* are removed from the *aron ha-kodesh* and carried in *hakafot*, a procession which takes them around the synagogue seven times. This ceremony is repeated the next morning, followed by the readings of the last chapter of the Book of Deuteronomy which closes the old cycle and the first chapter of Genesis which opens the new one. Reading during this service is a particular honour and readers are known as *Chatan Torah* (Bridegroom of the Torah) and *Chatan Bereshit* (Bridegroom of Creation).

For *Chanukah* children get *chanuke gelt* (coins) as presents and play with a *dreydl* (spinning-top) decorated with Hebrew letters.

Chanukah

Chanukah or Renewal or the Feast of Lights starts on the 25th day of *Kislev* and lasts eight days. It commemorates the victory of the Maccabees over the armies of Syria and the resumption of religious practices in the Temple. The festival of *Chanukah* is celebrated by lighting candles, which stand in an eight-branched candelabrum called a *menorah*. There is also an extra branch, usually in front, for the *shammes*, the candle used to light the others. On the first night one candle is lit. On the second day, two are lit, and so on, until, on the final day, eight candles are burning. Lamps filled with olive oil may also be used. This festival commemorates the miracle which took place after the rebuilding of the Temple, when the lights on the *menorah* burned for eight days, even though there was only enough oil for half a day. Meals eaten during *Chanukah* are traditionally fried in oil and in Poland potato pancakes were a speciality. Gambling, though usually forbidden, was allowed.

Tu B'shevat

This festival which falls on the 15th day of *Shevat* is also known as New Year for Trees and, while it does not appear in descriptions of the customs of Polish Jews, it is usually found nowadays in Jewish calendars printed in Poland. In Israel this is a day when trees are planted. Diaspora Jews would organise a celebratory feast consisting of seven (in some cases, fifteen) different types of fresh and dried fruit. During the meal, the *Torah* and the *Zohar* would be discussed.

In some communities it was considered sufficient to take just one piece of fruit to say the prayer *Shehechiyanu* over it and for it to remain uneaten during the following year.

During the festival of *Purim*, *Megilat Ester* (the Book of Esther) is read in the synagogues from a special scroll.

Purim

"Therefore the Jews of the villages, that dwelt in the unwalled towns, made the fourteenth day of the month

When the name of Haman, the persecutor of the Persian Jews, is mentioned during the reading from the Book of Esther, it is drowned out by the sound of rattles and the stamping of feet.

of Adar a day of gladness and feasting, and a good day of sending portions one to another" (Esther 9:19). *Purim*, known in Poland as Shrovetide or the Festival of Lots, is of lesser importance than, say, *Pesach*, but is extremely popular because of the joy and happiness that is associated with it. *Purim* commemorates the miraculous salvation of the Jews in Persia. Young boys dressed up as characters from the Book of Esther went from house to house acting out scenes taken from the text and collecting gifts in a ritual known as *Purimshpil*. People gave each other presents and threw noisy parties, as tradition dictated that you should get drunk. There is even a law to this effect. It is called *ad lo yada*, which means "until he does not know what is going on", the idea being that a reveller should not be able to differentiate the words "Cursed be Haman" from "Blessed be Mordechai". In some communities *Purim* was a time for making fun of others. A special "Purim rabbi" was elected and it was his job to joke and laugh at people, in this way settling a number of outstanding scores. Purim is also a time for baking *Homentashen* (Haman's Ears), triangular-shaped biscuits made with nuts.

PESACH

Pesach (Passover) commemorates the Exodus of the Jews from Egypt and is a very important festival, falling on the first New Moon after the vernal equinox. It begins on the 15th day of *Nisan* and lasts eight days, the first of which is the anniversary of the deliverance from Egypt. The four days in the middle are working days and the final day marks the crossing of the Red Sea by the Children of Israel. With the passing of time *Pesach* assumed the characteristics of an agricultural festival, as in Palestine it was associated with the end of the rainy season.

Seder, the celebratory supper beginning the festival of *Pesach*, requires the use of special tableware (below: a *Seder* plate).

Pesach begins with the *Seder* (Passover meal) at which the service, in accordance with tradition, is read from a book called the *Haggadah*. The following dishes of great symbolic significance appear on the *Seder* table: the *aphikomen* (three pieces of *matzah*, usually concealed from the children), *zeroah* (meat on the bone), *beytsa* (a burnt or roasted egg), *maror* (horseradish and parsley leaves dipped in salt water, commemorating the tears and suffering in Egypt) *charoseth* (a paste made from minced apples, almonds, cinnamon and wine). Each person must drink four cups of wine to commemorate the words of the Lord: "I will lead you out and I will save you and I will set you free and I will take you in".

Matzah is eaten instead of bread, recalling the unleavened bread consumed in the wilderness. In Poland during *Pesach* one was not allowed to use yeast or even keep it in the house. Any leftovers were to be sold to a non-Jewish neighbour and bought back afterwards. The custom of *B'dikat chametz* (search for *chametz*, or fermented yeast) on the eve of *Pesach* had a similar purpose and was designed to remove all trace of yeast from the house. A glass of wine was kept on the table for the Prophet Elijah, whose arrival presages the coming of the Messiah. As the prophet may assume the guise of any one of the guests, visitors were warmly welcomed and the front door was left ajar.

Lag B'Omer is believed to be a very good day to get married.

After *Pesach* comes the period of mourning known as *Omer* (Sheaf), a reference to work in the field at that time of year.

Lag B'Omer

A minor holiday celebrated on the eighteenth of *Adar*, the thirty-third day after the second day of *Pesach*. It commemorates the anniversary of the death of Shimon bar Yochai, allegedly the author of the Kabbalistic text *Zohar*. Unlike the preceding period of the *Omer*, this is a joyous holiday. In modern Jewish tradition it is "Schoolchildren's

Dates of Jewish Holidays

Holiday	Date	5765 (2004/2005)	5766 (2005/2006)	5767 (2006/2007)
Rosh Hashanah	1–2 Tishri	16/17 IX 2004	4–5 X 2005	23–24 IX 2006
Yom Kippur	10 Tishri	25 IX 2004	13 X 2005	2 X 2006
Sukkot	15–23 Tishri	30 IX–7 X 2004	18–25 X 2005	7–14 X 2006
Simchat Torah	23 Tishri	8 X 2004	26 X 2005	15 X 2006
Chanukah	24 Kislev–2 Tevet	8–15 XII 2004	25 XII 2005–1 I 2006	15–22 XII 2006
Tu B'Shevat	15 Shevat	25 I 2005	13 II 2006	3 II 2007
Purim	14 Adar	25 III 2005	14 III 2006	4 III 2007
Pesach	14–22 Nisan	24 IV–1 V 2005	13–20 IV 2006	3–10 IV 2007
Lag B'Omer	18 Iyar	27 V 2005	16 V 2006	6 V 2007
Shavuot	5 Sivan	13–14 VI 2005	2–3 VI 2006	23–24 V 2007
Tisha B'Av	9 Av	14 VIII 2005	3 VIII 2006	24 VII 2007

Day" and also a day of sport. In Sephardic tradition *Lag B'Omer* is a day for going on a pilgrimage to one of two places: the first being the village of Meron in Galilee where Shimon bar Yochai died, the second the El-Ghriba synagogue on the Tunisian island of Djerba. Ashkenazi Jews go no further than the forest where they take a walk or have a picnic.

The Festival of *Shavuot* recalls the events surrounding the receiving of the *Torah* on Mount Sinai.

SHAVOUT

Shavuot falls on the sixth and seventh days of *Sivan*, seven weeks after the second day of *Pesach*, and , for this reason, is also known as the Feast of Weeks. Once upon a time on this festival Jews would travel to the Temple in Jerusalem, taking with them fruit and grain from the harvest. These days the entire night preceding this festival is taken up with the reading of *Tikkun Lail Shavuot* (the Reparation of the Night of Shavuot). The synagogue service is taken from the Book of Ruth, the heroine whose conversion to the Jewish faith symbolises the receiving of the *Torah* by the Jews. The 19th century saw the introduction of paper cut-outs which were stuck on the windows. They were known as *shevuosl* or *royzelech* (little roses) and some experts claim that they were the inspiration for Polish folk cut-outs.

TISHA B'AV

Tisha B'Av (the ninth of Av) is the saddest day in the Jewish calendar, as it commemorates the destruction of the First and Second Temples in Jerusalem.

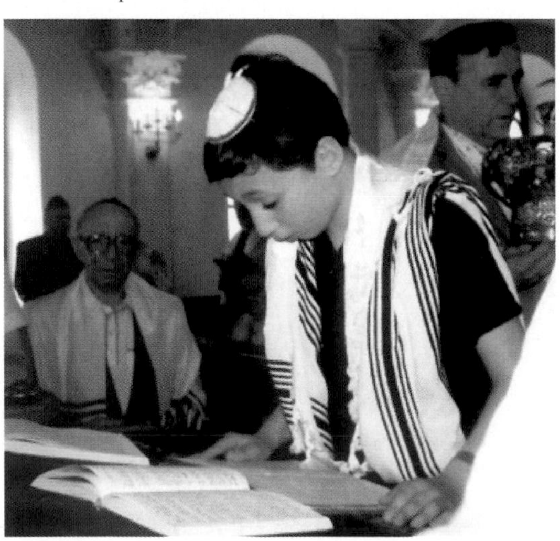

During the *bar mitzvah* ceremony the thirteen year old boy is called up to read a portion of the *Torah*. He then delivers a commentary and receives a blessing from his father who hands him responsibility for his future deeds.

From dusk until dusk the following things are forbidden among Orthodox Jews: eating, drinking, washing, wearing leather shoes and sitting in chairs. All work is prohibited, as is study of the *Torah*. During morning prayers men do not put on *tefillin*. This holiday contains an element of expectation, as it is thought that *Tisha B'Av* is the day when the Messiah will come.

CUSTOMS AND TRADITIONS

On the occasion of *bar mitzvah*, a celebratory feast is organised in the Jewish home. During the feast the youngster shows off his knowledge and receives presents: his first *tallit* and also *tefillin* (above).

Bar mitzvah and Bat mitzvah

Bar mitzvah, from the Aramaic, "son of the commandment", is probably one of the best-known Jewish customs and according to rules laid down in the 15th century, should take place in the synagogue on the first Sabbath after a boy's thirteenth birthday. The ceremony celebrates the recognition of the boy as a full member of the adult community with all the rights and religious obligations that this entails. Part of this is the duty to perform a *mitzvah* (commandment), and there are 613 of them governing everyday life, with 248 regulating what one should do and 365 what one should not. Performing a *mitzvah* is considered to be character building as well as an excellent way of directing one's thoughts towards God.

There is also a coming-of-age ceremony for girls, called *bat mitzvah*, which takes place at the age of twelve. It is a comparatively recent phenomenon, dating from the 19th century and associated more with freedom for women than with tradition. In a reform synagogue a *bat mitzvah* follows a similar pattern to a *bar mitzvah*. In some Orthodox synagogues it will probably be on a Sunday, with the girl reading Psalms, in others it may just involve a party in the home.

Folklore

The folklore of Polish Jews is made up of two categories: common tales which everyone knew and stories set locally.

There is a classical myth about Behemot, based on an extract from the Book of Hiob (40:15–24), which describes a monster (in Hebrew the word *Behemot* means beast) living on land and as huge as a thousand mountains. Once a year, in the month of *Tammuz*, the monster emits a frightening roar. When the Messiah comes, Behemot will perish in a struggle with his counterpart from beneath the waters, the sea monster Leviathan, and their meat will be served at the feast of the righteous.

Leviathan

Musicians called *klezmorim* formed bands, which usually contained a violin, a double bass, a trumpet and a dulcimer.

Music was very closely connected with dance which in Poland also betrayed the influence of various Mediterranean cultures, both in the figures (a circle, steps, gestures) as well as in its dynamic (among *Chasidim* even ecstatic) nature. Women and men danced separately. The *hora*, in which dancers move in a circle and hold one another's arms, is still considered as the national dance (below).

The latter were about everyday life in Poland and well-known characters would appear, very often borrowed from Slavonic folklore. One particular story concerns how some Jews believe each generation to contain 36 righteous people, any one of whom may turn out to be the Messiah. Other tales involved the ten lost generations, the Messiah or the Promised Land. Examples of local colour can be found in the stories about the love affair between King Casimir the Great and Esther; the jokers Hershele of Ostropol and Motke the Thief; Elimelech of Leżajsk and numerous other *tzaddikim*, as well as places like Chełm and Lesko where the inhabitants were considered to be delightfully stupid. There was also widespread belief in a *dybbuk* (evil spirit) which *Chasidim* believed to be that of a sinner unable to leave this world. The *dybbuk* apparently manifested itself through the secret little sins that people committed. Only a *Baal Shem* or a *tzaddik* were able to drive it out.

Folk Music

Music and religious songs have always been an important part of Jewish tradition. Examples that spring to mind include *niggun*, a tune without words to put you into a trance, *zmirot*, containing a text from the *Midrash* or *Zohar*, as well as songs for children and those derived from historical sources. It is quite possible to identify the part of Poland that Jewish songs come from as they were sometimes influenced by the local culture and klezmer groups would very often include in their repertoire lots of different types of Polish music. Some of these musicians were extremely talented and the most famous one of all, the dulcimer player Jankiel Liebermann, found his way onto the pages of *Pan Tadeusz*, the great epic poem by Adam Mickiewicz.

On festivals, in addition to *yarmulkes Chasidim* also wore large fox or sable fur hats (*shtreiml*). Women were forbidden to wear low-cut dresses or show their elbows (above: exhibits on display in the Old Synagogue in Cracow).

Dress

In the 16th century Jews still dressed in the same way as the local townspeople or peasants, but Orthodox Jews gradually began to stand out by the clothes they wore. They favoured black coats as a result of laws passed by the *kahal*, limiting the wearing of expensive clothing. The women were noticeable for their Levantine tastes, opting for satin, lace and silk as well as gold jewellery. In 1595 the *kahal* in Kazimierz went as far as to forbid residents to leave the Jewish quarter, so as not to irritate their poorer neighbours.

In the period from the 18th to the 20th century, the outfit of an Orthodox Jew consisted of the following: a long coat, in Yiddish known as *kapote*; long black outer clothing; *tallit katan*, a kind of under-waistcoat not sewn up at the sides with *tzitzit* (fringes) at the bottom; trousers to the knee; stockings and boots with leggings. A *yarmulkeh*, traditional Jewish head covering, was worn at all times, usually being removed only before going to bed.

Men wore *payes* (side-curls) and untrimmed beards. These curls were a result of careful grooming of side-burns and go back to a biblical decree forbidding the cutting of hair above the ears. A married woman was required to cut off her hair and to cover her head with a *sheitl* (wig), scarf or hat. This was for reasons of modesty and not a religious requirement, although it was common belief that a *yarmulkeh* and a *sheitl* gave protection from *shedlim* (demons). These days it is only usually *Chasidim* who observe these dress codes and it is possible to identify exactly which group they come from by the way they curl their side-burns.

CUISINE

The basic tenet of Jewish cooking is the law of *kashrut*, requiring that food be *kosher* (suitable for consumption).

Food which conforms to the requirements of religious law is considered to be *kosher* (right: dishwashers making utensils *kosher* for the festival of *Pesach*, photo from 1914).

If it does not fulfil this requirement then it is *trayf*. The meat of only certain animals is permitted, provided that they have been slaughtered according to ritual practice. One is forbidden to mix dairy and meat dishes and separate sets of crockery and cutlery are used for each. Meat is allowed an hour after drinking milk, but six hours must elapse before drinking milk after meat. All of the animal's veins are removed, as food may not contain even the slightest trace of blood. The following are considered to be *trayf*: uncloven ruminants, such as camels, and non-ruminants, such as pigs or horses; fish without scales, for example eel; shellfish and water fowl, such as duck. In all, there are forty-two different groups. Plants are *parve*, that is to say neutral, but their derivatives such as wine or vodka must fulfil certain requirements (e.g. grapes must be washed) before they can be considered to be *kosher*. Certain items are *trayf* only at certain times, for instance bread during *Pesach*, whereas others, such as all dairy produce, must be prepared in the presence of an adult. These complicated laws

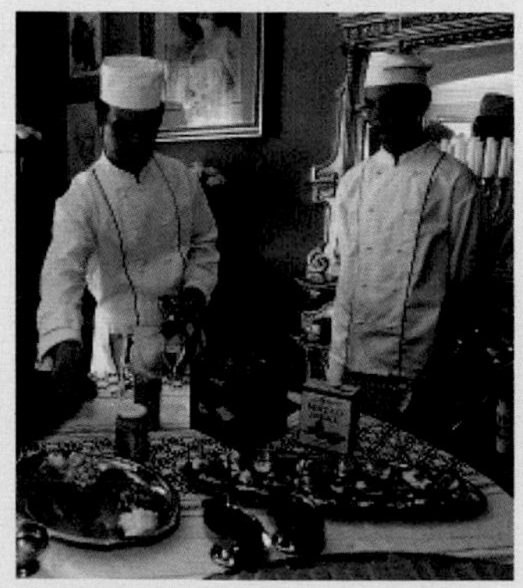

Many **Ashkenazic dishes**, served on festivals, are today *specialités de la maison* at Jewish restaurants in Poland.

Tzimmes – a casserole of cooked carrot, apple and dried fruit, sprinkled with sugar and cinnamon.

Chulent – a dish made of peas, potatoes, buckwheat, onions and scraps of meat, simmered in a heated oven for 16 hours.

Gefilte Fish – fish stuffed with *matzah* and vegetables. Served cold in jelly with raisins and almonds.

Kugel – a casserole made of potatoes or rice or pasta, as a side-dish to go with meat or as a separate dish with fruit, honey and nuts.

are strictly observed by Orthodox Jews, with the rest of the community varying in their approach.

ART

Painting

Apart from one or two exceptions, Jewish artists only began to make their mark in the middle of the 19th century, this being due to a traditional ban on portraying the human form. Abraham Neumann (1873–1943) specialised in painting scenes, such as synagogue services. Samuel Hirszenberg (1865–1908) is known for his depiction of Jews and their lot, as in *The Eternally Wandering Jew* or *The Prophet Jeremiah*. A little later on, the following avant-garde painters were predominant: Jankiel Adler (1895–1949), Jonasz Stern (1904–1988), Bruno Schulz (1892–1942), Mark Włodarski (Henryk Streng, 1903–1960), Erna Rosenstein (b. 1913) and Artur Nacht-Samborski (1898–1974).

There were also other artists in the vanguard of European painting, with close ties to Poland. Marc Chagall (1887–1985, born in Vitebsk) and Chaim Soutine (Chaim Sutin, 1894-1943, born in Minsk) are two outstanding painters to hail from the eastern edges of the borderlands. El (Eliezer) Lissitzky (1890–1941) and Mojżesz Kisling (1891–1953) also, allegedly, had Polish roots. Warsaw was the birthplace of Mela Muter (Maria Melania Mutermilchowa, 1873–1967), who later found fame in Paris and New York.

The works by Maurycy Gotlieb (1856–1879) are good examples of realism (*A Reconciliation Day*, *A Portrait of a Bride*, *Ecce Homo*; below: *Self-Portrait in the Arab Costume*).

Music

Jewish classical music began to develop in the 19th century and these are the names of some of the more important composers: Henryk Wieniawski (1835–1880) who was also a renowned violinist; Ludwik Grossman (1835–1915), famous for *The Fisherman of Palermo*; David Aizensztadt (1890–1915), creator of the musical drama *The Golem*. Even greater heights were scaled by the conductor, Grzegorz Fitelberg (1879–1953); the violinists, Eli Kochański (1885–1940) and Paweł Kochański (1887–1934); and last but by no means least, the pianist Arthur Rubinstein (1886–1982). A number of Jewish composers of light music enjoyed

Jerzy Petersburski and Henryk Wars

Many of their hits, once made popular by the cinema, are still very much part of the classical repertoire of Polish theatre. Petersburski composed such tunes as the world-famous tango *Oh, Donna Clara*, as well as a great number of songs known to everyone in Poland. Both composers survived the Second World War. After many years spent in South America, Petersburski eventually returned to Poland, while Wars settled down in what for him was the best place on earth, Hollywood.

a lot of success in Poland during the inter-war period, including Zygmunt Białostocki (d. 1942), Jerzy Petersburski (1897–1979) and Henryk Wars (1902–1977). Juliusz Feigelbaum, founder of the Syrena-Rekord studio, was a pioneer of the Polish music industry.

Theatre

Jewish theatre in Poland can be traced back to *Purimshpil*, when scenes from the Book of Esther would be staged. Until as late as the 19th century it was the only form of acting to exist, as rabbis forbade everything connected with lay theatre, including the attending of plays. The turning point came with the emergence of the *Haskalah* movement. It was then that artists, such as "the Brody Singers", often from

After the Second World War, in the 1940s, two Jewish theatre ensembles started up again: one in Łódź, directed by Ida Kamińska, the daughter of the pioneers of Jewish theatre in Poland, the other in Dzierżoniów, although it soon moved to Wrocław. During the dark days of Stalinism, Jewish theatre was non-existent. One of the ensembles, the E.R. Kamińska State Jewish Theatre established in Warsaw in 1955 survived the period of Communism in Poland and is still operating today (right: a scene from its production *Monish or Satan made in Ararat*, based on a poem by Y.L. Peretz).

the town of the same name, started to appear at inns and taverns and they were joined by travelling comedians, satirists and minstrels. The year 1875 saw the emergence of professional groups, the most important of which was the wandering troupe formed in 1900 by Abraham Izaak Kamiński (1867–1918) and featuring Ester Rachel Kamińska (1870–1925), the first Jewish theatre star.

The inter-war period was the heyday of Jewish theatre in Poland. In Łódź there were two revues, Azazel and Folks Teater, Warsaw had the Ararat cabaret and the Krakover Yiddish Teater performed regularly in Cracow. The avant-garde movement was also strongly represented, with the Sambation burlesque theatre in Warsaw, the Chad Gadyo puppet theatre in Łódź, as well as many ambitious Warsaw troupes, such as Yung Teater, WIKT and Varshever Nayer Yidisher Teater. We should also not forget Henryk Vogelfaenger (1906–1990), whose light entertainment programmes on the radio were incredibly popular, nor should we leave out Tońcio from the great pair of comedians Szczepcio and Tońcio from Lvov.

A Magic World – Chagall, a production at The Jewish Theatre in Warsaw, featuring Szymon Szurmiej, who also directed the show (above).

Photography

Polish Jews played a leading role in the development of photography in Poland and they were among the first to set up photographic studios, turning this particular service into something of a national speciality. Maksymilian Fajans (1827–1890) was the first photographer of repute and, having studied daguerreotypy in Paris, he opened the Studio Leonard in Warsaw. People quickly spotted the potential of photography in documenting history, with Michał Greim (1828–1911) being responsible for the collection of 160 photos entitled *The Jews of Kamieniec Podolski*. Mosze Raviv-Worobejczyk, the first person to create montages, was heavily involved in artistic photography, as was Stefan Themerson (1910–1988), who was probably better known in the West than he was in Poland. The post-war generation is represented by Ryszard Horowitz (b. 1939), who lives in the USA.

Szymon Zajczyk (1901–1944) took thousands of pictures of wooden synagogues (below: the synagogue in Wołpa).

Film

Jewish cinematography in Poland was already in existence before the First World War. The 1920s saw only isolated works, such as Jonasz Turkow's *In the Forests of Poland* (1929) based on the writings of Józef Opatoszu. The first "talkie" was the avant-garde picture about settlements in Palestine, entitled

The first Yiddish film-making company was Siła (Power), owned by Mordechai Towbin. Its first production was a silent film *A Chasidic Woman and an Apostate* from 1911, by Marek Arnstein (1879–1943). By 1914, twelve more films had been made there, in most cases starring Ester Rachel Kamińska (above).

Films in Yiddish Produced in Poland

Mir kumen on (The Path of the Young, 1936) by Aleksander Ford; *Yidl mitn fidl* (Yidl with a Fiddle, 1936) by Józef Green and Jan Nowina-Przybylski; *Dybbuk* (1937) by Michał Waszyński; *Freyleche kabtzunim* (Merry Poor People, 1937) by Zygmunt Turkow; *Der Purimshpiler* (The Purim Clown, 1937) by Józef Green and Jan Nowina Przybylski; *Al chet* (For the Sins, 1937) by Saul Goskind; *Mamele* (Mummy, 1938) by Konrad Tom and Józef Green; *A briwele der mamen* (A Letter to Mum, 1938) by Leon Trystan and Józef Green; *On a heym* (The Homeless, 1939) by Aleksander Marten, the last film made before the outbreak of war; *Mir lebngeblibene* (We, Who Have Survived, 1948) by Natan Gross; *Unzere kinder* (Our Children, 1948) by Saul Goskind and Józef Juszyński; *From Ruins to Homeland* (1949) by Saul Goskind.

Chalutzim (1933), which gained widespread publicity for Aleksander Ford (1908–1980), the man who was later to direct *Krzyżacy* (The Teutonic Knights), a film based on the famous novel by the Nobel laureate Henryk Sienkiewicz.

In the second half of the 1930s, Yiddish cinema reached its zenith, mainly due to the creation of Greenfilm and Kinor, two commercial studios involved mainly in the production of comedies. The former, set up by Józef Grinberg, a repatriate from America, was of particular significance. Jewish artists also figured prominently in Polish cinematography, with three names springing to mind: the actor Michał Znicz (1888 or 1892–1943), star of the film *Forgotten Melody* (1938);

The most important film from the late 1930s, broadly regarded as a masterpiece of Jewish cinematography, was *Dybbuk*, by Michał Waszyński (1937), with the outstanding part of the Miropol *tzaddik* played by Abraham Morewski. The film was based on a play by Sh. An-ski, with a script by Alter Kacyzne, Marek Arnstein and Anatol Stern.

Selected Films by Polish Directors and Containing Jewish Themes, made after 1945

Ulica Graniczna (Border Street, 1948) by Aleksander Ford; *Samson* (1961) by Andrzej Wajda; *Świadectwo urodzenia* (Birth Certificate, 1961) by Stanisław Różewicz; *Salto* (1963) by Tadeusz Konwicki; *Niekochana* (The Unloved Woman, 1966) by Jerzy Nasfeter; *Wniebowstąpienie* (Ascension, 1969) by Jan Rybkowski; *Sanatorium pod klepsydrą* (Sanatorium under the Sign of the Hourglass, 1973) by Wojciech Hass; *Ziemia Obiecana* (The Promised Land, 1975) by Andrzej Wajda; *Austeria* (The Inn, 1982) by Jerzy Kawalerowicz; *Europe, Europe* (1990) by Agnieszka Holland; *Wielki Tydzień* (Holy Week, 1997) by Andrzej Wajda; *Daleko od okna* (Far from the Window, 1999) by Jan Jakub Kolski; *Pianista* (The Pianist, 2002) by Roman Polański.

the composer Henryk Wars (1902–1977); and Henryk Szaro (1900–1942), director of the box-office hit *Ordynat Michorowski* (Michorowski – Lord of the Manor, 1937).

The war was by no means the end of Yiddish cinema in Poland and Kinor started up again soon after, producing two feature films dealing with the tragedy of those who had lost their lives. Only the Communist clampdown, together with mass emigration, finally put paid to any chance of a revival. The last film to be made was the Zionism inspired *From Ruins to Homeland* (1949), which had to be completed in France.

Literature

Works of literature by Polish Jews appear in any one of three languages: Hebrew, Yiddish and Polish, with anything written in Hebrew originally designed to serve a purely religious function. Books by Sephardi writers made their way through the Turkish border to Poland, where they found readers and imitators.

Famous early writings include: *Yeven Metzula* (The Deep Swamp, 1653), by Natan Hanover, dealing with the fate of Jews during the Chmielnicki uprising, and *Divrei Binah* (The Word of Reason, 18th century) by Ber of Bolechów. The first works connected with Chasidism, that is to say, aphorisms and parables, as well as biographies of *tzaddikim*, came out in Hebrew.

More modern forms of Hebrew literature developed hand in hand with the *Haskalah* movement and in connection with this the name of Chaim Zelig Słonimski (1810–1904) should be mentioned. Its focus, though, soon moved together with waves of emigrants to Palestine, such that writings in this language are of rather marginal significance in Poland. Nevertheless, a number of outstanding authors writing in Hebrew hailed from the Polish Jewish community, with Nobel laureate Shmuel Josef Agnon, a native of Buczacz, at the very top.

Sholem Aleichem (1859–1919).

Shmuel Yosef Agnon (1888–1970)

Yiddish literature had a much wider range, initially being spread by word of mouth. Some written texts did occur, for instance, in books for women who were not familiar with Hebrew, a good example being *Tsene Urene* (Come out and Have a Look) by Yaakov ben Itzhaak Ashkenazi of Janów Lubelski. As with Hebrew literature, great strides were made during the *Haskalah* era, with the first short stories being published in 1864. The author was Mendele Moicher Sforim (1835–1917), considered by many to be the father of Yiddish literature. Very soon, two major authors, Sholem Aleichem and Yitzchak Leibush Peretz, came to prominence. Sholem Aleichem, who lived in the Podole region in the far reaches of the borderlands, would eulogise about Kasrilevka, a tiny little Jewish town. His most famous work *Tevye der Milchiker* (Tevye the Milkman, 1894–1916) was finally turned into the stage musical *Fiddler on the Roof* in 1964 and was made into the famous film of the same name by Norman Jewison in 1971. Yitzchak Leibush Peretz (1852–1916) was born in Zamość but lived in Warsaw, where he wrote first in a positivist and then in a modernist style, his influences being Wyspiański and Przybyszewski. His best-known works are his reports, *Bilder fun a Provinzrayze* (Pictures from a Trip in the Provinces, 1891), the short stories, *Chasidish* (1900) as well as the plays *Churban Beit Tzaddik* (The Fall of the Tzaddik's House, 1903) and *Baynacht oyfn Altn Mark* (On the Old Square by Night, 1906).

The heyday of Yiddish literature was the period of the Second Polish Republic. Various groups formed, such as Yung Yiddish from Łódź, the Warsaw-based Chaliastre or Jung Vilne from Vilna. Surrealism was represented by the poet, Itzik Manger (1901–1969), local folklore by the Cracovian from Kazimierz, Mordechai Gebirtig (1877–1942). The most outstanding, however, were these prose writers: Shalom Ash, author of *Miasteczko* (Little Town, 1904) and *Motke Złodziej* (Motke the Thief, 1916); Józef Opatoszu (1888–1954), author of *W lasach polskich* (In the Forests of Poland, 1921); Israel Joshua Singer (1893–1944), author of *Josie Kalb* (1932), and last, but not least, Nobel laureate Isaak Bashevis Singer, born in Leoncin near Radzymin and author of *Satan in Goray* (1932), *The Magician of Lublin* (1960), *The Mannor* (1967), *The Estate* (1969), and many more. To read Isaak Bashevis Singer is a wonderful introduction to Yiddish literature, and his works have been translated into many languages.

Mordechai Gebirtig (1877–1942)

After the Second World War, Yiddish literature ceased to exist in Poland as an identifiable genre and today it may be regarded as a closed chapter. The last Yiddish writer was the poet from Szczecin Eliasz Rajzman (1909–1975), whose little tome of verse, entitled *Di Shprach fun Dayne Oygen* (The Way Your Eyes Speak, 1967) was the final book of its kind published in Poland.

Jewish jokes were a separate phenomenon entirely. A distinction was made between a *vitz* (joke), which is short and concise, and the longer *shmontzes* (anecdote). Jewish humour blossomed in Poland during the inter-war period, producing several masters of the form, with Marian Hemar in a class of his own. After the war, the Dudek cabaret revived this particular art.

A third trend, that of Jewish literature written in Polish, is the oldest of all and represents by far the greatest output of work by Polish-Jewish writers. The first pieces of writing by Jewish authors in the local language appeared in the circle of Frankists around the year 1800 and further development was closely linked to the process of assimilation in the middle of the century. The first poems by Aleksander Kraushar were published, as were short stories by Wilhelm Feldman and a novel *From a Tight Sphere* by Malvina Meyersonova. The Jewish contribution to more recent Polish literature is enormous. All one has to do is mention

Shalom Ash (1880–1957)

Marian Hemar (1901–1972)

Bruno Schulz (1892–1942) self-portrait

these names: Jan Brzechwa (Jan Wiktor Lesman, 1900–1966), Marian Hemar (Jan Marian Hescheles, 1901–1972), Benedykt Hertz (1872–1952), Bruno Jasieński (Wiktor Zysman, 1901–1938), Mieczysław Jastrun (M. Agatstein, 1903–1983), Bolesław Leśmian (Bolesław Lesman, 1877–1937), Tadeusz Peiper (1891–1968), Julian Stryjkowski (Pesach Stark, 1905–1996), Julian Tuwim (1894–1953), Aleksander Wat (Aleksander Chwat, 1900–1967), Adam Ważyk (Adam Wagman, 1905–1982), Józef Wittlin (1896–1976) and finally Henryk Grynberg (b. 1936).

THE ALPHABET

The Hebrew alphabet is one of the oldest known to mankind. It was created somewhere around 700 B.C.E. and based on the Phoenician alphabet which in turn, developed from the Assyrian cuneiform version. The twenty-two letters signify consonants. In modern-day pronunciation there is no difference between "tet" and "tav" or "kaf" and "kof"; the letters "alef" and "ayin" now also denote the vowels "a" and "e".

As with other alphabets which are ancient in origin some of the letters change shape depending on whether the vowels ascribed to them are within the word or at the end of it. The Hebrew alphabet had a much wider application than the language, as all texts which originated in a Jewish culture were written in it, including Yiddish and Ladino.

The letters of the Hebrew alphabet are also used for indicating numbers. *Alef* denotes 1 and so on, up to *yod*, which is 10. The next letters are used for the tens, so *kaf* is 20, up to *kof*, which is 100. In order, starting with *resh* (200), the letters indicate the hundreds, up to *tav* (400). Higher numbers are made up of combinations of letters. Certain combinations are forbidden, an example being, the number 15 which in Hebrew is *tet-zayin* (9+6), instead of 10+5 which would require letters that form part of the name of the Lord.

Hebrew Alphabet

א	alef	מם	mem
ב	bet	ןנ	nun
ג	gimel	ס	samech
ד	dalet	ע	ayin
ה	he	ףפ	pe
ו	vav	ץצ	tsadi
ז	zayin	ק	qof
ח	chet	ר	resh
ט	tet	ש	shin/sin
י	yod	ת	tav
ךכ	kaf		
ל	lamed		

WARSAW

•

Once the Largest Jewish City in Europe

•

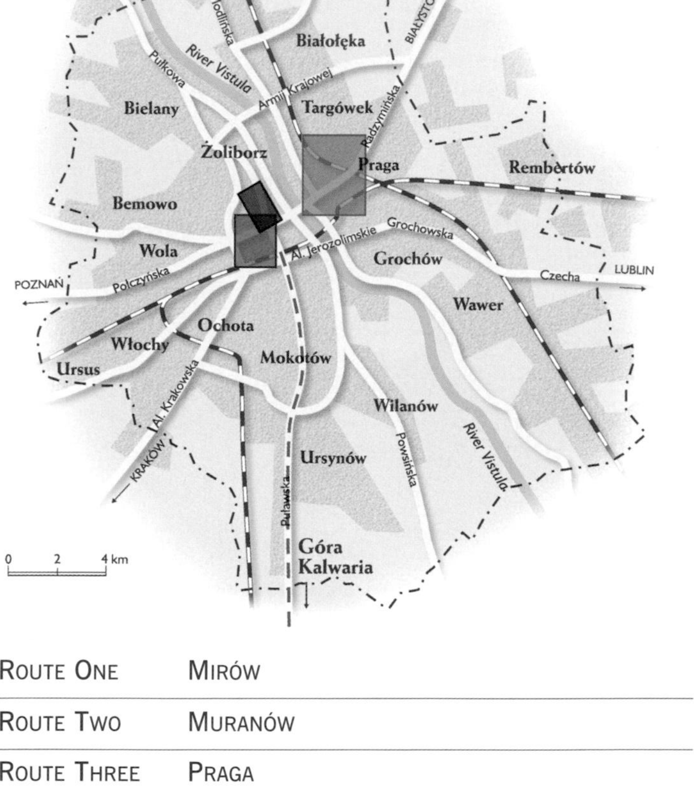

▬	ROUTE ONE	MIRÓW
▬	ROUTE TWO	MURANÓW
▬	ROUTE THREE	PRAGA
▬	ROUTE FOUR	WARSZAWA → GÓRA KALWARIA

FOR PRACTICAL INFORMATION SEE PAGE 275

RECOMMENDATIONS

Visit the **Nożyk Synagogue**, see a performance at the **Jewish Theatre**, go for a walk along **ul. Żelazna** and **ul. Chłodna**, visit the **cemetery in ul. Okopowa**, be sure to take a look at **ul. Tłomackie** and the pavement of the former **ul. Nalewki**, and also go to **Umschlagplatz**.

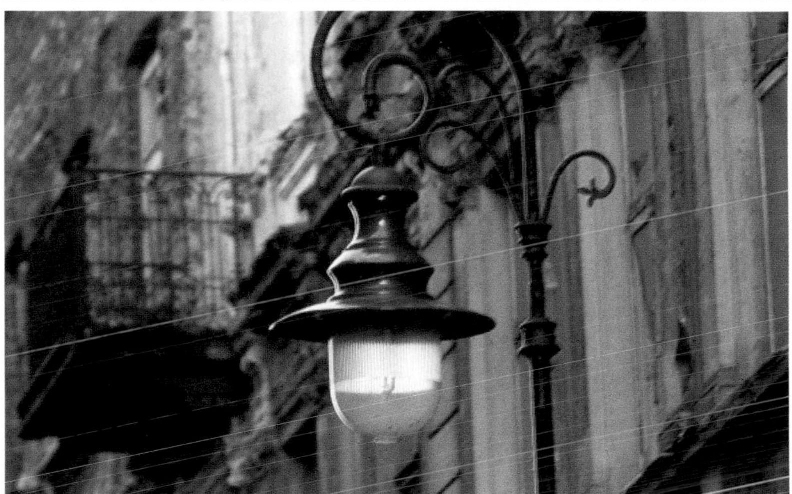

Historic Warsaw perished during the Second World War and with it all the monuments testifying to a Jewish heritage in this city: the Great Synagogue in ul. Tłomackie, the "round synagogue" in the Praga district and a great number of smaller but also very significant buildings.

The earliest material evidence of the existence of Jews in Warsaw is a record from 1414. The first known Jewish quarter, according to a description from 1430, was situated somewhere in the vicinity of the following streets: ul. Rycerska, ul. Piwna, ul. Piekarska and ul. Wąski Dunaj (some people claim that the name comes from the Hebrew word *Adonai* meaning "Lord" and also from the first Warsaw synagogue, which was presumably somewhere here). In the Middle Ages ul. Wąski Dunaj and ul. Piekarska were linked by ul. Żydowska, which disappeared a very long time ago. The first Jewish cemetery was established outside the city walls, east of Krakowskie Przedmieście.

From 1483 Warsaw was closed to Jews. They were only allowed to attend fairs. From 1774 the estate refered to as New Jerusalem (the street called Aleje Jerozolimskie gets its name from this) existed on land owned by the Potocki and Sułkowski families (now Plac Zawiszy). Jews also lived in the Praga district and in some of the small towns outside Warsaw, among them Raszyn and Golędzinów. It was here that the local Jewish community (which included among its number Szmul Zbytkower, confidant to the king and ancestor of Henri Bergson, the famous French philosopher) established the first cemetery (on the corner of what is now

Warsaw, Sienna Street
number sixty nine
The evening pours
golden wine
over windowpanes
On a narrow balcony
Just you and me
Is this true?
It cannot be.

From a poem
by Aron Cejtlin
Once in Poland
based on a translation
into Polish by Zew Szeps

Little slivers of Warsaw's past which survived the war: backyards, old tram rails in the cobblestones, parts of walls and even empty places at meaningful locations (ul. Sienna 69, ul. Miła 18) are often of special significance (above: the former ul. Nalewki, now ul. Bohaterów Getta).

ul. św. Wincentego and ul. Odrowąża). A census from 1793 (after Warsaw and Praga were joined in 1791) indicated that the enlarged town was home to some 7,000 Jews.

In 1795 the Prussian invaders quashed the *privilegia de non tolerandis Judaeis* and from then on Jews began to migrate to Warsaw. Many wealthy families arrived from Berlin, Koenigsberg and Riga. Self-governing bodies were formed, including two Jewish communities in Warsaw and Praga, as well as hospitals, brotherhoods and schools. Together with the arrival of Jews from Germany came the idea of the *Haskalah*. Jacob Flatau set up the first progressive synagogue, known as the German synagogue, in ul. Daniłowiczowska. The Prussians gave an order which required surnames to be given to the entire Jewish population and this was carried out between 1804 and 1807 by the romantic writer Ernst Theodor Amadeus Hoffmann (1776–1822), who was employed as an official in the

Tourist Attractions

The rebuilt **Old and New Town**: the Royal Castle; the 14th century arch-cathedral basilica of the Decapitation of St John the Baptist; St Martin's Church with a convent (built in 1356, the church reconstructed in 1744); the church of the Visitation of the Most Holy Virgin Mary in Nowe Miasto, built some time after 1411; the Jesuit church (1608–1626); the church of St Jack (1612–1639); the church of the Holy Spirit (1699–1717); the beautiful church of St Casimir (the Sisters of the Sacrament, 1688–1692), designed by Tylman of Gemeren; the Franciscan church (1679–1733); the walls of the Old Town (the second half of the 15th century) with a Barbican (1548), as well as the column of King Sigismund III from 1644. Since 1980 the Old Town of Warsaw has been an UNESCO World Heritage site.

In **Śródmieście** (city centre) you should visit the Łazienki park with the Palace on the Water (1683–1690), the Theatre on the Island and the Old Orangery. The churches, such aş St Ann's, built sometime after 1454 and remodelled later; the church of Visitandines (1727, 1754–1763); the Evangelic-Augsburg church (1777–1781). Other palaces and castles: the Ujazdów Castle (1619–1620, remodelled in 1975–1983), now home to the Centre of Contemporary Art; the Presidential Palace (The Koniecpolski Palace, 1643–1645, later extended); The Lubomirski Palace (Pod Blachą); the Krasiński Palace; the Pac Palace; the Czapski Palace; the Primate's Palace. The monuments to Sobieski (1788), Poniatowski (1826–1832), Copernicus (1830), Mickiewicz (1898), Chopin (1904), and the Grave of the Unknown Soldier (1925). In Warsaw you will also find dozens of museums.

In the **Czerniaków** district: the baroque church of St Anthony of Padova (1690–1693). In the **Mokotów** district: the Królikarnia Palace (1786–1789). In the **Praga** district: the Loretanian chapel (1640–1644) in ul. Ratuszowa, the Metropolitan Orthodox Christian church (1867–1869), the cathedral church of St Florian (built after 1902, its two tall towers are visible from the Old Town bank of the Vistula). The palace in **Wilanów**, the suburban royal residence with a museum and a magnificent park area, is a compulsory part of a visit to the capital of Poland.

Warsaw municipality office. This is how many family names originated, including those of Eisenberg, Rosenthal, Tonenblat and Vogelsang.

In the 19th century, the quarters of Warsaw known later as Muranów and Nalewki were populated mostly by Jews (above: the corner of ul. Leszno and ul. Okopowa, photo from before 1939).

In the era of the Duchy of Warsaw, Jews were allowed to live in certain parts of the town only and required to move out to the area of what is now ul. Okopowa, in the direction of ul. Nowolipie, ul. Bonifraterska, ul. Franciszkańska and ul. Gęsia. The Napoleonic era was very favourable for the Jews, who quickly became rich through deliveries of military supplies. It was then that huge fortunes were made by some Warsaw Jewish families, among them the Fraenkls, the Bersons, the Kronenbergs, the Rosens, the Epsteins, the Glueckbergs the Natansons as well as by the above-mentioned Szmul Zbytkower.

In 1821 the Russian authorities removed the *kahal* and replaced it with a government-controlled Board of the Jewish Community. This reform deprived the Warsaw Orthodox Jewish community of its principal bastion. The School of Rabbis opened in 1826 was another important institution whose mission was the victory of the followers of the *Haskalah*. Its programme of study included not only elements of religious education but also a more secular approach.

Jan Gotlib Bloch, the railway king, was born in Radom in 1886, the son of a dyer. He settled in Warsaw in 1851 and this is where his great career began. After some fifteen years he became one of the top financiers in the world. His ability to make the right choices was the basis of his extraordinary success. He invested the money he had made from the manufacturing of timber and plywood in the development of a railway line between the town of Koluszki and the factory district of the city of Łódź. In the context of the industrial boom in Łódź, this investment proved to be extremely lucrative. He soon built another railway line, from the depths of Russia to Lipava in Latvia, and took over the transporting of goods from the Russian Empire. In addition to the construction of railway lines and train stations, he manufactured railway sleepers and rolling stock. He also wrote an astonishing book *Future War*, which contained his speculations on the development of military technology and infrastructure. Despite the fact that he had converted to Christianity while still living in Radom, he never broke from his Jewish compatriots. He was, for instance, a patron of the literary works of Yitzchak Leibush Peretz. Modern-day Warsaw is indebted to Jan Gotlib Bloch for his contribution to the development of the water supply and sewage systems. He helped Sokrates Starynkiewicz in communal investment projects, but was opposed to the disposal of sewage into the Vistula. He lived in a house on the corner of ul. Królewska and ul. Marszałkowska. He died in 1902.

Thanks to two eminent Jewish families: the Glueckbergs and the Orgelbrands, Warsaw became a great publishing centre printing books in Hebrew, Yiddish and Polish. In 1823 the first issue of the Polish-Jewish periodical "Der Beobachter an der Weichsel" (The Vistula Observer) was published by Antoni Eisenbaum, today regarded as a pioneer of Jewish press.

The second half of the 19th century brought with it enormous changes in the position of Jews in the town, with a resilient group of wealthy members of the community paving the way for change. This they achieved in various ways, including the publishing of "Gazeta Polska" and involvement in charitable activities. Assimilation began to take place, and with it the emancipation of a group constituting more than a quarter of the population of Warsaw. Total equality came in the years preceding the January Uprising and the dramatic events of 1863. It was then that the first Jewish newspapers appeared: in Yiddish, Hilel Gladsztern's "Varshoyer Yidishe Tzaytung" (Warsaw Jewish Gazette) in 1867 and in Hebrew, Chaim Zelig Slonimski's "Hatzefira" (Morning Star) in 1862.

One of the key figures in these processes was Dov Ber Meisels (1797–1870), known for his patriotism and support for the independence revolts in 1830, 1846 and 1848. He also awakened patriotism in the Jews. Thanks to his efforts a uniform list of merchants was drawn up, in which nationality was no longer a criterion. The breakthrough came at a demonstration of patriotism on 8 April 1861. By firing into the masses, the army shot dead a young craftsman in the first row, who was carrying a cross. Michael Landy, the son of a Jewish merchant, picked up the cross and raised it above the crowd, only to be killed by a bullet. This tragic event left its mark on both communities. The Jews under the leadership of Meisels were shocked and adopted an openly anti-Russian stance. When on 8 November 1861 all Catholic

Patriotic manifestations in Warsaw were attended by the representatives of both Polish and Jewish communities (below: the march of the rabbinate on 3 May 1916).

Leopold Kronenberg (1812–1879; a portrait by Leopold Horowitz) came from a Jewish family. He converted to Calvinism in 1845. Having inherited a substantial fortune, he increased it enormously within a short space of time, trading in tobacco and snuff. He built the largest sugar-mills in the Polish Kingdom. Both the Vistula Railway Line connecting Mława, Warsaw and Kowel and the strategic line between Warsaw and Brest on the River Bug were among his achievements. He also established several financial institutions, such as the Trade Bank, the Credit Society and the Industrial Fund. He supported the January Uprising against Russia, becoming a leader of the Directorate of the "Whites". He was also active in social work. He organised the Higher School of Commerce, managed the stock exchange and published "The Polish Gazette" (whose editor-in-chief was the famous Polish writer Józef Ignacy Kraszewski). Leopold Kronenberg's work was carried on by his descendants. His third son Leopold Jan (1847–1937) was one of the founders and benefactors of the Warsaw Philharmonic Society (now the National Philharmonic) and he was also behind the initiative to erect in Warsaw a monument to the great Polish poet Adam Mickiewicz. He also financed Polish support for the national plebiscite in Silesia.

churches were closed as a result of the protest against an incursion by Cossacks into a Bernardine church, some of the Warsaw rabbinate came out in support of the action. The Russians arrested Meisels as well as six high-ranking officials and locked them in the Citadel. After this episode the atmosphere was unequivocal; the patriciates of both nationalities attended joint receptions and young Jews went about in traditional Polish national costume. When the uprising took place, Warsaw Jews followed their hearts. The ranks of the insurgents were reinforced even by *Chasidim*, who as a matter of general principle did not participate in political life. Henryk Wohl became director of the National Government Finance Department and Leopold Kronenberg was his advisor.

There were 213,000 Jews in Warsaw around 1900 (35% of the population). In 1916 this proportion went up to as much as 44%. Malicious elements from other cities, particularly Lvov and Vilna, sometimes called the Polish capital "the Jewish town in the West".

In the main Jews made their living from commerce, handicraft and transport services. They traded in wood, dyes, metal wares, leather goods and haberdashery. Publishing

Dov Ber Meisels, formerly the rabbi of Cracow, came to Warsaw in 1852 to take up the post of Chief Rabbi.

houses and bookshops were their domain, an excellent example being the Orgelbrand family. The electric trams, the life work of Maurycy Spokorny, are a wonderful memorial to the Jewish contribution to Warsaw transport.

However, at the beginning of the 1930s an incredible 75% of Warsaw Jews were estimated to be living in poverty. *Di yidishe prostitutkes* was a real social problem for the Jewish community. Ul. Kamienne Schodki, a little street in the Old Town, had a rather unsavoury reputation, as did ul. Kępna and ul. Białostocka in the Praga district. Streets such as ul. Stawki, ul. Niska, ul. Miła, ul. Pawia, ul. Dzika and, above all, ul. Krochmalna, formed a "forbidden area". The criminal Yitzchak Farberowicz became famous as a writer, having published his book *Biography of a Criminal* under the pseudonym Urke Nahalnik. All kinds of stories circulated about the safe-breaker Leyzor Floksztrumf. The Jewish criminal world lived from passing stolen goods, giving bribes and forging documents.

During the two decades of the inter-war period the majority of Jews lived in the north-west part of the city. In the streets there one could see numerous signs advertising little shops and handicraft workshops.

There were several Orthodox synagogues, including the Nożyk Synagogue in ul. Twarda, functioning to this very day

In the first half of the 20th century, the Jewish population of Warsaw was larger than in any other European city.

The corner of ul. Franciszkańska and ul. Nalewki was one of the most Jewish places in Warsaw. Another large group of Jews lived in the Praga district (below: the place where ul. Nalewki crossed ul. Gęsia and ul. Nadwiślańska, photo from 1910).

Shoemaking and tailoring were among the main Jewish crafts (above: the Jewish shoe market in ul. Stawki, photo from 1933).

and the "round synagogue", no longer to be found. The latter was erected in 1835 and situated in the Praga district (on the corner of ul. Jagiellońska and ul. Szeroka, now ul. Kłopotowskiego). So-called progressive synagogues also existed, an example of which was the Great Synagogue on Tłomackie, opened on 14 September 1878 (today on this site there is a sky scraper referred to as the Blue Tower). More than three hundred houses of prayer were in operation at that time. Many Chasidim made use of the *shtiblech* (prayer rooms) on a daily basis. They spent *Shabbat* at the courts of the *tzaddikim* in Góra Kalwaria, Radzymin, Przysucha, Kozienice, Warka or Kock. Many *tzaddikim* had their own houses in Warsaw, spending more time there than they did in their home towns, especially the Alters from Góra Kalwaria. Among community institutions, two hospitals for Orthodox Jews stood out: the one in ul. Pokorna and the other at Czyste established in 1902, at that time the most modern in Warsaw (now the Wolski hospital in ul. Kasprzaka). There were also old people's homes and orphanages, not to mention two cemeteries which can still be found; the first in ul. Okopowa (measuring 33 hectares) and the second in ul. św. Wincentego in the Bródno district (formerly 12.4 hectares in size).

At the outbreak of the Second World War there were 380,567 Jews living in Warsaw. In September 1940 the Germans established the Warsaw Ghetto, which occupied part of the pre-war district mostly populated by Jews. The Ghetto was closed on 15 November 1940. Approximately 450,000 Jews had passed through it. After several reductions in its area, the Ghetto was made up of two parts joined in February 1942 by a wooden bridge over ul. Chłodna. In total it measured little more than three square kilometres, which meant about 120,000 people living in each square kilometre. The daily food ration amounted to 230 calories and everybody received only 2 kg of bread per month. Between 1940 and 1942, 100,000 people died of hunger and illness. From 22 July to 21 September 1942, approximately 300,000 were deported to the death camp in Treblinka by way of *Umschlagplatz*, part of the freight station

The Philharmonic

The rather modest building of the contemporary National Philharmonic is but a shadow of the glamorous home of the Warsaw Philharmonic Society from the time before the Second World War. The magnificent edifice was the great concept of Aleksander Rajchman, financed by 270 industrialists, including many Jews. Jews were not only among the main benefactors of the Philharmonic (testimony to which is now to be found on commemorative plaques unveiled in 2001) but also constituted a major part of the audience. When in 1909 this musical institution fell into financial difficulties, its debts were paid by Maurycy Zamoyski, the Polish count and Leopold Jan Kronenberg, the Jewish banker.

area in the north of the city. On 23 July 1942, Adam Czerniaków, the chairman of *Judenrat* (the Jewish Council established by the Germans) chose to take cyanide rather than give into the demands of the Nazis. Some of the inhabitants of the Ghetto decided to take their fate into their own hands and fight against the Germans. On 19 April 1943, with 60,000 people still trapped inside, an uprising started and marked the beginning of the end of the largest Jewish community in Europe.

Approximately three hundred thousand Warsaw Jews perished during the Second World War (above: a photograph of the memorial to the children murdered by the Nazis).

After the war a revival within the Jewish population of Warsaw gradually took place. However, it was followed by several waves of emigration due to the terror of Stalinism as well as the anti-semitic events of March 1968.

The present Warsaw Jewish community is one of the largest in Poland. The nationwide headquarters for all Jewish organisations can be found in the building at ul. Twarda 6 and Plac Grzybowski 12/16. Warsaw also sees the publication of the most important Jewish newspapers and magazines, including "Midrash", "Jidele" for children, as well as "Dos Yidishe Vort – Słowo Żydowskie" (The Yiddish Word).

Religious life among the Jewish community is undergoing a revival nowadays (below: *Purim* celebrations).

MIRÓW

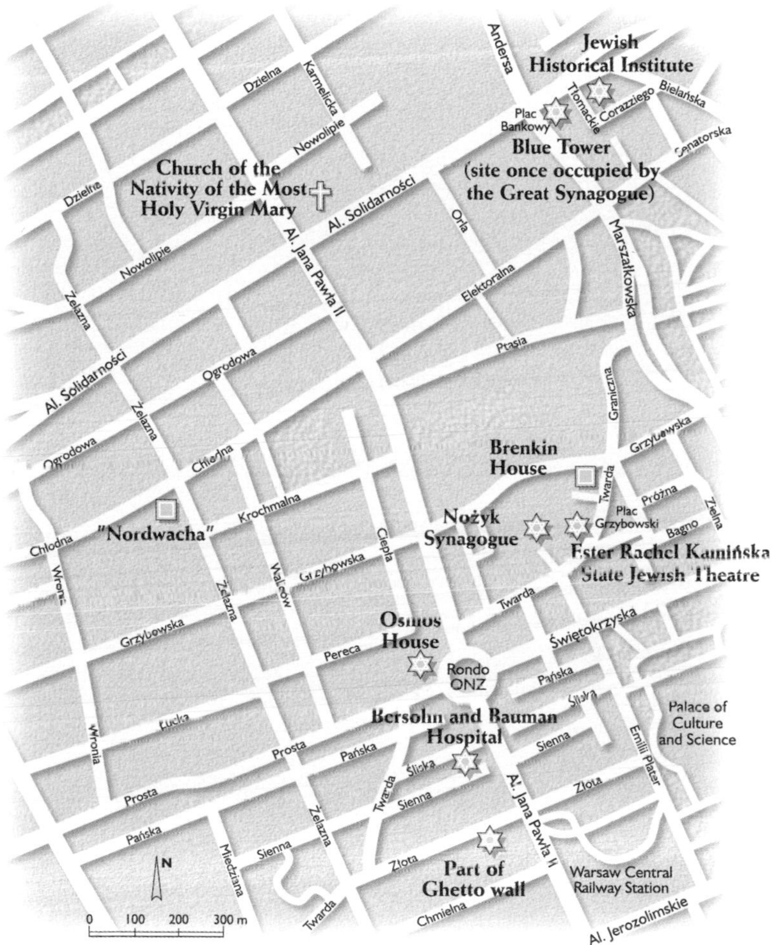

Suggested Route

Plac Grzybowski → the Nożyk Synagogue → the Jewish Theatre → ul. Próżna → ul. Twarda (the osnos house) → al. Jana Pawła II → ul. Złota (remains of the ghetto wall) → ul. Żelazna → ul. Chłodna → ul. Elektoralna → Plac Bankowy (the blue tower) → ul. Tłomackie (the Jewish Historical Institute)

The Nożyk Synagogue, the only pre-war Jewish house of worship still remaining in Warsaw, dates from 1902.

The synagogue was designed to hold 565 worshippers. The seats were sold by auction. Those closest to the *aron ha-kodesh* were the most expensive.

You should begin your search for Warsaw's Jewish monuments from Plac Grzybowski. Before the war this square, now somewhat out of the way, was one of the most important places in the city. Each hectare was inhabited by an average of 729 persons. Ul. Bagno and ul. Graniczna, the two streets leading away from the square, were busy arterial roads. All that remains of the latter is a magnificent pastoral street light at the crossing-point with ul. Grzybowska. Trams ran here and you can see their tracks in the asphalt in the square.

The Nożyk Synagogue

This house of worship was founded as an Orthodox synagogue by the Nożyks, a wealthy Warsaw couple. Their gift to the community came with the following conditions: "The synagogue should exist on this property for ever and ever, and always bear the name of Mr and Mrs Zalman and Rivka Nożyk" (quote from J. Kasprzycki, *The Roots of the City*, vol. II). The building is a good example of the eclectic architecture from the turn of the 20th century. Here we find a mixture of Neo-Romanesque features and what is known as Byzantine style, typical for the fading years of the Russian Empire. During the Second World War the synagogue was inside the boundaries of the "Little Ghetto". It was used by the Germans as a storehouse. Its furnishings were destroyed during the Warsaw Uprising, as were parts of the walls. Immediately after the war the building was provisionally made secure. Proper repair works, however, did not began until 1977, completion being celebrated on 18 April 1983.

Ul. Twarda 6. The synagogue is open on Saturdays, admission 5 zl.

Mr Szyc's little shop situated near the synagogue and probably the only *kosher* shop in Poland is well worth visiting. Members of the Jewish community can also use the *kosher* cafeteria on the first floor of the adjacent building (referred to as "the old congregation").

The Jewish Theatre

In the vicinity of pl. Grzybowski there are a number of other buildings linked to Warsaw's present-day Jewish community.

The Ester Rachel Kamińska State Jewish Theatre (pl. Grzybowski 12/16) is Polish Jewry's largest cultural institution and continues a more than 150 year tradition of performances in Yiddish. The theatre can hold 390 people and its most important post-war figures are the actress Ida Kamińska (the daughter of the founder), Jakub Rotbaum, Szymon Szurmiej and Chevel Buzgan.

On the other side of the square, on the corner of ul. Bagno, you will find the Jewish restaurant called Menorah. Walking from the square in the direction of ul. Grzybowska you go past a row of shops selling ladders and ironware, which take up the ground floor of what is called the Brenkin House. It is the only remaning enclave of commerce from pre-war Warsaw.

The repertory of the Ester Rachel Kamińska State Jewish Theatre includes plays by writers such as Sholem Alejchem, Sh. An-ski and Y.L. Peretz (below: *Monish or Satan made in Ararat* based on the poem by Y.L. Peretz).

The tenement house at ul. Próżna 14 once belonged to Mayer Wolanowski.

Ul. Próżna

Find some time to visit ul. Próżna, as its pre-war appearance remains intact, even though the surrounding area was almost completely razed to the ground. For a few years now there have been plans to open here a street museum with little shops, restaurants and exhibition rooms illustrating the history of Jewish Warsaw. Costly and time-consuming repairs to buildings of historical importance are under way. The houses here date from 1880 to 1890. House No 7 belonged to Szejwach Batawia, and No 9 to Naftali Perlman and Zalman Nożyk, the synagogue's founder. Before the war this street specialised in the selling of ironware and cheap literature from Szrajgold and Zyskind's paper recycling plants.

Along Ul. Twarda to Ul. Żelazna

From pl. Grzybowski, ul. Twarda leads to the Rondo ONZ. One thing that sticks out here is a large pre-war building which does not fit in with the more modern surroundings. It is the Osnos House (which belonged to the family of Leyb Osnos) built in 1912 and its address conforms to the pre-war network of streets (ul. Twarda 28, corner of ul. Ciepła 1). In old photographs we can see it as a mass of small shops including Grubstajn's butcher's stall, Lipman and Ret's smoked meats, Widerszal's grocery, Merder's dairy products, Frosz's cake shop, Lustman's soaps, Borensztajn's laundry and Geller's barber shop.

Approaching Aleja Jana Pawła II and all the way to Aleje Jerozolimskie, we can see many more such jewels. The street names say as much to lovers of old Warsaw as they do to readers of Hebrew or Yiddish writers. They include: ul. Pańska, ul. Śliska, ul. Sienna, ul. Złota and ul. Chmielna. You might like to end your visit to the monuments of pre-war Jewish Warsaw in the courtyard at ul. Złota 60, where a small piece of the Ghetto wall remains. It bears a commemorative plaque and a recess in which pilgrims from all over the world place candles.

At ul. Sienna 60 (between ul. Śliska and ul. Sienna) the Bersohn and Bauman Hospital (now Warsaw Children's Hospital) existed from 1878. It gained fame as the place where Janusz Korczak worked for 7 years.

Ul. Żelazna

Ul. Złota leads to ul. Żelazna and the first turning on the right beyond the point where it crosses with ul. Prosta is ul. Pereca, which before the war was called ul. Ceglana. Here, in house No 1, Yitzchak Leibush Peretz, one of the greats of Jewish literature, used to live. The next turning is ul. Grzybowska and here, at the crossroads, used to be one of the gates of the Ghetto.

Now you should go to the next crossing on ul. Żelazna. On the right hand side there is ul. Krochmala, street of legend, vividly portrayed by Isaac Bashevis Singer, but now nothing more than an empty, shrunken version of its former self, and becoming a park alleyway a little further on. Before the Second World War it had been one of Warsaw's most characteristic thoroughfares and a place where many merchant families chose to live. The Tykociners, the Kohns, the Kleins and the Gurewiczs all made their homes here. The famous bakeries of Enoch London, Murawski, Grynzang and the Kurant family also had premises in ul. Krochmalna.

Another crossing, another turning and you will reach ul. Chłodna. Anyone interested in the history of the Jews of Warsaw has almost certainly seen a photo from the Ghetto, portraying a crowded wooden viaduct above a street in which tramlines are visible in the paved road. You will find this very place and that very track right here, preserved as a memorial along with the original paving. Here, in house No 20, Adam Czerniaków, the chairman of the Ghetto *Judenrat* (Jewish Council), used to live. The building on the corner was once a guardhouse in which the *Nordwache* was stationed. It used to terrorise the Ghetto and "Aryan" districts alike. At the nearby crossroads of Aleja Solidarności and Aleja Jana Pawła II, some twenty or so metres removed from its original site, there remains the church of the Nativity of the Most Holy Virgin Mary, which during the war served Jewish converts to Catholicism. From here make your way along the historic ul. Leszno (now Aleja Solidarności) in the direction of Plac Bankowy.

Isaac Bashevis Singer (1904–1991) was awarded the Nobel Prize in 1978.

Mirów, Grzybów and Leszno, the parts of Warsaw evoking Jewish connotations quite obvious to the pre-war Varsovian, mean very little to contemporary inhabitants of Warsaw. It is a pity because the western parts of the city centre, and especially streets such as Chmielna, Srebrna, Sienna, Złota, Twarda, Chłodna, Krochmalna and Żelazna are the sections of Warsaw with which Isaac Bashevis Singer was familiar (left: Plac Piłsudskiego, former Plac Saski, photo from 1915).

The Main Judaic Library and the Great Synagogue (photo from 1936)

An Old Jew
by Maurycy Gottlieb

The Jewish Historical Institute

Before the Second World War, the Jewish Historical Institute building was the home of the Main Judaic Library situated next to the Great Synagogue in ul. Tłomackie and the Institute for Judaic Studies. It is one of the few relics of Jewish life in Warsaw, which at that time was the most important Jewish centre in the world. It is not just the building itself but the rich collection of archives and museum exhibits, as well as the library it houses, that are reminders of the past, gathered together in a place that was once completely plundered and partly wrecked by the Nazis (ul. Tłomackie 3/5, ☎ +22 82779221, www.jewishinstitute.org.pl.; Mon–Wed 9am–4pm, Thu 11am–6pm). In 1947 the building was restored thanks to the joint efforts of Jewish organisations. It houses two permanent displays. The first of them depicts the history of the Warsaw Ghetto, the largest in the territories conquered by the Third Reich. It shows the consecutive stages of the crime: the first regulations and practices of the Nazis, the imprisonment of 450,000 people in the Warsaw Ghetto and finally the mass murder of almost all its inhabitants. The photographs and documents in the exhibition show everyday life in the Ghetto, its economic, cultural and religious aspects, as well as

The exhibition "Life and Extermination in the Warsaw Ghetto (1940–1943)"

The Jewish Historical Institute and the sky-scraper known as the Blue Tower (photo from 2002)

the political underground movements and the struggle against starvation and disease. It also gives evidence of the activities of Jewish Mutual Social Aid, of slave work enforced by the Germans on those trapped in the Ghetto, and of Jewish armed resistance.

The other permanent exhibition is "The Gallery of Jewish Art". It is divided into two sections. The first shows objects of Jewish ritual art and the second those of Jewish secular art, including painting and sculpture. One of the most eye-catching displays in the section devoted to ritual art is the hall depicting the interior of a 19th-century synagogue. It has been arranged with the use of original, restored and, in some cases, reconstructed furnishings. A rich collection of Jewish ritual textiles and silverware has also been gathered here. Among the pictures shown at the exhibition there are paintings by some of the most famous Jewish artists, including Maurycy Gottlieb (1856–1879) and Samuel Hirszenberg (1865–1908). The Institute building also houses a bookshop which offers the largest selection of Judaica in Poland (mail order is also possible). It is open from Monday to Friday (9am–4pm) and the library with a reading room on Monday, Tuesday and Wednesday (8am–4pm), Thursday (8am–6pm) and Friday (8am–2pm). Temporary exhibitions are also organised here on a regular basis.

A *parochet* depicting the Sacrifice of Izaak (1774)

A reconstruction of a synagogue interior

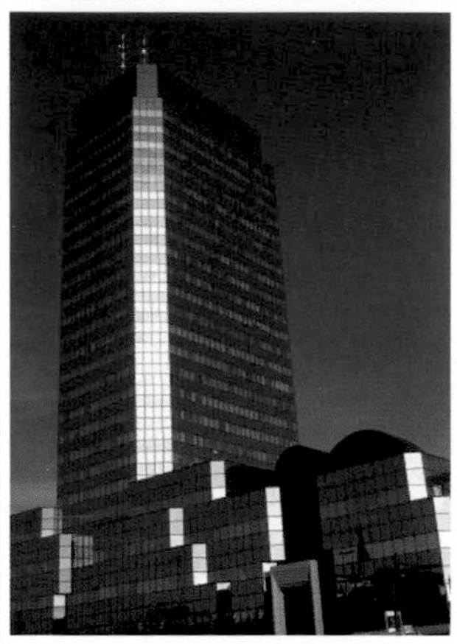

The so-called Blue Tower rises above Plac Bankowy.

Plac Bankowy

The Great Synagogue stood in ul. Tłomackie until 16 May 1943. This magnificent building, once the pride of the Jews of Warsaw, was erected from 1876 to 1878 and based on a design by Leandro Marconi, who gave it an impressive Classicist appearance. It could hold 3,000 worshippers and contained prayer halls, a religious school and archives. The synagogue was blown up by the Germans on 16 May 1943 as a definitive sign of victory over the rebellious Warsaw Ghetto.

After the war the erection of the present sky-scraper began on this site. Things, however, did not go quite as planned. The construction work took as long as thirty years. The legend of the "rabbi's curse" which forbade the completion of the building began to circulate in Warsaw. Fortunately the "curse" was lifted with the collapse of communism.

The Jewish Historical Institute

Behind the tower, in a little street known before the war as ul. Tłomackie, you can find the Jewish Historical Institute. (JHI, see page 74).

Prior to 1939, ul. Tłomackie was a much larger street and stretched as far as the Gruba Kaśka, a drinking water pumping station not far from the tram stop. After the war this street name disappeared for a few decades, making a comeback at the beginning of the 1990s.

MURANÓW

The district of Muranów no longer has the tightly packed buildings and narrow streets that it once contained. Nor is there any trace of the interminable courtyards with dozens of little shops, ateliers and basements. A walk around Muranów mainly involves looking for and finding famous addresses and significant places commemorated by stones or memorials.

Before the Second World War the Muranów district was an area populated mostly by Jews (below: the former Plac Muranowski, photographed in March 1939).

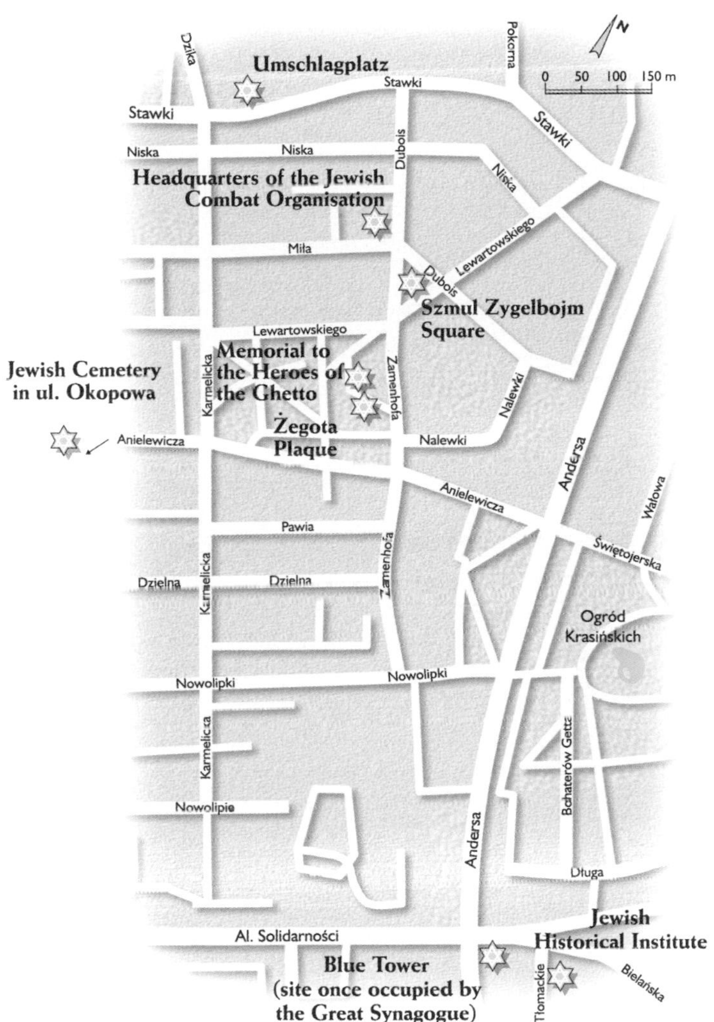

Suggested Route

ul. Bohaterów Getta → Ogród Krasińskich → ul. Anielewicza → Memorial Lane (ul. Zamenhofa, Shmul Zygielboim Square, ul. Stawki → Umschlagplatz) → the Jewish Cemetery in ul. Okopowa

The story of the survival of **Władysław Szpilman** (1912–2000) is just one of many episodes depicting the dramatic fate of Warsaw Jews. He was well-known as a pianist before the Second World War and referred to as the "man in whom music lives". He was also the hero of the last broadcast of pre-war Polish Radio (on 23 September 1939). He ended up in the Ghetto and this is where an amazing sequence of coincidences began. During the loading of the trains in *Umschlagplatz*, he was picked out of the crowd by a Ghetto policeman who happened to know him. He then managed to escape from the Ghetto, having mixed in with a group of "Aryan" workers, and began to live in a small deserted flat in Aleja Niepodległości. After the collapse of the Warsaw Uprising, the Germans began to set fire to each building in town. When it came for the house in which Szpilman lived to be burned, he took a lethal dose of sleeping tablets and opium, but woke up the following day to find out that the fire started by the Nazis stopped one floor below and the poison he had taken was not strong enough. Szpilman would not have survived the final weeks had it not been for help from a German captain Wilhelm Hosenfeld, a declared anti-facist who saved the lives of many people. Władysław Szpilman has described his dramatic life story in his book *The Pianist* (initially entitled *Death of the City*), later made into a film by Roman Polański, the winner of the Palme d'Or award at the 55th Cannes International Film Festival.

Ul. Bohaterów Getta (Heroes of the Ghetto Street)

You can get here either from ul. Tłomackie or from in front of the Blue Tower (*Ratusz* metro station). On the other side of the road you will see the Arsenal building, which today houses the Archaeological Museum. Next to it is ul. Bohaterów Getta, a dead-end and closed to traffic. It is hard to believe that this was once the beginning of ul. Nalewki famed for its bustling noisy crowds. The way this street looks today gives a feel of what the Nazis did to the pre-war district of Muranów. Pavements leading nowhere and old tram lines are the best preserved parts of this area.

The Memorial to the Heroes of the Ghetto, designed by L.M. Suzin in 1948, was sculpted by Natan Rappaport.

Ogród Krasińskich

One of the pavements ends in Ogród Krasińskich (the Krasiński Garden). Before the war the Jewish inhabitants from the neighbouring districts often used to go for a walk here. Behind the park ul. Świętojerska joins with ul. Mordechaja Anielewicza, named after one of the leaders of the Jewish Combat Organisation. This part of the street was laid out after the war. Its other segments correspond to pre-war ul. Gęsia. Follow it as far as the crossroads with ul. Zamenhofa, which is where the Memorial Lane begins.

Memorial Lane

If you go along the left hand side of ul. Zamenhofa, you will come across all the points of interest in the Memorial Lane. First of all there is the stone delineating the boundary of the Jewish quarter

during the Nazi occupation. Then you will find the first memorial to the Ghetto victims, dating from 1946, and also a plaque dedicated to *Żegota*, an organisation which was part of the Polish underground resistance units of Armia Krajowa (Home Army) and which helped imprisoned and persecuted Jews. Then, there is the Memorial to the Heroes of the Ghetto and further on ul. Zamenhofa which leads to Skwer Szmula Zygelbojma (Shmul Zygelboim Square). Opposite, there is a historic address, ul. Miła 18, the headquarters of the Jewish Combat Organisation. Rather than surrender to the Germans who had surrounded the building, on 8 May 1943 the leaders of the Ghetto Uprising committed suicide. Today on the corner of ul. Miła and ul. Dubois there is a commemorative mound dedicated to Mordechai Anielewicz. The last part of the Memorial Lane is the monument designed by Władysław Klamerus and Hanna Szmalenberg in what was *Umschlagplatz*, the platform from which over three hundred thousand Jews were deported to the death camp in Treblinka.

Umschlagplatz is often on the itinerary of visiting heads of state to Poland Pope John Paul II has prayed here.

The Jewish Cemetery in ul. Okopowa

The cemetery in ul. Okopowa measures some 33 hectares and contains about 250,000 tombs. Its size helps us to grasp just how huge the Warsaw Jewish community once was.

The Jewish Cemetery in ul. Okopowa was marked out in 1806 at the end of the former ul. Gęsia (now ul. Anielewicza). Since that time it has been the main burial ground for the Jews of Warsaw.

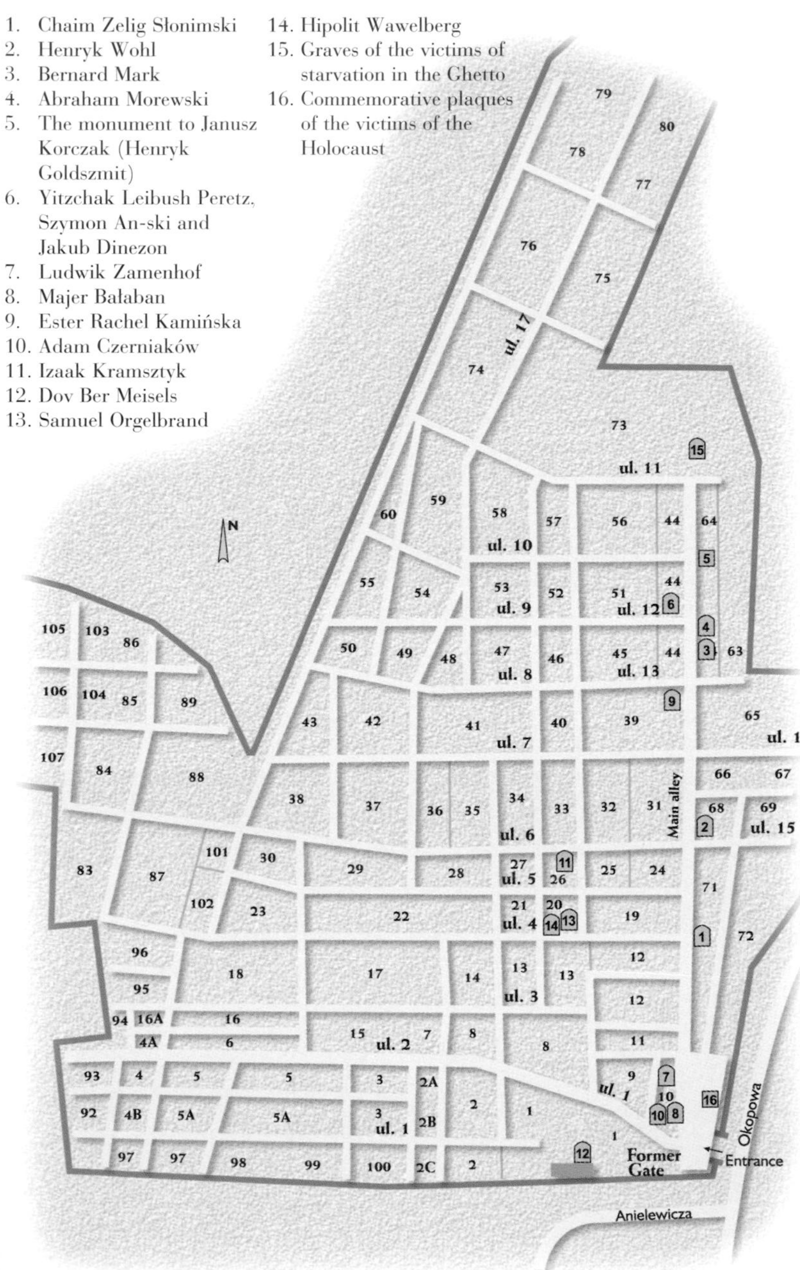
1. Chaim Zelig Słonimski
2. Henryk Wohl
3. Bernard Mark
4. Abraham Morewski
5. The monument to Janusz Korczak (Henryk Goldszmit)
6. Yitzchak Leibush Peretz, Szymon An-ski and Jakub Dinezon
7. Ludwik Zamenhof
8. Majer Bałaban
9. Ester Rachel Kamińska
10. Adam Czerniaków
11. Izaak Kramsztyk
12. Dov Ber Meisels
13. Samuel Orgelbrand
14. Hipolit Wawelberg
15. Graves of the victims of starvation in the Ghetto
16. Commemorative plaques of the victims of the Holocaust
N
ul. 17
ul. 11
ul. 10
ul. 9
ul. 12
ul. 8
ul. 13
ul. 7
ul. 14
ul. 6
ul. 15
ul. 5
ul. 4
ul. 3
ul. 2
ul. 1
Main alley
Former Gate
Entrance
Okopowa
Anielewicza

An alms box depicted on a headstone emphasises the generosity of the deceased, a feature considered a great merit in Jewish tradition. The box might also denote the resting-place of a community treasurer or a person who collected donations for charitable purposes.

Among the graves in the main alley there are those of Henryk Wohl (1836–1907), the minister of finance in the National Government at the time of the January Uprising (section 68, row 1); Bernard Mark (1908–1966), the first director of the Jewish Historical Institute (section 64, row 1); and Abraham Morewski (1886–1964), actor and director (section 64, row 1). One can also find here a symbolic memorial to the outstanding educator Janusz Korczak (Henryk Goldszmit, 1878–1942). In the western part of the cemetery there is the common gravestone of two great writers: Yitzchak Leibush Peretz (1852–1915) and Sz. An-ski (1863–1920) as well as the political activist Jakub Dinezon. Then, in section 10, row 2, you can see the graves of the creator of Esperanto Ludwik Zamenhof (1859–1917) and the great historian Majer Bałaban (1877–1942). Other famous Jews buried here include: the translator of the Bible into Polish Izaak Cylkow (1841–1908; section 33, row 1), the Jewish Council (*Judenrat*) chairman Adam Czerniaków (1880–1942; section 10, row 5), the rabbi-patriot and Siberian

The eminent Hebrew writer Chaim Zelig Słonimski (1810–1904) is buried in the cemetery in ul. Okopowa (section 71, row 11).

Building a colony of houses containing inexpensive flats, assigned to poor people regardless of their origin, was one of the most spectacular examples of philanthropy in Warsaw. The generous founder was **Hipolit Wawelberg** (1844–1901; section 20, row 3), an eminent Jewish banker. The housing estates he built in ul. Górczewska and in ul. Ludwiki (named after his wife) are still there today. Even the original inscriptions on the buildings remain. A technical college known as the Wawelberg and Rotwand School was another of Wawelberg's successful projects. In the 1950s the college became part of Warsaw Polytechnic.

exile Izaak Kramsztyk (1813–1889; section 26, row 11), Rabbi Dov Ber Meisels (1798–1870; section 1, row 6); as well as the printer Samuel Orgelbrand (1810–1868; section 20, row 7). The cemetery functions to this very day.

After visiting the graves you might like to have a look at the corner of the wall almost opposite the exit in ul. Anielewicza. Here, between the wall and the Skra stadium, the mass graves of starvation victims from the Ghetto were discovered. A memorial to them was erected thanks to the efforts of the Nissenbaum Foundation.

Ul. Okopowa 49/51. Open: Sun 9am–4pm; Mon–Thu 10am–5pm; Fri 9am–1pm. Autumn–Winter until sunset. Closed on Saturdays and Jewish holidays. Admission 4 zł.

Ester Rachel Kamińska (1870–1925) was a star of the pre-war Jewish theatre (sec. 39, row 1).

In Praga there were storehouses for goods from the entire Mazowsze region. This is where big trade deals were struck and commodities loaded onto the barges on the Vistula as well as standard and narrow-gauge railway carriages.

PRAGA

The district of Praga occupies a separate place in the history of the Jews of Warsaw. From 1768 the *privilegia de non tolerandis Judaeis* no longer applied and for this reason the Praga Jewish community was older and initially larger than the one in Warsaw. Also after the ban forbidding settlement on the left bank of the river was lifted, this suburb managed to retain its specifically Jewish commercial character. Praga was known for the good relations between its Polish and Jewish communities. This was always emphasised in comparisons with the situation of Jews on the left bank of the Vistula.

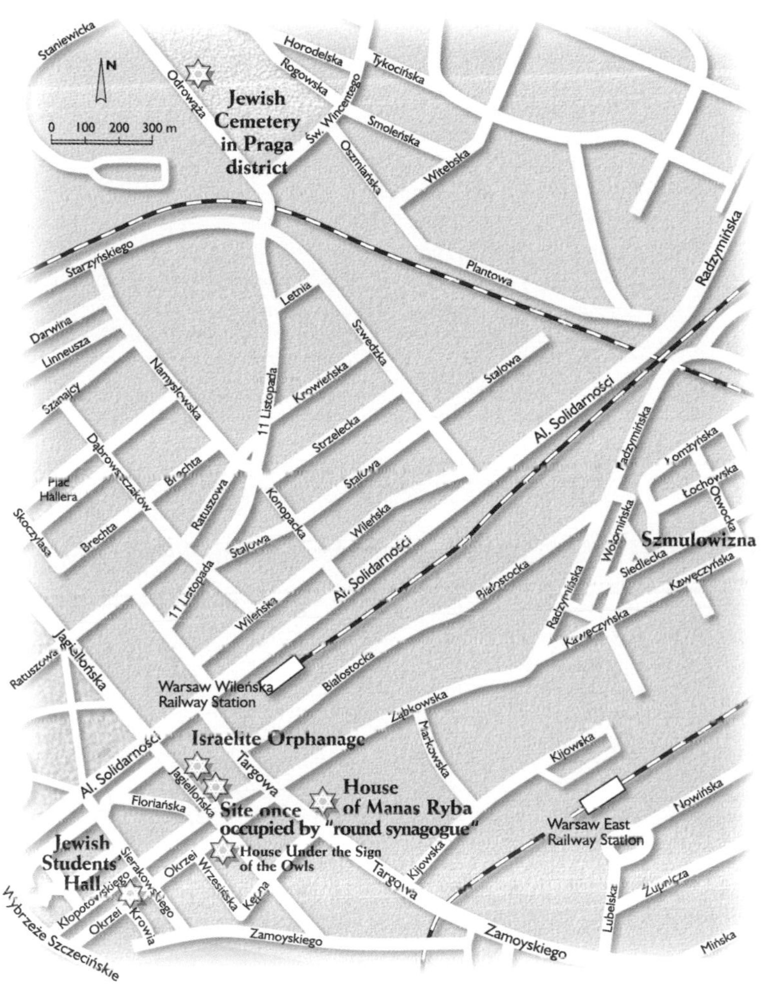

Suggested Route

ul. Jagiellońska (the site once occupied by the round synagogue, the orphanage) → ul. Kłopotowskiego → ul. Sierakowskiego (the Jewish students' hall of residence) → ul. Okrzei (the house under the sign of the owls) → the Jewish Cemetery on the corner of ul. Odrowąża and ul. św. Wincentego

Manas Ryba (1843–1938), the founder and administrator of the Różycki bazaar, was one of Praga's most interesting characters. This merchant from Nowy Dwór Mazowiecki arrived in Praga long before the First World War and lived in the house at ul. Targowa 56, which exists to this day. Ryba was a real lord of the bazaar, famous for an iron fist, but also for a sharp mind when it came to making a profit. He was probably the inspiration behind the construction of the Marki railway line. He was the subject of countless stories, including the one about how his wife married him because his name was Ryba (Fish) and her maiden name was Halbfisz (Half-fish). He seemed indestructible and at the age of 95 was still keeping an eye on his business. He died before the war and so, fortunately, he did not have to witness the end of the colourful world with which he was so closely identified.

The easiest way to start your visit to Praga is from outside St Florian's Cathedral, whose towers can be seen from far away. There is a large tram and bus stop next to it. (Trams # 13, 23, 26, 32; buses # 125, 160, 162, 170, 190, 192, 512).

To the left of the cathedral's facade you will find a pretty street called Floriańska which will take you straight to the centre of Jewish Praga at the point where ul. Jagiellońska crosses with the historic ul. Szeroka (now ul. Kłopotowskiego).

Praga is the only place in Warsaw which has retained its historic pre-war atmosphere. Unfortunately, this is also true in the case of theft and robbery, for which the district had a something of a reputation even before the First World War. During a visit to Praga bear your safety in mind. Do not go out alone or after dark. Leave cars in a guarded parking area. Do not leave anything of value inside them, particularly radios, cameras or documents. Take special care when visiting the Jewish cemetery as it is known for attacks in broad daylight. To be on the safe side it is better to go in a group.

The "round synagogue" was erected in 1835 (on the site of the earlier wooden house of prayer). The plans were drawn by Józef Lessel, in an unusual form of a roundhouse.

The Site Once Occupied by the Round Synagogue

A nursery school playground opposite the Praha cinema is where the Orthodox "round synagogue", the main synagogue on Warsaw's right bank, used to stand. The construction of this impressive building is linked to the decision of several wealthy Jewish families (the Pasmenters, the Posners, the Dancygiers, the Rubinlichts, the Bergsons and the Feigenbaums) to settle in Praga.

Sad to say, the synagogue did not fall victim to the Germans who only set fire to it, but to the Communists. In 1961, in the name of "changing the bourgeois character of the district", the authorities ordered that the walls be pulled down. This barbaric act was part of a plan which included the removal of balconies and plaster from neighbouring houses.

The Orphanage

Fortunately, the neighbouring building at ul. Jagiellońska 8 still remains. The plaque there says that it is the headquarters of the "Michał Bergson Educational Centre for the Warsaw Orthodox Jewish Community". One is struck by the beauty and solidity of this edifice visible in all its magnificence from some distance away. The architect Henryk Stifelman was alluding here to the Renaissance architecture of Kazimierz Dolny. In this surviving complex there was also a *mikvah*. In the words of Jerzy Kasprzycki in *Roots of the City*: "After the war, a few Praga Jews who had survived the Holocaust and returned to their home town found a haven here for their beliefs and customs. Until the 1950s kosher meat was sold in the annexe at the back of the building, the animals having first been killed in an old ritual slaughterhouse under the supervision of a rabbi". The *kosher* butcher Zygmunt Warszauer died in 1997.

The Israelite Orphanage was named after Michał Bergson, eminent curator of child-care institutions and initiator of the "palace for the orphans of the Praga district". There is a commemorative plaque on the building.

Szmulowizna

Opposite ul. Okrzei, ul. Ząbkowska starts and leads to the crossing with ul. Radzymińska. Here you will find another trace of Warsaw's Jewish past: the part of Praga known as Szmulowizna. It is made up of ul. Kawęczyńska, ul. Otwocka, ul. Siedlecka and neighbouring streets. It gets its name from the royal banker Szmul Zbytkower, who owned the land here at the end of the 18th century We can get a whiff of the character of this area from the following extract taken from "Wędrowiec" (The Wanderer, 1893): "Szmulowizna became a hotbed for all the outcasts from the big city. All the suspicious characters being at odds with public order found a sure and safe haven in the nooks and crannies and the network of tiny little streets here. These individuals even had their own nickname 'ravens', known to everyone in the neighbourhood, as ravens would always throw themselves on anything they could lay their claws on". Szmulowizna, however, had other faces apart from this one. To this day some of the older inhabitants of Praga retain in their memories images of Friday nights, where the windows of all the houses would suddenly come alight with thousands of *Shabbat* candles.

The Jewish Student Hostel was erected in 1926 thanks to the efforts of the Auxilium Academicum Judaicum society (above: a detail from the facade of the building).

The Jewish Students' Hall of Residence

Further on in the direction of the Vistula ul. Kłopotowskiego (formerly ul. Szeroka) leads to the crossing with ul. Sierakowskiego. Here you will see the impressive building that used to be the Jewish Students' Hall of Residence. It occupies all of the land between ul. Kłopotowskiego (ul. Szeroka) and ul. Okrzei (ul. Brukowa). It is now a police hostel.

The House Under the Sign of the Owls

From here ul. Okrzei leads to ul. Targowa, to the stop from which trams 3 and 25 will take you close to the local Jewish cemetery. The building on the corner of ul. Okrzei and ul. Sierakowskiego is known as the "House Under the Sign of the Owls". Before the war, in what is now a pharmacy one could find Abraham's, the restaurant of Abraham Kronenberg. When the troublemakers from the Radical National Faction repeatedly destroyed the sign outside, the owner changed the name to Adolf's.

The Jewish Cemetery in Praga

The Jewish Cemetery in the Praga district is the oldest Jewish necropolis in Warsaw.

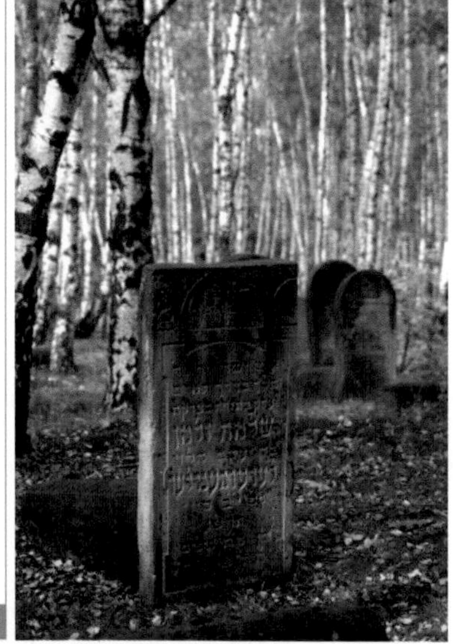

The Jewish cemetery in Praga is a rather strange place. After many years of total neglect, renovation work was begun. However, financial and organisational problems meant that conservation work came to a halt with only a new gate and the adjustment of a few dozen *matzevot* to show for it. Behind the elegant fence everything is once again overgrown with birchwood thicket, among which some five thousand well preserved *matzevot* are gathered in random piles. The cemetery functioned from 1780–1939. In 1870 the Praga Jewish community joined with the one from Warsaw and from then on the cemetery was used by both. During the Second World War it was devastated and in the years that followed it was consigned to oblivion. Officially it was a "recreational park", but in actual fact it was an abandoned collection of wild trees and bushes. In 1985 a clearing-up operation was begun and in 1989 the area was fenced off.

The main entrance is next to the wooden building by the roundabout. The columns near the gate are in memory of the cemetery's founder Szmul Zbytkower (d. 1802). From here the main alley leads to the piles of *matzevot* (on a hill to the left)

Abraham Stern, the brilliant inventor, was born in 1769 in Hrubieszow. This talented watchmaker was brought to Warsaw by Stanisław Staszic, who saw that he received a good education in mathematics, physics and foreign languages. Stern was the only Jew to be made a member of the Warsaw Society of Science and he was responsible for a considerable number of inventions, including a triangle for surveying and threshing. But his greatest achievement was a counting machine which could carry out basic mathematical calculations. And so, he may be regarded as the inventor of the automatic calculator. To his dying day he did not renounce his traditional gabardine or his customary appearance, his beard becoming a thing of legend. He died in 1842.

and to a memorial in the form of a podium into which the most precious of the preserved gravestones have been walled. The cemetery is the resting-place of Abraham Stern, inventor and great-grandfather of Antoni Słonimski.

The main gate is locked but the entrance from ul. Odrowąża is open. To get to the main alley, follow the wall of the Catholic cemetery almost as far as another open gate (from ul. Rogowska), but before you reach it, follow one of the paths leading up on the right to the lapidarium.

Please bear in mind that the Jewish cemetery is very isolated and not visible from the outside. For this reason it is extremely inadvisable to go there alone or after dark. To get to ul. Odrowąża from the centre of Warsaw, take trams # 1, 2, 3, 25, 32. Get off at the first stop after the railway viaduct for the main gate, at the second one for the open gate.

GÓRA KALWARIA | Yiddish: Ger, Gur

It is certainly worth making a trip to Góra Kalwaria, which was once one of the largest centres of Chasidism in Poland. Jews first arrived here around 1800, as before that time the *privilegia de non tolerandis Judaeis* laws were in force. In 1859 Yitzchak Meir Rothenberg Alter (1789–1866), also called *rebe* Itchie Majer, settled here. This outstanding preacher continued the teachings of Menachem Mendel Morgenshtern from Kock. He wrote *Chiddushei ha-RIM* (The New Interpretations of Rabbi Yitzchak Meir), published posthumously in 1875; the work which is studied in *yeshivot*

The *ohel* of Yitzchak Meir Rothenberg is a destination for pilgrims from Israel and the USA.

In Góra Kalwaria, the house of prayer (rebuilt after the Second World War) still exists, as does the house of the *tzaddik* at ul. Pijarska 10–12.

to this day. *Rebe* Majer often spoke about the joy of studying the *Talmud*. His court became so popular that it was deemed worthwhile building a narrow-gauge railway line for the pilgrims going from Warsaw to Góra Kalwaria. When, during the course of a dispute, one of the *tzaddikim* forbade Jews to travel by train, within a week the service was on the verge of bankruptcy. After pleas by the owners the ban was lifted. Another consequence of such an enormous number of visitors was the construction of a local sewage system, which at that time was unheard of for a small town. At the beginning of the 20th century the Chasids from Góra Kalwaria (*Gerer Chasidim*) became the dominant Jewish community in the Kingdom of Poland. They stood out because of their willingness to participate in political life.

From close-up this well-known town appears miserable and grey, but many monuments belonging to *Chasidim* remain, in particular the *ohel* of Yitzchak Meir Rothenberg Alter, which was rebuilt in 1991 along with the cemetery. This *ohel* is also the resting-place of Yehuda Arieh Leib. The Jewish cemetery is situated behind the Roman Catholic cemetery, between ul. Zakalwaria and ul. Wiejska.

Góra Kalwaria does not have particularly good transport connections with Warsaw. You can get here either by bus from Dworzec Zachodni (West Bus Station), by car along road 79 (37 km) or possibly by bicycle along the path to Powsin and then on through Konstancin and Brześce (a nice ride). The railway line from Skierniewice to Pilawa was closed to passengers in 2000.

The Alter Dynasty from Góra Kalwaria

Yitzchak Meir Rothenberg Alter (1789–1866)
Yehuda Arie Leib Alter (1847–1905)
Abraham Mordechai Alter (1866–1948)
In 1940 he managed to leave Poland for Jerusalem.
Israel Alter (1892–1977)
Pinchas Menachem Alter (1926–1996)
Jacob Arieh Alter (1939–)

Podlasie

•

In the Lithuanian Borderlands

•

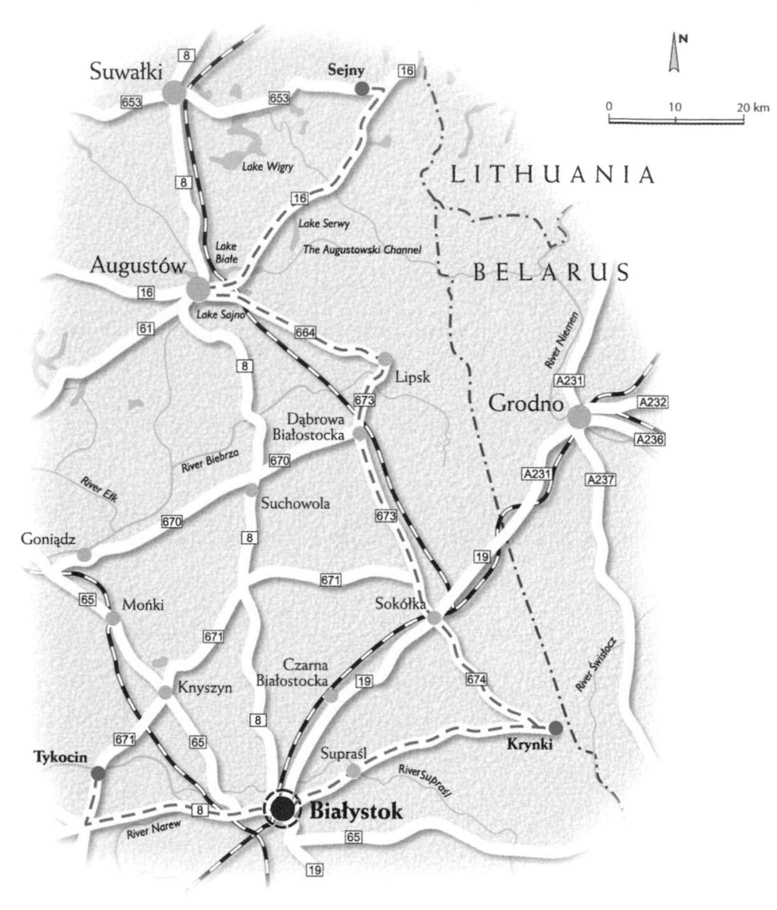

Route One Białystok

Route Two Białystok → Tykocin → Krynki → Sejny

For practical information see page 280

Recommendations

In **Białystok** take a walk around the area of Rynek Sienny (The Hay Market), go down ul. Waryńskiego to Cytron Beit Midrash and walk along ul. Warszawska; visit **Sejny**, especially when the local *klezmer* bands are performing; see the synagogue in **Tykocin** as well as the town.

Podlasie is situated between the pre-war frontier territories of Poland, with their famous centre in Vilna, and the Mazowsze and Lublin regions, each with a large Jewish population. In Podlasie the only Jewish centre of considerable size (though established somewhat later) was Białystok, the capital of the region. The importance of Tykocin should also be borne in mind. In the other towns of Podlasie, the Jewish communities were relatively small. The region was passed over by major historical events and the expansion of chasidism was limited. Chasidic houses of prayer, called *kloyzn*, were usually to be found in people's homes as the movement had few supporters.

Before 1939 local examples of Jewish culture were mostly limited to provincial cemeteries and wooden synagogues, which, being easy to destroy, did not survive the war.

Only a few interesting monuments of Jewish culture still remain in Podlasie, including one high class example, the synagogue complex in Tykocin (above; a part of a wall painting from the Great Synagogue).

BIAŁYSTOK

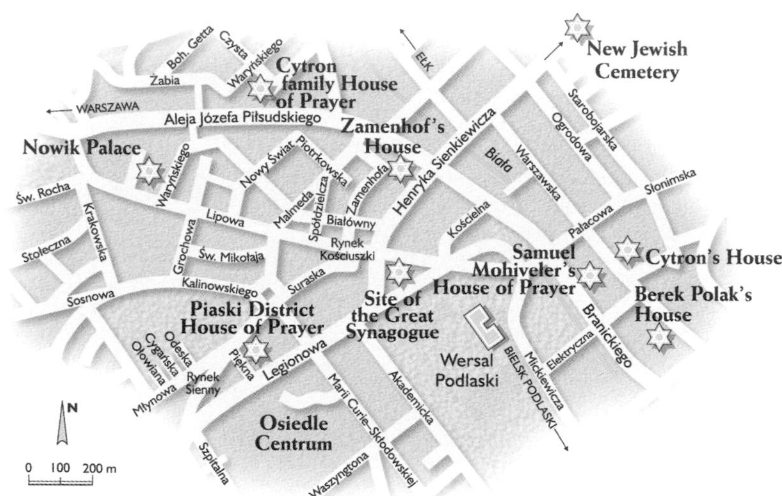

There were about 80,000 Jews in Białystok at the outbreak of the Second World War.

Suggested Route

Rynek Sienny → ul. Piękna (the Piaski district house of prayer) → ul. Suraska → the Site of the Great Synagogue → ul. Zamenhofa → ul. Waryńskiego (the Cytron family house of prayer) → ul. Warszawska → ul. Branickiego (Samuel Mohilever's house of prayer) → the New Jewish Cemetery

Tourist Attractions

Wersal Podlaski (The Podlasie Versailles) is one of the most magnificent 18th-century palace and park complexes in Poland, once owned by the Branicki family; the town hall and the 18th-century army commander's armoury; the former parish church, dating from the 17th century and the Neo-Gothic cathedral (1905); the Orthodox Christian Church of St Nikolaus with replicas of frescos from the Kiev Sobor (1846); the church of St Roch (1927), one of the most interesting instances of modernist sacral architecture; the 19th-century palace of the Ruediger Family in Dojlidy.

First accounts of Jewish settlement in Białystok date from 1658 to 1661. In 1692 there was a branch of the *kahal* of the Tykocin community operating in Białystok to serve the needs of local Jews. Along with the rapid development of the town in the second half of the 19th century, its Jewish community grew in size, reaching 70% of the local population (61,500) in 1913.

In the 1930s the Białystok Jewish quarter stretched over the territory west of the Branicki Palace and south of Rynek Kościuszki and ul. Marszałka Piłsudskiego (today renamed ul. Lipowa). Life was concentrated mainly around Rynek Rybny (The Fish Market), now Osiedle Centrum, and Rynek Sienny (The Hay Market). It absorbed the oldest district called Shulhof, as well as the Chorshul district, established in the second half of the 19th century and named after the Choral Synagogue located in that part of the town. Shulhof was the central area, containing streets such as ul. Lipowa, ul. Suraska, ul. Mikołajewska (now ul. Sienkiewicza), as well as the valley of the River Biała. It was inhabited by Orthodox Jews, the Great Synagogue being its focal point. Chorshul was made up of streets such as ul. Kupiecka (now ul. Malmeda) and ul. Giełdowa (now ul. Spółdzielcza). In 1939 the Rabbi of Białystok was Gedali Rozenman. There were approximately 100 synagogues and houses of prayer. The examples of Jewish culture in Białystok bear testimony to the glory as well as to the poverty within the local Jewish population.

In his *Guidebook to the Białystok Region*, Mieczysław Orłowicz wrote: "The Jewish quarter, as in other Polish towns, forms a series of short, dirty and bustling streets filled with noisy crowds typical of the East". Nevertheless, many picturesque little streets with old wooden houses still remain (below, a photograph from the time of the First World War).

The Białystok Jewish Quarter had two main market squares: Rynek Sienny and Rynek Rybny (above photo from 1917).

Rynek Sienny (the Hay Market)

There are several places of interest in the area around Rynek Sienny. On the west side, from ul. Młynowa, you will find a few pre-war buildings containing old shops with shutters. The paving is also authentic. The little streets leading away from the market (ul. Udeska, ul. Cygańska, ul. Ołowiana) are also worth a look. Depressing, though picturesque, these ramshackle houses tilting towards the streets, or rather paths, are not so much a tourist attraction as testimony to the way the quarter used to look. Maurycy Szymel captured this in his poem *In the Jewish Provinces*:

"Cottages sway like women walking in their sleep
And winding little streets run down in panic deep".

Be sure to take a look before the bulldozers working on the other side of the square make their way here.

The windows were restored to their original appearance during repair work to the former Piaski District House of Prayer.

Piaskover Beit Midrash (the Piaski District House of Prayer)

At ul. Piękna 3, a pretty little street on the northern side of the Rynek Sienny, you will find one of the three synagogue buildings still existing in Białystok.

At present it houses "Wersal Podlaski", the firm which carried out a thorough reconstruction after a fire in 1989. The edifice, which dates from around 1893, replaced the wooden synagogue built here in 1820. This main House of Prayer in the Piaski District functioned until the Second World War. From 1945 it was the centre of the Jewish community and from 1948 it was home to the Social-Cultural Society of Jews in Poland. From 1968 the building was left empty, and a dozen or so years later it burned down. The outside walls, vaults and windows are part of its original features. The front wall has been recreated with the help of old photographs. The only remaining elements of the original interior decor are the recess for the *aron ha-kodesh* (behind the reception) and the cast iron columns in the hall, which support the gallery. The roof is totally different from that of the original building and dates from 1994.

The remains of the old building can be viewed in the reception hall open during working hours.

Ul. Suraska

Ul. Suraska runs to the north of Rynek Sienny. At one time it was the main street of the Shulhof district. A visitor may be somewhat bemused by the total inconsistency in pre-war accounts of the place. While some people emphasised the street's picturesque nature, others saw "long and winding backyards, across which you can sometimes walk through several household between shabby huts and pigsties. Often without any gates, everything here is wide-open; a sorry sight of human misery..."

Orłowicz wrote: "Long and narrow backyards linking the streets are one of the peculiarities of the Białystok Ghetto. Somehow typical of all the nearby small towns in Podlasie, it was full of small, picturesque, wooden houses with tiled roofs, their gable walls facing onto the street" (above: ul. Młynowa; below: Jewish shops on the southern side of the main square; photo from 1917).

The Great Synagogue was designed by Shlomo Rabinovich (photo from 1920).

Unfortunately, there are no "huts and pigsties" here any more, as in the 1950s the street was turned into a socialist-realist promenade with each and every element completely lacking in taste. The only gate you can enter is the one to the right of Rynek Kościuszki. On the housing estate erected on the site of former ul. Głucha, ul. Gęsia and ul. Ciemna, there once stood the Great Synagogue, situated at ul. Bóżnicza 14.

The Site of the Great Synagogue

This square, now situated in the yard, is one of the most important places in the history of the Jews of Białystok. Here you will find a memorial reminiscent in shape of the synagogue's dome twisted by flames. It was designed by Samuel Solasz from the United States and Michał Flikier from the Białystok Society in Israel. The inscription recalls the tragedy: "This magnificent holy shrine of ours fell victim to flame on 27 June 1941, and 2000 Jews were burnt alive by the German murderers".

Somewhere here, in what is now a car park, once stood the oldest synagogue in Białystok, founded in 1715. It was built of wood and had no section for women. The Great Synagogue was erected on the same spot, its construction taking from 1909 to 1913. Funds were collected

Ludwik Zamenhof created Esperanto, the international language, which still has thousands of enthusiasts all over the world (in the picture below, taken in Frankfurt, he is in the company of his wife, Klara).

The house in which Ludwik Zamenhof was born burned down during the Second World War (photo from 1935).

from the charges for *kosher* meat and also from donations. The result was a square building, characteristic, though reflecting no particular style. Its most striking feature was a massive dome with a spire. The alcoves were crowned with other domes in Neo-Byzantine style. It also had Neo-Gothic windows. There were galleries for women on three sides.

The easiest way to get here is from ul. Legionowa, between houses 14, 16 and 18.

Ul. Zamenhofa

After crossing ul. Lipowa you should make your way towards ul. Zamenhofa, which runs through the territory of the second of the old Jewish quarters, known as Chorshul.

The Choral Synagogue, built in 1834, was in ul. Żydowska (Jewish Street), now Białówny. It was renowned for its magnificently decorated interior. The Germans burnt it down in 1943. Apart from a few old houses (ul. Zamenhofa 19, 20 and 25), the most important spot here is the birth place of Ludwik Zamenhof (on the corner of ul. Biała, and according to the present numbering system ul. Zamenhofa 22). Until the Second World War a "small, green, wooden house" stood here, and you could sign your name in a memorial book.

A building in socialist-realist style, bearing a commemorative plaque, was erected where Zamenhof's house once stood.

Ludwik Lazar Zamenhof (1859–1917) was brought up in a wealthy family. His father was a language teacher and one of the founders of the Choral Synagogue. Having already become a respected oculist, Ludwik Zamenhof decided to create *Esperanto*, an artificial language, the name of which means 'having hope'. In 1887 he began publishing textbooks from which people could learn this language based on two thousand elements taken from Romanic, Germanic and Slavonic languages. The title of his fundamental work, which consisted of a grammar book and a dictionary, was *An International Language*.

From Zamenhof's house you have a choice of two routes. The first takes you through the area of the former Chorshul, with streets such as ul. Kupiecka (ul. Malmeda) and Giełdowa (ul. Spółdzielcza), to ul. Waryńskiego. On your way you will pass old houses randomly situated among the post-war buildings. Ul. Waryńskiego, the nicest in the town centre, leads to the Cytron Family House of Prayer. The second option is a walk in the direction of ul. Sienkiewicza and the bridge on the River Biała. On the other side of the river you will find ul. Warszawska, a former promenade with palaces and houses once belonging to factory owners. Nearby, in ul. Branickiego, you will find the third remaining synagogue building.

Cytron Beit Midrash (the Cytron Family House of Prayer)

The building was completed and ready for use just before the outbreak of the Second World War. The governor of the Białystok region took part in the opening ceremony. The founders also raised 75,000 zł for the purchase of an aircraft for the Polish armed forces.

During the war the synagogue was within the borders of the ghetto and performed religious services illegally. After 1945 it also served the Jewish community as a place of mourning as well as a stage for theatre performances. It functioned until the 1960s, when it was turned into a tailoring co-operative. In 1993 part of the building was taken over by the Ślendziński Gallery.

The Cytron Family House of Prayer was erected in 1936.

Close to the intersection of ul. Waryńskiego and ul. Lipowa you can still find the eclectic Nowik Palace. It was built from 1900 to 1910 for Chaim Nowik, a cloth and hat tycoon (ul. Lipowa 5).

The synagogue's original decor bore testimony to the high social status of its founders. The ceilings were made of exotic wood. The paintings depicted biblical themes as well as animal and plant motifs. Its candelabrum for 150 candles was a work of art. The interior of the synagogue was later destroyed. Sad to say, the coffered wooden ceiling adorned with paintings was removed as recently as 1979. The large building next door to the former house of prayer (now the Białostoczanka tailoring co-operative) was once home to the Druskin High School, an educational institution well-known before the Second World War.

Ul. Waryńskiego 24a. The street name suddenly changes, but you should go straight on up to al. Piłsudskiego and then cross over. Such streets, somewhat oddly broken up, are a consequence of the post-war reconstruction of Białystok's transport system. Visiting these places, now considerably altered, is rather complicated as they have been divided up among several different companies. Not much remains of the former interior. A look inside the Ślendziński Gallery where you can find a text about the history of the building should suffice. Open 10am–5pm.

The former house of the Cytron family, at ul. Warszawska 37, is now the History Museum.

Ul. Warszawska

Białystok's dynamic development, similar to that of Łódź, brought about the transformation of ul. Warszawska into an

Berek Polak's house, at ul. Warszawska 50, was built at the turn of the 20th century.

attractive promenade where *nouveau riche* factory owners erected their magnificent palaces. The Cytron House built from 1905 to 1914 is representative of an Art Nouveau style rarely found in Białystok. It was erected as a memorial to the success achieved by Samuel Hersh Cytron, the maker of the family fortune. In the 1930s his son and heir Benjamin also lived here. Berek Polak's house at ul. Warszawska 50 has a Neo-Renaissance style facade. It belonged to a well-known Białystok factory owner whose plant was at the back of the building. From 1941, adorned with the Star of David, it served as the headquarters of the Gestapo.

Samuel Mohilever

Ul. Branickiego runs parallel to ul. Warszawska and also very close to the River Biała. Here, at No 3, you will find the former *Beit Shmuel* (the progressive synagogue of Great Rabbi Samuel Mohilever). It was erected in 1902 outside the former Jewish quarter. The synagogue was burnt down during the war and rebuilt afterwards. A visit to the backyard is all that is necessary. Only from here will you see the contours of the original windows; the facade having been remodelled. From this side you can also see the recess for the *aron ha-kodesh*, not visible from the inside. The building now belongs to a local sports club.

Samuel Mohilever (d. 1898), the patron of the synagogue, was a Białystok Rabbi known for his Zionist activities. He was buried in the Jewish cemetery in ul. Wschodnia. In the 1990s his remains were taken to Israel.

The New Jewish Cemetery

There were four Jewish cemeteries in Białystok and the only one to remain is in the attractive suburban district of Wygoda. It was established in 1890. The *matzevot* which survived the Second World War occupy one sixth of its area. The location is well mantained although partly overgrown with shrubs.

The cemetery is located in ul. Wschodnia, opposite house No 43. Access by buses # 3, 9, 27 and 100. Get off after the Wasiłkowo–Krynki road junction, four stops after the bridge over the River Biała. The walk from the bus-stop to ul. Wschodnia takes 15 minutes. The gate is open.

TYKOCIN | Yiddish: Tiktin

Of all the Jewish towns in Podlasie, Tykocin is without doubt the one which is most worth a visit. Jews arrived here in 1522, invited by Olbracht Gasztołt, the governor of the Vilna and Troki (Trakai) regions, to enhance local trade and handicraft. The undertaking was supported by two Polish kings: Stefan Batory, who granted Jews the privilege of settlement in 1576 and Ladislaus IV, in 1633. The Tykocin *kahal* achieved great significance. It encompassed every Jewish community within a radius of 150 km and played an important role in the Diet of Lithuanian Jews. In the second half of the 19th century Tykocin began to lose out to its competitor Białystok and the town started to fall into decline. In the 19th century Jews formed over 60% of the population, but because the railway line avoided the town an economic crisis ensued, causing people to emigrate. Before the outbreak of the Second World War Jews constituted 44% of the population, approximately 2,000 people. One of the ways they made a living was from the production of *tallitim*.

There was a Hebrew school as well as the Zionist youth movement He-chalutz. The last rabbi was Abraham Zwi Pinchos. The Holocaust reached Tykocin on 5 August 1941 when the Germans shot dead 1,400 people and deported the rest to the Białystok Ghetto. The largest

This miniature model of Tykocin, located in the museum in the Great Synagogue, will help you to plan a walk around the town, whose layout remains almost unchanged. Only the wooden Chasidic synagogue no longer exists. The roads are still paved with cobblestones. In the streets you can see cats basking in the sun. All around there is silence.

Tourist Attractions

The main market square and the memorial to Stefan Czarniecki (dated 1763); a magnificent post-missionary monastery complex, founded by J.K. Branicki, with the Church of the Holy Trinity (1742–1749); the military seminary (1634–1638); the houses from the 18th and 19th centuries; the remains of the Renaissance castle of King Sigismund Augustus on the right bank of the River Narew.

The figure of **Rivka Tiktiner** who lived in the first half of the 16th century is closely connected with the history of Tykocin. She was one of the very few women who gained respect as a religious authority in Judaism. As daughter of rabbi Mayer from Tykocin, she learned Hebrew and studied the *Torah.* She published her work *Meneket Rivka* (Rebeca the Feeder) about raising children and the duties of women. The book, published in 1609 in Prague and in 1618 in Cracow, was written in Yiddish in order to reach the greatest number of uneducated female readers. Rivka Tiktiner, an extraordinary character for her time, was the focus of great interest in Europe. In 1719 her monograph was published in Germany, under the title: *De Rebecca Polona eruditarum in gente Judaica Foeminarium rariori exemplo* (On Rebecca of Poland, the Rarest Example of a Female Scholar from the Jewish Nation).

Jewish presence was in the neighbourhood of the Jewish market and the Great Synagogue in the western district of Kaczorowo, along ul. Holendry and ul. Piłsudskiego. The community institutions: the rabbi's house, smaller houses of prayer, and the ritual bath all concentrated around the spot where the River Motława flows into the River Narew.

A walk in Tykocin, taking around an hour, is an indispensable part of the trip. The most interesting streets are ul. Piłsudskiego and ul. Kaczorowska. In ul. Piłsudskiego, opposite the synagogue, you will find a plaque commemorating Markus Zamenhof, the father of Ludwik. The house at ul. Kaczorowska 1 is adorned with the Star of David. The Tykocin Jewish cemetery is located in ul. Piłsudskiego and surrounded by a concrete wall. The fairly large site contains numerous toppled gravestones with the illegible inscriptions. By the road to Łopuchowo there is a place marked with a memorial, where the execution of Jews by the Nazis took place in 1941. It is accessible by taxi from the bus stop.

The Great Synagogue

The synagogue was erected on the site of the former house of prayer in the centre of the Jewish quarter of Kaczorowo situated on an island which existed there at that time. Its

This magnificent synagogue built in 1642 has survived to this very day.

construction was inspired by the desire to erect a synagogue worthy of the local *kahal* which exercised authority over the communities of Białystok and Grajewo. According to some sources, it is modelled on the fortified synagogue in Pińsk, built in 1640. It is a square building (18m by 18m) with a tower in the north-east corner. It used to perform many functions, being home to institutions such as the *kahal* and the court of law. The tower was used as a prison. In the 17th and 18th centuries it was a great centre of intellect. The Talmudists studied and taught here, and among them scholars such as Menachem David ben Yitzhak, the pupil of Moses Isserles (Remuh) from Cracow, Shmuel Eliezer ben Yehuda ha Levi Edels, Joshua ben Josef Elijahu Shapira and Eliezer Rokeach. Redecorated in the 1840s, it was renowned for its rich furnishings, including valuable ark curtains. The Germans stripped it bare during the Second World War. The looted building was restored in the 1970s and turned into a museum. The nearby market stalls were never rebuilt.

The *bimah* bears numerous inscriptions. One of them features the date 1662.

The walls of the Great Synagogue are covered in polychromies restored in the 1980s.

The entrance leads you through the *pulish*, a spacious hallway which once housed the *kahal* and the court. From here you can walk into the main prayer hall for men. The lowering of the level of the floor is the

implementation of the words of a psalmist: "From the depth I call Thee, Lord". The hall is nine meters high. The exhibition in the synagogue is one of the most interesting displays of Jewish heritage in Poland. The *bimah* occupies the centre of the prayer hall. It does not contain a chair for circumcisions.

The nine-bay vaulting is typical of Polish synagogues. The wall paintings are very interesting. They contain biblical texts in Aramaic and Hebrew, as well as painted decorations depicting twigs and animal motifs. New discoveries are being made in the building all the time. The oldest and most original features show up only when surface layers are removed. Some items from the interior, for example the candlesticks, have been re-created with the aid of old photographs taken by Szymon Zajczyk. The *parochet* is completely new (a gift from rabbi Schudrich and the Ronald S. Lauder Foundation). The collection of artistic handicraft is quite astounding. Here you can find silver spice boxes, eight-light *Chanukah* lamps, and vessels used during the festival of *Pesach*. The phylacteries, little boxes made of leather which contain verses from the Bible written on parchment, are particularly special.

The eastern wall is adorned with a beautifully surmounted *aron ha-kodesh* with the inscription: "Here is the crown of the Torah".

The synagogue is encircled by prayer rooms for women and a spacious hallway.

The building next to the synagogue, now housing the museum and the Tejsha restaurant, is the former *beit ha-midrash* (house of study). It was erected in the period from 1772 to 1798. Totally destroyed during the Second World War, it was rebuilt in 1972. In recent years it underwent repair and remodelling during which a new roof was put on.

The Tykocin Museum, a branch of the Podlaskie Museum in Białystok, ul. Kozia 2, ☎ (85 7181626. The synagogue is open from 10am to 5pm with the exception of Mondays, Fridays and the days following major holidays. Last visitors are admitted at 4.30pm. Tickets 5 zł, concessions 3 zł; Saturdays entrance free.

Two interesting exhibitions are housed in the tower of the Tykocin synagogue. One shows the rabbi's room and the other, called *Seder Pesach*, a table laid for the Passover meal (above).

KRYNKI | Yiddish: Krienek, Krinek

In Białystok people say, "At the sight of Krynki crows turn round and fly away".

This is slightly unfair, but you do get the feeling here that you are visiting the end of the world. This small borderland town, cut off from the rest of Podlasie by the primeval forests of the Puszcza Knyszyńska, is in fact part of the Grodno region, a most interesting territory though these days somewhat isolated and forgotten. A multitude of cultures and languages was one of its greatest attributes. Apart from Poles and Belarusians, who form a majority in the area (Sokrat Janowicz, one of the most distinguished Belarusian writers, lives there), Krynki is also home to Tartars (their village of Kruszyniany is only 10 km to the south). Until the outbreak of the Second World War Jews were very much a part of this mosaic.

Jews first came here in the beginning of the 16th century. As in other towns of Podlasie, their arrival was connected with the wish to develop trade and handicraft in the area. At the end of the 18th century the local Jewish community totalled 700 and was more numerous than that of Białystok. The town's location at the crossroads of trade routes was advantageous for its development. In the 19th century

Tourist Attractions

The only 18th-century urban complex preserved in Poland: a hexagonal market square from which 12 streets lead away; the church of St Anne from 1907–1913 designed by S. Szyller; the 18th-century belfry gate; the de Virion manor house park; the 18th-century wooden Orthodox Christian cemetery church of St Anthony; the Orthodox Christian church of the Nativity of the Holy Mother (1868).

Many old houses as well as the cobblestone paving and even names of streets remain in Krynki. Little is left to the imagination here, with the possible exception of the Great Synagogue.

the Jews themselves were the driving force behind the town's growth. In 1827 Józef Giesl set up the first garment workshop, which put Krynki on the road to becoming a centre for the textile and tanning industries. At the beginning of the 20th century Jews made up as much as 90% of the local population. They ran political organisations, *chadarim* and even a *yeshivah* for 80 students. The inter-war period saw the town fall into an economic decline from which it has never recovered. Jews emigrated *en masse* to Palestine and America and the town's population fell by 50%.

In 1939 Krynki was annexed to the Belorussian Soviet Socialist Republic and deportations to Siberia began. In June 1941 the Soviets were expelled by the Germans. The inhabitants were enclosed in a ghetto, which was liquidated in January 1943. The Krynki Jews were not passive and put up resistance, killing 12 Germans. Some of them escaped to the forest and formed an underground unit led by Moses Slopak whose pseudonym was Mohryn.

The Jewish quarter stretched over the main square, ul. Garbarska, some of the northern and all of the western parts of the town. Józef Hazekiel Miszkowski was the last rabbi of Krynki.

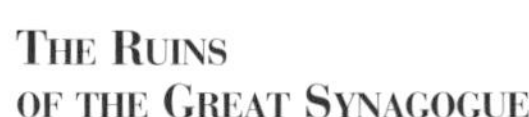

The Ruins of the Great Synagogue

A huge pile of rubble, regular in shape, located by one of the main streets, is all that remains of the Great Synagogue. In 1944 the Germans decided to blow it up, but though the roof was destroyed the

A boy with the four plants used during the celebration of the festival of *Sukkot* (an old post card of a painting by Izydor Kaufmann).

powerful building survived. The act of destruction was completed by Communist Party activists from Białystok who laid another set of explosives in 1971, this time with greater success. The only parts to survive were the walls of the main hall, built from glacial erratics and granite.

Ul. Grodzka 5 (on the corner of Zaułek Szkolny), a two-minute walk from the main square and on the road to Kruszyniany.

The Great Synagogue was erected at the beginning of the 19th century (although some sources mention 1756). It was square in shape, with prayer rooms for women on three sides.

The Caucasian Beit Ha Midrash

This beautifully preserved building from 1850 was used by the Krynki tanners. It is square in shape (16m x 16m) with a vestibule, a prayer hall and a section for women. It was burnt down during the Second World War. In 1955 it was reconstructed and turned into a cinema. In the process the *bimah* was destroyed and the openings to the women's prayer room as well as the windows above the former *aron ha-kodesh* were bricked up. Today it houses a Community Centre for Sport and Culture.

Some of the local inhabitants remember the building's original purpose and object to its being used for occasions such as weddings, which is seen as being comparable to the fate of Catholic churches similarly misused in the former Soviet Union. The building nearby, which now accommodates the post office, was probably also used for religious functions.

Ul. Piłsudskiego 5. A two-minute walk to the west along one of the streets leading away from the main square.

The name of the Caucasian House of Learning has a rather interesting origin. "Caucasus" was the nickname given to the section of the town inhabited by tanners who imported hides from as far away as the Caucasus.

The Slonim Chasidim House of Prayer

Take a look at this building, even though it is now a neglected storehouse. It is one of the very few Chasidic prayer houses still existing in Poland. The *Chasidim* often prayed in *kloyzn* (private prayer rooms) but they also used wooden synagogues, which were mostly destroyed during the Second World War. This building, erected in brick in the second half of the 19th century, once belonged to an exotic group of Chasids from Slonim (now

The Slonim Chasidim were part of the Lithuanian Chasids, as were the Chasids from Stolin in the Polesie Region, also present in Krynki (their house of prayer *Chasidim Shtibl Beit Midrash* did not survive the Second World War). In the Grand Duchy of Lithuania Chasidism met with strong resistance from numerous co-believers supported by the authority of the renowned Elijahu ben Shlomo, the *Gaon* of Vilna. The Lithuanian *Chasidim* whose homes were beyond the post-war eastern borders of Poland are the most forgotten in the history of Polish Jews. They are worth a mention, however, as several of their communities exist to this very day in the USA or Israel. There are the *Karliner Chasidim* from Karlin near Pinsk, the oldest Chasidic group in the Grand Duchy of Lithuania and *ChaBaD*, a particularly interesting community.

This name, the abbreviation deriving from *Chochma, Bina, Dea* (Wisdom, Reason, Learning), is still used by the Chasidic group from Lubavitchi. The *Lubavitcher* group enjoys the continuity of the Schneerson dynasty *(tzaddik* Josef Yitzhak Schneerson survived the war in the Soviet Union) and has its headquarters in the USA. It is the only Chasidic community which is increasing in size, mainly through conducting missionary work amongst Jews in the former Soviet Union.

in Belarus). It burned down around 1880 but was then rebuilt. Two floors served as a synagogue and religious school. Its characteristic semi-circular windows are still there.

Ul. Czysta 10 (off ul. Garbarska between the Great Synagogue and the main square, a two-minute walk from the square).

The Cemetery

The local Jewish cemetery is a spacious field (2.25 hectares) surrounded by a stone wall and overgrown with weeds. All you will find in the long grass are bits of broken gravestones. Only in the middle can you see complete *matzevot* placed in rows. The area is wild and forlorn.

Having visited the Jewish cemetery, make sure to go further along the Zaułek Zagumienny to the Orthodox Christian cemetery which you will see on the nearby hill. It is one of the most picturesque cemeteries in Podlasie.

It is not difficult to get to the cemetery, though the directions may seem to be a little complicated. From the main square take ul. Legionowa and walk to the spot where it crosses ul. Grodzieńska and ul. Polna. On the left hand side there is a house behind which there is a road called Zaułek Zagumienny. You should walk up here as far as the overground cellars hidden in the bushes, which you will see on your left hand side. Behind them there is a stone wall and behind the wall the cemetery. Getting here takes a quarter of an hour.

The Jewish cemetery in Krynki was established in the 18th century.

There are many old houses in Sejny, including the buildings on the right side of ul. Piłsudskiego and in ul. Ogrodowa, which once constituted the Jewish quarter (above: the model of the town). Sightseeing takes two to three hours.

SEJNY

Sejny, although part of the Podlasie administrative province, is in fact very much a part of the Vilnius region. Jews arrived in Sejny in the 17th century. In this idyllic little town, which brings summer holidays to mind, a particularly large influx of Jews took place after 1770, when the Dominicans who then owned the town invited Jewish artisans to come in order to help the town to compete with neighbouring Krasnopol. To make the place more attractive, in 1778 the Dominicans built a synagogue (since replaced by the existing one). The idea for this unusual undertaking came from Prior Bortkiewicz. As Polujański wrote in his *Roaming around the Augustów District*, quoted from Rąkowski: "In order to bring Jews to Sejny and with their help enliven trade thereabouts, he built a magnificent synagogue to which the people of Israel gladly came and by widening the scope of their trading contacts they contributed to the decline of fairs and commerce in Krasnopol. In gratitude to their benefactor, prayers for Bortkiewicz were

Tourist Attractions

The listed urban complex in the shape of the letter X; the church of the Visitation of the Most Holy Virgin Mother Mary, with a cloister (1610–1619), remodelled in 1760, with a Rococo decor; inside the church there is a figurine of the Holy Mother and Child (ca 1400), which is famous for miracles; the 19th-century crest-house architecture on the eastern side of the main square; the Town Hall (1840), the Classicist bishops' palace from the first half of the 19th century, now a post office.

The synagogue, erected sometime after 1856, underwent a thorough repair in 1885 (the building of the former *yeshivah*, now the "Papuciarnia" gallery, is visible on the right).

said in the synagogue each day". Nevertheless, the Sejny community was a peripheral one. However, it played an important role as a centre of the *Haskalah* for the Grand Duchy of Lithuania.

Jewish settlement kept increasing here until it reached a record level of 72% of the population in the middle of the 19th century. Later, for economic reasons, an equally rapid decrease took place. Poverty was so great that the local Jews could not afford the upkeep of the synagogue and many emigrated. In this way Sejny became a "temporary stop" for one generation on its way from east to west. In 1931 only

The "Pogranicze" (Borderland) Foundation is a very active cultural institution located in Sejny. It was established in May 1990 by Krzysztof Czyżewski. In January 1991 the Borderland of Arts, Cultures and Nations Centre came into being. The cultures of the national minorities living in the borderlands are the focus of its activity. There are several permanent organisations based at the Foundation: the Documentation Centre of Borderland Cultures, the Class of Cultural Heritage, the Sejny Theatre, the Klezmer Band, the "Papuciarnia" Gallery and the Borderland Publishing House (the publisher of the book *Neighbours* by Jan Tomasz Gross, to mention but one). Other activities take the form of cyclical projects, such as: "Człowiek Pogranicza" (Borderlander), "Pamięć starowieku" (Memory of Ancient Time), "Spotkanie innego" (Encounter with the Other), the Central-European Forum of Culture, "Camera Pro Mineritate". Jewish themes are approached here on very many levels: the Klezmer Band gives regular concerts and the Sejny Theatre's repertoire includes *The Dybbuk*, a play by Sh. An-ski. The Centre for the Documentation of Borderland Cultures collects books, films, musical recordings, photographs and old postcards. It also publishes the cultural magazine "Krasnogruda".

819 Jews lived here, which was some 24% of the population. They mostly traded in farming products and fruits of the forest. Some of them also worked as craftsmen or had jobs connected with the Augustów Channel. In November 1939 they were deported to Lithuania and later murdered by the Germans who invaded the territory in 1941.

An engraving depicting a wandering Jew has been placed on the front wall of the Borderland Foundation building (adjacent to the former *yeshivah*).

The White Synagogue and Yeshivah

Moses Becalel Luria played the leading role in the construction of this synagogue. During the Second World War the Nazis turned it into a fire station. It was used later as a garage, then a community co-operative storehouse and later a fuel depot. The renovation works (1978–1982) brought the period of destruction to an end and the original exterior of the synagogue was restored. It is a building with three naves, rectangular in shape (19m by 25.5m). The recess for the *aron ha-kodesh* has remained, as have four richly shaped pillars between which the *bimah* once stood.

The blue and white building by the synagogue, now the premises of Fundacja Pogranicze (the Borderland Foundation), is the former *yeshivah* from the mid-19th century. It was built by Moses Yitzhak Avigdor. It also contained the *kahal* and Hebrew High School of Tuvie Pinkas Shapiro. The building was the main centre of the *Haskalah* for the entire Grand Duchy of Lithuania. During the period of Communist rule it served as a factory manufacturing footwear and this is how it got its nickname *papuciarnia* (slipper-house).

The interior of the synagogue is now used as an exhibition hall for the Borderland Foundation. Concerts of *klezmer* music also take place here.

The Sejny Klezmer Band

The band was formed in 1995 during preparation for the staging of *The Dybbuk* by Sh. An-ski, as its members were playing a group of wedding musicians. Their performances delighted the audiences so much that they decided to start out on their own. They gradually built up a repertoire of traditional horas, shers, doinas and bulgars, being inspired by the works of Dave Tarras and Naftule Brandweine. The band polished its act at folk dance parties organised in fire stations and barns in villages on the River Bug and in Belarus around Grodno and Lida, as well as in Drohobych in Ukraine. Eventually, the band were invited to the Cracow Festival of Jewish Culture, where its members started to collaborate with the famous *klezmer* musician David Krakauer. The result was the music workshop The Musicians' Raft, attended by such masters of the genre as Dave Krakauer himself as well as Michael Alpert, Stuart Brotman, Jeff Warschauer and Deborah Strauss. The band is led by Wojciech Schroeder and the instruments are: the double bass, mandolin, drum, clarinet, accordion and viola. There is also a female vocalist. *All concerts start at 7pm in the White Synagogue; tickets cost 10–15 zł. For dates contact the Borderland Centre.*

The building is administered by the Borderland Foundation, which runs the Centre named the Borderland of Arts, Cultures and Nations. Ul. Piłsudskiego 37, ☎ +87 5162765 or 5162189; e-mail: fundacja@pogranicze.sejny.pl. Visitors are welcome between 10am and 4pm. The key is in the office of the Foundation (at the beginning of 2002 the Foundation was in the process of moving offices to the building adjacent to the former yeshivah*).*

Other Monuments of Jewish Culture

If you are looking for a little nostalgia, take a stroll on the right side of ul. Piłsudskiego in the direction of the church, where you will find some small houses with no modern conveniences. They were once inhabited by poor Jews. Old cobblestone paving has also withstood the passage of time unscathed. In one of the buildings you will discover a characteristic gate, in another a little shop. After a walk around the Town Hall in the market square you should go along ul. Ogrodowa, the best preserved old street in town.

Very little has remained of the Jewish cemetery. It used to occupy a hill overgrown with pine-trees and situated on the road to Augustów, a twenty five minute walk from the town centre (just past the modern-looking building at ul. 1 Maja 43 but on the opposite side). At present you will find here over a dozen complete *matzevot* from the 20th century as well as some broken ones.

Houses characteristic of the region can still be found in the little streets of Sejny.

Łódź

•

In the Promised Land

•

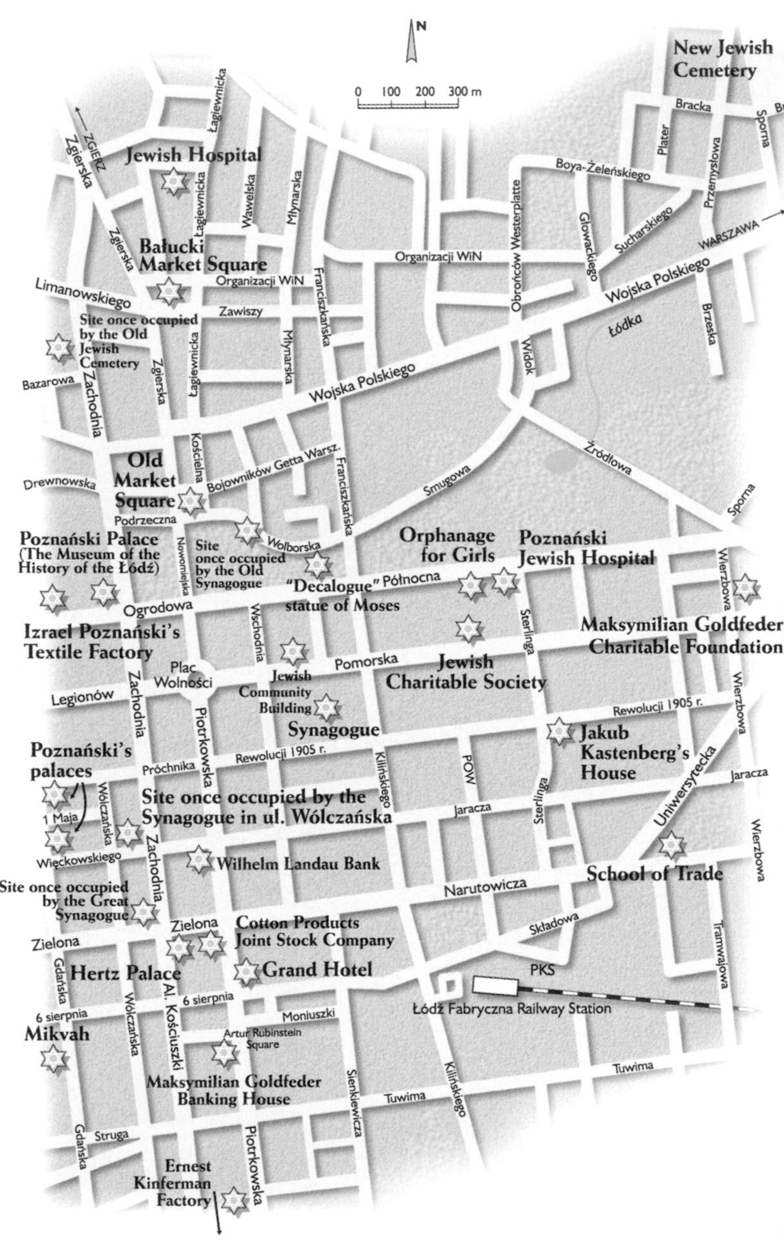

FOR PRACTICAL INFORMATION SEE PAGE 282

"It was a total jumble, a scrap-heap of all possible styles used by brick-layers, with turrets poking out here and there and stucco decorations all over the place forever dropping off; with a multitude of windows, balconies, caryatids and dormer windows, supposedly decorative in character; with roof balustrades and magnificent gates by which liveried footmen were dozing in velvet armchairs; with simple hatches through which mud from the street poured into horrid backyards similar to dunghills; with lots of stores, counting houses, warehouses and squalid little shops full of dirt and shoddy goods; with poverty swarming all over the streets; their lips blue with despair; their eyes sharp from permanent hunger."
(from *The Promised Land* by W.S. Reymont, 1924 Nobel Prize winner)

In Łódź (Yiddish: Lodz) the Jewish community gained autonomy in 1811. Its first rabbi was Jehuda Arie from Widawa. Jewish settlement was concentrated around the Old Market Square as well as ul. Wolborska, ul. Drewnowska, ul. Nowomiejska, ul. Podrzeczna and ul. Kościelna. In 1882 the authorities restricted the Jewish area of residence to what was known as "the district", containing only ul. Wolborska and ul. Podrzeczna. Jews who wanted to live outside the area had to obtain permission. They were also required to know Polish, German or French, and to refrain from wearing traditional attire. These restrictions were lifted in 1862.

When in 1864 the Kingdom of Poland became part of the Russian Empire, the town found itself in an

A huge city, similar to Liverpool or Manchester, with vast industrial areas surrounded by poverty, was created here in the 19th century (below: the gate of Poznański's factory at ul. Ogrodowa 15).

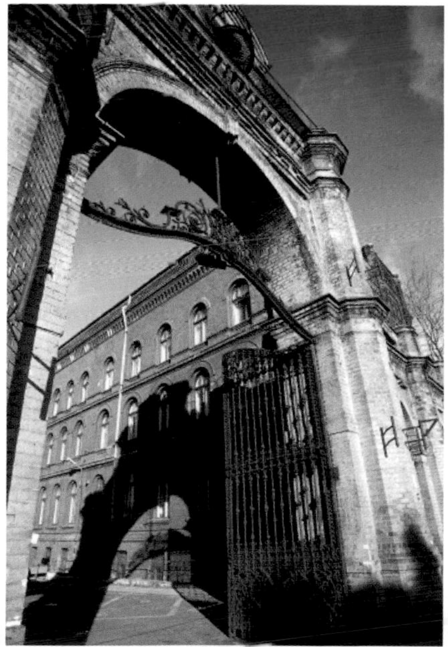

Suggested Route

UL. PIOTRKOWSKA → THE AREA BY UL. ZACHODNIA (POZNAŃSKI PALACE – THE MUSEUM OF ART, THE SITE ONCE OCCUPIED BY THE GREAT SYNAGOGUE) → THE ŁÓDŹ FABRYCZNA RAILWAY STATION (THE SYNAGOGUE, ONCE WOLF REICHER'S PRIVATE HOUSE OF PRAYER, UL. POMORSKA) → BAŁUTY (POZNAŃSKI PALACE, THE MUSEUM OF HISTORY OF THE CITY OF ŁÓDŹ, THE SITE ONCE OCCUPIED BY THE OLD CEMETERY, RYNEK BAŁUCKI, UL. WOLBORSKA) → THE NEW JEWISH CEMETERY

Recommendations

Go for a walk along **ul. Piotrkowska**, visit the only functioning **synagogue**, take a look at the details of the magnificent interior of the **Poznański Palace** in ul. Więckowskiego, see the **New Jewish Cemetery**.

excellent geo-political location, which resulted in large-scale investment. This is how Alexander Janowski described it in his work *Excursions Around the Country* (1903): "The waters here are of extraordinary colours, as they contain industrial waste from various dye-works. The trees drawing moisture from the poisoned soil wither or twist in sickness, the grass dries out and plant life suffocates in dense clouds of smoke and the nauseous smell of contaminated water".

Jewish settlement in the suburb of Bałuty began in 1858 along with investments made by Yitchak Birenzweig and Shlomo Yitchak Bławat. After being accorded rights of citizenship in 1862, Jews also moved to ul. Wólczańska, ul. Zgierska, ul. Zachodnia and ul. Spacerowa. The most spectacular careers were those of the great industrialists Izrael Poznański and Markus Silberstein, and also, after the First World War, of Aszer Kon as well as Borys and Naum Eitingon. (It is interesting to note that some of the family names of Łódź industrialists, for instance Grzywacz or Lesman, occur later on among the founders of industry in Israel). At the outbreak of the Second World War the 233,000 Jews constituted 33% of the town's population.

99,000 Jews lived in Łódź in 1899 (32% of the city's population).

Although industrial in character, the town was a centre of Chasidism, which radiated from the nearby town of

Arthur Rubinstein (1886–1982), the famous pianist, is one of the best known figures of Jewish Łódź, although he only spent the first 20 years of his life there. He made his first public appearance in Berlin as early as in 1897. His decision to emmigrate to the USA in 1906 was a turning point in his career. He settled down in Philadelphia, where, linked with the distinguished local orchestra, he became world-famous, especially for his interpretations of Frederic Chopin. He also collaborated with the composer Karol Szymanowski. He visited Poland several times. After the Second World War he set up the Department of Musicology at the Hebrew University in Jerusalem.

Aleksandrów (Yiddish: Alexander). There were even periods when the Alexander Chasidim were in charge of the Łódź Jewish community, having won the elections. They described themselves on the electoral roll as the "Non-party Religious Jews". Political life thrived and Agudas Isroel, with leaders such as Moses Halpern, Usher Mendelsohn and the community's last chairman, Leib Mincberg, was the dominant party. The Zionists were much weaker, but they had their groupings such as Mizrachi and the New Zionist Organisation. The left-wing Bund achieved some success every now and then, but not as much as one would expect in a town with such a large working class.

Łódź was an important centre of learning and culture. This is where the pianist Arthur Rubinstein (1886–1982) and the great Polish poet Julian Tuwim (1894–1953) were born. The Łódź group Yung Yiddish brought together a distinguished circle of avant-garde artists and writers, the poet and graphic artist Moses Broderson (1890–1956), the painter Yitchak (Vincent) Branner, the sculptor Mark Szwarc (1895–1942), to name but a few. In the house at ul. Więckowska 21, the mathematician Arie Sternfeld (1905–1980) wrote his work entitled *Introduction to*

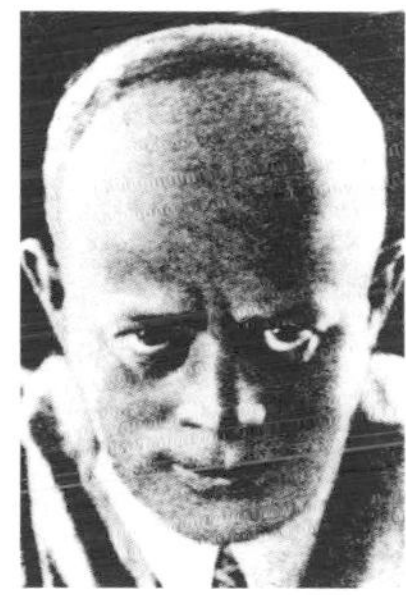

Yitzchak Katzenelson (1886–1944), the poet who wrote *The Song of the Murdered Jewish People*, lived in Łódź.

Tourist Attractions

The city of Łódź is less than 200 years old. Apart from its main street, ul. Piotrkowska, the following monuments are worth mentioning: the church of the Elevation of the Holy Cross (1867); the cathedral church of St Stanislaus Kostka (1912); the Russian Orthodox cathedral church (1884); the palaces of factory owners: Biedermann (second half of 19th century), Eisert (1890), Heinzl (1882), Hertz (1892), Kohn (sometime after 1850), three palaces of the Poznański family (1896, 1902, 1904), as well as those of Scheibler (1865–1885), Schweikert (1912), Steinert (1909–1911) and Stiller (1893); residential houses of Grohman (1881), Herbst (1877), Kindermann (1903), Kupiec (1896), J. Richter (1898), R. Richter (1904), Siemens (end of 19th century); the town hall (1827); Meyer's passageway, now ul. Moniuszki; and also the examples of industrial architecture: the "White Factory" of Geyer (1835–1837), the Księży Młyn housing estate (second half of 19th century), the spinning factory of Scheibler (1873), the weaving plant of Grohman (1896); excellent museums including the Museum of Art housing one of the largest collections of modern art in Europe.

The Łódź cab driver, shown in the painting by Samuel Finkelstein (1895–1942) was a typical feature of the town's landscape.

During the inter-war period Łódź was the place with the second largest Jewish population in Poland (photo from 1918).

Cosmonautics (in 1933 he left for Moscow). In Łódź there were several newspapers published in Yiddish: "Lodzer Tugblat" owned by the Hamburski family and "Nayer Folksblat" owned by Brzustowski, as well as some in Polish: "Republika", addressed mainly to supporters of Marshal Piłsudski, and "Głos Poranny" (The Morning Voice).

During the Second World War, the Third Reich's minister of propaganda, Joseph Goebbels, decided to organise a "show ghetto" here for over 200,000 people, of whom 5,000 were Gypsies. He used it for many propaganda exercises. Films made there depicted Jews as happy with their lot. The Nazi press published their photographs. Chaim Rumkowski (1877–1944), the local industrialist and head of the *Judenrat*, adopted a rather peculiar strategy. He played for time, avoided contact with the resistance and carried out the demands of the Germans, including the preparation of transports to death camps. Eventually he himself fell victim to the Nazis, but the Łódź Ghetto lasted longer than any of the others, until September 1944. Eight hundred and eighty seven people survived the war hidden in the Ghetto. Immediately after the German occupation, Łódź became

Julian Tuwim (1894–1953), one of the greatest Polish poets, came from an assimilated Jewish family. Although his literary works are very much part of Polish culture, on several occasions he made reference to the complexity of his mixed identity. During the Second World War, he emigrated to Brazil and the USA, and often spoke in public about the fate of Jewish people in Poland and in Europe. In 1944 he published his famous poem *We, Polish Jews.* After the war for some time he was chairman of the Society of Friends of the Hebrew University in Jerusalem and the Committee for Polish-Israeli Friendship.

for a while the main centre for those Jews who had survived the Holocaust. Home to the Central Committee of Polish Jews and the only *yeshivah* still functioning after the war, as well as the newspapers "Arbeter Tzaytung" and "Naye Lebn", Łódź had one of the two largest Jewish communities in Poland (the other one being Wrocław). In 1968 there were still 4,000 Jews living in Łódź. To this very day this city has one of the larger Jewish communities in Poland, although it possesses neither a kindergarten nor a school of its own. The synagogue still functions and funerals take place at the Jewish cemetery.

The inspiration for the tourist route described here comes from trips suggested in Jerzy Maleńczyk's book *A Guide to Jewish Łódź* (Warsaw, 1994).

In ul. Piotrkowska you can sit on a bench which is part of the memorial to Julian Tuwim and have a photograph taken at the sculpture of a grand piano being played by Arthur Rubinstein (below).

UL. PIOTRKOWSKA

This legendary street is to Łódź what the Champs Élysées is to Paris. For ten years now the authorities have been taking good care of its numerous charms. You can even do your sightseeing riding in the comfort of a reasonably priced rickshaw.

It is worth stopping at house No 29, dating from 1902, where a bank owned by Wilhelm Landau used to be. It was designed by a distinguished Łodź architect Gustaw Landau-Gutenteger (1870–1917). House No 32 from 1896 is another of his creations. A little further on, in house No 40 dating from 1904 there used to be the offices of one of the city's wealthiest industrialists Markus Silberstein (1837–1899), a well-known trader and owner of a cotton mill. The headquarters of the rival firm, Israel

Ul. Piotrkowska, the main artery of the city, was there a long time before being officially marked out in 1825.

Poznański's Towarzystwo Akcyjne Wyrobów Bawełnianych (The Cotton Products Joint Stock Company), were at ul. Piotrkowska 51. This building's elaborate details are very impressive.

The Grand Hotel is situated on the corner of ul. Piotrkowska and ul. Traugutta. It owes its present form to reconstruction carried out in 1911 and was designed by the eminent architect Dawid Lande (1868–1928). Ul. Moniuszki, formerly a privately owned street called Pasaż Meyera (Meyer's Passageway) is located nearby and worth seeing for its Neo-Renaissance residential buildings. The edifice at ul. Piotrkowska 77 is the Neo-Baroque Maksymilian Goldfeder Banking House erected between 1891 and 1892 and designed by Hilary Majewski. Buildings Nos 99, 109 and 137–139 are yet more creations of Gustaw Landau-Gutenteger. The last one in particular, built for Ernest Kinderman's factory, is of great interest as it still houses its historical interior decor.

Jankiel Adler, one of the most eminent Jewish painters in Poland, was born in 1895 in Tuszyn near Łódź. He graduated from art college in Duesseldorf and then returned for a short while to Poland, where he became one of the first and most important members of the Yung Yiddish group. In 1920 he left Poland for good. Jewish folklore was the dominant theme in his works. His best known paintings are *Rabbi Eleazar's Last Hour* (1917; stolen from the Łódź Museum of Art in 1981), *Ecstasy* (1919) and *My Parents* (1921; see left). His paintings in the Duesseldorf planetarium were destroyed by the Nazis. During the Second World War, Adler fought in the Polish Armed Forces in Western Europe. He died in 1949 in Aldbourne, England.

Izrael Poznański (1833–1900) was the son of a merchant from Kowal near Włocławek. He married Leonia Hertz, whose dowry enabled him to set up large factories manufacturing cotton products in ul. Ogrodowa. He also owned warehouses and a chain of shops. He even tried to establish his own cotton fields in Turkestan. He was the founder of a hospital and the New Jewish Cemetery. His fortune was one of the largest in Europe.

AROUND UL. ZACHODNIA

Many important monuments of Jewish culture remain in the central part of Łódź, west of ul. Piotrkowska. You should turn from ul. Piotrkowska into ul. Próchnika to get to ul. Wólczańska. Here, at No 6, used to be one of the city's largest Jewish synagogues, known as the Synagogue in ul. Wólczańska. It was a handsome Neo-Romanesque building designed by Gustaw Landau-Gutenteger and erected from 1899 to 1904. The Nazis destroyed it during the Second World War.

From ul. Wólczańska, ul. 1 Maja will lead you to ul. Gdańska, where you will find the impressive Poznański Palace dating from 1904. The style of this building alludes to Italian Renaissance architecture. Its decorations as well as the finish of the remaining interior features are of a delightfully subtle nature. As the building now houses the Academy of Music, visiting it is somewhat difficult.

The Poznanski Palace (the Museum of Art)

On the corner of ul. Gdańska and ul. Więckowskiego there is another one of Izrael Poznański's palaces. It was designed by Adolf Zeligson and erected between 1896 and 1900. It was built for Poznański's eldest son Ignacy and became the actual home of the Poznański family, who lived here until 1940. The Museum of Art, now housed in the palace and containing one of the best collections of modern art in Europe, is well worth a visit.

The museum does not collect Judaica in the strict sense of the word but works of art created by Jewish artists. Among the more

In the Łódź Museum of Art there is a picture by Maurycy Gottlieb (1856–1879) entitled *The Expulsion of the Moors from Grenada.*

The Neo-Renaissance residence of the Poznański family in ul. Więckowskiego is adorned with stained-glass windows depicting themes from mythology.

At the Museum of Art it is worth having a look at the picture entitled *A Saturday Siesta*. It was painted by Samuel Hirszenberg (1865–1908), the best known Jewish painter from the turn of the 20th century. His works were created thanks to the patronage of great Łódź factory owners.

important exhibits on display, the following deserve a mention: a series of graphics (*My life – a Teacher of the Talmud*) by Marc Chagall (1887–1985) as well as some of his illustrations. The museum also contains the works of the members of the group Yung Yiddish, in particular those of Jankiel Adler (1895–1949). Another impressive collection is that of avant-garde art. It contains works by Henryk Berlewi (1894–1976), a constructivist, and by Louis Marcoussis (1883–1942), a Parisian painter and acquaintance of Guillaume Apollinaire. There is also a picture entitled *Landscape from Southern France* painted by Moses Kisling (1891–1953), a well-known representative of École de Paris and several works of the Seidenbeutel brothers (both 1903–1945), known from their work in Kazimierz Dolny. You can also see the works of Henryk Streng alias Marek Włodarski (1903–1960), Bruno Schulz (1892–1942), 23 pictures by Jonasz Stern (1904–1988), as well as some by Erna Rosenstein (born 1913), Artur Nacht-Samborski (1898–1974), Otto Axer (1906–1983) and finally the collection of sculptures by Alina Szapocznikow (1926–1973). The famous photographs of Kazimierz Dolny by Benedykt Dorys (1901–1990) can also be found here.

Ul. Więckowskiego 36, ☎ +42 6339790, www.muzeumsztuki.lodz.pl; open Tuesdays 10am–7pm, Wednesdays and Fridays 11am–5pm, Thursdays noon–7pm and Sundays 10am–4pm.

The Great Synagogue, which no longer exists, was one of the most magnificent in all of Poland (photo from 1915).

The Site Once Occupied by the Great Synagogue

Ul. Gdańska leads to the former *mikvah* (at ul. Gdańska 77), now converted into a school. The Art Nouveau house at No 42, designed by David Landy and built in 1895, is particularly eye-catching.

The now empty square in ul. Kościuszki was once the site of the Great Synagogue, also known as the Synagogue on the Promenade. It was built from 1883 to 1887 with funding provided by a group of wealthy Łódź citizens headed by Izrael Poznański. The designer was Adolf Wolff from Stuttgart. This huge edifice was reminiscent of Christian basilicas. Its dominant central dome was surrounded by several others smaller in size. It combined elements of Romanesque and Moorish styles and its exquisite mosaics were particularly outstanding. On 16 November 1939, fifty-seven years to the day after its foundation committee was established, the Germans burnt the synagogue down and in the years that followed demolished its ruins.

At ul. Kościuszki 14 there is another palace of the Poznański family. It was erected in 1892 for Izrael Poznański's daughter Anna. This building, known as the Hertz Palace (after her husband's surname), now houses part of the Medical Academy.

NORTH OF ŁÓDŹ FABRYCZNA RAILWAY STATION

The area north of Łódź Fabryczna Railway Station is now the centre of Jewish life

Artur Szyk (1894–1951) is one of the better-known artists from Łódź. His miniature graphics depicting Jewish themes are of particular interest. Initially, he was part of the Yung Yiddish group. He created his own style, which showed his fascination with medieval illuminations and Jewish symbolic representations, as well as Baroque and Art Nouveau decorative features. He devoted several cycles of graphics to religious themes, among them: *Shir ha-shirim* (The Song of Songs, 1919–1920) and *Megilat Ester* (The Scroll of Esther, 1922). He also explored historical motifs in a cycle called *Statut kaliski* (The Kalisz Statute, 1926–1928) and social themes in *Hagada shel Lemberg* (The Lvov Haggadah, 1938). He escaped the Holocaust and from 1941 lived in New York. This postcard reproduction of his portrait of the Polish-American freedom fighter Kazimierz Pułaski was published within the cycle *Pictures of the Glorious Days of Polish-American Brotherhood* (1939), devoted to Poles who gained fame in the United States.

in the city. The offices of the Łódź Jewish community are also located here.

Ul. Składowa leads from Łódź Fabryczna to ul. Narutowicza, in which building No 68, now part of the university, was once the School of Trade. The edifice, erected in 1907, is representative of the Art Nouveau style which was very fashionable at that time. From here, across Plac Dąbrowskiego, you can get to ul. Sterlinga. Its patron, Seweryn Sterling (1864–1932), was an eminent doctor and director of the Poznański Foundation hospital and member of the Polish Academy of Science. He contributed greatly to the battle against tuberculosis.

On the corner of ul. Sterlinga and ul. Rewolucji 1905 (at ul. Sterlinga 26) there is another magnificent building in Art Nouveau style. It is the house of Jakub Kestenberg (1864–1921), an industrialist and owner of a company manufacturing cotton products. He unfortunately lost everything when he went bankrupt towards the end of his life.

The Synagogue of Wolf Reicher was designed by a well-known Łódź architect Gustaw Landau-Gutenteger.

The Synagogue, Once Wolf Reicher's Private House of Prayer

The synagogue was built from 1895 to 1900 for the warehouse owner Wolf Reicher. During the Second World War it was used for the storage of salt.

In 1945 the Reichers donated the building to the Łódź Jewish community, which turned it back into a house of prayer. After the tide of emigration in 1968, religious services were no longer performed here, although formally the synagogue was still functional. For religious purposes the community gathered in a hall at ul. Zachodnia 78. The synagogue burned down in 1987. It was renovated thanks to the efforts of rabbi Chaskiel Besser and the Ronald S. Lauder Foundation. With the revival of the Jewish community in Łódź after 1989 the synagogue became once more a house of religious worship.

It has a handsome facade and contains a vestibule, a prayer hall for men and galleries for women. There is also a post-war plaque in memory of its founder who died of starvation in the Łódź Ghetto.

Ul. Rewolucji 1905, No 28. From the main door go through to the second yard. The key is kept at the Jewish community office at ul. Pomorska 18. Buses # 86, 96.

Gustaw Landau-Gutenteger, the famous Łódź architect and one of the main creators of the Art Nouveau image of the town, was born in 1870. He returned to his home town after completing his studies at the Institute of Civil Engineering in St Petersburg. His best known creations are the Wilhelm Landau Banking House (1903, ul. Piotrkowska 29) and the School of Commerce (1911, ul. Narutowicza 68), which was one of the first buildings of those days erected with the use of cement. He also designed the houses at ul. Piotrkowska 32, 37, 99, 109, 128 and collaborated with David Lande on the reconstruction of the Grand Hotel. He died in 1917 at the early age of 47.

Ul. Pomorska

You can get to ul. Pomorska from the synagogue by way of ul. Wschodnia. Here, in building No 18, you will find the offices of the Jewish community. In the same street (at 46/48) there is the lodge of the former Jewish Charitable Society. From here you should make your way to

There is a functioning prayer room at the Jewish Community offices.

Before the First World War Jews lived mainly in the Łódź suburb of Bałuty.

ul. Północna along ul. Sterlinga. At the point where these two streets cross there stands the edifice of the Izrael and Leonia Poznański Jewish Hospital established by the great charitable foundation of this family of industrialists, at that time the wealthiest in Łódź. Another interesting building is the former Orphanage for girls, founded by Anna and Jakub Hertz (at ul. Północna 39). The next place worth a visit is the house at ul. Pomorska 92, the former Maksymilian Goldfeder Charitable Foundation for the poorest members of the Jewish community. You can get there by walking along ul. Wierzbowa.

BAŁUTY

Ul. Ogrodowa is a convenient starting point for a trip around the oldest Jewish quarter in Łódź. Its northern side is occupied by Izrael Poznański's huge textile factory (ul. Ogrodowa 15). Built in the last two decades of the 19th century, the plant was one of the largest in Europe. In order to provide dwellings for his numerous employees, Poznański built houses situated along ul. Ogrodowa and ul. Gdańska, many of which have remained to this very day.

The original idea for the construction of the Poznański Palace in ul. Ogrodowa arose in 1880, but it received its present Neo-Baroque look in the years 1902–1903 when it was remodelled by the eminent architect Adolf Zeligson.

The Poznański Palace (the Museum of the History of Łódź)

One of the palaces of this industrial magnate was erected in the immediate vicinity of his factory. The interior of the palace is very impressive. One of the most elegant halls is the ballroom arranged in Empire style and also referred to as the "mirror hall". At present it hosts symphony orchestra concerts and theatre performances. The exquisite dining hall will take your breath away with its extremely rich decor of oak panelling and paintings by Samuel Hirszenberg.

Some of the tables, armchairs and chairs, marked with the initial "P" carved in wood or impressed on leather, are part of the palace's original furniture. At warmer times of the year you might want to take a walk in the palace garden. You should also spare some time for the Arthur Rubinstein Gallery of Music, although it is not part of the original contents of the palace. The gallery keeps a copy of the 1970 film *L'amour de la Vie* about the life of the famous pianist.

Themes connected with the Jewish inhabitants of Łódź can be found on permanent display in several places.

The magnificent details of the interiors in the Museum of the History of Łódź are worth particular attention.

The Neo-Baroque dining room is adorned with sculptures depicting allegorical scenes.

At the Museum of the History of Łódź, a permanent place has been given to the exhibition entitled "But I still prefer Łodź! The literary trail of Julian Tuwim".

These include exhibitions such as: "From the History of Łódź (History, Culture, Everyday Life)"; "Jerzy Kosiński. Life like a best-seller", about the famous writer and author of *The Painted Bird* (see below); "The Triad of Łódź – Three Great Societies: Poles, Germans, Jews" and "Professor Jan Karski's Study". Among the exhibits there are items related to religious rituals, mostly serially produced in Warsaw. There are also some exhibits ethnographic in character: a silk *tallit* and several types of *yarmulkeh*. The section on old Łódź contains many prayer-books (the oldest printed in Hamburg at the end of the 18th century), two parchment *Torah* scrolls (possibly from one of the Łódź synagogues) as well as a wide array of printed matter documenting social life: copies of periodicals (such as "Poylishe Manchester" from the 1920s and 1930s), a stamp with the word *kosher* on it, posters and examples of company stationery. Wartime is illustrated by intriguing bank-notes and postage stamps from the Ghetto. The collection also includes several dozen paintings by Jewish artists (Samuel Hirszenberg, Maurycy Trębacz and Bolesław Utkin) depicting precious views of pre-war Łódź.

Born in Łódź in 1933 **Jerzy Kosiński** is most probably the best known writer of the post-war generation of local Jews. He graduated from the local university and then emigrated to the United States. There he began his career as a writer. He was chairman of the American Pen-Club (1973–1975). His most famous books are *The Painted Bird* (1965), *Steps* (1968), *Being There* (1971) and *Cockpit* (1975). He wrote in English. His works were not published in Poland until the abolition of censorship. Both the author and his books still remain the subject of controversy. He committed suicide in 1991.

Ul. Ogrodowa 17, by the factory, on the corner of ul. Zachodnia, ☎ +42 6540323 and 6540082, www.poznanskipalace.muz.pl. Open Tuesdays and Thursdays 10am–4pm, Fridays to Sundays 10am–2pm and Wednesdays 2pm–6pm. Tickets 6 zł and 3 zł. Saturday – entrance free. Trams # 2, 5, 11, 21, 22, 45, 46.

Personal objects, photographs and documents are shown in the reconstructed apartment of Arthur Rubinstein (above, a cast of the pianist's hands).

The Site Once Occupied by the Jewish Cemetery

From the Poznański palace head north along ul. Zachodnia. The third turning on the right is called ul. Bazarowa. Before the war this was the site of the oldest Jewish cemetery in Łódź, situated between ul. Bazarowa, ul. Zachodnia, ul. Limanowskiego and ul. Rybna. Marked out in 1811, it functioned officially until 1892 and unofficially until as late as 1922. It was the resting-place of Moses Fajtłowicz (1757–1837), the first head of the Łódź Jewish community; the Hamburski family, owners of "Lodzer Tugblat"; Kalman Poznański (1786–1856), forefather of the most powerful dynasty of Łódź industrialists, and Abraham Prussak who imported the first spinning machines from England. Already defunct, the cemetery was destroyed by the Germans during the Second World War. The vestiges were removed after the war and the iron gate was taken to the cemetery in ul. Bracka.

Rynek Bałucki (The Bałuty Market Square)

Ul. Limanowskiego leads to Rynek Bałucki, the former centre of the Bałuty district and a place full of symbolism for the Łódź Ghetto. At ul. Limanowskiego 1 there is a plaque commemorating the 210,000 victims of the Holocaust. The street on both sides of the Market Square is ul. Łagiewnicka, in which at No 36 there is the building erected in the 1930s by the local health care authority. During the Second World War it housed the Ghetto hospital and today it is the Dr Wolff Hospital. This street also leads do the Old Market Square, the very place where the first Jews in Łódź settled.

Bałuty is a former Jewish quarter with administrative boundaries from the earliest period of the history of Łódź (below: the extension of ul. Wschodnia, referred to as the "thief market", now within the area of Staromiejski Park.

Because of its beauty, the Old Synagogue in ul. Wolborska was one of the greatest tourist attractions of Łódź in the inter-war period.

Ul. Wolborska

At ul. Wolborska 20, there once stood the synagogue built in the 1860s and known as the "old one". In 1897, Adolf Zeligson had it reconstructed in original Moorish style. Unfortunately, the Germans set fire to it in November 1939 and then gradually demolished the building in 1940 and 1941. This is where a statue of Moses called *The Decalogue* and sculpted by Gustaw Zemła towers over the square.

THE NEW JEWISH CEMETERY

The largest Jewish cemetery in Europe, within boundaries set out in 1912, is spread over 42 hectares. It was established in 1892 in response to the rapid growth of the city and a cholera epidemic. Its layout conforms to tradition. There are separate sections for women, men and children. The cemetery was equipped with electricity and a drainage system. During the Second World War it became the final resting-place of over 40,000 victims from the Łódź Ghetto. This section is now referred to as "the Ghetto Fields". Only a few of its *matzevot* have survived, as well as several dozen family vaults and the mausoleums situated by the main avenue.

Right behind the main gate there is the largest pre-burial house in Poland, built from 1896 to 1898. It contains a memorial to the Victims of the Łódź Ghetto.

The most impressive of all the vaults situated by the main avenue is the mausoleum of Izrael Poznański, dating from 1902 and designed by Adolf Zeligson (section I on the

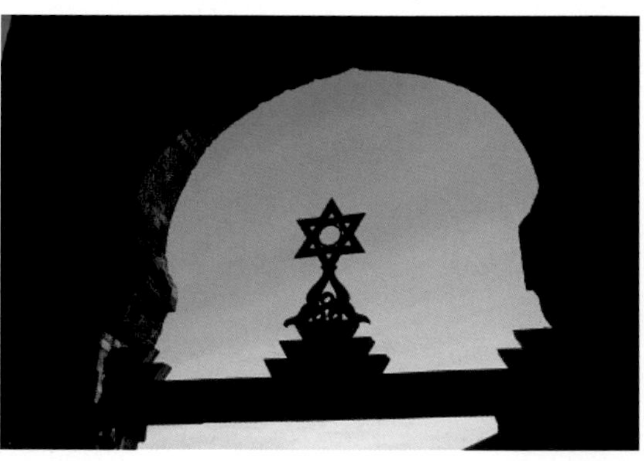

An internal gate behind the pre-burial house leads to the cemetery proper.

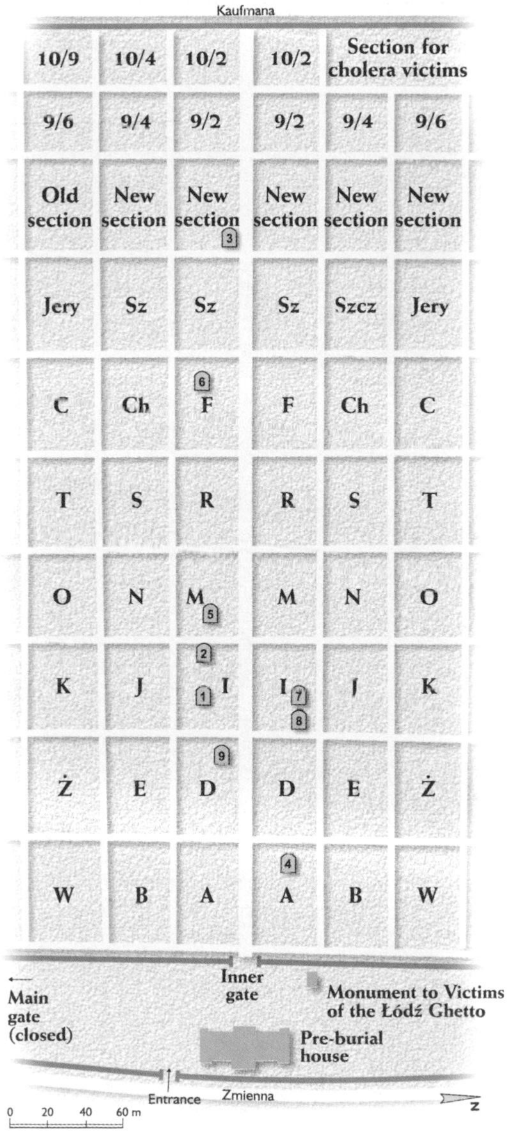

Kaufmana

10/9	10/4	10/2	10/2	Section for cholera victims	
9/6	9/4	9/2	9/2	9/4	9/6
Old section	New section	New section (3)	New section	New section	New section
Jery	Sz	Sz	Sz	Szcz	Jery
C	Ch	(6) F	F	Ch	C
T	S	R	R	S	T
O	N	M (5)	M	N	O
K	J	(2) (1) I	I (7) (8)	J	K
Ż	E	(9) D	D	E	Ż
W	B	A	(4) A	B	W

Inner gate

Main gate (closed)

Monument to Victims of the Łódź Ghetto

Pre-burial house

Entrance

Zmienna

Z

0 20 40 60 m

1. Izrael Poznański
2. Markus Silberstein
3. Izrael Lichtenstein
4. Herman Abzac
5. Stanisław Heyman
6. Adela and Izydor Tuwim
7. Felicja and Izzak Rubinstein
8. The Stillers
9. The Jarosińskis

Some of the most wonderful examples of sepulchral art from the Jewish history of Łódź are to be found in the New Jewish Cemetery.

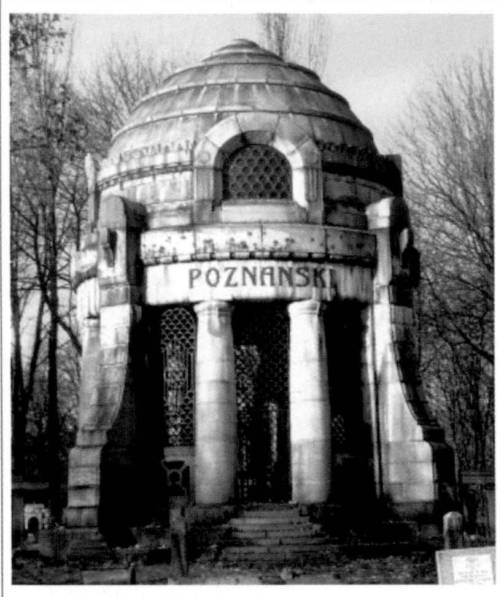

left side). Its main part built in the style of Art Nouveau was made of marble, cast iron, glass and grey granite. Its dome, adorned with an internal mosaic made up of two million pieces of glass by the Venetian artist Adrea Salvati is supported by pillars resting on a round base. The pillars bear reference to palm-trees, symbols of the righteousness of the deceased. The verses in Hebrew praise him: "And the time came for Israel to die / And the sons of Israel sighed as well, for He was the pride of Israel and did much good in Israel". In the first verse quoted here Israel is a first name, while in the second it refers to all Jews. The mausoleum was refurbished in 1992.

Poznański's Mausoleum, a monument to his earthly significance and wealth, breaks with the traditional image of a Jewish grave.

Although now in a state of neglect,. Markus Silberstein's mausoleum (section I, left side) was described by the author of the cemetery's monograph Izaak Kersz in the following way: "Many thousands of visitors are struck by its beauty". The memorial to Izrael Lichtenstein, built in constructivist style, will almost certainly be of great interest to those fascinated by Jewish sepulchral art (left-hand side, section J, grave 30). The leader of the Łódź branch of the Bund has been honoured with four granite blocks in the shape of Hebrew letters which together form the name of the party. The graves of Herman Abzac (designed by M. Broder; right-hand side, section A) and Stanisław Heyman (designed by Abraham Ostrzega in Expressionist style, left-hand side, section M) are also interesting in form. Among the remaining graves the following are worth a mention: the tomb of Adela and Izydor Tuwim, parents of the famous poet Julian Tuwim (left-hand side, section F, grave 138); of Felicia and Izaak Rubinstein, parents of the famous pianist Arthur Rubinstein (right-hand side, section I) as well as the graves of the Stillers, built in Art Nouveau style with old-Egyptian decorative motifs (right-hand side, section J) and the eclectic tomb of the Jarocińskis (left-hand side, section D).

Another millionaire, Markus Silberstein, rests in an eclectically styled vault situated close to that of Izrael Poznański.

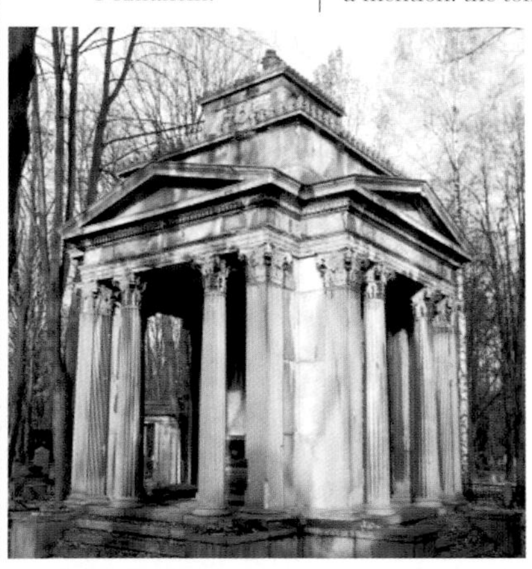

The main gate in ul. Bracka is rarely open. Tourists are welcome to enter from 9am to 4pm (6pm in summer) through the gate in ul. Zmienna. Closed on Saturdays and Jewish holidays. Men are required to cover their heads. Trams # 1, 15, 19 to the ul. Strykowska / ul. Inflancka terminal.

The Kielce Region

•

"The Polski Hotel (run by an Israelite)"

•

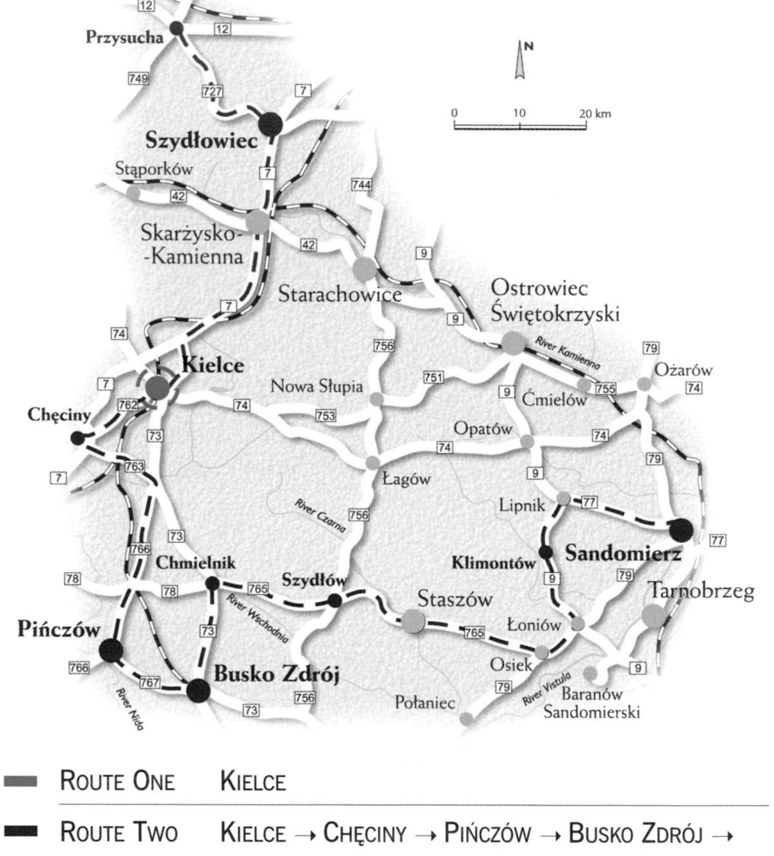

▬	ROUTE ONE	KIELCE
▬	ROUTE TWO	KIELCE → CHĘCINY → PIŃCZÓW → BUSKO ZDRÓJ → CHMIELNIK → SZYDŁÓW → KLIMONTÓW → SANDOMIERZ
▬	ROUTE THREE	KIELCE → SZYDŁOWIEC → PRZYSUCHA

FOR PRACTICAL INFORMATION SEE PAGE 284

RECOMMENDATIONS

Look for traces of Jewish heritage in **Kielce**, climb up to the Old Cemetery in **Chęciny**, visit the exhibition in the **Pińczów** synagogue, have a look at the synagogue in **Szydłów** and the monuments in **Sandomierz**.

The route goes through the territories of the Kielce Region, which before the Second World War was the area with the highest density of Jewish population in Poland. Jews came here at different times in history. They arrived in some places (Pińczów, Sandomierz) in the Middle Ages and in others only after the Tsar's edict of 1862 lifting restrictions on their place of residence (Busko Zdrój, Kielce). Local Jewish communities were not at all wealthy. They did not erect school or *kahal* buildings. They lived in meagre wooden houses, none of which now remain. And so the local remnants of the Jewish presence are mostly synagogues, sometimes of great historical significance. When you travel through these towns devoid of any traces of their Jewish past, keep in mind that they also have a story to tell.

The Polski Hotel (Run by an Israelite)

In the small towns of the Kielce region Jews were mainly involved in providing services. They also ran small hotels and Inns. For marketing reasons, as we would say today, they often gave them fancy names. There was the "Cracow Inn" in Klimontów and the "Warsaw Hotel" in Opatów. The authors of 19th-century guidebooks usually marked their descriptions of such places with a note "run by an Israelite", which suggested that the reader should not be over-impressed.

KIELCE | Yiddish: Kielc

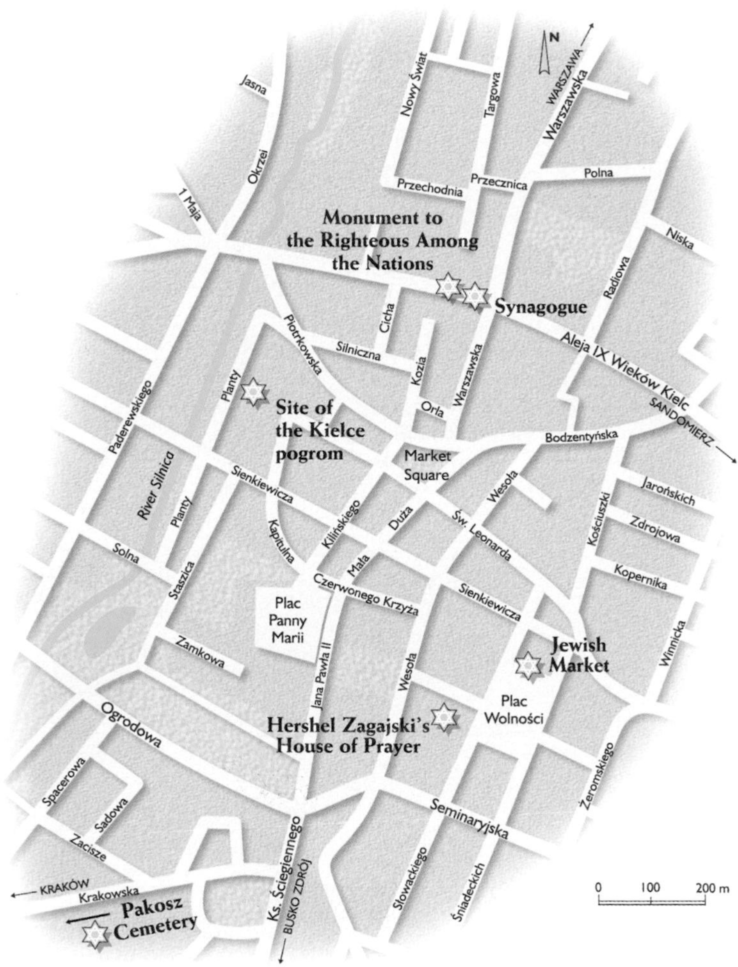

Suggested Route

The Synagogue → Town Centre (ul. Przecznica, ul. Nowy Świat, ul. Targowa, ul. Warszawska, ul. Orla, ul. Kozia and ul. Cicha) → Hershel Zagajski's House of Prayer → the Site of the Kielce Pogrom → the Pakosz Cemetery

Jews began to settle in Kielce comparatively late. The decree preventing Jewish residence within the town borders was in force until 1868, requiring Jews to remain in neighbouring Chęciny. An enormous influx began after the collapse of the January Uprising of 1863. A *kahal* district was established in 1868, and in 1874 the town already had over a thousand Jewish settlers. Eventually the proportion of Jews in the population reached 30–35%, which in 1939 meant 21,000 people. Depending on their material status, they lived either in the town centre or in the suburbs of Szydłówek, Psiarnia, Piaski and Barwinek. The first *mikvah* was in ul. Nowotarska and the first *kosher* meat-stall in ul. św. Tekli. The cemetery, still in existence, is located in the Pakosz District.

The Jewish community in Kielce reflected the character of a society of factory owners and the working class (photo from 1908).

The lifting of the ban on Jewish residence in Kielce occurred at the same time as the construction of the railway, which was then the main factor in the development of the economy. Taking advantage of this new means of transport, Jews set up many different enterprises. They invested in stone-pits (Zagajski's "Wietrznia"), limestone quarries (Lipszyc's "Międzygórze"), brickyards (owned by the Rozenholc family) and glassworks ("Leonów" owned by the Heiman brothers). Intensive urbanisation and industrialisation was accompanied by political and racial tensions. Organisations, such as the PPS (Polish Socialist Party), the Zionists and the Bund actively operated in Kielce. Although no pogroms took place here at the beginning of the 20th century, there are records of attempts to boycott Jewish shops (the "Us for Us" campaign of 1912–1913), that resulted in Jewish emigration (the Kielce *Landsmanshaft* was established in New York in 1905).

Tourist Attractions

The early Baroque Palace of Cracow Bishops on the castle hill (1637–1641), extended by Kacper Bażanka from 1720 to 1746, housing the National Museum and the Gallery of Polish Art and an excellent display of folk art; the cathedral of the Assumption of the Most Holy Virgin Mary (1632–1635) with rich Baroque furnishings; the church of the Holy Trinity (1640–1644); the Zieleński Manor House (1846–1858) with pretty garden pavilions; the houses from the 18th and 19th centuries; numerous museums, such as the Museum of School Years of Stefan Żeromski (Polish novelist, 1864–1925); the museum of the villages of the Kielce region (the skansen in the village of Tokarnia); the museum of toys in Karczówka; the 17th-century post-Bernardine monastery; the monuments of industrial architecture in the Białogon district including a factory (1814–1816) with working class housing from the first half of the 19th century; wonderful surroundings: hiking routes in the Świętokrzyskie Mountains, picturesque landscapes (Sufraganiec), deserted quarries with exposed cross-sections of rock (Biesak-Białogon).

In the inter-war period, the Jewish community in Kielce set up many important institutions. Those worth a mention are the charity societies, the Jewish High School (for boys), the Zimnowoda School (for girls), the Hazomir Jewish Musical and Literary Society, the Peretz Library, and two sports clubs (Maccabi and Stern). It also published newspapers: "Kielcer Cajtung", "Kielcer Radomer Wochenblatt" and "Kielce Unzer Express".

The inter-war years were for Kielce the next period of industralisation in which Jews were prominent. Famous local firms of that period were the Sitówka-Nowiny quarries owned by the Goldfarb family, the "Henryków" bowed beech furniture factory owned by the Nowaks and the Tenenbaum tannery. In all, about 62% of trade outlets belonged to Jews.

German occupation created a scenario here just as dreadful as in other Polish towns. Jews were deprived of all rights, their bank accounts were blocked, their businesses and schools were shut down, and each was forced to wear a Star of David. On 1 April 1941, 27,000 people were enclosed in the Kielce Ghetto stricken with starvation and typhus. From 20 to 25 August 1942, around 20,000 people were deported to the Treblinka death camp. The Ghetto was liquidated in 1944. Seven hundred people survived the war; two hundred in Russia and five hundred in the Ghetto. In this way, 97% of the Kielce Jews were exterminated.

Immediately after the war, the local Jewish community numbered approximately 200 people. They lived at ul. Planty 7/9 and ul. Focha 18/20. On 4 July 1946 a tragic event which has passed into history as the Kielce pogrom took place. A crazed mob murdered 42 Jews in revenge for the alleged detention of a boy called Henryk Błaszczyk in cellars which did not even exist. This horrifying act has not been clarified to this very day. In particular, the role of the secret security forces and the militia (Communist police), which had been spreading rumours that Jews were kidnapping children, was unclear. Regardless of the obvious influence of political agitation, the participation in this crime of the workers of the Ludwinów Factory and of the local sawmill is not in doubt. The nine provocateurs of the pogrom were sentenced to death, but after 4 July 1946 there was no way a Jewish community could exist in Kielce. The Kielce pogrom also prompted nationwide Jewish emigration from Poland.

Near the entrance to the synagogue there is the monument to the Righteous Among the Nations, the title given to those who were helping Jews during the Second World War. It bears the following inscription: "I hear these words and with all my might I think of those who protected me, and I ask myself again and again: Dear God, had I been in their place, would I have been able to do the same?"

The Kielce synagogue was founded by Moses Pfeiffer (photo from 1916).

Remnants of a Jewish past in Kielce are comparatively few and quite recent. They are linked more with historical events than with any aesthetic or artistic value.

The Synagogue

This immense building towering over the roundabout on the corner of ul. Warszawska and al. IX Wieków Kielc was built in 1902. It was designed by municipal architect Stanisław Szpakowski. It had three naves; those on the sides containing the galleries for women. The facade was decorated with Oriental motifs. After the Second World War the synagogue was remodelled and converted into a building serving the needs of the state archive bureau, which is there to this day. As a result the synagogue is not accessible to the general public.

Ul. Warszawska 17.

The original outline of the synagogue (above) did not have its present socialist-realist appearance (below).

A Walk in the Centre

Very little remains nowadays of the area of ul. Nowy Świat which was referred to as "an enclave of Jewish Kielce"; just a few old houses, several others rebuilt and changed out of all recognition, and contours of foundations overgrown with thick bushes. Despite this, it is worth having a walk around the area of the present Sady housing estate. Make a point

The tragedy of the Kielce pogrom is commemorated by a plaque on the wall of the house at ul. Planty 7/9

of visiting the old houses at ul. Przecznica 4, ul. Nowy Świat 18/18b and 30, ul. Targowa 8 and 10, as well as the whole row of houses around ul. Warszawska. The most charming, although different in character to those mentioned above, are the streets in the town centre: ul. Orla, ul. Kozia and ul. Cicha. At ul. Słowackiego 4 there still stands Hershel Zagajski's house of prayer built in 1922. Today it is used as a storehouse. In Plac Wolności you can see the municipal trade halls, the work of Chaskiel Landau from Chęciny.

The house in which the Kielce pogrom took place can be found at ul. Planty 7/9. This past tragedy is recalled in a memorial chamber with interesting decorations made by students from the Szermentowski School of Art in Kielce.

The Cemetery in the Pakosz District

The present condition of the cemetery is a clear indication that Jewish Kielce is now consigned to history. The cemetery was marked out in 1868, coinciding with the first wave of Jewish settlers to the town. It functioned until the Second World War and then remained in a state of neglect. In 1987 the Nissenbaum family together with the New York City Jewish Kielce community represented by William Mandel took up its renovation.

The path west of the gate leads to the corner grave of 45 children murdered by the Germans on 23 May 1943. According to local sources these children have yet another tomb situated by the gate and purely symbolic in its character. The next path leads from here to the collective grave of the victims of the Kielce pogrom of 4 July 1946. Apart from these two individual memorials the cemetery today is but a large, empty meadow.

The house at ul. Targowa 8 is one of the very few remaining pre-war buildings.

You can get to the cemetery by bus # 44 which goes to the Pakosz terminal. The key is kept by Ms Irena Kowalczyk (also known in the neighbourhood as Ms Sikorówna), address: ul. Marmurowa 9, ☎ +41 3616210. The bus stops 300 metres from the gate. Access on foot along ul. Pakosz and ul. Osobna.

A lapidarium has been created right behind the gate of the Kielce cemetery. After the war a large part of the *matzevot* were retrieved from the waters of the nearby River Sinica. The gravestones are worth a closer look. In the higher rows there are many examples of outstanding stonework.

CHĘCINY | Yiddish: Chenczin

The first mention of Jews in Chęciny dates from 1564. The local Jewish community was linked to Kielce, where Jews could stay only temporarily and were not allowed to reside until 1833. The development of the community was a consequence of a series of privileges obtained from the Polish kings: Michael Korybut Wiśniowiecki, John III Sobieski and Stanislaus Augustus Poniatowski. The average proportion of Jews in the local population ranged from 60% to 70%. In 1939 they numbered 2,825 (56%). On 1 September 1942 the Germans deported all of them to the Treblinka death camp. Much of the historical housing has remained, including the buildings once owned by Jews in the Rynek (Main Square) and ul. Długa.

The Synagogue

Since its construction in 1638 the synagogue has been remodelled several times (in 1905 it also caught fire). Nevertheless its exterior has remained almost unchanged. Erected on the basis of the privilege granted by King Ladislaus IV, the synagogue is a stone building, rectangular in shape (14m by 26m). It has a vestibule on its western side and a prayer room for women located above it. The present roof dates from 1959, when it replaced the former pavilion roof. In 1939 the synagogue was shut down by the Germans. After the war it was used as a cinema and a library. It now houses a cultural centre.

Tourist Attractions

The ruins of the bishop's (and later royal) Gothic palace (1269–1306, enlarged in the second half of the 15th century); the church of St Bartholomew (1600, with features from the second half of the 15th century) and the Kasper Fodyga chapel (1614); the Franciscan monastery; the church of the Assumption of the Most Holy Virgin Mary (second half of the 14th century, remodelled) and the cloister buildings; the nunnery of the order of St Clare (1643–1685, remodelled in the 19th century); the Niemczówka Inn (1570); the wooden granary (18th century); the historical lay-out of the town with its two market squares.

The interior of the Chęciny synagogue still contains part of the stucco decor, the Renaissance stone alms boxes, and the beautiful marble frame of the *aron ha-kodesh*

The stone framework of the synagogue's interior portal is adorned with a Hebrew inscription visible from the vestibule.

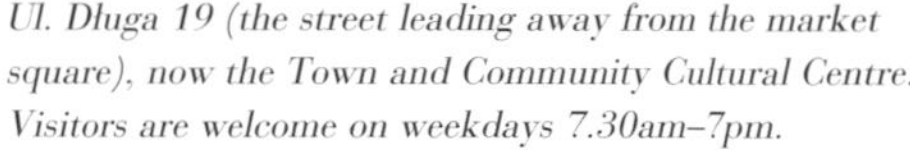

Ul. Długa 19 (the street leading away from the market square), now the Town and Community Cultural Centre. Visitors are welcome on weekdays 7.30am–7pm.

The Cemetery on Zamkowa Góra (Castle Hill)

Here you will find approximately 100 *matzevot*. They are made of the unique local marble. Many of them show evidence of superb stonework and the oldest one dates from 1638. The cemetery functioned for several centuries (1581–1833) and also served Jews from Kielce, who were not allowed to bury their dead in the town cemetery. Its appearance today calls to mind the Lemko and Boyko cemeteries of south-western Poland; it is just as picturesque and wild and in a similarly high location. The beautifully engraved *matzevot* are sinking under the bushes, falling apart from rain and frost and becoming overgrown with wild fruit trees. Nothing will be visible here in the not too distant future.

The walk to the Chęciny cemetery is a real adventure. It was once possible to get here from the foot of the mountain, but as the old paths are now overgrown with bushes and the pre-war property borders have been changed you should take the following route: from the synagogue go to ul. Krzywa and then walk along ul. Radkowska (with the house numbers getting bigger) up to the border of the town. There, on your left you will see a house with a sign "kamieniarz-plastyk" (artistic stone-masonry). Opposite this house, on the other side of the road, you will find a beaten track (with the remains of asphalt at the beginning). Having walked approximately 150 meters up

this road, look out for a poorly visible path situated on the slope on the right-hand side leading to Zamkowa Góra (Castle Hill). As you walk up, the path will become clearer. You should keep going up until you reach the top of the hill. Than walk across its flat top. After 90–100 paces you will see a birch-tree marked with spray paint and a house below. There is also an electricity pole nearby. A very steep path to the right will lead you from there straight to the cemetery (you will see the matzevot from above). The walk from the synagogue to the cemetery takes 25–30 minutes.

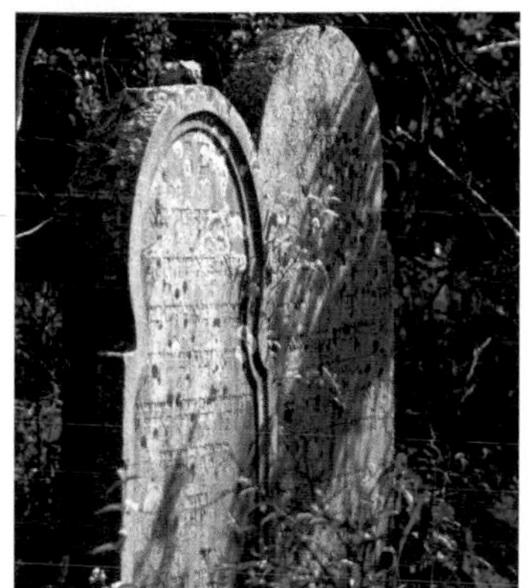

The beautifully situated cemetery at the foot of Góra Zamkowa (Castle Mountain) may have been established as early as in 1581

PIŃCZÓW

This beautifully situated town is distinguished by the fact that it contains the only exhibition of Jewish heritage in the Kielce region to be housed in a historical synagogue.

Jews came to Pińczów sometime before 1576. The owners of the town, the Myszkowski family, brought the settlers in from royal and church towns which had introduced the *privilegia de non tolerandis Iudaeis* (it is not improbable that one of the groups came from the Kazimierz district in Cracow). In accordance with the expectations of their patrons, Jews working in trade, handicraft and services kept the economy vibrant even in times of crisis. Merchandise from Pińczów was often exported abroad, aided by institutions such as the Leipzig trade fairs. In the 17th century the proportion of Jews in the population exceeded 60% and the town became the main Jewish centre in the Małopolska region, closely linked to the Kazimierz district of Cracow by ties of both family and trade. In 1738 Jakub Felczer and his Jewish compatriots contributed to the strengthening of cult of the Holy Mother of Mirów, which exists to this day. During a fire at the monastery they saw "a beautiful lady" (The Mother of God), "a monk in a garment of the Reformed Franciscan Order" (St Francis the Seraphic) as

Elias from Pińczów (ca 1710–1770) is one of the town's better known Jews. Born into a poor family, he completed medical studies thanks to a benefactor. He gained an excellent reputation as a doctor but his great passion was mathematics. He published a dissertation on arithmetic (in Żółkiew) and a geometry textbook for schools (Berlin, 1760).

Tourist Attractions

The Pauline monastery (1436); the church of St John the Evangelist (1642, parts from the first half of the 15th century); the monastery from the middle of the 15th century, today housing the Regional Museum (archaeological and historical exhibitions); the monastery of the Reformed Franciscan Order; the church of the Visitation of the Most Holy Virgin Mary (1615–1640); the chapel of St Ann (1600, S. Gucci's atelier); the remains of the Oleśnicki Family Castle (1424–1454): the tower, the garden pavilion; the Wielopolski Palace (1780), now a school; the so-called Arian print-shop from the 16th and 17th centuries, now an archive bureau; the fountain in the main square (1593); the 18th and 19th-century houses; the narrow-gauge railway to Jędrzejów; the kayak trail to Wiślica and Nowy Korczyn.

The majority of the inhabitants of pre-war Pińczów wore side-curls, skull-caps and gabardines. In the censuses, however, they declared themselves to be "Poles of the Mosaic faith".

well as "a soldier" (St Prosper). The fire soon went out and the Jews were the only eyewitnesses to the miracle. The 19th century saw great progress in the town's industrial development. Rosenberg opened his cloth factory, and Barenstein his dye-works and a factory manufacturing cotton textiles. Printing and the book trade also began to thrive.

Pre-war Pińczów was a bustling town. Streets such as ul. Klasztorna, ul. Złota, ul. Krakowska, ul. Gęsia, ul. Krzywa and ul. Słabska were considered Jewish. Much of the land around the main square also belonged to Jews. There was a Jewish amateur theatre and several sports clubs. The town council, headed by a Catholic priest, was made up of 15 Jews and 15 Poles. The last Rabbi of Pińczów was the conservative Shapsha Rapaport (1888–1942). Among well-known local characters was a certain Kasztański who knew all the personal details of every Jew in town, as well as Herszkowicz, the owner of the pub in the main square. During the Second World War the Germans murdered most members of the local Jewish community.

It Is Dawning in Pińczów

The colourful world of the Pińczów Jews has survived the passage of time in several common sayings used in Polish even today. The multitude of Jews in the town's population gave rise to the following simile referring to a crowd "as many people as Jews in Pińczów".
As their taste in clothes and sense of elegance was less than exquisite, local Jewish women were described as "Parisiennes from Pińczów". As Pińczów Jews manufactured a well-known cheese, another saying goes "as salty as Pińczów cheese". According to some accounts, the cheese would mature on the roof, giving off a peculiar glow. This gave birth to the incomprehensible saying: "It is dawning in Pińczów". Others attribute the origin of this line to the novel *The Magician of Lublin* by Isaac Bashevis Singer.

The Old Synagogue

The Pińczów synagogue, built in late Renaissance style, dates from the turn of the 17th century. Inscriptions discovered during repair work lead us to believe that the foundations were laid in 1594 and the construction completed from 1608 to 1609. As tradition requires, the entrance leads us through the vestibule to the main prayer hall for men located on the ground floor. The prayer room for women is on the first floor. The interior was destroyed during the German occupation from 1939 to 1944. After the war it was used as a fertiliser storehouse and a shop.

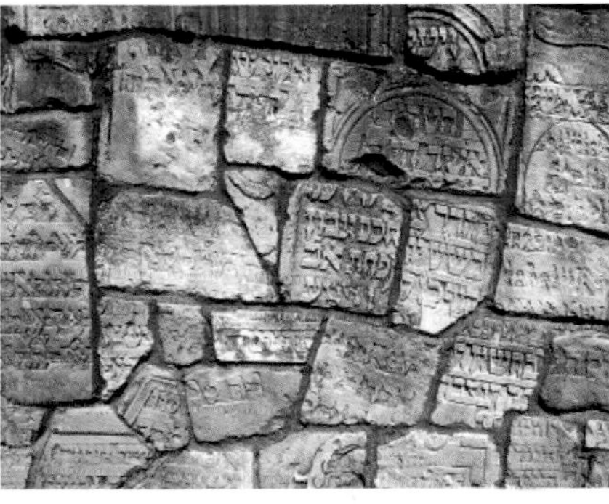

The *aron ha-kodesh* fell off the wall in 1974. Renovation works began in the 1990s and in 1997 it was restored, the reconstructed parts constituting slightly more then 10% of the whole. Also the floor was repaired and the spot where the *bimah* once stood was marked. Inside the synagogue you can see the richly decorated wooden ceiling and approximately seventy inscriptions discovered during conservation work. One of those on the western wall, dating from around 1608, translates as "Shibtai, the son of Mister Abraham of blessed memory". You can also see the exhibition entitled "The Jewish Community in Pinczów", with the original 17th-century local *Torah* and photographs of the New Synagogue once situated in ul. Złota and destroyed by the Nazis. Fragments of the 18th-century polychromy in the vestibule are particularly impressive. Paintings are also visible in the *kahal* room, and among them inscriptions from the time of its foundation in 1608 1609. The synagogue has been visited by Józef Glemp, Primate of the Catholic Church in Poland and Tadeusz Mazowiecki, the former Prime Minister.

Ul. Klasztorna, a two-minute walk from Plac Wolności (the main square). The synagogue is maintained by the Regional Museum in Pińczów (☎ +41 3572472). Open: Tue, Fri 9am–3pm; Wed, Thu 9am–4pm (1 May–30 Sep 10am–5pm); Sat, Sun 10am–3pm. Tickets: 2 zł or 1 zł.

Since 1990 fragments of *matzevot* have been placed on the inner side of the wall built around the synagogue in 1979.

Until the Second World War the Old Synagogue stood in what was then Plac Bóżniczy (Synagogue Square). New buildings have been added since that time.

BUSKO ZDRÓJ | Yiddish: Busk Zadroy

Just 16 km east of Pińczow (road 767) there is the well-known spa Busko-Zdrój. It was once a church town, and Jews were not allowed to settle there until 1862. This, however, did not prevent many of them from being treated at the local sanatorium. From 1862 the number of Jews in Busko increased rapidly, such that just before the war the proportion of Jews in the local population had reached approximately 40%.

A brick synagogue at ul. Partyzantów 5 is a relic of the former local Jewish community. Its interior has not been preserved. The building has been turned into a department store.

The synagogue in Chmielnik was erected sometime after 1638 and remodelled after a fire in 1876.

CHMIELNIK

Chmielnik could well be your next stop on the way to Szydłów. The local Jewish community had a much longer history than the one in Busko. The first Jews arrived here in the first half of the 16th century. By the beginning of the Second World War, they were by far the largest ethnic group, constituting as much as 77% of the population. You can find a synagogue building in ul. Wspólna. Its rich interior furnishings were destroyed when an intermediate ceiling was added in 1942. After the war the synagogue was turned into a storehouse. It now stands empty.

SZYDŁÓW

Szydłów was a royal town established in 1329. Jewish settlement most probably began at the end of the 14th century and its Jewish community has existed since the first half of the 15th century. It belonged to the Cracow and Sandomierz regions of the Diet of the Four Lands. In the 16th

Tourist Attractions

The panorama of Szydłów, visible from the road, will encourage you to have a look at the town. It is surrounded by defence walls from the second half of the 14th century, with loop-holes, merlons and crenels. Here you will find such historical monuments as Brama Krakowska (the Cracow Gate) with a well preserved forecourt (second half of 14th century) and the Gothic church of St Ladislaus (mid-15th century); the Gothic affiliate church of All Saints; the ruins of the church and hospital of the Holy Spirit (16th century) and the castle (second half of 14th century); the so-called Little Treasury (second half of 14th century), now the Regional Museum: geological, archaeological, historical and ethnographic exhibitions.

century there were only four brick-buildings in town: the parish church, the castle, the town hall and the synagogue. In 1577 and 1588 agreements between the Jews and the citizens of Szydłów were signed regarding production and sale of alcohol. In 1662 the community obtained numerous privileges, confirmed by King Stanislaus Augustus in 1767.

Szydłów never managed to develop into anything more than a provincial centre. A lack of investment caused a reduction in size of its Jewish population in the 19th and 20th centuries. The proportion of Jews dropped from 53% in 1827 to approximately 30% at the outbreak of the Second World War. In January 1942, a ghetto was formed here, from which all the Jews were deported to the Treblinka death camp.

The oldest house in the main square, on the corner of ul. Łokietka, belonged before the war to Nachman, a local man of wealth nicknamed "the Heir". Nachman survived, as during the war he was in Russia. He returned to visit his home town in 1949.

The inhabitants of Szydłów who can still recall the friendly way in which the two societies lived together before the Second World War have fond memories of their Jewish neighbours.

The Synagogue

The synagogue, the only significant Jewish memorial in Szydłów to remain, was erected from 1534 to 1564. Apart from one modification it has survived in its original form to this day. After the war it was used as a library and a cinema. It underwent a complete overhaul from 1978 to 1981, which rescued the building from complete ruin. Built of

The Szydłów Synagogue is a top-class historical monument.

This is what the *bimah* of the Szydłów synagogue looked like (photo from before 1939)

stone, it has walls with buttresses and a crenellated parapet. The interior is painted white, concealing polychromies by Yehuda Leib. The stone framework of the *aron ha-kodesh* in the shape of a portal, the alms box bearing the motif of hands in the act of giving a blessing and the acoustics of the interior make the place very special. The upper wooden part of the vestibule is also of great interest, although it is an addition from 1979, distorting the historical character of the building.

At ul. Targowa 1 there is a community centre open Tue–Fri noon–8pm, Sat–Sun 4pm–8pm. Mr Krzemiński, who lives opposite at Osiedle Łokietka 2/1 is likely to appear with the keys, should visitors arrive outside opening hours. The synagogue is visible from the main square.

KLIMONTÓW

According to accounts from a hundred years ago, the local Jews, engaged mostly in small trade and the manufacture of low quality products, remained in poverty and ignorance. But at the same time these very people established the Klimontów Company Limited, which ran shops selling foodstuffs and farming equipment, as well as the Loan and Savings Society protecting people from usury.

A local physician Dr Zysman, was one of the initiators of these enterprises, which a century ago were not common practice deep in the provincial parts of Poland. Next to the Klimontów synagogue there was a cemetery, which was turned into a playground in 1962.

There are several routes going from Szydłów to Sandomierz (a distance of 57 km). The easiest connection is road 765 which goes through Staszów to Osieka, from where you take road 79 to Sandomierz via Łoniów. In Łoniów turn left onto road 9 and after a dozen or so kilometres you will get to Klimontów.

Not far from the market square in ul. Szkolna in Klimontów there is a well preserved synagogue built from 1851 to 1862. Wrecked after 1945, it was renovated in the second half of the 1980s.

SANDOMIERZ | Yiddish: Sudomir, Tzoyzmir

Jews lived in Sandomierz from the Middle Ages. At the time of the Commonwealth of Poland, the local community was one of the most important in the entire country and equal in rank to those of Cracow and Lvov. King Sigismund III limited the number of Jews in Sandomierz to no more than 11 families domiciled in any one street. These restrictions were lifted by King John Casimir, and his successors granted the Jews further rights of residence and work (1696, 1745, 1774). In the 19th and 20th centuries Jews consituted 30–40% of the town's population. The Jewish quarter in Sandomierz occupied the area along the city wall in the western part of the town. In April 1942 the Nazis set up the Sandomierz Ghetto, from which most of the detained were deported to the death camp in Bełżec. About a thousand of those remaining were shot dead in the Ghetto on 10 January, 1943.

Sandomierz is one of the most glorious historical urban complexes in Poland.

The Synagogue and the Kahal House

The synagogue dates from 1768. Next to it, on the northern side, there is a *kahal* building, added in the 19th century.

Tourist Attractions

The Gothic Town Hall (14th century, extended in the 16th century); the Gothic cathedral of the Nativity of the Most Holy Virgin Mary (founded by King Casimir the Great, from 1360–1382, remodelled); the 15th-century Gothic house of Jan Długosz (an early Polish historian), now housing the Diocesan Museum of Church Art; the Dominican monastery (1226) with the famous church of St Jacob; the Benedictine monastery (1613) with the church of St Michael (1686–1696); the Reformed Franciscan Order monastery with the church of St Joseph (from 1679–1689); the Gothic church of St Paul (from 1426–1434); the late Renaissance Gostomianum Jesuit College (1605–1615); the castle, of which the main body and two towers remain (ca 1480, remodelled in the 16th century); parts of the city walls (the Opatowska Gate); the Oleśnicki House (1770–1780) containing the exhibition of the District Museum (including the treasure of Roman Denarii); the underground tourist route (entrance from ul. Oleśnickich); the beautiful surroundings: loessial gorges, including The Queen Jadwiga Gorge and the Piszczele Gorge, as well as the Góry Pieprzowe (Pepper Mountains) reserve.

According to a local legend, the first synagogue in Sandomierz was founded by Esther from Opoczno, the lover of King Casimir the Great.

A lapidarium in a shape of a pyramid is a characteristic feature of the cemetery established in 1850.

Both buildings are situated in ul. Żydowska, at the main axis of the old Jewish district. The square-shaped prayer hall, bearing traces of wall paintings on the vaulting and walls, has remained, although at present it is subdivided by an intermediate ceiling. The entrance to the synagogue leads from the *kahal* house through a late Gothic portal transferred here from the castle. The synagogue functioned until the Second World War, when it was wrecked by the Nazis. After the war it was renovated and given over to the local archives office. Next to it, on the side of an adjacent slope, there are parts of the defence walls and also the remains of a tower. The Sandomierz synagogue is a very pretty building and one is tempted to say it would be an ideal place for a museum. Unfortunately, at present access is extremely difficult. The building houses the municipal archives storing the town's records dating back to the 16th century, as well as 19th-century documentation from the entire Kielce region. It ensures that this listed building is well preserved but makes a visit impossible.

Ul. Żydowska. The Archives Bureau working hours are: Mon, Wed, Thu, Fri 7.30am–3.30pm and Tue 8.30am–4.30pm. Entrance from the main square via ul. Oleśnickich.

The Cemetery

In the fairly small and only partly preserved Sandomierz cemetery you can see pieces of *matzevot* placed along a path. The graves here are richly decorated. A memorial plaque

Charges of **ritual murder** have accompanied Jews since the time of ancient Greece. Several different explanations have been given for the supposed reason for this alleged crime: the need for blood, apparently necessary for the preparation of Passover *matzah*, a wish to repeat the Passion of Christ, or even medical experiments conducted by Jewish doctors. Some people believed that the blood of Christian infants healed the wounds after circumcision or removed the unpleasant smell supposedly emanating from Jews. In the Middle Ages, the first court trial concerning ritual murder occurred in 1144 in Norwich, England. In Poland these allegations started in the 13th century and reached a peak in the second half of the 17th century. Both church and state authorities attempted to protect Jews from the consequences of such superstition. From 1540 several papal bulls were issued on the subject and even Polish Kings intervened (1531, 1557, 1576, 1633, 1766). A recurrence of these spurious claims accompanied the anti semitic campaign in Russia in the 1890s. The alleged ritual murder was a pretext for the pogrom in Kishniev in 1903 (400 dead). The last instances of such allegations in Poland took place in Cracow on 11 August 1945 and in Kielce on 4 July 1946.

funded by the Szafran family has also been put here. The gravestones with the dates 1942–1943 are elements of a monument built after the war and commemorating the victims of the Holocaust.

Ul. Sucha. The gate is locked but you can enter through a broken fence on the right hand side. The cemetery is not far from the PKS bus station. Just make your way towards the huge building which is the student hostel of the local catering school.

The Paintings in the Sandomierz Cathedral

Jewish motifs in the paintings on the walls of the cathedral are rather peculiar in character. As part of the cycle produced between 1708 and 1737 by Charles de Prevot and entitled *Martyrologium Romanum*, they depict the martyrdom of the Catholic church as well as of Christians in Sandomierz. It contains scenes of the Tartar siege of the town in 1260. One of the paintings on the west wall entitled *The Slaughter of the Innocent* contains anti-Jewish elements. The scene of ritual murder depicted here most certainly bears reference to the charges brought in the trial for such a crime in Sandomierz in 1710. This historical picture is a source of controversy. The recurring disputes over it emphasise on the one hand the historical nature of Prevot's painting and, on the other, stress the unacceptability of displaying content which for

In 1689 and 1710 court trials on cases of alleged ritual murder took place in Sandomierz. In the second instance, in 1712, the Crown Tribunal ordered Jews to be banished from the town. Fortunately, royal intervention prevented this from being carried out (below: part of the painting by Charles de Prevot).

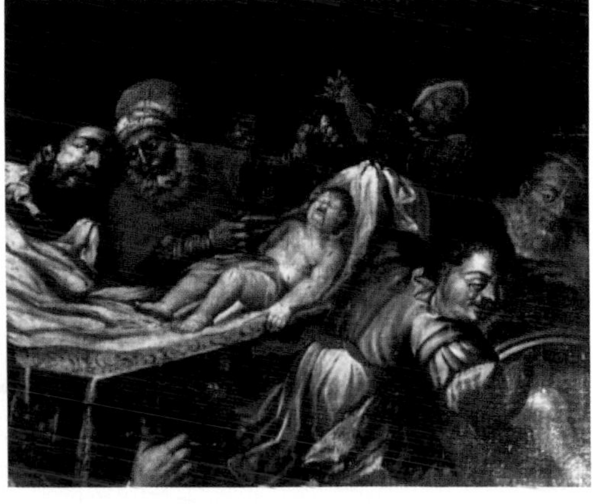

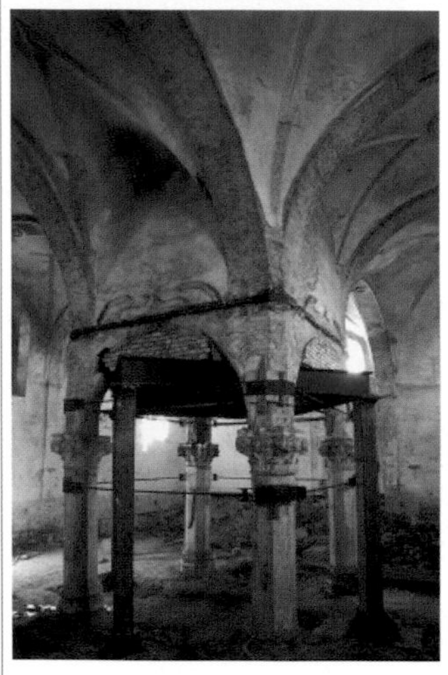

centuries has been a rallying cry for pogroms. Similar pictures can be found in St Paul's church.

The church is open to visitors daily 3pm–5pm. The taking of photographs is forbidden.

SZYDŁOWIEC

In Szydłowiec there are several remnants of the town's Jewish past, such as the Ajzenberg factory synagogue built before the Second World War, a wooden *Sukkah* on the house adjacent to the synagogue and, above all, a large Jewish cemetery, a good part of which is well preserved. It contains over 3500 gravestones, the oldest dating from 1831. The Jewish community in Szydłowiec developed along with the growth of local quarries and the tanning industry.

The *bimah*, the framework of the *aron ha-kodesh* and some traces of wall paintings still remain in the partly destroyed interior of the synagogue in Przysucha.

PRZYSUCHA | Yiddish: Pshiskhe

The magnificent local synagogue has survived the passage of time. After a ten-minute walk from the bus station along ul. Warszawska, on your left hand side you will see the impressive synagogue building (address: Plac Stefana Żeromskiego). The synagogue was built from 1764 to 1777.

Oholot of the following distinguished figures may be found in the Jewish cemetery: Abraham (d. 1806), Symcha Bunem (d. 1827) and, most importantly, Jacob Yitzhak ben Asher known as the Holy Jew of Przysucha (1766–1813), the first propagator of Chasidism in central Poland and the representative of its intellectual faction. "It is not difficult to perform miracles. To be a Jew, however, is really hard" is one of his famous sayings.

The key to the synagogue is with Ms Maria Gajda, in the house next door at ul. Konopnickiej 6. Access to the cemetery is somewhat complicated. From the synagogue you should go out onto ul. Wiejska and walk past the end of ul. Brzozowa as well as the large building with the "Skup" sign. Opposite, on the right hand side, there is an opening to a path by which there is a large container for waste. You should go approximately 100 metres up this path and get the key from Mr Werenc, who lives nearby at ul. Wiejska 50a.

The impressive *oholot* in the Przysucha cemetery, reconstructed in 1990.

The Lublin Region

•

Amidst Hills of Chalk and Fields of Green

•

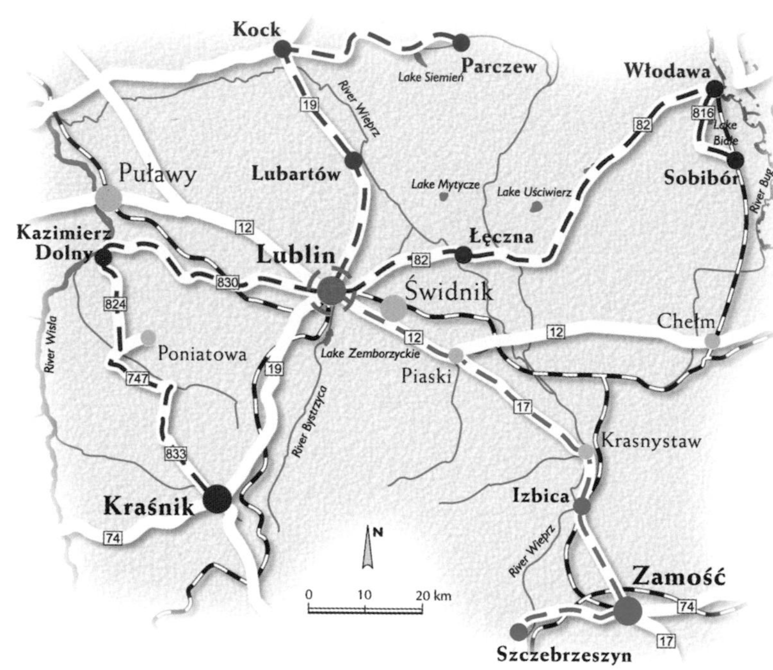

▬	Route One	Lublin
▬	Route Two	Lublin → Lubartów → Kock → Parczew
▬	Route Three	Lublin → Łęczna → Włodawa → Sobibór
▬	Route Four	Lublin → Kazimierz Dolny → Kraśnik
▬	Route Five	Lublin → Izbica → Zamość → Szczebrzeszyn

For practical information see page 287

Recommendations

Visit the old Jewish Cemetery in **Lublin**, look in at the Lublin Yeshivat Chachmei (The Lublin Academy of Sages), walk along ul. Lubartowska as far as the Chevrat Nossim (Funeral Society) Synagogue; visit the synagogue complex in **Włodawa** and Rynek II in **Łęczna**; go for a walk in the old town of **Zamość**; visit **Kazimierz Dolny**.

Until the middle of the 16th century, Jewish communities existed only in Lublin and Kazimierz and maybe also in Chełm. The migration of Jews to the Lublin region began with the founding of new private towns, to which they were brought to develop trade and services. New towns were in economic competition with existing ones and so Lublin, Krasnystaw and Urzędów tried to limit the influx of people of the Jewish faith. As a result of high demographic growth in the second half of the 18th century, Jews began to dominate in many places (such as Kraśnik, Lubartów and Łęczna). At the beginning of the 20th century, in eleven towns more than 70% of the population was Jewish, while in Łaszczów and Izbica it was close to 100%. Jewish settlement in rural areas was sparse and mostly limited to single families engaged in trade, craftsmanship or tavern keeping. At the outbreak of the Second World War there were about 300,000 Jews living in the Lublin region.

Being a centre of Jewish culture and tradition for over three hundred years, the Lublin lands (excluding the city itself) produced many *tzaddikim*, such as Mordechai Josef Leiner of Izbica, Chaim Israel Morgenstern of Puławy or Motele Rokeach of Biłgoraj, as well as the family of the famous Jewish writers, Israel Joshua and Isaac Bashevis Singer.

Let's get
to the point...
I'll draw a horse
running
Amidst the hills
of chalk and
the fields of green:
On this side
– the mountains
like a stairway
to the sky,
And on the other
– the fields and
the river sweetly
humming nearby.
Farewell, you
wonderful, humble,
little town!

From the epic poem by Zusman Segałowicz (1884–1949) *In Kazimierz on the Vistula* (1912)

Getting Around

All the buildings are very close to each other and the best way to see them is on foot. It will take 2–3 hours, including sightseeing. If you prefer to go by bus, take # 5, 6, 10, 11, 16, 22, 33, 34, 35 or 39, each of which will take you to the roundabout at the corner of al. Tysiąclecia and al. Unii Lubelskiej. Buses # 2, 18, 24, 156 and 160 run along ul. Lubartowska. Tickets are valid for limited time periods (10 or 30 minutes). On private lines tickets should be purchased from the driver.

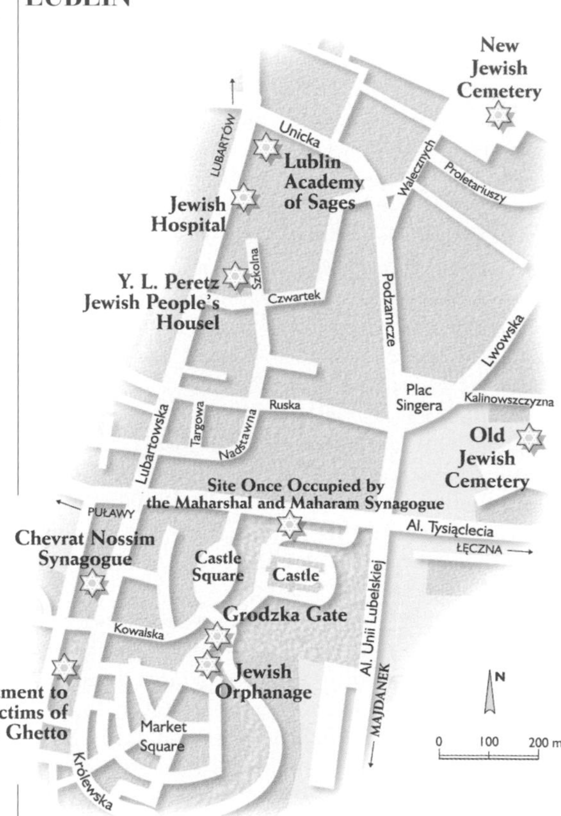

Lublin was one of the oldest and most important Jewish centres in Poland. It was called the Jerusalem of Poland as well as the Mother of Israel.

Suggested Route

Brama Grodzka (the Grodzka Gate) → Plac Zamkowy (Castle Square) → the Site Once Occupied by the Maharshal and Maharam Synagogue → ul. Kalinowszczyzna (Old Jewish Cemetery) → ul. Walecznych (New Jewish Cemetery) → ul. Lubartowska (the yeshivah), the Jewish Hospital, the Y.L. Peretz Jewish People's House, Chevrat Nossim Synagogue → Plac Ofiar Getta (the Square of the Victims of the Ghetto) → ul. Kowalska – Majdanek

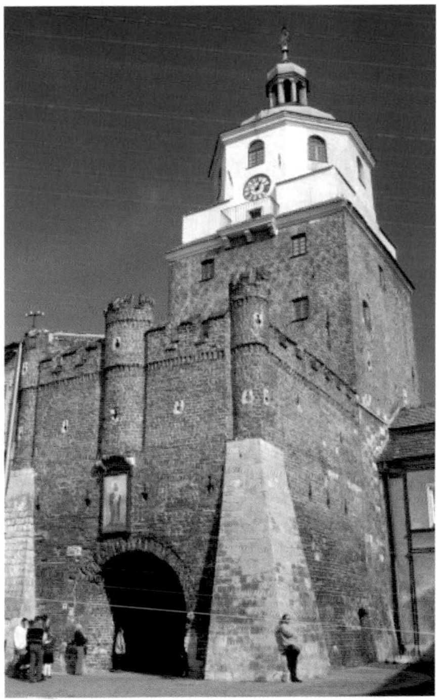

Brama Krakowska (the Cracow Gate) was a part of the medieval city walls

The foundation of the town dates from 1317, and the first mention of the Jewish community from as early as 1336. In 1453, Kazimierz Jagiellończyk (King Casimir of the Jagiellonian dynasty) bestowed the privilege of free trade upon the Jews and in 1523, in return for participation in the construction of fortifications, they were made equal in the eyes of the law with the rest of the townsfolk. In 1568 the two communities became completely separated as the Jewish quarter obtained the *privilegia de non tolerandis Christianis*. This resulted in an isolation which lasted until the middle of the 19th century, so that one can speak of the presence of Jews in the old town of Lublin only from 1862.

Lublin's function was that of a centre of intellect. It was the home of Talmudic schools and Hebrew printing houses. The most renowned 16th-century Lublin institutions of learning included the schools of Ya'akov ben Yehuda ha-Levi Kopelman, Shalom ben Yosef Shachna and Shlomo ben Yechiel Luria also known as Maharshal. The most important printers were the houses of Kalonymos (from 1578) as well as Kalmen and Levi (from 1630) which published prayer books and Talmudic texts for "all the towns from the River Bug to the River Spree". From 1580 to 1725, together with Jarosław, Lublin became the centre of Jewish self-government in the Polish Republic. This is where the *Vaad Arba Aratzot* (Diet of the Four Lands) conventions took place. The situation within Poland worsened and Jews embarked upon a difficult period and

Tourist Attractions

The Royal castle founded by King Casimir the Great, its 13th-century donjon and 14th-century chapel (wall painting from 1418); the old town complex; St John the Baptist and St John the Evangelist's cathedral (1592–1604) designed by J.M. Bernardoni, facade by A. Corazzi from 1819 (the "acoustic sacristy" is well worth a visit; the Dominican monastery with the late Gothic Church of St Stanislaw the Bishop (remodelled in the 17th century); the Old Town Hall, from 1579 the seat of The Crown Tribunal, rebuilt in 1781 by D. Merlini, at present the Wedding Palace, the 16th and 17th-century tenement houses; the Classicist New Town Hall (1827–1828), at present the seat of the municipal authorities; the gates: Brama Krakowska and Brama Grodzka.

There used to be a bridge going from the Grodzka Gate to the castle (photo from 1931).

Many distinguished Jews hailed from Lublin. In 1740 Zalkind Hurwitz gained fame in France as a philosopher and became a member of the Paris Royal Society of Science and Art. In the following century Emil Mayerson (1859–1933) also made a name for himself in Paris as the creator of the philosophical movement known as casualism. Samuel Arzt (1818–1900) moved to Warsaw, where he became an eminent publisher and bookseller. He converted to Calvinism and changed his name to Stanisław Arct.

during the war of 1655 the armies of Bohdan Chmielnicki burnt down the Jewish quarter and 2,000 people were killed. In memory of this tragic event the Jews of Lublin held a special fast until midday on the eve of the festival of *Sukkot.*

The end of the 17th century brought religious conflicts. First, in 1670, the "messiah" Sabbatai Tzvi and his followers were declared an anathema. Then, with the emergence of Chasidism and the development of the court of *tzaddik* Yaakov Yitzhak ha-Levi Horovitz also known as the Seer of Lublin, a long-lasting split began in Jewish society.

At the outbreak of the Second World War, 42,000 Jews lived in Lublin (31% of the population). This large community published its own daily "Lubliner Tugblat", ran sporting organisations (Samson, Hapoel, Maccabi), amateur theatres, political parties (Bund, with one of its famous members Bela Shapiro) and strong trade unions. Jews maintained good relations with the Poles, although the cultural differences between the two communities led to the creation of two separate societies.

In 1945 there were still 4,553 Jews in Lublin. In 1990 there were 45. At present efforts are being made to re-create the Lublin Jewish community under the leadership of Roman Litman. The Polish-Israeli Friendship Society is also active here. It was established in 1989 by a group gathered around Andrzej Nowodworski. The Society numbers 50 members and is focused mostly on information and education. Meetings are held on the first Tuesday of the month at 5 pm (holiday periods excepted) at Centrum Kultury w Lublinie (The Lublin Cultural Centre), ul. Peowiaków 12, ☎ +81 5360322, e-mail address: tppilub@poczta.onet.pl, www.tppilublin.of.pl.

From the Jewish community of Lublin came the family of the famous composer **Henryk Wieniawski** (1835–1880), who also gained fame as one of the greatest violinists of the second half of the 19th century. His father, Tobiasz Pietruszka, a physician, converted to Catholicism and changed his name to Tadeusz Wieniawski, taken from the place where they lived, called Wieniawa, now a district of Lublin.

Brama Grodzka (the Grodzka Gate)

Begin a trip around Jewish places of interest in Lublin with the Grodzka Gate. It was erected as part of the town fortifications during the reign of King Casimir the Great and obtained its present form in 1787. Behind the gate, in the direction of the castle, there stretched another world full of houses in which the light of Sabbath candles could be seen on Friday evenings. Here one entered what was called the "Jerusalem of Poland". Today the Grodzka Gate is the home of the NN Theatre. Szeroka 28, the only Lublin restaurant offering Jewish cuisine, is located next door. Before you get to the gate from the square at ul. Grodzka 11, you will see the *Ochronka* building which was purchased in 1870 to serve the needs of the Jewish Orphanage run by Joseph Goldstern.

Brama Grodzka (the Grodzka Gate, once also known as the Jewish Gate) was a traditional border between the Christian and the Jewish parts of Lublin.

Plac Zamkowy (Castle Square)

From the Grodzka Gate it is easy to get to Plac Zamkowy where you will find a commemorative plaque bearing an engraving of the pre-war network of streets in this part of town. The town quarter shown here (ul. Cyrulicza, ul. Furmańska, ul. Jateczna, ul. Kowalska, ul. Krawiecka, ul. Mostowa, ul. Nadstawna, ul. Podzamcze, ul. Ruska and ul. Szeroka), today just a green area surrounding the castle, once constituted the heart of Jewish Lublin, though the poor also lived in the suburbs of Piaski, Kalinowszczyzna and Wieniawa. The Jews

Strolling across the open spaces surrounding the castle, it is hard to imagine the intricate network of streets tightly packed with houses which once filled this place. The language heard here was mostly Yiddish; unlike in Cracow, many Lublin Jews (about 20%) spoke no Polish at all. They could be identified by a specific pronunciation of the personal pronoun "I" – *yech*. (It was pronounced *yach* in Warsaw, *ech* in the Małopolska region and *ich* in The Grand Duchy of Lithuania.) Ul. Szeroka stretching from ul. Kowalska to ul. Ruska was regarded as the wealthiest street. Many of the houses suffered from neglect. Flats lacked toilet and sewage facilities. The spot separating ul. Szeroka from ul. Krawiecka and ul. Podzamcze was, in a somewhat vulgar fashion, referred to as "Zasrana Brama" (the Shitty Gate) and the poor lived in the area behind it. Ul. Kowalska and ul. Cyrulicza belonged to merchants, ul. Furmańska was known for the sale of poultry. *Bubelach* (buckwheat cakes eaten warm with butter), a delicacy characteristic of the Lublin Jews, were sold near the Grodzka Gate.

drained the swamp around the castle and finally the area was incorporated into the Jewish quarter (known as the Jewish Town). All traces of it finally disappeared in 1950, when this part of Lublin was redeveloped.

The Site Once Occupied by the Maharshal and Maharam Synagogue

The route from Podzamcze to the Old Jewish Cemetery goes along al. Tysiąclecia. Take the right side of this street at the foot of the castle and walk across the area of the former synagogue square in ul. Jateczna, a street which no longer exists. On the raised part of the pavement you will see a memorial stone. It is on the site where a Lublin Jewish community landmark, the Maharshal and Maharam Synagogue, once stood. It was also known as The Maharshal-shul, in honour of Rabbi Shlomo ben Yechiel Luria.

The Maharshal-shul was erected in 1567 and destroyed by the Germans in 1942. In fact it was not one but two synagogues: the Maharshal on the ground floor and the

All traces of the former centre of the Jewish quarter were erased in 1950 (below: Plac Zamkowy).

At the foot of the castle one can see the characteristic roof of the Maharshal-shul Synagogue (archive photo).

Maharam on the first, together accommodating 3,000 worshippers. In keeping with the contour of ul. Jateczna the wall of this edifice was somewhat rounded. The vestibule has an interesting story. This is where, until the 19th century, the convicts sentenced by the *Beth Din* (Rabbinical Court) were detained, tied to the wall. Daily prayers took place in a small room next to the vestibule. The main part of the synagogue was opened on *Shabbat* and on other holidays. During the period between the First and the Second World Wars, Jewish soldiers of the 8th Regiment of the Polish Legions prayed here as well and sang the hymn *Boże, coś Polskę* (God who protected Poland) in front of the synagogue.

Sections for women were on the ground floor on the north and south sides and on the first floor next to the northern wall. The most prestigious places were to be found next to the eastern wall. Eminent members of the congregation sat here, as did the wealthy, who paid for the privilege. Opposite the Maharshal Synagogue, where the street runs today, the Kahal Synagogue used to stand. Other famous Lublin synagogues included the Leifershul at ul. Podzamcze 12, the beautiful Kotlarshul at ul. Szeroka 2, as well as the Rebbe's Beth Hamidrash in the courtyard of the house of the Seer of Lublin at ul. Szeroka 28. There is no trace of any of them today.

Rabbi Shlomo ben Yechiel Luria (1510–1574), known as **Maharshal**, was one of the most brilliant Talmudic scholars of his time. In 1555 he arrived in Lublin to take up the position of Rector of the Yeshivah founded by another distinguished scholar Shalom ben Yosef Shachna. He soon became involved in a conflict with his protector (regarding the methodology of teaching) and in 1567 he founded his own *yeshivah* called *Maharshal-shul* (The Maharshal Synagogue). He became a great authority by resolving numerous religious questions. His solutions to various problems were published in Lvov (1574) in the collection *Yam shel Shlomo* (The Sea of Salomon). The second of the patrons of the largest Lublin synagogue was Mayer ben Gidali (d. 1616) also known as Maharam, a commentator on the Talmud. The name of the last *gagbai* (governor) of the Maharshal synagogue was David Keller. His splendid *baal-kore* (recitations of the Torah) have passed into legend.

The Old Jewish Cemetery

Al. Tysiąclecia leads to ul. Podzamcze, which will take you to the crossing with ul. Lwowska. On top of the hill above the Statoil petrol station you will find one of Lublin's most wonderful Jewish monuments – the Old Jewish Cemetery.

The cemetery, which functioned from 1541 to 1829, is one of the oldest and most precious Jewish necropolises in Poland (some sources mention burials as early as 1489). From the beginning

Shalom ben Yosef Shachna (d. 1558) took over the Talmudic School in Lublin and made it into one of the most important centres of learning in Europe. None of the works by this scholar has survived. His views are known thanks to the writings of his students, the most famous of whom was Moses Isserles also called Remuh, renowned for his work in Cracow.

The grave of the Seer of Lublin is the most important place in the Old Jewish Cemetery.

of the 20th century it has been recognised as a historic monument, but despite this it has been wrecked several times. After a period of neglect during the Communist era, in the 1980s the cemetery was finally tided and catalogued by the Society for the Care of Jewish Cultural Monuments in Lublin. Unfortunately, as a result of acts of vandalism between 1988 and 1991, forty of the eighty remaining gravestones were destroyed.

A concrete path runs from the gate, leading successively to all the most significant monuments. The first *matzevah* dates from 1541 and marks the resting-place of the famous Talmudist Yaakov ben Yehuda ha-Levi Kopelman (d. 1596). It is the oldest *matzevah* in Poland still to be found at the original place of burial. The next two *matzevot* belong to Abraham the Cantor (d. 1543) and the Talmudist Yehuda Leib (d. 1596). The tomb enclosed in a special barred cage, with the remains of wall paintings covered in numerous *kvitlech*, is the grave of the Seer of Lublin.

Further on the path splits in two. The path to the side leads to an unadorned slab where there are even more lamps and *kvitlech* than on the tomb of the Seer. It is the grave of Shalom ben Yosef Shachna, the great scholar and Talmudist. The third most important *matzevah*, damaged and surrounded with candles, was erected in 1574 in memory of Shlomo ben Yechiel Luria known as Maharshal. Others at rest here are: Moshe Montalto (d. 1637), a famous physician; Abraham ben Chaim (d. 1762), president of the Diet of the Four Lands (his unique gravestone bears the engraving of Artemis with a bow); Rabbi Israel ha-Levi Horovitz (d. 1819), known

Yaakov Yitzhak ha-Levi Horovitz (1745–1815) known as **ha-Hose (the Seer) of Lublin** was one of the creators of Polish Chasidism. A disciple of Elimelech of Leżajsk and Dov-Ber of Międzyrzec, he was most famous for his extraordinary skills such as treatment of infertilty, clairvoyance and levitation, thanks to which he became one of the heroes of Jewish folklore. His teachings focused on ethical perfection. He cut himself off from the wickedness of the world by wearing a blindfold all the time. The circumstances of his tragic death are a mystery. According to his followers, in a state of religious ecstasy he was to levitate out of the window of the house at ul. Szeroka 28, loudly demanding the arrival of the Messiah. The urgency of this demand did not please the Lord, who brought him down to earth by making him fall from the second floor. It happened during the festival of *Tisha B'Av*, on the day of the fast in memory of the destruction of the First and the Second Temple. This only enhanced the legend of the *tzaddik*.

as Eisenkopf (Ironhead), the rival of the Seer (inscription illegible). The wall around the cemetery was erected in the 17th century.

The cemetery is on Grodzisko hill between ul. Sienna and ul. Kalinowszczyzna (where you will find the gate behind the Salesian Church). Despite its official status as a historical monument, the cemetery is closed to tourists. The key is with Mr Józef Honig who lives on the nearby housing estate at ul. Dębowskiego 4/17. It is easy to reach the cemetery by bus. Get off at Plac Singera-Kościół. Buses # 1, 5, 6, 10, 11, 16, 57, 58, ZA.

The New Jewish Cemetery

The new cemetery was established in 1829 thanks to the efforts of Nachum Morgernstern. It is located in ul. Walecznych, not far from the Old Cemetery (access from ul. Podzamcze). In its present day form it is made up of two extensive lots (3.5 hectares) with a fence around it. Two structures worthy of attention can be found here: the restored *ohel* of Meir Shapiro, visible through the fencing (the tomb is only of symbolic significance as in 1958 the remains of Rabbi Shapiro were transferred to the *Har Hamenuchot* cemetery in Jerusalem), and the so-called Memorial Chamber containing the symbolic *matzevot* of the Bass, Wulfman and Frenkel families.

The New Jewish Cemetery owes its present appearance to renovation work undertaken thanks to financial support from Sara and Manfred Bass-Frenkel in homage to the members of their families murdered by the Nazis. The cemetery has been functioning since 1830. It is the final resting-place of over 50,000 people, including the members of the dynasty of *tzaddik* Jacob Leib Eiger, whose "court" existed from 1851 until 1942.

Engravings of animal motifs are often found on the headstones in Jewish cemeteries.

The Lublin Yeshivah enhanced the city's status as a leading intellectual centre.

Only one section of the cemetery is accessible; the other, containing the Memorial Chamber and the ohel, *is closed to visitors.*

Yeshivat Chachmei Lublin (The Lublin Academy of Sages)

The impressive edifice of the former Lublin Academy of Sages stands on the corner of ul. Unicka and ul. Lubartowska. It is hard to miss, as it is on the approach road from Lubartów to the town centre and the PKS bus station. The school was founded by Rabbi Yehuda Meir Shapiro, the site having been donated by Shmul Aichenbaum and the plans drawn up by Agenor Smoluchowski. Construction went on for six years (1924–1930), swallowing up considerable funds which came mostly from the USA and Western Europe. The school operated for nine years only, yet it achieved great fame. Lecture halls took up five floors, the dormitory housed 200 students and the library contained 10,000 volumes of Talmudic literature. To complete things there was a garden of 12,000 trees. Study began with *Mechina* (preparatory courses). At the entrance examinations prospective students had to prove that they knew as many as

Yehuda Meir Shapiro (1887–1933), who rests in a newly renovated *ohel* at the New Jewish Cemetery, brought credit upon the town, particularly as the creator of the Lublin Yeshivah, although he was a towering figure for all of Polish Jewry. He was born in Suczawa in Bukovina. During his career (one of the posts he held was that of Rabbinate of Sanok) he published two works which brought him universal acclaim: *Imrei Daat* (The Word of Knowledge, 1919) and *Or Hameir* (The Light of Brightness, 1926). From 1922 until 1927 he was a member of the Polish Parliament. His greatest dream was to create a worldwide Rabbinical-Talmudic college. It came true in the form of the Lublin Yeshivah (The Lublin Academy of Sages).

200 pages of the *Talmud* by heart. The brightest students took up higher Talmudic studies, obtaining the title of *Tzurva de-rabanan*. The first graduates left the college in 1934.

The building still serves educational purposes as the Collegium Maius of the Medical Academy. After the collapse of Communism the Academy authorities allotted special premises (well worth seeing) to visitors to the former Yeshivat Chachmei Lublin. The first room you enter is a spacious lecture hall, which was once also used as a synagogue. It occupies the second and third floors of the building. It is rectangular, with galleries situated on three sides and resting on circular columns. Nothing remains of its rich pre-war furnishings, nor of the windows on the eastern wall (now bricked up). The second hall of particular interest is the library which contains a separate prayer room. Here you will find a new *aron ha-kodesh*, a *parochet* (ark curtain) and the texts of prayers

The school at ul. Lubartowska 85 is part of the premises of the Medical Academy, used for lecture purposes. The wardens, however, are ready to help visitors and will willingly take you to both places.

Ul. Lubartowska

A walk up ul. Lubartowska will take you through the area of what was known as the new Jewish quarter. It has managed to retain much of its original character. Though the original Jewish district was spread over the territory around the castle, in the second half of the 19th-century Jews began to settle along ul. Lubartowska and on Czwartek hill. Take the left side of the street.

Before the Second World War ul. Lubartowska was the most elegant street in Jewish Lublin. Kopel Wurman was the owner of house No 15, once inhabited by wealthy families. The most expensive Jewish restaurant, Dornfeld's, was also located here. It was a place where deals were struck over a glass or two. The "Jewish market" spread from ul. Lubartowska along ul. Czechówka to ul. Nadstawna (known nowadays as al. Tysiąclecia). The first row of stalls belonged to fishmongers, while the second, by the river, was taken up by forty five stalls selling *kosher* meat.

The plaque on the building of the present Obstetrics Clinic (formerly the Jewish Hospital) commemorates those patients who were murdered by the Nazis on 27 March 1942.

The Memorial Chamber of Lublin Jews in the former Synagogue of Chevrat Nossim houses a collection of items reflecting the life of the town's pre-war Jewish community.

The edifice adjacent to the Lublin Yeshivah is the former Jewish Hospital (today an obstetrics clinic) established in 1886. In the 1930s it had a hundred beds at its disposal and employed many famous physicians, including Jacob Cynberg. In 1986 the site was marked with a commemorative plaque in Polish and Yiddish. Keeping on the same side, go to the corner of ul. Czwartek, where the atmosphere is reminiscent of bygone days. In the yard opposite building No 7, there is a place very important in the history of the Lublin community – the Y.L. Peretz Jewish People's House (ul. Szkolna 16). Erected on the initiative of the Lublin Bund and completed in 1939, the building was never used for its original purpose as a centre of Jewish life. For a few years after 1945, it was the headquarters of the Jewish Committee, the library and a cultural society. At present it houses the local healthcare authority. From here go back to ul. Lubartowska and walk up to the only remaining Lublin synagogue.

The Synagogue of Chevrat Nossim

This synagogue was established at the end of the 19th century as a house of prayer and learning for the Funeral Society Chevrat Nossim. *Shi'ur be-tsibur* (Talmudic lectures) which were given here by Moshe Aisenberg and David Mushkatblit achieved great popularity. The synagogue functioned until 1984, when services on Saturdays and festivals were suspended for want of a *minyan*. The building was then renovated and since 1987 one of its sections has served religious purposes (joyous occasions, such as the *bar mitzvah* of Jacob Mushkatblit, great-grandson of the former lecturer). A part of it is used as the Memorial Chamber of the Jews of Lublin, displaying old photographs and Hebrew books and items used in religious rituals. Unfortunately many of the exhibits gathered over the past fifty years or so were stolen on 27 May 1995. Only part of the collection has been retrieved.

The synagogue is situated in ul. Lubartowska, in the part closest to the town centre. Go through the gate of house

*number 8 (where you see the sign "Pawilon 19 – Płaszcze"). At present it is possible to visit the synagogue on Sundays only, from 1pm to 3pm. Regular services do not take place. On certain Jewish festivals (*Pesach, Chanukah, Purim*) meetings are sometimes organised here by the Polish-Israeli Friendship Society in Lublin.*

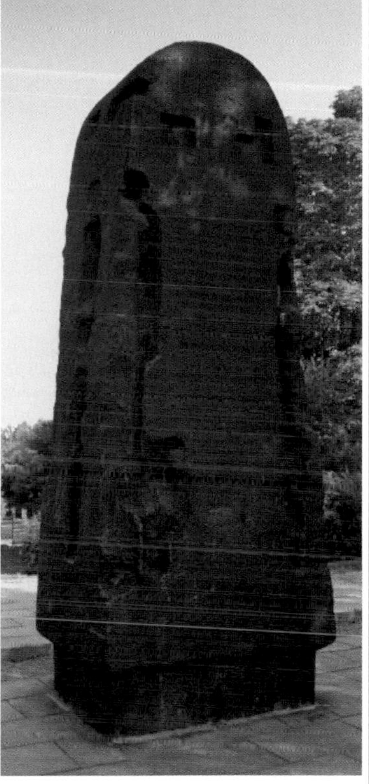

The tragic fate of the Jewish inhabitants of Lublin is commemorated by this monument in Plac Ofiar Getta (The Square of the Victims of the Ghetto).

Plac Ofiar Getta

Further along ul. Lubartowska you come to Plac Ofiar Getta (Square of the Victims of the Ghetto) where you will find a memorial with the following quotation: "In every handful of ashes I seek those close to me" from *The Song of the Murdered Jewish People* by Yitzchak Katzenelson. The square was laid out in 1951. There was a large Jewish market-place here until the end of the 1920s.

Ul. Kowalska

End your trip to the most important Jewish places of interest in Lublin with a walk along the charming ul. Kowalska. It is one of the few places in Lublin where you can still feel *genius loci* of the old Jewish quarter.

Majdanek

The concentration camp in the Majdanek suburb of Lublin, established in the autumn of 1941 on the orders of Heinrich Himmler, is the place where the history of the Jews of Lublin came to a tragic end. The camp was 270 hectares in size and contained 280 buildings. Its central section consisted of barracks for 25,000 prisoners at a time. The camp was liquidated in July 1945. A museum exhibiting some of its structures (barracks, gas chambers, crematoria, mass execution ditches and SS-women's living quarters) was set up here after the war. A huge memorial in the form of a mausoleum designed by Witold Tołkin has been built to pay homage to the 360,000 victims (of whom 100,000 were Jews).

A permanent exhibition "Majdanek in the System of Camps" by Anna Wiśniewska and Czesław Rajca, with art design by Brunon Nagrodzki, is located on the former camp site. On display you will find archive materials, including photographs as well as various exhibits: articles of clothing, instruments of death, items used for

Majdanek is not the only place in Lublin where a mass murder of Jews took place. The remains of 190 victims were exhumed in 1988 at Majdan Tatarski and later interred at the New Jewish Cemetery.

Lubartów left its mark on literature in works such as *Sketches* (1887) by Adam Szymański (1852–1916). In his book entitled *Srul from Lubartów* he describes his meeting with "a fanatical Chasid", who has lost his entire family in exile in Russia. Engraved on Szymański's memory most of all is a Jew's incredible longing for his homeland, for the tiniest little bit of Lubartów, which is "just a stone's throw from Lublin, just a stone's throw".

religious purposes and objets d'art. The exhibition is housed in barracks 43, 44, 45, 52, along with the baths, gas chambers and crematorium. In barrack 47 there is the multimedia installation entitled "Shrine", created by Tadeusz Mysłowski with music by Zbigniew Bargielski. It was created to commemorate the 55th anniversary of the liberation of the camp. The museum organises history workshops, readings and meetings with former camp inmates as well as documentary film shows about the war and the camps in Polish, English, French, German and Russian. It also publishes its own periodical "The Majdanek Booklets".

State Museum at Majdanek, ul. Droga Męczenników Majdanka 67, 20-325 Lublin, ☎ +81 7442640; 7442647.
The easiest way to get to the museum is along the road to Zamość (ul. Droga Męczenników Majdanka). Buses # 23, 28, 153, 156, 158. The exhibition "Majdanek in the System of Camps" is open daily (except Mondays and holidays) from 8am to 6pm (May to September) and 8am to 3pm (October to April), prior notification required.
The installation can be seen from May to September, from 8am to 3pm. Entrance is free.
Charges are made for guide services and film shows only.
Children under the age of 14 are not admitted.

LUBARTÓW | Yiddish: Levartov

Situated 23 kilometres north of Lublin, Lubartów is a place well-known in Jewish culture. All the sadder that so little remains of its past, as Jews were once 45% of the town's population. Jews first came to Lubartów in around 1567 to work in the wholesale trade of grain which was transported up the Wieprz and Vistula rivers to Gdańsk. Until the

Second World War the Jewish quarter was made up of the main square and the houses along ul. Lubelska. Unfortunately everything here was meticulously destroyed. In ul. Cicha you will find what is referred to as the New Cemetery, and it is all that is left. It was first established around 1819. Its only remaining parts are a dozen or so *matzevot* bearing traces of polychromy.

KOCK | Yiddish: Kotzk

Jewish settlement began here relatively late, at the beginning of the 17th century. Two events brought fame to this little town situated far away from the flow of history: the battle with the Austrians in 1809 and the arrival of Menachem Mendel Morgenstern in 1829. In the 20th century Jews made up the large majority of the local population (64–68%; about 2,500 people). They worked as traders, tailors, hat-makers and shoemakers. During the Second World War the Germans set up a local ghetto. Its inhabitants were then deported to the concentration camp at Treblinka.

A tour around the monuments of Jewish culture in Kock will take about two hours.

The Ohel of Menachem Mendel Morgenstern

Little remains of the Kock cemetery, although the area is fenced off and well maintained. The *ohel* of Menachem Mendel Mongerstern, on which renovation work was carried out in the 1990s, is the most important site and a destination for pilgrims to this very day. Apart from the

Tourist Attractions

The parish church in the main square (1779–1782) designed by S.B. Zug; the A. Jabłonowska palace (1780) designed by S.B. Zug, remodelled in 1840 by H. Marconi; the geometric landscape park around the palace complex; the cemetery of the Polish soldiers fallen in the last battle of the Second Polish Republic between 2nd and 5th May 1939, and the grave of their commander, general F. Kleeberg (d. 1941), who was laid to rest here in 1969.

Menachem Mendel Morgenstern (1787–1859), called *Kotzker Rebe* (the Teacher of Kock), was one of the most famous Chasidic leaders and disciple of the Seer of Lublin and the Holy Jew of Przysucha. Hostile to ritual, he taught that "one cannot serve God out of habit". He coined many aphorisms which illustrated perfectly his way of thinking. A good example is "People have souls, not watches". In 1829 he came to Kock and changed this little town into a powerful centre of Chasidism and a focal point for pilgrimages from all of Central-Eastern Europe. He supported the November Uprising, which he paid for with several years in exile. In 1839 he decided to "leave this world" and had himself bricked up in the prayer room in his house. He remained in seclusion for 20 years, until the end of his days (below: the *ohel* of *tzaddik* Morgenstern).

Kotzker Chasidim

The *Chasidim* of Kock, first established as a community in 1829, based themselves on the teachings of Menachem Mendel Morgenstern, who they recognised as the first *tzaddik*. In 1830 they supported the November Uprising, supplying the Polish armies with shoes, clothes and food. After the death of their leader, a large part of them changed their alliegance to the dynasty from Góra Kalwaria. A few remained with the Morgernstern family and the new *tzaddik* David (1809–1873). *Kotzker Chasidim* also supported the January Uprising. Their positive stance on Polish independence was described by Józef Opatoszu in his novel *In the Forests of Poland* (also entitled: *Jews in the Struggle for the Independence of Poland*), made into a film by Jonasz Turkow in 1929. Chaim Israel Morgernstern (1840–1905), who then moved to Puławy, was the third *tzaddik* of Kock. Chaim Israel's successor was Moses Mordechai (1862–1929), domiciled in Warsaw between 1914 and 1929. The last *tzaddik*, once again with headquarters in Kock, was Josef Morgenstern, who perished on 9 September 1939 during an air-raid on the town.

grave of this well-known *tzaddik*, you will also find stone fragments lying here and there in the grass. They are characteristic remains of *matzevot* made of granite blocks. People say that before the war the cemetery caretaker was a local German.

Getting there takes 25 minutes. Starting from Plac Jabłonowskiej, walk along ul. Hanki Sawickiej to the roadside shrine of St John the Baptist and then follow the route marked in red. The monument is locked. The key can be obtained from Mr Roman Stasiak, a farmer living in the first house behind the cemetery. He takes care of the cemetery, repairs ohelim *and cuts the grass.*

Tzaddik Morgenstern's House

A large number of pre-war houses characteristic of Jewish towns of Eastern Poland have been preserved in Kock. You can see some of them on the way to *tzaddik* Morgenstern's house. The tourist route goes from Plac Jabłonowskiej (the main square) along ul. 1 Maja (the path is marked in black) to the second turning, ul. Wojska Polskiego. Here you should go left and having passed two characteristic

wooden houses, at ul. Wojska Polskiego 30 and 32, you will come to a rather striking building which architecturally is anything but typical. It brings to mind a Polish manor house combined with a peculiar corner tower, and is the only one of its kind in the whole country. The locals reckon that this is where *tzaddik* Menachem Mendel bricked himself in. Historical sources prove only that after 1924 the house belonged to Joseph Morgenstern who was pronounced *tzaddik* of the *Kotzk Chasidim* in 1929.

These days there are private flats in *tzaddik* Morgenstern's house on the corner of ul. Wojska Polskiego and ul. Polna. The tower remains empty and unused.

The Grave of Berek Joselewicz (Yoselevich)

Another walk you may wish to take from Plac Jabłonowskiej goes along ul. Berka Joselewicza (the tourist route marked in green). There you will see the grave of Berek Joselewicz, which is situated in the village of Białobrzegi, outside the boundaries of Kock. It is quite a hike but worth it, even just to see the row of old houses (all of them in ul. Joselewicza; the most typical being numbers 11, 25, 27, 41, 46 and 90). The picturesque surroundings and the unusual roadside shrines are also worth seeing.

The monument to Berek Joselewicz consists of two boulders surrounded by a fence. The higher one, put there more recently, gives only his first name, surname and two dates. The lower one is from 1909 and was funded by Count Edward Żółtowski. The fading inscription reads: "Berek Joselewicz, Józef Berkowel Berkowicz, born in Kretinga in Lithuania. Polish Army colonel, squadron leader of the 5th Regiment of the Mounted Fusiliers of the Grand Duchy of Warsaw, knight of the crosses of the Legion of Honour and of Virtuti Militari. He died in the Battle of Kock in 1809. Here

Many streets and squares in Poland bear the name of Berek Joselewicz.

Berek Joselewicz (1760–1809) spent some time in Paris, where he witnessed the outbreak of the French Revolution. He returned to Poland and when the Kościuszko Insurrection took place, Joselewicz, driven by the concepts of brotherhood and equality, suggested to general Kościuszko that a Jewish cavalry regiment should be formed to support the Polish troops. This unit, numbering 500 volunteers, fought in the Insurrection and its presence in the Polish ranks was of extraordinary significance for the image of Jews in the eyes of Poles. After the collapse of the uprising, Joselewicz emigrated from Poland and was a member of the Polish legions in Italy. He returned to his homeland with Napoleon's troops and took command of two squadrons in the army of Prince Poniatowski. His son, Yosek Berkowicz (1789–1846) also fought for independence. During the November Uprising he persuaded Jewish soldiers from the Russian army to come over to the Polish side and made attempts at the creation of Jewish front line units.

he lies. Neither with trick nor with drink but with blood his fame did link. On the centenary of his death. 1909".

The grave is situated under a lime-tree on the right side of the local road from Kock to Białobrzegi, 50 paces from the road sign indicating sharp bends.

PARCZEW

Many of the buildings connected with pre-war Polish Jewry, once 50% of the local population, remain here. They are: the synagogue at ul. Piwonia 3 (ul. Szeroka), rebuilt in 1924 and converted into a clothing factory after the Second World War; the *beth ha-midrash* (house of learning); the *mikvah* (ritual bath) from the beginning of the 20th century (ul. Piwonia 1), later turned into a cinema; and the former Jewish Community centre (ul. Zjednoczenia 31).

There is no convenient direct road from Kock to Parczew, only the local one through Tarkavica, Czemierniki, Siemień (40 km). You can also continue on road 19 to Radzyń Podlaski and turn here onto road 814 to get onto road 815 to Parczew (in all 52 km). From Parczew to Lublin you can return directly on roads 815 and 19 (41 km).

The Death of Berek Joselewicz in Kock by Henryk Pillati (second half of 19th century).

ŁĘCZNA | Yiddish: Lenchna

Jews lived in Łęczna as early as in 1501 and the community was established in the first half of the 16th century. From 1668 to 1685 the town hosted sessions of *Vaad Arba Aratzot* (Diet of the Four Lands). The first half of the 19th century saw the heyday of the Chasidic movement. This is when the town of Łęczna was home to the court of *tzaddik* Shlomo Yehuda Leib Lechner (d. 1843) whose *ohel* was in the cemetery (no longer existing) by the road to Lublin. Chasidism also created a division between the members of the local community; its followers prayed in private houses of worship known as *klozyn*, while other Jews, referred to as Orthodox *Mitnagdim*, kept to the synagogue.

In the19th century Łęczna was renowned for its local rabbi Chaim Boruch Kowartowski (d. 1885) who was held in great esteem. From 1879 to 1902 the town belonged to Jan Gotlib Bloch, the European "railway king" (described more fully in the chapter on Warsaw). The merchant families of Geldman and Handelsman, as well as the descendants of rabbi Kowartowski, were among the most influential people in town. Abraham Rachmil Bromberg (1879–1939) was the last rabbi of Łęczna. At the outbreak of the Second World War, Jews made up 53% of the local population (2,300 people). They perished in the extermination camps of Sobibór and Trawniki; the last group in April 1943 in Łęczna itself.

The heart of Łęczna's Jewish quarter is the now somewhat sleepy Rynek II (Second Market Square). It is worth having a walk around it and taking in the atmosphere of this perfectly preserved *shtetl*. Here you will find everything: the single storey houses, tiny little shops, original shutters. When you look at the outer sides of the doorframes you can still see here and there the indentations left by *mezzuzot*. The "tight" system of house numbering (sometimes you can find as many as three numbers on one house) proves how densely populated the town once was. At the same time it shows the scale of the division of property and the degree of poverty. Ul. Partyzancka (see picture above) leads away from the square.

Tourist Attractions

The Mannerist parish church of St Mary Magdalene from 1618–1631 (belfry from 1827) and the 17th-century parish house, as well as the Town Hall and the cloth stalls from the 19th century.

The synagogue in Łęczna was erected from 1648 to 1655, most probably on the site of the former wooden house of prayer.

The Synagogue and House of Learning

This magnificent rectangular building measures 9.5m by 15m. Particularly noticeable are the strong walls (up to 2.4m in thickness) and the traditional Polish mansard roof, which once may have been even larger and crowned with an attic. There are unconfirmed reports that the Jews were forced to make the synagogue lower, as it left the local parish church in the shade. After the fire of 1846, extensive reconstruction work was carried out and the women's prayer room was enlarged. During the Second World War the Germans used it as a storehouse.

After the war, the locals dismantled the floor, stole the windows and the doors and destroyed the vestibule as well as the neighbouring *kahal* building (the more recent western part of the synagogue does not contain much in the way of historical value). The damage was so considerable (80%) that in 1952 a decision was taken, with the approval of the Lublin Union of Members of the Jewish Faith, to pull the building down. The monument was saved thanks to an absence of funds to pay for its demolition. A major overhaul was carried out from 1954 to 1964 and the synagogue was then converted into a museum. At first it was the Coalfields Museum of Lublin and at present it houses the District Museum.

The *bimah* is well preserved. It is one of very few originals in the Lublin area as well as the only one of its kind. It supported the dome as well as the decorative canopy over the place where the *Torah* was read. The interior, once covered in wall paintings, is now coated white.

Inside the building the Regional Museum has organised an exhibition of Judaica entitled "The Gates of Time". The exhibits are arranged according to the Jewish cycle of festivals, starting with *Rosh Hashanah* and going on to *Yom*

Only the *aron ha-kodesh* and the *Torah* scroll (now exhibited in a showcase) remain of the pre-war interior of the synagogue in Łęczna. The *parochet* (ark curtain) is a replica.

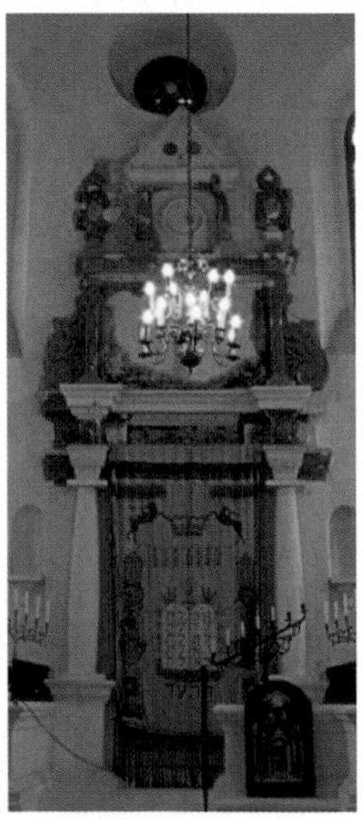

Kippur, *Sukkot*, *Chanukah*, *Purim* and *Pesach*. Here you will find objects used in religious ceremonies: vessels for the ritual washing of hands, *Shabbat* candles, *kiddush* cups, dishes for an *etrog* (citrus fruit), *Chanukah* lights, *Seder* plates and goblets, articles of clothing (such as a *tallit* from Kishinev, a gift from a descendent of the well-know Geldman family of Łęczna). The highlight of the exhibition is the extremely original part dealing with everyday life. Here you will find copper pots, snuff-boxes, wedding invitations, visiting cards and even actual bottles which once contained Haberfeld's famous Passover vodka. The original costume of a Jewish woman from Ostrowiec Świętokrzyski, composed of a sleeveless jacket and skirt, is an absolute rarity nowadays.

The *bimah* is the most impressive part of the Łęczna synagogue.

Take a walk around the synagogue. The neighbouring building, now a public library, is a former *beth ha midrash* (early 19th century). On request the staff will open the closet in which the ritual wash-hand basin is preserved. Remnants of polychromies, painted over in 1993, are still visible.

The Łęczna District Museum, ul. Bóżniczna 17,
☎ +81 7520869. Open 8am–1pm; Sundays 9am–4pm.
Tickets 2 zł, concessions 1.5 zł; guide 25 zł per group.

WŁODAWA | Yiddish: Vladova, Vlodova, Vlodave

Several examples of Judaica worth a special trip have been preserved in this beautiful borderland town (Belarus and Ukraine begin just outside it). What is more, it has all been organised in such a way that you can combine your visit with a spot of relaxation in really beautiful surroundings.

The Włodawa Jewish community, which was under the jurisdiction of the Brest *kahal*, emerged at the turn of the 17th century. It quickly developed thanks to trade with Ukraine and Włodawa's location near the Chełm–Brest railway line. At the outbreak of the Second World War 5,650 Jews (61% of the local population) lived here. The Jewish quarter consisted of the following streets:

On the other side of the Łęczna museum there is a lapidarium. It is all that remains of the Jewish cemetery by the road to Lublin (referred to as *gyergyel* and located in a cluster of trees next to a sports ground). The original cemetery no longer exists. The *matzevot* scattered around were found on the territory of local farms.

The building of the Great Synagogue is reminiscent of a palace.

Tefillin are small boxes containing parchments with verses from the *Torah*, worn by men on the arm and forehead during prayer (above: *tefillin* with decorated bag).

ul. Wyrkowska (now ul. Tysiąclecia Państwa Polskiego), ul. Solna (now ul. Czerwonego Krzyża), ul. Okunińska, ul. Furmańska, ul. Kozia (now ul. Witosa) and ul. Chełmska. Aside from its two synagogues, the town was home to two prayer houses, a *kahal* house, a *Talmud-Torah* and a ritual bath. The Włodawa cemetery was situated between what is now ul. Jana Pawła II and ul. Reymonta. The gravestones were removed by the Germans and used for paving the streets and building embankments on the River Włodawka. Mendele Morgenstern was the last rabbi of Włodawa.

Taking the train to Włodawa is not recommended as the railway station is located 5 km from the town.

The Museum in the Synagogue Complex

The main tourist attraction in Włodawa is the well-preserved synagogue complex situated in the area of ul. Korolewska, ul. Czerwonego Krzyża and ul. Hołoda.

The museum located here offers a good selection of brochures and objects related to the town Jewish past. The *beth ha-midrash* dating from 1928 houses the museum offices and storerooms.

Tourist Attractions

The Pauline Monastery (1711–1717); St Louis Church (1739–1780) with its Rococo decorations; the Uniate Church (1840–1842) with the parish house; the trader and butcher stalls from the second half of the 18th century, later remodelled, the cemetery of insurgents of the 1863 Uprising; Lake Białe with numerous holiday centres. Be sure to take a walk along the River Bug, particularly up past the church in Orchówek. The beauty of this river is a real feast for the eyes. Belarus is on the opposite bank.

Muzeum Pojezierza Łęczyńsko-Włodawskiego (The Łęczyńsko-Włodawskie Lake District Museum), ul. Czerwonego Krzyża 7, ☎ +82 5722178. Open 10am–5pm, Sat and Sun 10am–2pm. Tickets 2 and 5 zł. Sundays admission free.

The Great Synagogue

This mighty building was erected between 1764 and 1774, partly thanks to support from the Czartoryski Foundation. The architect is thought to have been P.A. Fontana. In the second half of the 19th century a second floor over the vestibule and alcove was added. The Germans demolished the interior and turned it into a storehouse, which functioned here until as recently as 1970. A complete overhaul was then begun and the museum was finally opened in 1986. The richness of the front elevation is amazing. The building is rectangular in shape (25.9m by 30.6m) with the prayer hall occupying its central part covered with a mansard roof. On the two sides of the main prayer hall there are sections for women, each with an attic. At the front there is a vestibule, above which there is the third women's prayer room with adjacent arcaded alcoves. Unique, rich adornments are the greatest attraction of the synagogue's interior. They date from 1934, when they replaced the original furnishings destroyed in a fire.

The symbolic meaning of the beautifully decorated *aron ha-kodesh* is worth decoding. In the upper part two griffins are expressing their adoration for the Tablets of the Covenant, surmounted, as the inscription tells us, with the Crown of the Torah. The interior of the tablets contains a skylight giving the effect of the light of the *Torah*. Lower down there is a representation of a *menorah*. The inscription above it reads: "In reverence will I bow down toward your holy temple" (Psalms 5:8) and the inscription below: "And soon, in our days, the Saviour shall come unto Zion. Amen". A fruit basket on

The Neo-Baroque framework of the *aron ha-kodesh* is made in painted stucco. It bears inscriptions situated below the centrally placed image of the *menorah*, as well as on its both sides. We are able to read the date of the construction, which was after the fire of the *aron ha-kodesh* in 5696 (1936).

Melamed Menachem's room has been re-created in the synagogue.

A *yad* (pointer in the shape of a hand) is used during the reading of the *Torah*.

the left-hand side of the *menorah* symbolises the festival of *Shavuot* (inscription: "The first fruits of the field"). On the right side we can see hands making a blessing (inscription: "the minister's blessing"). The adornments of the *aron ha-kodesh* itself are as follows: on both sides of the recess for the *Torah* scrolls there are images of musical instruments with texts from Psalm 150: "Praise him with the sounding of the trumpet, praise him with the harp and lyre, praise him with tambourine and dancing, praise him with the strings and flute". The engravings in the medallions from the 18th century original decor of the synagogue depict the following: symbols of the festival of *Sukkot* (edge of the eastern wall); a stork fighting with serpents – piety overcoming the powers of evil (south-east corner); an eagle – the symbol of divine providence; a deer – the pursuit of piety. The four posts are all that remains of the stone *bimah*. The Germans either plundered or destroyed all other elements of the interior. Here you can see the exhibition "From the History of the Włodawa Jews" which shows how the Jewish community organised itself, the activities of its members, well-known families, as well as political and sporting life. The museum also contains many objects donated by Jacob Friedmann from Sydney, who took part in the Sobibór uprising. Silver *Chanukah* lamps, spice boxes, and spoons were dug up during excavation carried out by the Włodawa Electricity Board.

Be sure to visit the prayer room for women, which before the war housed the *Beth Josef* (House of Josef), a *cheder* which was attended by 160 pupils. It was modelled on the Novogrod Yeshivah set up by Josef Hurvitz. In the school, along with the study of the *Torah*, great emphasis was placed on ethics and morality. After the Bolsheviks assumed power, it was no longer possible for a school of this kind to continue functioning in Russia. Therefore, in 1922 it was moved to Poland. Today, along with temporary exhibitions it offers a permanent display which is at once extremely valuable and educational. It is entitled "In the Room of the Melamed, a Teacher of Religion". The faithfully re-created room is that of *melamed* Menachem, an employee of the Novogrod Yeshivah. Various everyday items have been gathered here, including a kettle and an iron stove (almost all synagogues in Poland had heating problems).

The Little Synagogue

The building next door to the Great Synagogue is a good example of a small town synagogue. The vestibule and the prayer rooms for women are on the western side. It has existed in exactly the same form (22m in length, 14.8m in width and 5.8m in height) since 1786 and has never been remodelled. It had a dual role: synagogue and place for study of the *Torah* and the *Talmud*. During the war it was turned into an army storehouse and from 1945 to 1983 it was used for the same purpose by a local co-operative. It was re-opened in 1999 after renovation work which lasted from 1983 to 1988. It is worth visiting not just for the exhibition "Włodawa in Old Photographs" but also to see the numerous frescos and uncovered inscriptions. There is also a frieze depicting the signs of the zodiac, original wooden cupboard frames and the framework of the *aron ha-kodesh* inside which there is an unexhibited beam with the text: "In memory of the soul of Mrs Mendl Rachel from her husband Chaim Shloma, son of Iser ha-Levi".

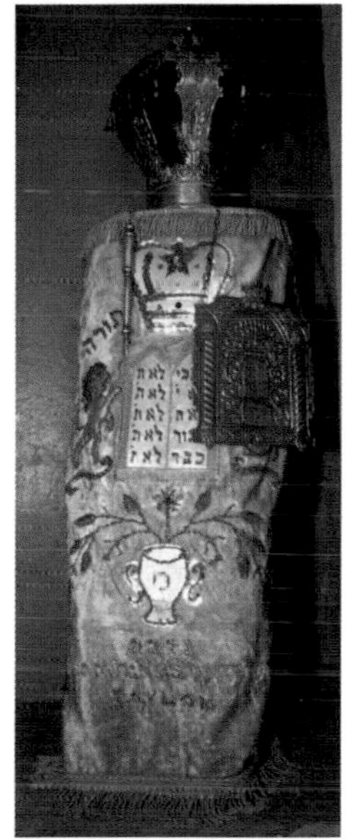

The *Torah* kept in the Great Synagogue is wrapped in a cover decorated with the *tas* (shield) and *keter Torah* (a characteristic crown-shaped silver adornment).

The walls of the Little Synagogue are adorned with beautiful frescos and inscriptions.

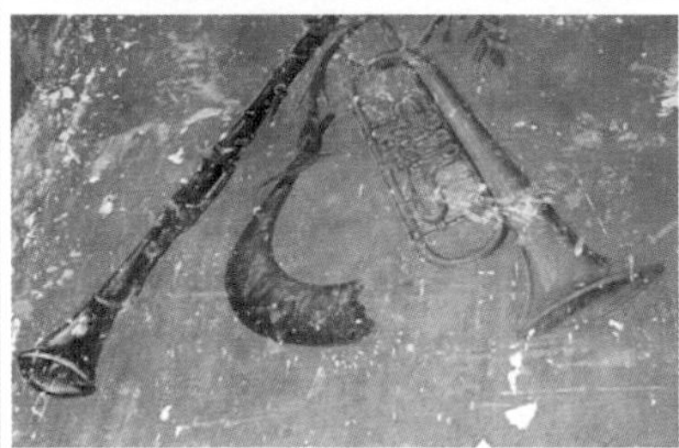

Among others things, the frescos in the Little Synagogue depict musical instruments.

The inscriptions also contain lines from a biblical text (Isaiah 55:6–56:8); the prayers *Modim dirabanam, Al ha-kol yitgadol, Al ha-rachamim* and *Binesoa ha-aron*, as well as Psalms 24, 111, 112. The largest of the inscriptions on the wall to the right of the door reads: "In eternal memory of the toils of the late Mr Yehuda Leib, son of the late Mr Moshe Elijahim Gecel, to the blessed memory of Lichtenberg; his generosity in the rebuilding of the house of study in the year 5676 (1915), after it was destroyed during the World War, in the year 5675 (1914). He died on the 15th day of Shevat 5691 (1931) in Siedlce". The dates on this description are given in the abbreviated form. The Little Synagogue also houses ethnographic exhibitions.

Sobibór witnessed one of the few Jewish victories to occur during the Second World War. On 14 October 1943, an uprising took place in the concentration camp, thanks to which 300 prisoners escaped. While some of them perished during the breakout, others managed to reach partisan units (some of which contained refugees from the Włodawa Ghetto) and took up arms against the occupants. Fifty escapees survived the war. In 1987 the American director Jack Gold made the film *Escape from Sobibor*, based on these facts.

SOBIBÓR

This forest colony is located 12 km to the south east of Włodawa (access by road 816). In 1942 and 1943 there was a death camp here, in which 250,000 victims were murdered by the Nazis. Since 1993 it has been possible to visit Muzeum Obozu Zagłady (the Death Camp Museum), ☎ +82 5719867, a branch of the Włodawa Museum. The exhibition details the history of the camp. There is also a mound made from the ashes of the victims and a monument with the words "In homage to those murdered by the Nazis".

Polish Jews were always part of the history of Kazimierz Dolny (photo from 1936).

KAZIMIERZ DOLNY | Yiddish: Kuzmir

Warsaw's favourite summer resort has always been connected with Jewry, with a community existing here as early as 1406. The 16th and 17th centuries were a time of great prosperity for the town situated near a ford across the River Vistula and the port from which grain was shipped to Gdańsk. This was particularly beneficial for the Jewish community engaged in trade, services and brewing. Shmul Jakubowicz, a Warsaw financier also known as Zbytkower the royal banker, was one of the owners of the local granaries. The 18th century brought a period of economic boom and the development of a new religious movement, Chasidism.

At the outbreak of the Second World War Jews made up 50% of the local population. Almost all of them perished in March 1942. Berek Cytryn managed to save his life by hiding first in Bochotnica and then in Warsaw. One of the Lihzons, a local family of chemists, also survived, as he spent the war in Russia. Afterwards he lived in Łódź and by emigrating in 1968 he brought the history of the Kazimierz Jews to an end.

The Jewish quarter, also called Na Tyłach (At the Back), with its own market square (Mały Rynek), stretched from the south-east part of the main square. One of the main streets was ul. Lubelska which, unlike the Christian part of town, was made up of wooden houses.

Tourist Attractions

The ruins of the royal castle with a 14th-century tower, the parish church (1586–1589, extended 1610–1613) housing an ancient organ (1607–1620); the houses from the turn of the 18th century, with late Renaissance and Mannerism decorations, such as Kamienice Przybyłowskie (1615), Kamienica Celejowska (1635); the Baroque monastery of the Reformed Franciscan Order (1630-1690) rebuilt in 1762–1768); on the Vistula: the former hospital together with St Anne's Church (1649–1670), the 17th-century late Renaissance granaries; the villas from the 19th and 20th centuries (the Potworowski villa from 1910, Zofia Kuncewicz's house from 1936, and others).

In the 19th century Kazimierz Dolny was famous as a summer resort and tourist centre. It attracted numerous Jewish artists, including the painters Natan Korzen and the brothers Efraim and Menashe Seidenbeutel, the photographer Benedict Dorys; the writer Adolf Rudnicki, author of *The Summer*; and the poet Zusman Segałowicz, author of *In Kazimierz*. It also drew filmmakers. Pre-war Kazimierz is the background to the film *Jidl mitn fidl* (Yidl with a Fiddle) by Józef Green and Jan Nowina-Przybylski. The script was written by Konrad Tom, the songs by Itzik Manger. The film features the American actress Mary Picon.

Around the year 1827, a former merchant from Płońsk, **Ezekiel ben Tzvi-Hirsh Taub** (d. 1857), one of the disciples of the Seer of Lublin, was drawn to Kazimierz and a Chasidic court was formed around him. One can say that Taub's views corresponded to the "artistic" atmosphere which prevailed in Kazimierz. He advocated the affirmation of life, nature and the Lord. His motto: "I cannot feel the joy of the Sabbath without a new melody", was a call for the creation of new Chasidic songs. Many of the tunes composed by Taub have survived to this day. The *tzaddik* is buried in the old cemetery (now a school playground). His beautiful tomb, along with the cemetery, did not survive the Second World War. Ezekiel ben Tzvi Taub founded a Chasidic group known as *Kuzmir Chasidim* and the Taub dynasty created several branches in central Poland, all linked by a common doctrine. David Tzvi (d. 1882) was leader of the Jabłonowo Chasids and Shmul Eliyahu (d. 1888) leader of those from Zwoleń. Moshe Aaron Taub (d. 1918) operated in Nowy Dwór Mazowiecki, Chaim Taub (d. 1942) in Warsaw and Mława and Eliezer Shlomo (d. 1938) in Wołomin. Many of the Kazimierz Chasids emigrated from Poland and survived the Second World War. Ezekiel Taub from Jabłonowo left for Palestine together with a group of followers as early as 1925. There they founded an agricultural settlement. The last Kazimierz *tzaddik* was Shmul Eliyahu Taub of Dęblin (1905–1984). After the war he moved to Tel Aviv.

The Castle

Strictly speaking, the ruins of the 14th century castle and tower do not have anything to do with Jewish culture, but they are linked to the legend of King Casimir the Great and his Jewish lover Esther from Opoczno. According to various people, including the early historian Jan Długosz, Casimir the Great and Esther had a steamy love affair, the background to which was the town of Kazimierz and neighbouring village of Bochotnica, where the ruler put his Jewish beauty in a specially erected castle. He went to her each night through a secret underground passage which ran from Kazimierz. The result of their passion (apart from two sons, Pelka and Niemir, and two daughters raised in the Jewish faith) was a wide range of rights which the king granted the Jewish people. Sceptics say that this legend is strangely similar to the biblical story of Esther, but it was without doubt a cause of pride for pre-war Kazimierz Jews. As Aleksander Janowski wrote in 1901 in his book *Trips around the Country*, "Berek, like all the poor people of the town, associates the buildings and legends with the epoch of King Casimir. What kind of king he was, when, where and over whom he ruled, is hard to tell, but anyway he

The best place to start a sight-seeing trip is from the ruins of the castle and tower.

was a great king, a good king, and, of course, the protector of Esther. These two names are the alpha and omega of the town's tradition". All over Poland, Esther was a symbol of the beauty of the Jewish women from Kazimierz. As Janowski wrote, "The tradition of the beautiful Esther is still alive in all attractive women, and the memory of the royal lover and protector of the people lives on in the minds of the local Jews. Even on the festival of Sukkot they say prayers to her memory".

Maybe the beautiful Esther looked like this?

The Jewish Quarter

To get to the former Jewish quarter from the castle it is best to take ul. Lubelska which will lead you to the part of town called Na Tyłach. Many buildings here, for example houses No 8 and 10, as well as the very typical 11 and 17, are characteristic of the town's past. On the right hand side you can see the synagogue in Mały Rynek. Take the steps and go down.

The Synagogue and Butchers' Stalls

The synagogue in Mały Rynek, built of local limestone, dates from the second half of the 18th century. It is rectangular in shape (14.8m by 16.9m) with the main hall on the south-western side and the prayer rooms for women to the north. The interior was once richly decorated with wall paintings. The vaulting composed of eight parts was covered with

The external appearance of the synagogue in the Mały Rynek remains unchanged.

Wooden stalls in Mały Rynek were reconstructed after the Second World War.

paintings depicting animal themes and the representation of the grave of Rachel and the Wailing Wall. Local Jewish tradition attributed many legends to this synagogue. It was said to have been founded by King Casimir the Great as a gift for Esther. The stones in the wall were alleged to have come from the Wailing Wall in Jerusalem. The ark curtains were said to be the work of Esther herself. The synagogue was partly destroyed in 1944 and vandalised after the war. It was rebuilt in 1953 but without any decoration. At that time the arcades were walled up, and did not return to their original form until 1995. Since its reconstruction, the synagogue has been used as a cinema, which makes visiting somewhat difficult. You will find a commemorative plaque on one of the walls.

"Horses, deer, castles, flowers, geese, scales, doves and symbolism in all its richness hovers over the crowd deep in prayer." This is how around 1900 Aleksander Janowski described his impressions of the synagogue. "The elevation with a wooden balustrade, brass candelabra with numerous arms, an embroidered silk curtain, enormous books on pulpits and several splendid silver-bearded types. This is the east – hot and fanatical. The east, in their long flowing garments and silver adornments on their foreheads. These nostalgic, passionate songs full of simplicity and woe, these sighs for the land once lost, for Mount Zion and the tomb of David, for the waters of Jordan and the cedars of Lebanon..."

Nearby, in the middle of Mały Rynek, there are some unique wooden stalls, very few of which remain in Poland to this day. At present they house a gallery and the offices of the nearby bazaar.

The Mały Rynek almost touches the south-east side of the Kazimierz main market square. You can get into the synagogue building when the cinema is open and visit the butchers' stalls during the working hours of the galleries and the little shops which are there now.

The Site of the Former Cemetery

From the Little Market Square go back up the steps to ul. Lubelska and take a walk down this street. On the bend you will see the school. The playground surrounded by a stone wall is on the site of the Old Cemetery dating from 1568. Not a single trace of it has remained, although the *matzevot* may have ended up in the local lapidarium. If you turn right here, you will cut across to ul. Nadrzeczna and head straight for ul. Czerniawy (the road to Opole Lubelskie). After a quarter of an hour you will come to the new Jewish cemetery in ul. Czerniawy.

The New Jewish Cemetery

The cemetery in ul. Czerniawy was established in 1851 on land belonging to Motek Herzberg. It is now situated behind Poland's most interesting lapidarium, the creation of Tadeusz Augustynek, completed in 1985 and built from the remains of 600 *matzevot*. Some of the gravestones may have come from the old cemetery in ul. Lubelska.

They were saved by Polish workers, who put the *matzevot* meant for paving the streets face down, against the instructions of the Nazis who had ordered the removal of all engravings and inscriptions. Through a "crack" in the memorial you can enter a very beautiful cemetery. Be sure to take a good look at each of the headstones, as many of them show traces of paintings and the refined forms create a true gallery of Jewish sepulchral art.

It is interesting to note that lamps still burn there on Saturdays. One can also find *kvitlech* in Polish. The cemetery is not fenced off and you can enter without any problem.

Engravings depicting candles and *Shabbat* candlesticks are frequent motifs on the gravestones of women. Hands raised in blessing symbolise *cohanim* (ministers), and books denote wisdom.

A jug and a bowl were put on the graves of *Levites*, the descendents of Levi, who helped the ministers at the making of sacrifices.

In the New Jewish Cemetery there is a wall-monument (visible in the background) made of pieces of *matzevot*.

Various items associated with the life of Kazimierz Jews can be found in the local museum. The exhibition is located in the house called Kamienica Celejowska, ul. Senatorska 11/3, ☎ +81 8810289 and open on Saturdays and Sundays 10am–4pm. It contains silverware used in religious ceremonies, *Torah* decorations, *Chanukah* lamps, *kiddush* cups, spice-boxes called *besamim* (see above) and *mezzuzot* (see below), as well as paintings inspired by Jewish themes. The Nadwiślańskie Muzeum, ul. Podzamcze 12a, ☎ +81 8810288, has old photographs and a pre-war film about Kazimierz, as well as some written accounts given by local people who remember the pre-war era.

By the River

You may want to end your walk around Kazimierz with a stroll by the Vistula, as the valley of this river is extraordinarily pretty here. An added attraction is the opportunity to take a boat to Janowiec on the opposite bank, where you can find the ruins of the Firlej and Lubomirski castle.

Before the war these trips were the domain of the ferrymen, who formed a sizeable group among Kazimierz Jews. The writer Shalom Ash is alleged to have said to the famous Polish playwright and painter S.I. Witkiewicz (also known as Witkacy): "In Kazimierz the Vistula speaks to me in Yiddish". The names of some of them, such as the Bendit family or Abram Tantzerman, are remembered to this very day. Janowski described the latter as follows: "Abram Tantzerman, the Kazimierz gondolier, a true child of the Vistula, a robust, swarthy, handsome lad; his body, as if made of bronze, burnt by the sun and hardened by the river winds, peers through the tattered sleeves of his shirt". Zusman Segałowicz described another ferryman in his beautiful poem entitled *In Kazimierz on the Vistula:* "The old, silver-haired ferryman by the Vistula prays / Silent, his kingly pride in my mind I keep / He looks like a High Priest standing in this place / Pouring his pain down to the deep..." Maybe Segałowicz had seen someone who looked like the famous Chaim from Wojszyn, immortalised by Shalom Ash in the novel *Shtetl* and a favourite model for the painters staying at the summer resort.

KRAŚNIK

We know about the Jewish presence in Kraśnik from accounts dated as early as 1531, but the right allowing Jews to settle here was granted only in 1584 (at once annulling the *privilegia de non tolerandis Judaeis*). The local community, quite numerous in size (it sent one of the three representatives from the province of Lublin to sessions of The Diet of the Four Lands) was prevented from expanding freely. In 1654 attempts were made to limit the area in which Jews could reside to the territory around the synagogue, but this was not observed. The former Jewish quarter stretches around ul. Bóżnicza and down ul. Bagno. At the outbreak of the Second World War, 5,000 Jews lived here, which was 40% of the local population. They were all murdered in the death camp in Bełżec in 1942.

Tourist Attractions

The Lateran Canons monastery complex: St Mary's Ascension church (ca 1469) with paintings by T. Dollabella and gravestones of the Tęczyński family and the monstery (15th–18th centuries); the Baroque former hospital church of the Holy Spirit (1758–1761) and the hospital from the middle of the 18th century; the ruins of the Zamoyski castle from the 17th century.

The Synagogue with an Annexe

Two badly destroyed buildings, the synagogue (erected 1637–1654) and its annexe, are to this very day powerful testimony to Kraśnik's Jewish past. The synagogue is square in shape (each side 20m in length). Its interior arrangement was typical: the prayer hall for men on the north-east side, two floors on the south-west side; the lower taken up by the vestibule and the upper by the prayer rooms for women. The single floor section is a part of the original building. The vestibule and the section for women were added later. The tablets containing the Ten Commandments, the recess for the *aron ha-kodesh* and the remains of wall paintings are all still there. The decorations once adorning the west wall depicted *Shor Habor* (ox) and *Leviathan* (fish). The dome was decorated with the image of an eagle surrounded by swallows, with an *etrog* in its beak and a sheaf of *lulavin* in its claws, a symbol of the feast of *Sukkot*. In 1945, the synagogue was designated as a workshop for the local handicraft co-operative. It remained empty from 1980 to 1989 when repairs were undertaken, but after a new roof in traditional Polish mansard style was put on, the works were unfortunately discontinued.

When the renovation is finally completed, the synagogue complex in Kraśnik may become one of the most attractive monuments of Jewish culture in the Lublin region.

The building on the right side is an addition to the synagogue and was used as an additional house of prayer and study. It was erected to support the main synagogue, which was not able to accommodate all of the worshippers. Construction took from 1823 to 1857. In 1948 a purchasing centre for agricultural products was organised there, and in 1966 some of the windows

The Decalogue Tablets still adorn the wall of the synagogue.

were bricked up. The additional synagogue was almost equal in size to the original one (19.5m by 22m). The interior was also laid out in similar fashion, with one and two storied sections. Even the framework of the *bimah* (four columns connected by archivaults) and the recess for the *aron ha-kodesh* survive. In the 1990s repairs to the annexe were started and soon abandoned, but not before the windows were faultily installed. It is not easy to have a look around either structure and it is advisable to do it in the company of Mr Chruściel (his address is given below), as it is not obvious which parts have been repaired and strengthened and which still might give way at any moment. To get to the synagogue from the annexe, there is a recently constructed underground passage, which lends atmosphere to the journey, particularly as the cellars are shrouded in total darkness. If the repair work is ever completed, the monument complex in Kraśnik might well become a major tourist attraction.

The synagogue and its annexe are in ul. Bóżnicza, very close to the square, on the left of the supermarket. The key is with Mr Chruściel, ul. Bóżnicza 12 (please ring), ☎ *+81 8843891.*

The Mikvah and the Cemetery

The building which housed the ritual baths is not far from the synagogue. Just go down ul. Bóżnicza and after crossing ul. Lubelska walk along ul. Bagno. It is a large and easily recognisable edifice which has been converted into an old people's home. The same road goes on further to the right (1 km) towards the cemetery, honoured today with a memorial to the Jews of Kraśnik. Unfortunately, most of the *matzevot* were stolen after the war and today serve as paving stones and steps.

One of the most extraordinary Jewish stories from the time of the Nazi occupation is associated with the history of Izbica. A Jew, Jacob Hersh Griner, hid among local Poles. He then converted to Catholicism, was later ordained a priest and as Father Grzegorz Pawłowski went to Jaffa in Israel. And it is Father Pawłowski and his brother Chaim Griner who are the benefactors of the cemetery's memorial to the Jews of Izbica, their parents among them, murdered by the Nazis.

IZBICA

Once a town with an almost entirely Jewish population (85–95%), Izbica was the seat of the Izbica-Radzyń *tzaddik* dynasty, existing until 1942 and having been established by Mordechai Josef Leiner (d. 1854), whose successors moved to Radzyń. Among several local examples of monuments of Jewish culture the ones worth a mention are the houses from the second half of the 19th century and the cemetery located between

the main road and ul. Fabryczna containing the *ohel* of the local *tzaddik*. In 2001 Izbica became a place of ecumenical prayer in memory of the Jewish community of the Lublin region. Józef Życiński, the metropolitan Archbishop of Lublin, was one of the organisers.

Arcaded houses are a characteristic feature of the main square in Zamość.

ZAMOŚĆ

Jews settled here some eight years after the town was founded. The area around Rynek Solny (the Salt Market) and ul. Żydowska (Jewish Street), now ul. Zamenhofa, was designated as the Jewish quarter. In the 18th century, Zamość became a centre of intellect and home to scholars such as Eliezer Lipman ben Manli and Shlomo ben Moshe. This is perhaps why later on the Jews of Zamość shared a fate unlike many of the others from the Lublin region. At the beginning of the 19th century the *Haskalah* under the leadership of Josef Cederbaum, Yakov Eichenbaum and Salomon Ettinger triumphed here. Zamość was home to Hebrew print shops, a Hebrew secondary school and even

In 1588, Jan Zamoyski invited to Zamość Sephardi Jews from Turkey, Italy and Holland. In the middle of 17th century, the Sephardi community began to disperse among the more expansive Ashkenazi Jews.

Tourist Attractions

Zamość is the only complete Renaissance urban complex in Poland. Established in 1589, the town was designed by the Italian architect Bernardo Morando and based on the concept of *citta ideale* (ideal town). Among its main attractions are the bastions including the Lubelska Gate (1588) and the Lwowska Gate (1599); the palace; the Town Hall (1591–1600) and its famous fan-shaped stairs; the buildings of the Zamość Academy (the second institution of higher learning in the Polish Kingdom, 1639–1648); the cathedral church (1587–1600); the Orthodox Christian church (1618–1631, now Catholic), and the arcaded houses from the 17th century. In 1992 UNESCO declared the historical monuments of Zamość a World Heritage Site.

Bolesław Leśmian (originally Lesman, 1877–1937), a great Polish poet of Jewish descent, lived in Zamość.

Another native of Zamość, known world-wide, but for different reasons, was the revolutionary, Rosa Luxemburg (1870–1937).

The Zamość Synagogue is one of the most precious monuments of Jewish culture in Poland.

a Jewish weekly, "Zamoishcher Shtimme" (The Zamość Voice). In 1939 Jews made up 45% of the town's population (12,000 people). Of these 5,000 managed to escape to the East. The Germans imprisoned the rest in the ghetto, from where they were deported to the death camp in Bełżec.

Many 16th and 17th-century buildings situated in the former Jewish quarter remain in good condition. In accordance with the plans made when the town was being established, the district once inhabited by Jews is spread over the north-eastern part of the town centre. It is delineated by ul. Pereca, ul. Zamenhofa and Rynek Solny. The centre of the former Jewish community was situated in the middle section of ul. Zamenhofa. There was a synagogue here, the *kahal* house and the *cheder*. Jews also lived in the Jewish suburb stretching from Stara Brama Lwowska in the direction of Nowa Osada set up at the beginning of the 19th century. There were once two cemeteries here. On the site of the Old Cemetery from the 17th century there is now a house of culture. In 1950 the new one in ul. Prosta was turned into a lapidarium in the form of a memorial made from the remains of *matzevot*. It is crowned with tablets bearing the inscription "Thou shalt not kill".

The other synagogue in Zamość is at ul. Gminna 32 in the Nowa Osada district. It was erected in 1872 and extended from 1909 to 1913. In 1948 it was turned into a kindergarten.

The Synagogue

Erected from 1610 to 1618, this Renaissance building, made of brick, was a place of religious worship until the outbreak of the Second World War, when the Nazis destroyed the interior and converted it into a joinery. Renovation work was undertaken in the 1960s.

This beautiful synagogue now houses a library. It is quite astounding that a historic monument of this class is not a museum. This situation, however, is due to change. In 2003 the library will move and maybe then the synagogue's richness will shine in all its glory.

Yitzchak Leibush Peretz (1852–1915) was the most famous Jewish citizen of Zamość. He was called the "Father of Jewish literature". The Peretz family had Sephardic roots. His father was a supporter of the *Haskalah*; his mother of Orthodoxy. This is perhaps why Peretz received a dual education: a traditional one (he completed courses of study both at the *cheder* and the *yeshivah*) and a secular (Law in Warsaw). In 1890 he moved to Warsaw and lived in ul. Ceglana (now ul. Pereca). His work was of particular importance for the development of literature in the Yiddish language. His most important works are short stories and plays, including the one translated into Polish and entitled *Nocą na starym rynku* (In the Old Square at Night) first published in 1906.

The present condition of the building does not mean that you cannot have a quick look inside. The main prayer hall is its oldest part, while the prayer rooms for women were added in the middle of the 17th century. The one on the north side was destroyed by the Germans during the Second World War and rebuilt in the 1960s. The vestibule was added in the 18th century. The attic has a rather interesting story. It was taken down in the 18th century and put back 200 years later. The entrance takes you through the Renaissance stone portal to the vestibule in which there is a reading room and an information desk. The ceiling in the main hall has been lowered. Between the bookshelves you can see the recess for the *aron ha-kodesh*. There is no trace of the *bimah*. Rich adornments, such as the crown of the *Torah* over the recess and the vessels (jugs and bowls used by *Levites*), are quite extraordinary. The walls here used to bear very rich paintings and numerous Hebrew inscriptions. The interior is begging to be renovated.

The synagogue is situated on the corner of ul. Zamenhofa and ul. Bazyliańska. The library is open 7.30am–6.30pm.

In the Old Square at Night by Y.L. Perec has been staged at the Jewish Theatre in Warsaw and directed by Szymon Szurmiej.

The Kahal House and Cheder

The building at ul. Zamenhofa 11, adjacent to the synagogue, is the former *kahal* house and *cheder*. The original building dated from the 17th century and served as a schoolmaster's

lodgings. The *kahal* house and *cheder* were set up here in the 18th century and extended in the 19th, with another floor being added. After the Second World War it was transformed into a hotel.

The Mikvah

The *mikvah* building from the middle of the 18th century, remodelled in the 19th century, can still be found ul. Zamenhofa 3. The ritual bath was located in the cellars.

You can go inside during the opening hours of the local club, from 6pm to 10pm.

Rynek Solny

You may want to end your walk around the Jewish monuments of the Old Town in Rynek Solny (the Salt Market). The houses on the northern and eastern sides of the square once belonged to Jewish merchants. Initially one-storied, they were built on in the 19th century.

The former *mikvah* is accessible from ul. Pereca through the gate marked Jazz Klub Kosz (the Mieczysław Kosz Jazz Club).

400 *matzevot* still remain in the Szczebrzeszyn cemetery.

SZCZEBRZESZYN | Yiddish: Shebreshin

This little town, where before the war 50% of the population was Jewish, has a handsome late Renaissance synagogue dating from the beginning of the 17th century and located at ul. Sądowa 3. It is now home to a local cultural centre. Its present appearance is the result of reconstruction works carried out between 1957 and 1963. Up to that time the synagogue was in a sorry state; in 1940 the vaults collapsed after being set on fire by the Germans. Here you can see the original stone framework of the *aron ha-kodesh* with the words "I keep the Lord always before me" (Psalm 16:8) and the stucco adorned with symbolic motifs. At the cemetery in ul. Cmentarna you can find *matzevot* dating from as early as the beginning of the 18th century. In keeping with ancient tradition the cemetery contains separate sections for men and women.

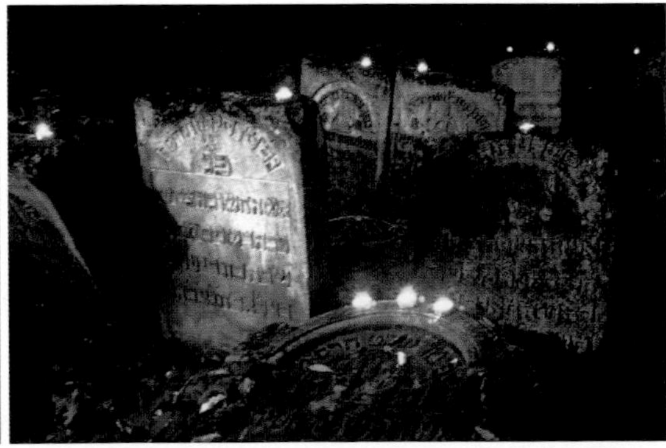

The Małopolska Region

•

From Cracow's Kazimierz to the Land of Tzaddikim

•

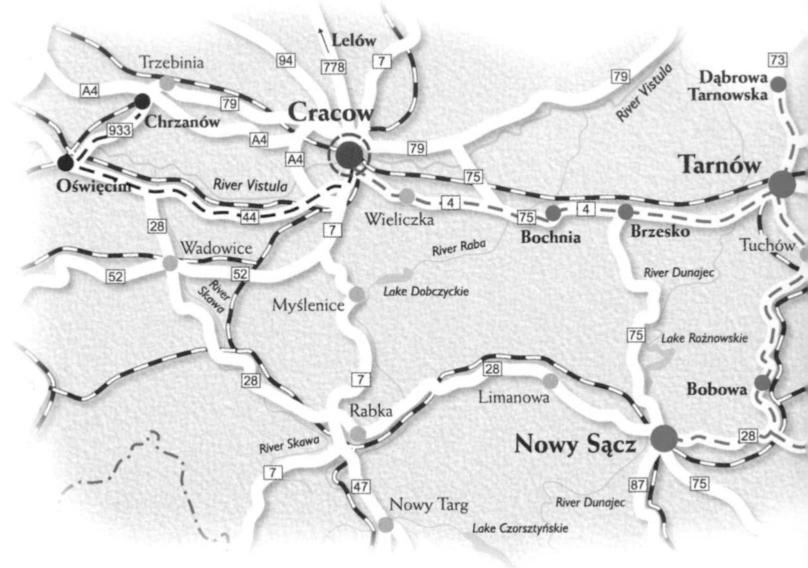

▬	ROUTE ONE	KRAKÓW
▬	ROUTE TWO	KRAKÓW → OŚWIĘCIM → CHRZANÓW
▬	ROUTE THREE	KRAKÓW → BOCHNIA → BRZESKO → TARNÓW → DĄBROWA TARNOWSKA → BOBOWA → NOWY SĄCZ → BIECZ → DUKLA → RYMANÓW → SANOK → LESKO → PRZEMYŚL → JAROSŁAW → SIENIAWA → LEŻAJSK → ŁAŃCUT → RZESZÓW

FOR PRACTICAL INFORMATION SEE PAGE 292

RECOMMENDATIONS

Visit the **Kazimierz district** of Kraków, find the Bays Nusn synagogue in **Nowy Sącz**, see the synagogue in **Bobowa** and go to the local ohel, take a trip to the synagogue and the Jewish cemetery in **Lesko**, see the wall paintings in **Łańcut** and go to **Leżajsk** on the 21st day of the month of Adar. Make a point of visiting **Auschwitz**.

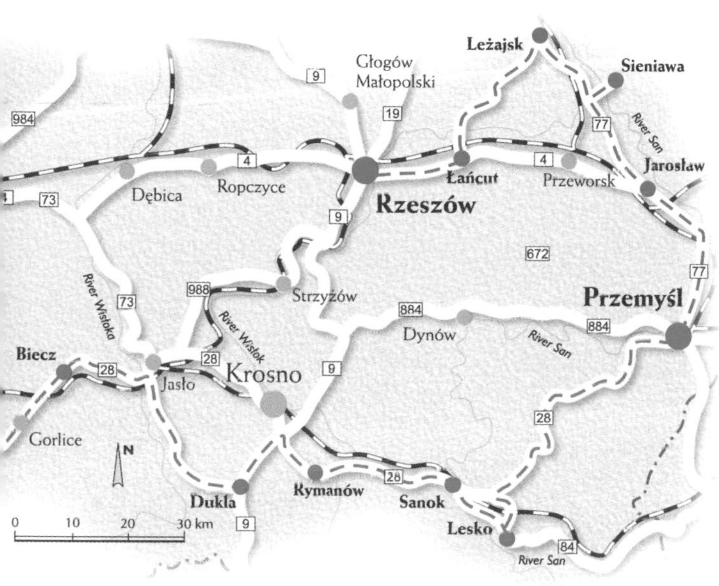

The Małopolska region is richer in monuments of Jewish culture than any other part of Poland. It was once home to a number of great centres of Jewish intellectual, political and religious life; among them Cracow, Przemyśl, Jarosław and Lvov. It was also an area where numerous Chasidic groups thrived: in Bobowa, Nowy Sącz, Dąbrowa Tarnowska and Leżajsk, to mention but a few. Along with Cracow, other towns in this region stand out for the number of their Jewish monuments of nationwide significance. This includes architecture of the highest class (Lesko) as well as testimony to Jewish spirituality in the form of the *oholot* in Bobowa, Brzesko, Dąbrowa Górnicza and Leżajsk. Many figures of international standing have roots in Małopolska, for instance Billy Wilder (1906–2002), born in Sucha Beskidzka, famous as the director of many Hollywood movies, including *Sunset Boulevard*.

The Jewish religion is coming back to life in the Kazimierz distict of Cracow (below: a service in the Remuh Synagogue)

CRACOW | Yiddish: Krake, Kroke

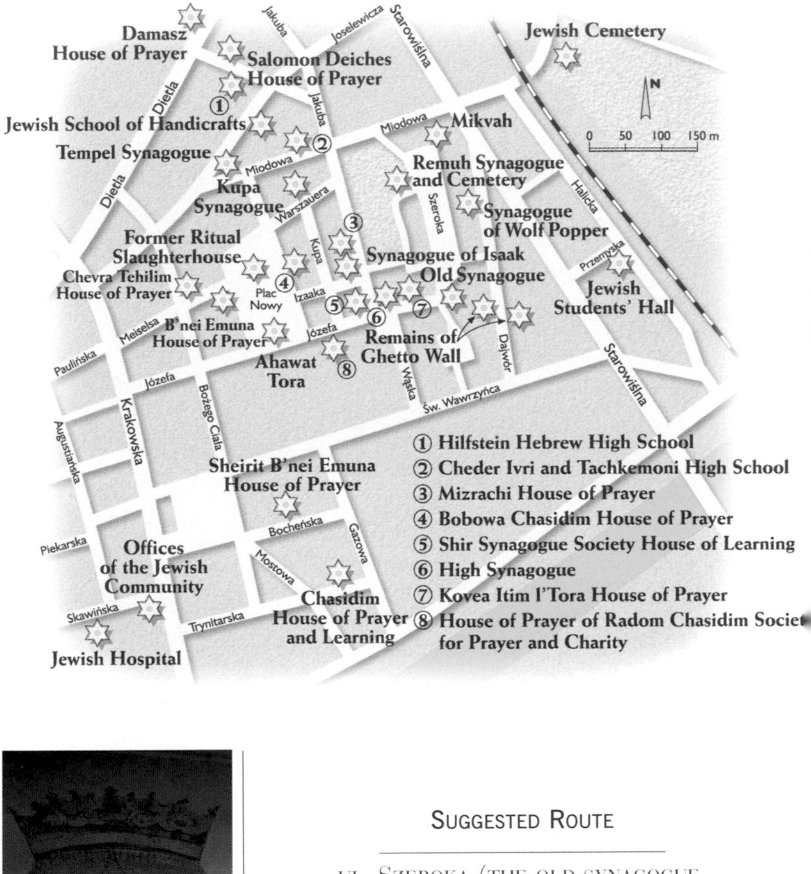

Damasz House of Prayer
Salomon Deiches House of Prayer
Jewish School of Handicrafts
Tempel Synagogue
Kupa Synagogue
Former Ritual Slaughterhouse
Chevra Tehilim House of Prayer
B'nei Emuna House of Prayer
Ahawat Tora
Sheirit B'nei Emuna House of Prayer
Offices of the Jewish Community
Jewish Hospital
Chasidim House of Prayer and Learning
Remains of Ghetto Wall
Old Synagogue
Synagogue of Isaak
Synagogue of Wolf Popper
Remuh Synagogue and Cemetery
Mikvah
Jewish Cemetery
Jewish Students' Hall

Jakuba, Joselewicza, Starowiślna, Dietla, Miodowa, Warszauera, Kupa, Szeroka, Halicka, Przemyska, Izaaka, Plac Nowy, Meiselsa, Józefa, Paulińska, Krakowska, Bożego Ciała, Augustiańska, Wąska, Dajwór, Św. Wawrzyńca, Bocheńska, Gazowa, Mostowa, Piekarska, Skawińska, Trynitarska

N
0 50 100 150 m

① Hilfstein Hebrew High School
② Cheder Ivri and Tachkemoni High School
③ Mizrachi House of Prayer
④ Bobowa Chasidim House of Prayer
⑤ Shir Synagogue Society House of Learning
⑥ High Synagogue
⑦ Kovea Itim l'Tora House of Prayer
⑧ House of Prayer of Radom Chasidim Society for Prayer and Charity

SUGGESTED ROUTE

UL. SZEROKA (THE OLD SYNAGOGUE, THE REMUH SYNAGOGUE AND CEMETERY, THE MIKVAH, THE SYNAGOGUE OF WOLF POPPER) → UL. JÓZEFA (THE KOWEA ITIM L'TORA HOUSE OF PRAYER, THE HIGH SYNAGOGUE) → UL. KUPA (THE SYNAGOGUE OF ISAAC) → UL. WARSZAUERA (THE KUPA SYNAGOGUE) → PLAC NOWY (THE RITUAL SLAUGHTERHOUSE FOR POULTRY) → UL. MEISELSA → UL. MIODOWA (THE TEMPEL SYNAGOGUE, THE CEMETERY)

Cracow has, without doubt, the most magnificent collection of monuments of Jewish heritage in Poland. However, it is not just the past which makes this city so special. Cracow today is also a vibrant centre of Jewish tradition and culture.

Jewish settlement began here sometime before 1304. It is assumed that Jews lived here as early as the time of the journey of the trader Ibrahim ibn Jacob (circa 965). The first Jewish institutions in Cracow had their seats in the vicinity of what is now ul. św. Anny, known then as ul. Żydowska (Jewish Street). Here you could find a synagogue, a *mikvah*, a hospital and a wedding house. But the medieval Jewish district was much greater in size. It spread from ul. Szewska to ul. Wiślna. In 1335 Kazimierz Wielki (King Casimir the Great) founded a separate town called Kazimierz on the site of the former village of Bawół. It soon became a dynamic centre of Jewish community life. The first well known Jewish historical figure was Lewko, the governor of the royal mint and the leaseholder of the Wieliczka and Bochnia saltmines. In 1407 a pogrom took place here, based on allegiations of ritual murder. In 1495, King John Olbracht banished all the Jews from Cracow and limited the area where they could live to the district of Kazimierz, the reason being the unresolved case of the fire at the church of St Ann.

The Kazimierz Jewish community was growing fast and in the 16th century it became the largest Jewish conglomeration

Alongside the monuments of Prague, Cracow's Kazimierz is the best preserved Jewish quarter in Europe, with as many as seven synagogues still remaining.

Tourist Attractions

Cracow is a city of such a multitude of monuments that the listing below should be considered only as an initial introduction. UNESCO has declared Cracow's Old Town and Kazimierz district a World Heritage site.

At Wawel Hill: the cathedral of St Vaclaus and St Stanislaus (1320–1364, and the remains of older buildings, from as early as the 9th century) with the King Sigismund Chapel (1519–1533) as well as crypts and tombs of Polish kings; the royal castle built in the early Middle Ages and remodelled in Renaissance style (1502–1536).

In the city centre: the old network of streets unchanged since the city was founded with a market square and the former site of the ramparts (the only remaining part being the Floriańska Gate from ca 1300). **In the Main Market Square**: the town hall tower built sometime before 1383, the Sukiennice (Cloth Hall), remodelled in Renaissance style, St Adalbert's Church (from the 11th and 12th centuries, remodelled in 1611), St Mary's Church, a great Gothic basilica (1355 and 1397; some features are even older) with its masterpiece altar (1477–1489) by Wit Stwosz (also known as Vit Stoss). Also more than a dozen magnificent churches, the buildings of the Jagiellonian University, as well as numerous tenement houses and palaces. The famous saltmine in Wieliczka (also a UNESCO World Heritage site) is close to Cracow.

Jews were mostly involved in trade and crafts on a small scale. Some of them were physicians and lawyers (the photograph on the right shows little shops in ul. Krakowska).

in Europe. In 1608 the size of the district was tripled, after the so-called *oppidum judaeorum* had been established on the basis of the *privilegia de non tolerandis Christianis* from 1566. The Jewish town was enclosed by the following streets: ul. Miodowa, ul. Dajwór, ul. św. Wawrzyńca, ul. Wąska and Plac Nowy. Kazimierz soon gained fame as a great centre of intellect. Its *yeshivah*, which opened in 1509, was renowned far and wide. It was headed by rabbi Moses Isserles, also known as Remuh, a distinguished philosopher and humanist. In the 16th century a group of Sephardi Jews expelled from Spain came to Cracow. Among them was Samuel Kalahora, later physician to King Stefan Batory.

The collapse of Kazimierz began at the time of the Swedish invasion (1655–1657) preceded by outbreaks of pestilence (1651–1652). The status of a separate town was maintained until 1800, when Kazimierz became part of Cracow. The period of the Republic of Cracow as well as equality of rights under Austrian rule in 1867 meant that Jews had more and more freedom and were now able to settle in the city wherever they chose. The area around ul. Stradom and the town centre was their favoured location. This resulted in Kazimierz being left *en masse* by wealthier Jews. In the 19th century, Cracow rose to become a significant centre of Jewish society in all its manifestations: Orthodox, Chasidic and Reform and by 1939 the city was home to nearly 60,000 Jews.

During the Second World War, the Germans imprisoned the Jews of Cracow in the ghetto in the Podgórze district (some remains of the wall can still be found in ul. Lwowska and ul. Limanowskiego), and in December 1942 they established a concentration camp in Płaszów. It was on land formerly occupied by Jewish cemeteries, which now became a place of extermination. In the middle of 1944, those Jews still alive were transported to Auschwitz.

Around the year 1900 there were ca 25,000 Jews in Cracow, constituting as much as 28% of the population.

The details of the extermination of Cracow Jews are known through the accounts of Tadeusz Pankiewicz, the only Pole who was allowed by the Germans to run a pharmacy. Now on this spot, situated in the former Plac Zgody, there is the National Remembrance Museum called the Pharmacy Under the Sign of the Eagle, pl. Bohaterów Getta 18, ☎ +12 6565625. Open: Monday–Friday 10am–4pm, Saturdays 10am–2pm.

After the war, efforts were made to revive Jewish institutions in Cracow. A synagogue with its own cantor held regular services and pilgrimages to the grave of Moses Isserles were organised. However, the deserted district of Kazimierz fell into decay. Some of the historic houses in ul. Kupa, ul. Estery and ul. Józefa were pulled down and replaced by buildings lacking in style and totally out of character. Interest in Jewish Kazimierz grew after the political changes of 1989.

Since 1989 the Kazimierz district of Cracow has been turning into an important destination for tourists (above: one of the Jewish restaurants in ul. Szeroka).

The seven large synagogues of Kazimierz constitute the biggest such complex in Europe, comparable only with the Jewish monuments in Prague.

The Old Synagogue

Begin your visit from ul. Szeroka. It is not so much a street as an elongated square, bearing clear traces of a medieval marketplace. On its southern side you will find the Old Synagogue. Built in the 15th century (exact date unknown), it is the oldest Jewish house of prayer in Poland. According to Jewish legend, the synagogue was founded by King Casimir the Great, for whom prayers were said until 1939. Yet historians maintain that it dates from the time of King John Olbracht. Initially Gothic, the synagogue was later rebuilt in Renaissance style. Its original form was modelled on the architecture of the synagogues in Worms, Prague and Ratisbon (now Regensburg). The reconstruction works undertaken in 1570, were based on plans by the Italian architect, Matteo Gucci. Apart from its religious function it was also the seat of the *kahal*, the court and the place where royal edicts were proclaimed. It was here, on 25 March 1785, that Tadeusz Kościuszko appealed to the Jews to take part in the insurrection against the Russian Tsar. The synagogue functioned until 1939 and during the war it was severely damaged by the Germans. Conservation work started in 1956 and lasted until 1959. From 1970 to 1972, the area around it was transformed; the wall surrounding it to the north and the west was demolished and its now characteristic broad terrace steps were built.

The present-day appearance of the interior of the The Old Synagogue is the result of reconstruction work carried out after the Second World War.

An eight-branched candelabrum is used during the eight-day long festival of *Chanukah*, when an additional candle is lit each day.

In 1958 the Jewish community of Cracow gave the building of the Old Synagogue to the Cracow Museum of History. An exhibition of Judaica is now housed here.

Few of the pre-war features of the synagogue remain. The *bimah* (modelled on the one from 1570), the platform with steps in front of the *aron ha-kodesh*, the *ner tamid* (ever-lasting light) on the left of the *aron-ha kodesh*, the "source of living water" (the well in the vestibule), and the iron door, are all replicas. Even the walls have been rebuilt, as it was necessary to replace damp bricks with new ones. Only some of the features made of stone are genuine: the Mannerist style framework of the *aron ha-kodesh* (from the 17th century), portals, collection boxes and the remains of paintings (such as the traces of the twigs in the men's prayer hall, dating from the 17th century).

The exhibition displayed here is divided into four sections: synagogue furnishings, Jewish festivals and rituals, Kazimierz, and the Holocaust. The exhibition contains a considerable number of paintings by artists such as: Gottlieb, Mehoffer, Popiel, Potrzebowski and Stern. There are also many items related to religious ceremonies, such as candle holders, *Chanukah* lamps, *menorot*, covers for the *Torah* scrolls, *parochot*, *tallitim*, and *kipot*. The museum also has a collection of books, containing 2,500 volumes of Hebrew manuscripts and old prints.

Ul. Szeroka 24, ☎ *+12 4220962. Open: Wed and Thu 9am–3pm; Fri 10am–3pm; Sat and Sun 9am–3pm (with the exception of the first weekend of the month); Mon and Tue 10am–3pm, but only after the first weekend of the month.*

The Remuh Synagogue and Cemetery

The most interesting of all Cracow's synagogues is in the western row of houses in ul. Szeroka. Izrael (Isserl) son of Joseph, a royal banker, founded it in 1556 for his son, the great rabbi and scholar Moses Isserles also known as Remuh. The layout was most probably designed by Stanisław Baranek, a builder from Kazimierz. Rebuilt several times (in the 17th and 18th centuries as well as in 1829 and 1882) it was restored in 1933. Re-opened in 1945, it functions to this day.

The synagogue's interior features include the original *aron ha-kodesh* (built sometime after 1557) as well as the steps, pulpit and eternal light, all of which are were added after the war. Also the foundation plaque has remained, as well as another one commemorating the place where Moses Isserles used to sit (next to the *aron ha-kodesh*). The stone collection boxes from the second half of the 16th century, the vessel used for *etrog*, and the candelabra (both hanging and free-standing) are all original. The commemorative plaques on the courtyard walls, however, were moved here from other sites in Cracow after the war. The building adjacent to the synagogue and visible from the courtyard is the caretaker's house (late 18th century).

The Remuh Synagogue building survived the Second World War without any damage. It lost, however, its interior features when the Germans turned it into a military storehouse.

The *bimah* from 1958 is an exact reconstruction of the one from before 1939. Both the southern door (from ca 1670) and the northern door (from the second half of the 18th c) are original.

The memory of **Moses Isserles also known as Remuh** lives on. His grave in Cracow is covered with lots of notes containing requests from pilgrims, who often come from far and wide. Remuh was a Cracow rabbi and also rector of the local *yeshivah*. Apart from his religious duties he was also a keen astronomer, geometrician, philosopher and historian. His popularity was secured by his commentary entitled *Ha-mapa* (Tablecloth), to the *Shulchan Aruch* (the code for everyday life). To this day every religious Ashkenazi Jew lives according to these rules.

The cemetery next door to the Remuh synagogue is one of the most important Jewish monuments in Poland. Established in 1533, it was one of the main Kazimierz necropolises until it was closed by the Austrians in 1799. Plans were then drawn up to build a street running through the cemetery but they were never implemented and, with the passing of time, the decaying cemetery was left to its own fate. Neglected and full of litter, it was not refurbished until 1959–1960. During the reconstruction works, several archaeological finds were made. It was discovered that the cemetery contained several layers of graves below the surface. The differences in the elevation of the cemetery are quite striking. Its south-eastern part, for instance, is four and a half metres higher than the rest. According to unconfirmed sources this is because that part is situated on top of a heap of the remains of old *matzevot*.

The cemetery is unique in Poland both in terms of the number of monuments as well as their historical and artistic value. Two types of gravestone can be seen here. First, there are those which are partly trapezoid in shape, with sloping ends and sides, and reminiscent of a sarcophagus, although in some cases they are more similar to a half-cylinder placed in a horizontal position. (Several of these can be found in the row adjacent to the corner of the Remuh synagogue). Second, there are also graves in the form of free-standing headstones. Among those buried here are the most eminent figures of the Cracow community from the period between the middle of the 16th century and the end of the 19th century. The grave of Moses Isserles Remuh, who died in 1572 on the festival of *Lag B'Omer*, is to be found at the back of the

The tomb of Moses Isserles Remuh is the most treasured of all the graves in the Jewish cemetery.

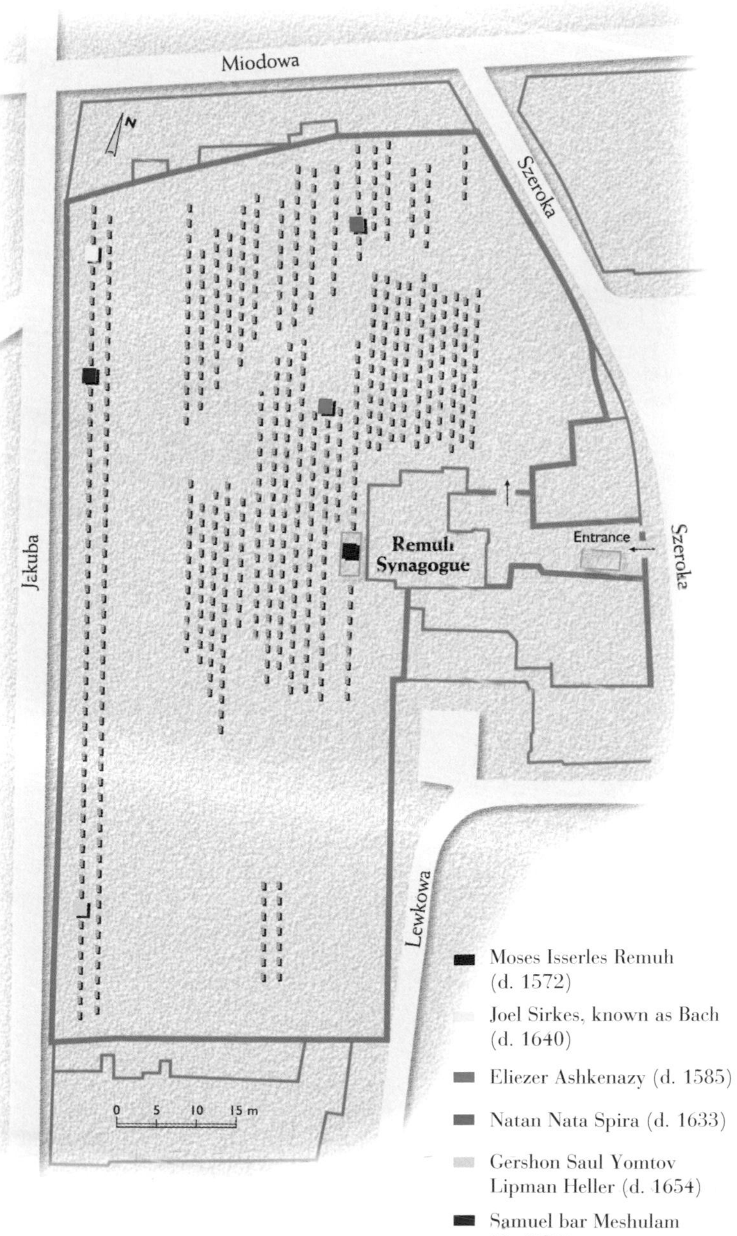
Miodowa
Szeroka
Jakuba
Remuh Synagogue
Entrance
Szeroka
Lewkowa
0 5 10 15 m
Moses Isserles Remuh (d. 1572)
Joel Sirkes, known as Bach (d. 1640)
Eliezer Ashkenazy (d. 1585)
Natan Nata Spira (d. 1633)
Gershon Saul Yomtov Lipman Heller (d. 1654)
Samuel bar Meshulam (d. 1552)

The wall of the cemetery is composed of pieces of broken gravestones.

synagogue on a stone dais. It is surrounded by iron railings. The tomb on the left is that of Izrael (d. 1568), Remuh's father and founder of the synagogue. The grave at the right end of the second row behind the tomb of Isserles, with a representation of the serpent of Aesculapius, is the resting place of Eliezer Ashkenazi (d. 1585), who was rabbi of Cairo, Cyprus (Famagusta) and Poznań. By the wall separating the cemetery from ul. Jakuba are the tombs of Joel Sirkes also known as Bach (d. 1640), head of the Talmudic School of Cracow and rabbi in Bełz, Szydłów and Cracow; Samuel bar Meshulam (d. 1552), physician to the Queen Bona and the last two kings of the Jagiellonian dynasty; Gershon Saul Yomtov Lipman Heller (d. 1654), rector of the *yeshivah*; and Natan Nata Spira, rabbi of Vienna and Prague and a renowned caballist (d. 1633).

The Remuh synagogue and cemetery, ul. Szeroka 46. Open: Mon–Thu 9am–2pm, Fri until sunset. Regular services are held in the synagogue at traditional hours.

Depictions of hands in a gesture of blessing were a regular feature of the graves of the families of *cohanim* (ministers). A crown signified piety.

The Mikvah

Directly opposite the Remuh synagogue, you will find the restaurant and hotel centre of Kazimierz. The first building on the left, now Klezmer-Hois, at the point where ul. Miodowa and ul. Starowiślna cross, is the former *mikvah*, which existed here in the basement as early as 1567. Its present form is the result of a complete remodelling of the building at the beginning of the 19th century. This ritual bath functioned until the Second World War.

The Ariel restaurant, in turn, occupies the inter-war house erected on the site of an 18th century building. It was once the home of the Levitans, a family of famous Cracow rabbis and opponents of Chasidism.

After a long period of neglect and decay, the *mikvah* was renovated (1974–1977) and converted into a hotel.

The Synagogue of Wolf Popper (Stork)

To the right of the *mikvah* there is a fence concealing a courtyard, deep into which you will find the synagogue of Wolf Popper, also known as Stork. He was a 17th-century financial magnate and five years before his death, in 1620, he founded a house of prayer, the most richly endowed of all the Cracow synagogues. Its costly upkeep impoverished the founders' heirs to such an extent that eventually the synagogue was taken over by the Kazimierz Jewish community. In 1827, the building underwent repairs and this is when the entrance hall was most probably added. The synagogue's historical furnishings were totally destroyed during the Second World War and the only item which survived, the wooden door of the *aron ha-kodesh*, was then moved to Jerusalem. The building was refurbished in 1964. Its wooden porches were removed, the recess for the *aron ha-kodesh* was bricked up and the entrance from ul. Dajwór was turned into a window. In this way the synagogues's interior lost its sacral character and a visit here is now more symbolic than illuminating.

The Synagogue of Wolf Popper is now a house of culture.

Ul. Szeroka 16, ☎ +12 4212987. The atelier housed here is open Mon–Fri 9am–2pm and 4pm–6pm and during the summer in July only, Mon–Fri 10am–2pm.

The Kovea Itim l'Torah House of Prayer

After a visit to the Stork synagogue and perhaps a bite to eat at one of the local Jewish restaurants, walk towards the passage to the right of the Old Synagogue which will lead you to ul. Józefa. Here, at No 42, you will find a building (from 1810) which once was the *Kovea Itim l'Torah* (Society for the Study of the Torah) house of prayer.

The facade of the building at ul. Józefa 42 is worth a closer look. The pre-war Hebrew inscription, "The Society for the Study of the Torah" is still visible.

THE FESTIVAL OF JEWISH CULTURE

This event takes place every year in the Kazimierz district of Cracow. It is the most significant Jewish culture festival in Poland and in 2002, which marks the twelfth time it has been held, it will be without any doubt one of the most important events of its kind anywhere in the world. The festival represents the triumph of life, the growth of a tradition rescued from oblivion and also, as with the reciting of *kaddish* (the prayer for the departed), it pays homage to the millions of Jews murdered by the Nazis. The final concert on the big stage in ul. Szeroka, with the participation of thousands of revellers, *klezmer* bands and the Festival Klezmer Orchestra brought together especially for the occasion, is always an unforgettable experience. Music is the festival's strong point and some of the world's leading artists, representing all kinds of musical trends, have performed and continue to perform here. They include: Itzhak Perlman, Shlomo Mintz, the great cantors Joseph Malowany and Benzion Miller, the groups Brave Old World, White Bird, The Klezmatics, The Klezmer Conservatory band, The Andy Statman Klezmer Orchestra, Shlomo Bar and Habrera Hativeet, Dave Krakauer Klezmer Madness, Jerusalem Jazz Band and many others. The festival is always inaugurated by a concert of synagogue music in the Tempel synagogue, but it is *klezmer* music which predominates, particularly the kind played at weddings. Occasionally you will also hear rather specific Chasidic or Sephardic music.

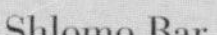
Shlomo Bar

A concert entitled "Leopold Kozłowski and Friends – The Most Beautiful Jewish Songs" takes place year after year at the Klezmer-Hois.

But the festival is also more than just a week of events featuring the most outstanding exponents in many different areas of Jewish art and culture, such as film shows (including screenings of Yiddish films made in Poland before the war), theatre and dance, literature and music. There are also classes in decorative paper-cutting, Hebrew calligraphy, dancing, cooking, Hebrew and Yiddish, instrumental music and also various forms of singing, among them cantoral, Chasidic and folk varieties. There are organised trips around old Kazimierz ("In the footprints of Bałaban") and the former Cracow ghetto (with a visit to the Pharmacy Under the Sign of the Eagle), as well as the Jewish cemeteries. The events that go to make up the festival usually take place in the following different locations: The Jewish Cultural Centre, ul. Meiselsa 17 (theatre performances, meetings and lectures); Galeria Shalom, ul. Józefa 16 (vernissages and exhibitions); Hotel Eden, ul. Ciemna 5 (Jewish cooking classes); Graffiti Summer Cinema, ul. św. Gertrudy 5 (film shows), Klezmer-Hois, ul. Szeroka 6 (concerts); The R. S. Lauder Foundation Club, ul. Kupa 18 (language classes); the Cracow Song and Dance Troupe Hall, ul. Meiselsa 18 (dance workshops); the Old Synagogue, ul. Szeroka 24 (open-air performances, exhibitions and the awarding of certificates to Poles who have helped to save monuments of Jewish history); the Kuźnica Society, ul. Miodowa 41 (meetings), the Popper synagogue, ul. Szeroka 16 (prayer, music workshops, exhibitions); the Tempel synagogue, ul. Miodowa 24 (concerts, prayer); Primary School No 11, ul. Miodowa 36 (art workshops and dancing); the Bagatela theatre, ul. Karmelicka 3 (concerts)

Shewach Weiss, ambassador of Israel to Poland

Janusz Makuch, director of the Festival of Jewish Culture

The Uri Caine Ensemble

The imposing building of The High Synagogue towers over the northern row of houses in ul. Józefa.

The High Synagogue

This synagogue was built from 1557 to 1563. It occupied the first floor only, its ground floor being used for the purposes of trade. With the passing of time, it became one with the building next door (ul. Józefa 40) and the two houses had one common entrance. Despite many attempts to renovate it, in 1935 the synagogue was in a sorry state; most of all this applied to its late Renaissance paintings. The gallery for women was situated in the second building and was added in 1939. During the Second World War all of the synagogue's furnishings and decorations were destroyed or stolen. The huge *menorah* ended up in the office of the Nazi governor Hans Frank, who resided in Wawel castle. The synagogue building was finally renovated in the period from 1969 to 1971, its interior being converted into a workshop for the conservation of historical monuments. A staircase was added as well as new entrances.

Ul. Józefa 38. The building is closed to visitors.

The Synagogue of Isaac

The Synagogue of Isaac (or the synagogue of Ajzyk Jakubowicz) was erected from 1638 to 1644. Its founder, whose grave can still be seen in the Remuh cemetery, was an elder of the Cracow Jewish community and a well known banker also referred to as Jacob the Rich. The plans of this early Baroque building were probably drawn by the local architect Jan Leitner, although the name of Giovanni Trevano also crops up. The building was considered to be over-imposing, which resulted in opposition from the diocesan chancery leading to a temporary break in construction. Like all other synagogues

The interior of the Synagogue of Issac is adorned with rich stucco decorations.

built with financial support of wealthy founders, the synagogue was renowned for rich furnishings, and in particular its silverware. Its lengthy peaceful existence, including several renovations and remodellings (in 1857 and 1924, to mention but two) was brought to an end by the outbreak of the Second World War. On 5 December 1939, the Germans ordered Maximilian Redlich, a Jewish community official, to burn the scrolls of the Torah. He refused and was shot dead. The Nazis destroyed all the furnishings, including the wooden frame of the *aron ha-kodesh*. In 1945 the building was made safe and allocated first to a sculpture and conservation atelier and then to a theatre company as a workshop and storage for props. In 1981 a fire broke out and and the interior was damaged. In 1983 yet another renovation was undertaken and in 1989 the synagogue was returned to the Jewish community.

The Treasure in Your Own Home

The founder of the synagogue is the hero of a well-known legend deriving from the *Tales of 1001 Nights*. Ayzik Jakubowicz, a pious but poor Jew, dreamed that there was treasure hidden under the old bridge in Prague. Without delay, he made his way there. On arrival, it turned out the bridge was guarded by a squad of soldiers and that digging was out of the question. Ayzik told the officer about his dream, promising him half of the booty. The officer retorted, "Only fools like Polish Jews can possibly believe in dreams. For several nights now I have been dreaming that in the Jewish town of Kazimierz there is hidden treasure in the oven of the home of the poor Jew Ayzik Jakubowicz. Do you think I am so stupid as to go all the way to Cracow and look for the house of this Isaac the son of Jacob?". Ayzik returned home immediately, took the oven apart, found the treasure and became rich. After this it was said: "There are some things which you can look for the world over, only to find them in your own home. Before you realise this, however, you very often have to go on a long journey and search far and wide."

At present a new project called "The Synagogue of Isaac" is beeing worked on, with the purpose of reconstructing the *bimah* and the steps leading to the *aron ha-kodesh*. Here you can see the exhibition entitled "In Memory of Polish Jews". It contains photograms of frames from unique documentary films found at the Documentary and Feature Film Studio in Warsaw. You can also see two films: *Cracow Kazimierz* (1936) by Julian Brian, an American documentary filmmaker, and the German documentary *Moving to the Ghetto in Cracow* (1941). Prayers are also said here on certain occasions.

Ul. Kupa 18, ☎ +12 4305577, e-mail: synagogaizaaka@eranet.pl.
Open daily 9am–7pm, except Saturdays and Jewish holidays.
Entrance fee: 7 zl.

The Kupa Synagogue

The synagogue was built in the 1740s, thanks to a donation made by the goldsmiths of Kazimierz. The word *kupa* means a contribution made by the members of a *kahal*. From the beginning of its existence the synagogue was linked with a Jewish hospital and poorhouse, thus resulting in two alternative names: the Hospital Synagogue and the Synagogue of the Poor. Its present form is the result of reconstruction works between

The *aron ha-kodesh* of the Kupa Synagogue dates from the 17th century.

1830 and 1834, although other modifications were also introduced later (the western wing was added in 1861). The interior furnishings were destroyed during the Second World War, but this did not prevent the synagogue from re-opening in 1945. It was, however, closed soon after and allocated to a co-operative for the disabled, which used it as a storehouse until 1991. The paintings in the prayer room for men depict the Wailing Wall and the Jaffa Gate (eastern wall), a view of Tiberias and the Mamre Oak Wood (southern wall), the panorama of Hebron and Haifa (western wall) and the panorama of Jerusalem and also of the Flood (northern wall). The foundations of the *bimah* also remain.

The original paintings (1830–1834 and ca 1930) have remained in the prayer hall for men.

The street, today called ul. Warszauera, was once named ul. Ubogich (Street of the Poor) as it was inhabited by impoverished craftsmen only. The name of the steet was changed in honour of a local physician, Jonatan Warszauer, who had made a great contribution to free healthcare for those in need.

Ul. Warszauera 8. The renovation of the synagogue was completed at the beginning of 2002. It will probably be open to visitors during the Festival of Jewish Culture.

The Ritual Slaughterhouse for Poultry

In Plac Nowy, take a look at the building in the centre. It is a circular pavilion built in 1900 for the purposes of trade. In 1927 the board of the Jewish community leased it out and converted it into a ritual slaughterhouse for poultry. This function ceased during the Second World War.

Ritual Slaughter

Jewish religious laws are very strict about the slaughter of animals. It is performed by a *shochet* (ritual butcher) and a *bodek* (assistant). The animals must be *kosher* and the knife perfectly smooth and sharp. The throat is slit using no more than three cuts. The meat is then inspected by the assistant. If there are signs of sickness he declares it to be *trayf* (contaminated). The object is to drain out the blood, which Jews are forbidden to consume.

Ul. Meiselsa

There are two houses of prayer here: *B'nei Emuna* (Children of Faith) from 1886 at ul. Meiselsa 17, now the headquarters of the Jewish Cultural Centre of the Judaica Foundation, and *Chevra Tehilim* (the Psalm Brotherhood) from 1896 at ul. Meiselsa 18, now used by the Krakus Song and Dance Ensemble.

The Tempel Synagogue

The walls of the Tempel Synagogue are adorned with geometric and plant motifs.

The most recent of the Jewish synagogues of Kazimierz is the so-called progressive synagogue built in 1860 thanks to the efforts of the Society for Religion and Civilisation and extended in later years (1868, 1883, 1893, 1924). Ozjasz Thon, the famous Zionist activist (d. 1936) was a preacher here before the war. The original exterior as well as wall paintings from 1904 and the stained-glass windows (ca 1890 and 1909, the only ones of their kind in Poland) are still there. The Neo-Renaissance *aron ha-kodesh*, the memorial plaques, the candlesticks and even the fence remain as well. The synagogue is open daily, although since the death of its last cantor Abraham Lesman in 1985, services rarely take place.

Ul. Miodowa 24. Open daily 10am–3pm, entrance fee: 5 zl. It is also open during services and concerts.

The Jewish Cemetery in ul. Miodowa

The Jewish cemetery in ul. Miodowa has functioned continuously since 1800.

Opened on the orders of the Austrian authorities, when Poland was partitioned and Cracow belonged to the Austro-Hungarian Empire, this new cemetery replaced the old one. The Nazis used some of the gravestones as construction material. It was restored by the American Joint Distribution Committee sometime after 1957. Several thousand gravestones are still there today. This cemetery is the resting place of such eminent persons as the distinguished Zionist rabbi Ozjasz Thon (d. 1936), a preacher at the Tempel synagogue and member of the pre-war parliament of the Polish Republic; the composer and conductor of Cracow Philharmonic Jerzy

Józef Sare (above: portrait by Jacek Malczewski) was deputy mayor of Cracow for over 20 years

Gert (d. 1968); the painter Maurycy Gottlieb (1856 –1879); and the deputy mayor of Cracow Józef Sare (d. 1929). Every kind of symbol and theme characteristic of Jewish sepulchral art can be found on the tombs situated here.

Ul. Miodowa 55. Official opening hours: Mon–Thu 10am–3pm (5pm in summer), Fri 10am–2pm; entrance through the hallway of the funeral home. One of the gates is often open outside official opening hours.

Other Monuments of Jewish Culture

There are many more places linked with the Jews of Kazimierz and Cracow.

Houses of prayer: Sheirit B'nei Emuna (The Remaining Children of the Faith) dating from 1914 (ul. Bocheńska 4); that of Salomon Deiches, from 1910 (ul. Brzozowa 6); that of the Bobowa Chasidim, from 1871 (ul. Estery 12, on the first floor); that of Mordechaj Tigner, from 1913 (ul. Grodzka 28–30); the Mizrachi (Eastern), circa 1939, next to the Isaac synagogue, now the Ronald S. Lauder Foundation (ul. Kupa 18); the prayer house of the Radom Chasids Society for Prayer and Charity, circa 1900 (ul. Józefa 22); the House of Learning of the Shir Synagogue Society from 1898 (ul. Kupa 20); Ahavat Re (Love of One's Neighbour) circa 1900, now an Orthodox Christian church (ul. Szpitalna 24); The Michał Hirsch Cypres Prayer and Charity Association, from 1887 (św. Agnieszki 5); Beit Midrash Chasidim (the Chasidic House of Learning), from 1881 (ul. Trynitarska 18 in the courtyard, and ul. Węgierska 5).

Schools: the Hilfstein Hebrew High School, 1917 (ul. Brzozowa 5); the Cheder Ivri School and the Tachkemoni High School, 1929 (ul. Miodowa 26); the Jewish School of Handicrafts, 1938 (ul. Podbrzezie 3); the Jewish Students' Hall of Residence, 1924, later the Tarbut School (ul. Przemyska 3).

The other remaining buildings are: the Jewish Hospital (ul. Skawińska 8, 1861–1866), remodelled and now part of Collegium Medicum at the Jagiellonian University of Cracow; Offices of the Jewish Community (ul. Skawińska 2, 1909–1911). There are also some remains of the Jewish town walls in Plac Nowy (17th century) between the houses at Plac Bawół 2 and 3 (1627) and in ul. Dajwór 19 and 21.

The Judaica Foundation – Centre for Jewish Culture is situated in ul. Meiselsa 17. It has been created for the protection of cultural heritage of Polish Jews as well as for educational and commemorative activities.

OŚWIĘCIM | Yiddish: Oyshvitzim, Oshpitzin Oshvitzin

Auschwitz is one of the 20th century's symbols of absolute evil. A visit to this death camp is everyone's moral duty, even though the installations designed and erected here so that man could more effectively murder his fellow man are truly appalling. Everything here is a warning to posterity and to omit Auschwitz would mean to turn a blind eye to the tragic fate of Polish Jews whose epilogue was so mercilessly written by history.

The beginnings of Jewish settlement in Oświęcim go back to the Middle Ages. The town developed as a dynamic centre of the salt trade. The influx of Jews must have been considerable, for as early as 1563 they were forbidden to build houses around the market square. A synagogue was erected in 1588 and a cemetery established nearby. According to records from 1561, Jews were required to pay their taxes with pepper and saffron. As time passed, the town fell into a long period of economic stagnation, interrupted in the middle of the 19th century by the construction of a railway station.

At the beginning of the 20th century Jews constituted 50% of the local population, and in 1939 as much as 58% (7,000). The Jewish quarter spread north of the market square and as far as the bank of the river. There were five sports clubs, an amateur theatre group and the Society of Hebrew Women.

Religious life was cultivated in the Jewish High School, eight *chadarim* and three *yeshivot* (in Bełz, Bobowa and Radomsko). Oświęcim was also a place where alcoholic drinks such as Haberfeld's famous Pesachówka (*Pesach* vodka) were produced.

No more than seventy Oświęcim Jews survived the war, and they all emigrated soon after. Services are held today in the synagogue of *Chevrah Lomdei Mishnayot* (The Society for the Study of the Mishna), but only on certain occasions.

The Synagogue of the Society for the Study of the Mishna and the Jewish Centre in Oświęcim

The synagogue of *Chevrat Lomdei Mishnayot* (Society for the Study of the Mishna), together with the adjacent buildings now housing the Jewish Centre, are the most important historical monument of Jewish Oświęcim from before the Second World War. The synagogue was once situated within the boundaries

Many monuments from Oświęcim's Jewish past still remain. There is the cemetery in ul. Dąbrowskiego which leads in the direction of Dwory (the key is available from the Jewish Centre). The present location of its several hundred gravestones does not correspond to the pre-war one, which often makes it difficult to find the right grave. In ul. Berka Joselewicza you can find what is left of the wrecked *yeshivah* of the Bobowa Chasids. At the rear are the huge ruins of the Jakub Haberfeld vodka and liqueur factory (below, original drink labels).

Tourist Attractions

The remodelled 13th-century castle on the River Soła; the remains of defence walls; the Gothic church of the Most Holy Virgin Mary the Succourer (first half of the 14th century, remodelled between 1899 and 1906). The Town Hall from the first half of the 19th century and several houses from the 18th century.

The synagogue's furnishings are contemporary in origin (late 20th century).

of the Jewish quarter. Its present building was erected in 1900. Its clearly defined taller northern section is quite eye-catching. Two original plaques remain; the first commemorating its foundation: "This synagogue was built by Minda Cwaijtel on the anniversary of the death of her husband Shlomo Zalman in the year 1900" (east wall), and the second commemorating officials linked to the synagogue, whose surnames were: Zinger, Goldsztajn and Nejberg (1928). The synagogue is looked after by the Auschwitz Jewish Center Foundation housed in the same building. The exhibition in the Center depicts the way of life of the former Jewish community in Oświęcim. It covers a wide range of educational and cultural activities, focusing mainly on commemorating the victims of the Holocaust by studying Jewish life and culture. On request you can also watch a film and hire a guide (prior booking by telephone required).

The Jewish Center in Auschwitz, Plac ks. Skarbka 3, ☎ +33 8447002, info@ajcf.pl; open: Sun–Thu 8.30am–5pm, Fri (in summer) 8.30am–5pm, (in winter) 8.30am–2pm. The Foundation also has an office in New York City: Auschwitz Jewish Center Foundation, 36 West 44th Street, Suite 310, NY 10036 (☎ +212 5751050, info@ajcf.org) and a web site in English: www.ajcf.org.

The Auschwitz Concentration Camp

The Auschwitz-Birkenau concentration camp was declared a UNESCO World Heritage site in 1979.

The first prisoners, 728 Poles from Tarnów, were brought here on 14 April 1940. The camp soon became a place for the extermination of Jews and Gypsies. As time passed the camp was extended and 40 sub-camps were set up nearby, including the death camp of Brzezinka (Birkenau), the largest cemetery in the world.

Deserted military barracks built before the Second World War were chosen by the Nazis as the location for their perfectly organised death machine. It led the victims from the gate with the inscription *Arbeit macht frei* to the flames of the crematoria, as if through the circles of hell.

In January 1942, the Nazis began the process of extermination, the main centre of which was the camp at Birkenau. The summer of 1944 was a period of intensive mass murder and twenty thousand people a day were killed here. The approach of the Soviet Army forced the Nazis to close the camp and its last 64,000 victims were marched into the depths of the Reich, this tragic evacuation being known as "the Death March". On 27 January 1945, the Russians arrived in Auschwitz, where they found seven thousand prisoners (including several hundred children) in a state of complete exhaustion but still alive. The exact number of people murdered in Auschwitz is unknown, but it is somewhere between 1,2 and 1,4 million people.

The entrance to the camp leads into a modern pavilion in which there is a tourist information desk where you can also hire a guide. It is advisable to follow the set route that starts here. It will take you to all the most important places. On the left-hand side there are some administrative buildings and the SS guardhouse, which once contained the office of the camp commandant. Next to it there is one of the best known gates in the world, with the derisive inscription "Arbeit macht frei" (Work sets you free) over it, although Dante's "Abandon all hope" would be more appropriate. The route takes you past the first camp alley and turns right into the second one. There are several exhibitions in the subsequent buildings in this alley. The blocks located near the wall contain more general displays (block 4 – extermination, block 5 – material evidence of the crime, block 6 – life of a prisoner, block 7 – living and sanitary conditions). Among these particularly shocking places on the same side of the camp

It was the custom among Chasidic Jews to travel all year long from town to town as beggars and in this way to learn humility. They never stayed in any one place for less than a day, regardless of the humiliation to which they might be subjected. They never remained anywhere longer than two nights, even if they met with hospitality. Somewhere around the year 1760 the young rabbi Elimelech of Leżajsk (see page 246) and his brother Zusya of Annopol wandered throughout Poland, going from place to place. One afternoon the two brothers, hungry and worn out, arrived in a small town. Although they were starving, they were unable to eat. Even though they were exhausted, they could not sleep. They sensed something which they had never before experienced. They were gripped by a feeling of inexpressible fear. They were struck by unbelievable terror. In the middle of the night they left the town and never returned. In Yiddish the town was called Oshpitzin – Oświęcim. (Quoted from Byron L. Sherwin, *The Spiritual Heritage of the Polish Jews*).

FORMER KL AUSCHWITZ I IN OŚWIĘCIM – ORIENTATION MAP

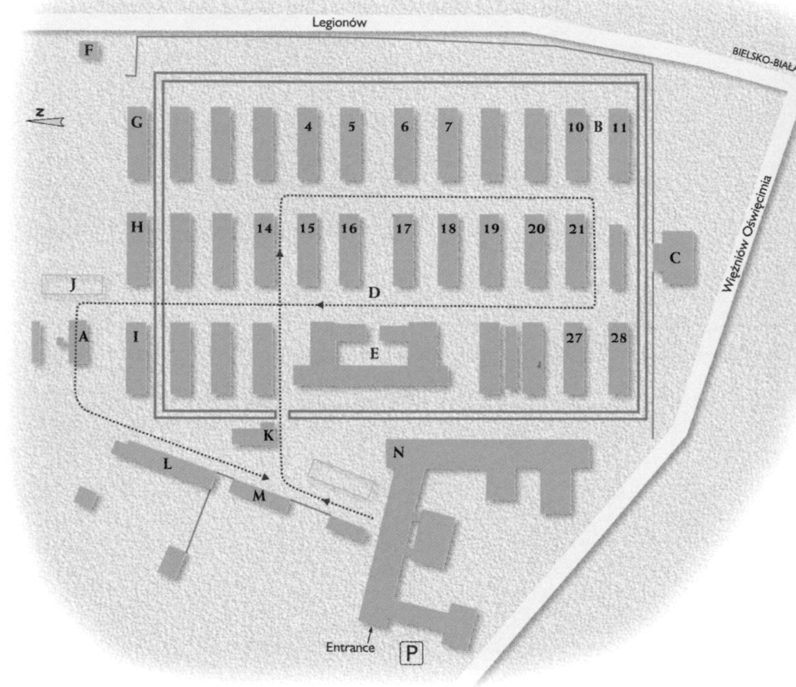

◄······ Route for visitors

Camp structures still remaining

Structures no longer existing

General Exhibition

4 Extermination
5 Material Evidence of Crime
6 Prisoner's Life
7 Living and Sanitary Conditions
11 "Death Block"

Other Displays

14 Former Soviet Union
15 Poland
16 The Czech Republic and Slovakia
17 Austria and former Yugoslavia
18 Hungary
20 France and Belgium
21 Italy and Holland
27 Jewish Martyrology and Struggle

Structures of greatest importance

A Gas chamber and crematorium
B Death Wall
C Storage for Zyklon B and property plundered from victims
D Roll-call square and multiple gallows
E Camp kitchen
F Camp commandant's house
G Administration Headquarters
H SS administration
I SS hospital
J Political Unit (camp Gestapo)
K SS Guardhouse and ca commandant's office
L SS garages
M Administration barrack
N Camp prisoners' registration building
10 Sterilisation experimen block
19, 20, 21, 28 Prisoners' hospital

The March of the Living

The March of the Living, the most important event commemorating the Holocaust and its victims, is organised every two years during the festival of *Yom ha-Shoah* (Holocaust Day, the 27th day of the month Nisan). The main ceremony takes place beneath the memorial in the former concentration camp at Birkenau. It is the crowning point of the march undertaken by several thousand people, starting at the Auschwitz museum. The names of those murdered are recalled, *kaddish* is recited, and some of those present record their experiences on wooden boards, which are then stored in the museum. The second part of the March of the Living takes place in Israel during the festivals of *Yom ha-Zikaron* (Remembrance Day) and *Yom ha-Atzmaut* (Independence Day).

there is block 10, where sterilisation experiments took place, and block 11, known as the "death block", where victims suffered unspeakable cruelty. Here in the courtyard there is a wall where thousands of innocent people were killed. It is known as the "death wall". In the blocks on the right-hand side there are memorial displays set up by the governments of European states in homage to their citizens (mostly Jewish) murdered in Auschwitz. In block 14, there is a display by the former republics of the Soviet Union; in block 15 – Poland; 16 – The Czech Republic and Slovakia; 17 – Austria and former Yugoslavia; 18 – Hungary; 20 – France and Belgium; 21 – Italy and Holland. After the Italian Dutch pavilion the route turns back into the first alley. Here you will pass a wall behind which there was a storehouse for the poisonous gas Zyklon B and property plundered from the prisoners. In the first alley there is block

Abraham Hirchson, the Israeli member of parliament, whose idea it was to have a March of the Living, justified the necessity of such an event for young people in the following way. "These youngsters will form a link between those who suffered and the next generation when those who survived the Holocaust will no longer be with us".

Concentration camps were of serious economic importance as the prisoners provided free labour to many German firms, such as IG Farben, Krupp or Siemens-Schuckert Werke AG. According to Odilo Globocnik's report, from April 1942 to December 1943 the Reichsbank received: 73 million German marks, 2,909.69 kg of gold, 18,733.69 kg of silver, 15.14 kg of platinum, 249,771 dollars in gold, 15,883 golden rings with diamonds, 2,511.87 carates of diamonds, 1,900 freight carriages of clothes.

Jews from many countries ended up in Auschwitz. The list is truly appalling: Austria, Belgium, Belarus, Bosnia, Croatia, the Czech Republic, Denmark, France, Germany, Great Britain, Greece, Holland, Hungary, Italy, Macedonia, Norway, Poland, Romania, Russia, Serbia, Slovakia, Slovenia, Spain, Switzerland, Turkey, Ukraine, and the United States.

27 containing the exhibition about the struggle and martyrology of Jews. This exposition (open to visitors 8.30am–6pm) devoted to the victims of the Holocaust, was opened in 1968. Further on in block 28 are the remains of the camp hospital. The route then leads straight on right across the camp and passes the large kitchen buildings. At the end there is a gas chamber and a crematorium, astonishingly small in size. Equally shocking are the "technical improvements", such as special carts on rails, once used to remove bodies. There are also the gallows on which in 1947 the commandant of the camp Rudolf Hoess was hanged in public after being tried and sentenced to death.

The Death Camp at Birkenau

The camp at Birkenau, built in 1942 at a distance of three kilometres from Auschwitz, had no other purpose than to create a centre of extermination operating on a scale unknown in the history of the world. Unlike the main camp in Auschwitz, there was no existing infrastructure in Birkenau before the Second World War. Therefore its 300 buildings stretching over a total area of 175 hectares had to be erected from scratch. Most of the instruments of mass-murder in the Auschwitz system of camps were installed there: the four crematoria with gas chambers, two provisional gas chambers as well as burning pits and furnaces. The number of prisoners at any time was as many as 100,000. Only 45 buildings and 22 wooden barracks remain. Follow the marked route. It starts by the death gate (the entrance by the former main SS guardhouse) and runs along the main alley to the railway unloading platform. On the right-hand side there are the following former camp sectors: BIIa, known as "the quarantine section" (the barracks are still intact); BIIb – the Theresienstadt family camp for Czech Jews from Terezin (one barrack); BIIc – the camp for Hungarian Jews. Here you should turn left to get to the adjacent alley, in which the

The two camps now form one Auschwitz-Birkenau State Museum, ul. Więźniów Oświęcimia 20, ☎ +33 8432022 or 8432077; opening hours 8am–3pm (16 Dec–29 Feb), 8am–4pm (1–31 Mar, 1 Nov–15 Dec), 8am–5pm (1–30 Apr, 1–31 Oct), 8am–6pm (1–31 May, 1–30 Sep), 8am–7pm (1 Jun–31 Aug). The museum has a guarded parking area (7am–7pm). Arrival in Auschwitz is usually at the combined bus and railway station. From here it is easy to get to the site of the Auschwitz concentration camp; take ul. Wyzwolenia as far as ul. Więźniów Oświęcimia or ul. S. Leszczyńskiej. Both streets lead straight to the museum. You can also go by local transport; bus #1, get off at the "Społem" stop. The site of the Birkenau extermination camp is situated 3 km away. To get there turn into ul. Leszczyńskiej from the roundabout in ul. Wyzwolenia and then immediately take the road on the right, leading to Katowice. A bus runs between the two camps (15 Apr–31 Oct).

Former KL Auschwitz II-Birkenau in Brzezinka
Orientation Map

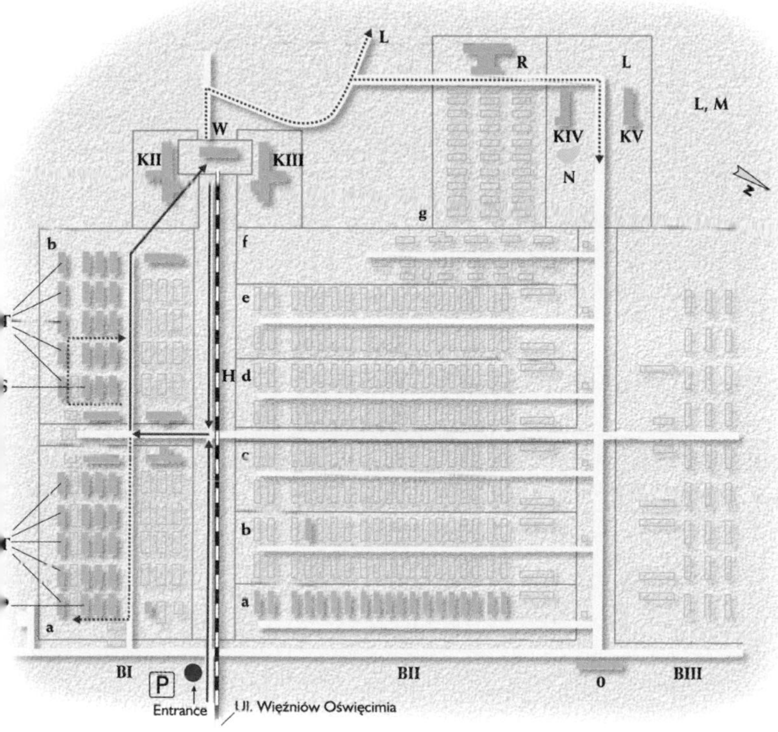

● Tourist information, former SS guardhouse

← Main route for visitors

←······ Additional routes for visitors

Barracks preserved in original condition

Structures no longer existing

- BIa Women's camp
- BIb Initially a men's camp, from 1943 a women's camp
- BIIa "Quarantine" section
- BIIb Theresienstadt family camp
- BIIc Camp for Hungarian Jews
- BIId Men's camp
- BIIe Family camp for Gypsies
- BIIf Prisoners' hospital
- BIIg Storage for property plundered from the victims ("Canada")
- BIII Camp extension under construction ("Mexico")
- H Railway loading platform
- KII-V The remains of crematoria and gas chambers
- L Burning furnaces
- M Collective graves of Soviet prisoners
- N The pond in which human ashes were disposed
- O Commandant's offices
- P "Death Block"
- R Camp baths
- S Penalty unit
- T Prisoners' latrines and washrooms
- W The International Memorial to the Victims of Fascism

CHRZANÓW

In Chrzanów, just 19 kilometres from Oświęcim (road 933), in ul. Borowcowa, a very interesting cemetery remains intact. It was established in 1759 and contains about a thousand tombs. Here you can find the *oholot* of these *tzaddikim*: David Halberstam (d. 1894), his sons, Józef (d. 1902), Józef Elimelech (d. 1907), Moses (d. 1915), Naftali (d. 1915) as well as Salomon Buchner (1928). Other local places of interest are the 19th-century synagogue converted into a covered market (ul. 3 Maja 9; the community synagogue was demolished in 1973) and exhibits connected with Jewish culture in the museum at ul. Mickiewicza 13, ☎ +32 6235173.

largest number of camp buildings have remained. The barracks on both sides once belonged to sections BIa and BIb which constituted the camp for women. Among the barracks are those of the penal colony, the latrines and the prisoners' washrooms. The remains of the crematoria and gas chambers are the focal points of the exhibition. Between them there is the International Memorial in Honour of the Victims of the Camp. The bathhouses, the pond into which human ashes were dumped as well as the administration headquarters also remain. This is the largest cemetery in the world and visitors should remember to conduct themselves accordingly.

Bochnia
In Bochnia, the synagogue (built in 1932–1939) is now a bank (ul. Trudna 13). There is also a ritual slaughterhouse for poultry and the flat where the butcher used to live. The local Jewish cemetery established sometime after 1862 contains a hundred gravestones, including the tomb of *tzaddik* Asher Maier Halberstam, the rabbi of Bochnia (d. 1932).

BRZESKO | Yiddish: Briegel

Jews first came to Brzesko towards the end of the 17th century. For a long time the local Jewish community was under the authority of the Wiśnicz *kahal*. In the 19th century two important Jewish families settled in Brzesko: the Lipszyc Chasidic dynasty and the Brandstaetters. In 1939 Jews formed half of the town's population and lived in the so-called Dolne Miasto (Lower Town) district, to the east of the town centre. The "most Jewish" streets were ul. Puszkina and ul. Długa. Many of the pre-war buildings still remain.

THE SYNAGOGUE

The local synagogue, with an exterior appearance and interior arrangement (main prayer hall for men – prayer rooms for women – vestibule) very typical of provincial synagogues serving the needs of the Jewish communities in Galicia, is still in quite good condition. It was erected in 1904 on the site of the former synagogue, which burned down during a fire in the town. The synagogue was also the

TOURIST ATTRACTIONS

The former urban complex with a market square, a parish church from 1447 (remodelled), and a palace from 1898, now housing a school. The town gained fame thanks to the local brewery established in 1845.

The Brandstaetters, renowned for their intellectual prowess, were one of the most eminent Polish-Jewish families. Their name was given its standing by Mordechai David Brandstaetter (1844–1928), a writer and follower of the *Haskalah* movement. He chose to write in Hebrew. His mode of expression is highly regarded and some of his output, translated into English and Russian, ranks among the jewels of Hebrew prose. His most important works are *Kfar mezagegim* (Village of Glaziers), *Zalman goy* (Zalman the Unbeliever) and his autobiography *Mi-toldot hayal* (The Story of my Life). Mordechai's grandson, Roman Brandstaetter (1906–1987) achieved true greatness with *The Wise Rabbi of Tarnów*, a work of Polish rather than Jewish literature. A graduate of the Jagiellonian University in Cracow, Brandstaetter began his career in 1927, writing exclusively in Polish. At first he concentrated mainly on poetry (four volumes between 1931 and 1935) and on relations between Poles and Jews, (*The Tragedy of Julian Klaczko, The Jewish Legion of Adam Mickiewicz, The Question of Polish-Jewish Poetry*). He replied to anti-semitic attacks with the brilliant essay *A Conspiracy of Eunuchs*. Having spent the war in Russia and the Middle East, he ended up in Rome, where, in 1948, he experienced a spiritual reawakening and was baptised. This heralded the most important period in the writing career of Roman Brandstaetter in which his creations were inspired by biblical themes (*Word of Words, Four Biblical Poems, Jesus of Nazareth* and *Biblical Circle*). Jewish motifs returned in *The Other Flowers of St Francis of Assisi*, with its allusions to Chasidic allegorical tradition, as well as in *I am the Jew from the Wedding* (a reference to *The Wedding*, a play by S. Wyspiański).

Roman Brandstaetter

seat of the *kahal* office. After the Second World War it was remodelled and became the home of a library which functions to this very day, as well as the workshops of the local co-operative for the disabled. Not far from the synagogue there is a 19th-century house of prayer (ul. Dluga 3) which now stands empty.

Ul. Puszkina 2; the library is open on Mondays, Wednesdays and Fridays 8am–6pm; on Tuesdays 8am–3pm and on Saturdays 8am–1pm.

The Jewish cemetery in Brzesko was established after the 17th century cemetery in the town centre had reached capacity.

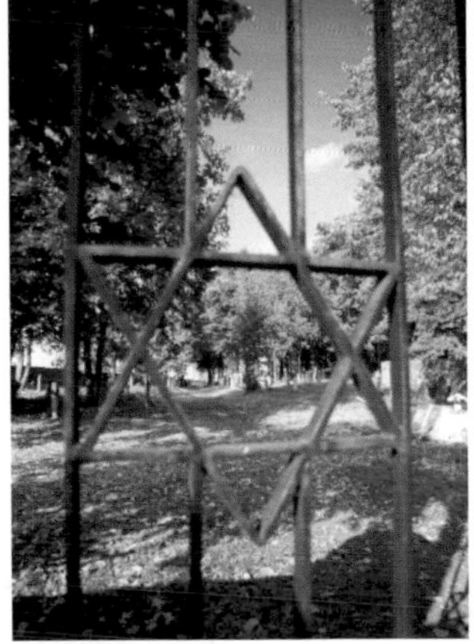

The Jewish Cemetery

The cemetery was marked out sometime around the year 1824 (in a monograph by Iwona Zawidzka the previous date of 1846 was put in doubt and revised). The most interesting landmarks here are the two *oholot*. The older of the two contains the graves of three rabbis from the Lipszyc family: Arie Leibush (d. 1846), his son Meshulam Zalman Jonatan (d. 1855) and the third member of the dynasty, grandson Tovie Lipszyc (1826–1912). The new *ohel* was built in the 1990s above the graves of Efraim Templer (head of *beth ha-midrash*; 1867–1938) and four members of the Templer family who were either rabbis or teachers. An enclosed memorial surrounded by a fence, was built

Rabbi Arie Leibush Lipszyc was a disciple of the Seer of Lublin (above: his headstone in the *ohel* at the Jewish cemetery in Brzesko).

in honour of the Jews murdered by the Germans on 18 June 1942. The last burial took place here in 1969.

Ul. Czarnowiejska. The key is available from Ms Maria Martyna, ul. Czarnowiejska 34 (opposite the cemetery gate).

TARNÓW | Yiddish: Tornev, Torne, Tarna

Tarnów once had one of the largest Jewish communities in the Małopolska region. First accounts of Jews settling here date from 1445. They were probably merchants trading in grain and wine. Initially the Tarnów community was a branch of the Cracow *kahal*. In 1581, the owner of the town Konstanty Ostrogski granted the Jews the privileges of trade from stalls, homes and on the marketplace, as well as of the production and sale of alcoholic beverages. Economic freedom was the main factor attracting Jews to the town. In the 18th century their number exceeded one thousand, which was more than 30% of the local population. They had several representatives in the Diet of the Four Lands. Towards the end of the 18th century new movements appeared: Chasidism (the influence of the Halberstam and Horovitz dynasties) and the *Haskalah*. In 1788, the first lay Jewish school was opened here thanks to the financial support of Naftali Herz Homberg.

At the outbreak of the Second World War, 25,000 Jews lived in Tarnów (48% of the local population). The Nazis created a ghetto for 40,000 people and from here they deported their victims to the concentration camps in Bełżec, Płaszów and Auschwitz. After the Second World War, a small group of refugees from the former Polish eastern borderland territories settled here, but with the passing of time they slowly disappeared as a result of several waves of emigration.

Tourist Attractions

The centre of Tarnów is one of the prettiest historical urban complexes in Poland. Its most precious monuments are: the 14th-century Town Hall, remodelled by J.M. Padovano in the second half of the 16th century (now the District Museum); the late Gothic cathedral church of the Nativity of the Most Holy Virgin Mary, ca 1400, later extended, with extremely rich interior decor and furnishings; the houses (16th–19th centuries); the remnants of the city walls (14th–16th centuries); the canonries from the first half of the 16th century (including the Mikołajowski House, now the home of the Diocesan Museum containing an interesting gallery of Gothic sculpture); the former Bernardine church from 1468, remodelled in 1823, now containing a historical exhibition; the former Bernardine nunnery from the 17th–18th centuries (now converted into a monastery); the ruins of the Tarnowski castle from 1340, situated on St Martin's Hill; the mausoleum of General Józef Bem in the city park. Numerous historical monuments can also be found in the suburbs: the mansion houses (18th–19th centuries) as well as the 18th-century palace (Gumniska); the 15th-century wooden church of the Most Holy Virgin Mary (na Burku), and the church of the Holy Trinity from 1562, also wooden (na Terlikówce).

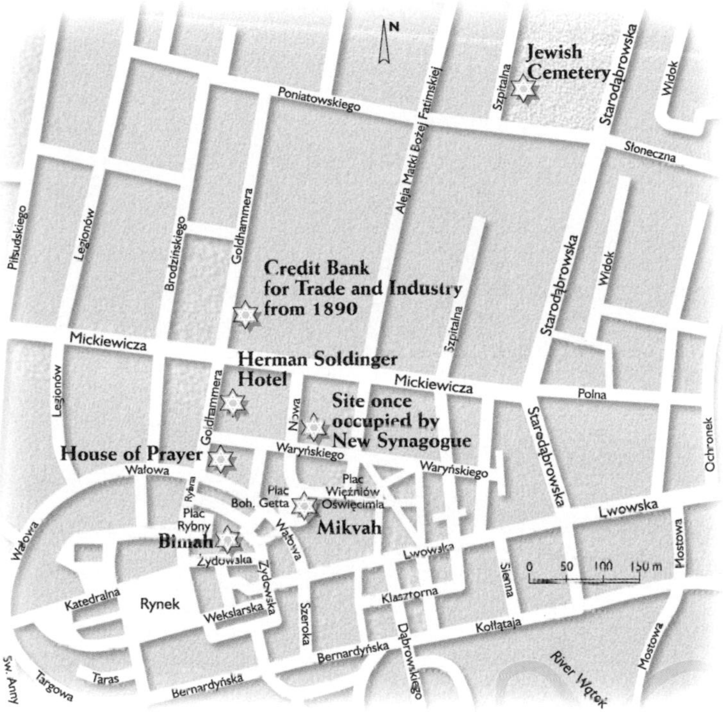

Suggested Route

MARKET SQUARE → UL. ŻYDOWSKA → THE BIMAH OF THE OLD SYNAGOGUE → THE MIKVAH → THE SITE ONCE OCCUPIED BY THE NEW SYNAGOGUE → UL. GOLDHAMMERA → THE JEWISH CEMETERY

The history of Tarnów Jews seemingly came to an end in 1993, when the last caretaker of the house of prayer (ul. Goldhammera) passed away. The synagogue's furnishings were moved to the Regional Museum and the keys transferred to the Jewish community in Cracow. *Landsmanshaftn* of Tarnów Jews operate today in France, Israel, Canada and the United States.

The Jewish quarter stretched over the north-eastern part of the centre. The district of Grabówka was the area inhabited by Chasids. In 1833 the Jewish community applied to the municipal authorities for permission to extend their area of residence. Permission, however, was

A walk around the landmarks of Jewish heritage in Tarnów takes about 90 minutes.

In the 19th century many Jews lived in Tarnów's main square.

not granted. Therefore, a proposal was made to build "a truly Jewish town" outside the city walls. The project never materialised, but several buildings which bore testimony to the concept were erected. In particular the New Jubilee Synagogue (built between 1865 and 1908), which no longer exists, and the ritual bath (built in 1904 in Moorish style), which still remains.

The Market Square

On the doorframe of house No 21 one can still see the indentations where the *mezzuzot* used to be. The building now houses the Tarnów District Museum (☎ +14 6212149), which has an interesting collection of Judaica. The original privilege document from 1667 and three scrolls of the *Torah* as well as documents and photographs from the last Tarnów synagogue (closed in 1993) are its most precious exhibits. The Market Square is also a place of Jewish martyrology. From 11 to 19 June 1942 it was the arena for the first act of murder of 10,000 local Jews. For the Jewish *Landsmanshaftn* these dates are days of remembrance. In 1997 a commemorative plaque in honour of the victims of the tragedy was erected on the corner of ul. Żydowska; the pavement there having been sanctified with their blood.

Ul. Żydowska

From the Market Square walk along ul. Żydowska (Jewish Street). Many 17th and 18th-century tenement houses with typical narrow entrance halls and front walls still remain. You will easily spot the iron display windows which belonged to former shops. On the left-hand side of ul. Żydowska you will also see an enclosure made of iron bars (from 1900) and a spacious square behind it. Towering above it is the only remaining part of the oldest Tarnów synagogue.

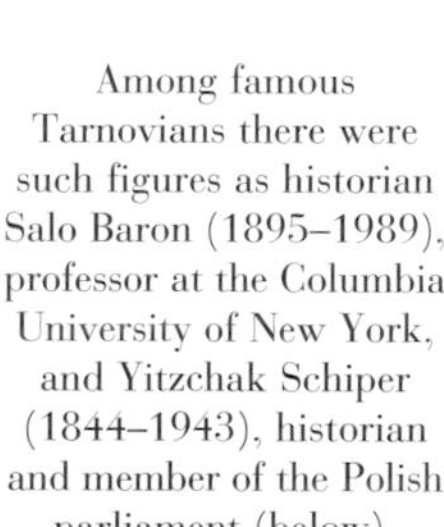

Among famous Tarnovians there were such figures as historian Salo Baron (1895–1989), professor at the Columbia University of New York, and Yitzchak Schiper (1844–1943), historian and member of the Polish parliament (below).

The Bimah of the Old Synagogue

The *bimah* is all that remains of the Old Synagogue.

The Old Synagogue, almost certainly dating from the beginning of the 17th century, stood here until the outbreak of the Second World War. It was on the site of an even older synagogue built sometime before 1581. The Old Synagogue was burnt down in November 1939 and then demolished. Only the *bimah* survived. You can still see some remains of the floor as well as of stucco decorations crowning the columns. Traces of the fire are still visible. In 1987 the *bimah* was covered with a roof in order to protect the monument from the weather.

Ul. Żydowska, a square on the left between the market square and the little turning to the right.

The Mikvah

The *mikvah* was built in 1904 in Moorish style, much in vogue at that time. The plans were drawn by F. Hackbeil and M. Mikos. During the Second World War this building witnessed particularly tragic events, as it was turned into a temporary concentration camp for prisoners awaiting deportation to Auschwitz-Birkenau. Some of the most eminent Tarnów Jews of the pre-war period passed through here, including Maksymilian Rozenbusz, the headmaster of the Hebrew High School; Jakow Szwarc, industrialist; Emil Wider, attorney; and also a distingushed geographer Zdzisław Simche, a Catholic. Not one of them survived. They became the first victims in the history of the Auschwitz death camp. Both the memorial situated here and the very name of the square (The Square of the Prisoners of Auschwitz) pay homage to the victims

The building of the *mikvah* (ritual bath) is one of the most impressive edifices left to posterity by the Jews of Tarnów.

of racism. For many years after the Second World War the *mikvah* was used as a public bath. Later, after an overhaul, it was turned into a department store.

Plac Więźniów Oświęcimia.

Ul. Goldhammera (Goldhammer Street)

Elias Goldhammer (1851–1912) was the son of a tailor from Dynów. He graduated in law from the Jagiellonian University in Cracow and then settled in Tarnów, where he later became deputy mayor. He was a distinguished orator and attorney specialising in penal law. When Goldhammer passed away in 1912, the City Council of Tarnów decided to honour this great man by naming the most Jewish street in the city after him.

Some say that the famous ul. Goldhammera is still remembered in Israel. It was a a symbol of splendour and wealth of Tarnow's Jewish elite and known as the "Wall Street of Tarnów".

It is worth taking a look at the building at ul. Goldhammera 6, where an inscription in Yiddish and Polish, visible through the peeling paint, advertises a restaurant from the 1930s.

The easiest way to get here from the main square is via ul. Piekarska, Plac Rybny and ul. Rybna. Ul. Goldhammera contains several places of interest. In house No 1, on the first floor, there was Tarnow's last *beth ha-midrash* (house of study), which functioned until 1993. There is not much left to see nowadays. The *aron ha-kodesh*, the *bimah* and the benches were moved to the Regional Museum at Rynek 21. The next building, at ul. Goldhammera 3, is Herman Soldinger's hotel designed by I. Apperman and erected in 1904. After the end of the Second World War, this is where the Jewish community of Tarnów had its offices and house of prayer. The later fate of Soldinger's hotel is the story of the collapse of this prestigious establishment, once advertised in old Austrian-Hungarian guidebooks. At first it was turned into a hotel called Leliva and then converted into headquarters of the regional committee of the Communist Party. At ul. Goldhammera 5 there is an eclectic 1890 edifice of the Credit Bank for Trade and Industry. In its hallway you can still see plaques commemorating the founder of the building Herman Merz, chairman of the Jewish community, as well as the eminent deputy mayor Elias Goldhammer himself.

The Site Once Occupied by the New Synagogue

The New Synagogue on the corner of ul. Nowa and ul. Waryńskiego was opened on 18 March 1908 (the birthday of Franz Josef, the Austrian Emperor). This is how it got the name "Jubilee Synagogue", and even the "Franz Josef Synagogue". Photographs taken before the Second World War show its imposing dome. Set on fire in 1939, for a long time it resisted attempts by the Nazis to destroy it, until they finally managed to blow it up with explosives. The place where the synagogue

The New Synagogue was considered to be one of the most beautiful buildings in Tarnów.

once stood was honoured with a commemorative plaque in September 1993. Its only remaining element, a single column, can now be found in the Jewish cemetery, where it forms part of a memorial.

The Jewish Cemetery

The Jewish cemetery in Tarnów, comparable with those of Cracow, is one of the oldest and most interesting cemeteries in southern Poland. It was established beyond the historical boundaries of Tarnów in the second half of the 16th century. Its several thousand gravestones from the period between the 17th and the 20th centuries are situated in an area of 3.2 hectares. Among them there are the tombs of the most important Jewish families of Tarnów: the Aberdams, the Brandstetters, the Maschlers, the Merzes and the Szancers. Many local rabbis are also buried here: Samuel Shmelke Horovitz (d. 1713), Yitzchak Ayzik (d. 1756), Eliezer ben Yitzchak (d. 1811), Izrael Rapaport (d. 1881), Abele Sznur (d. 1917) and Mayer Arak (d.1925). In the eastern part, behind a concrete wall, there is the resting place of Arie Leib, son of Ezechiel Shraga from Sieniawa, the great *tzaddik* from the Halberstam dynasty. This tomb is visited by pious Chasids belonging to the groups from Bobowa and Nowy Sącz. There are also the graves of over 50 Jewish soldiers from the Austrian army of the First World War. From April 1942 to November 1943 many cases of mass murder took place at the cemetery. In 1946, a memorial designed by Dawid Beckert in the form of a broken column, which in sepulchral symbolic representations means a tragically interrupted life, was built over one of the local collective graves. The inscription inspired by a biblical text was taken from the poem by Chaim Nachman Bialik *Be-ir ha-harega* (In the City of Slaughter) written after the 1903 pogrom in Kishinev. It reads: "And the sun shone and was not ashamed".

The column in the memorial at the Jewish cemetery comes from the New Synagogue and is all that remains of it.

Other Monuments of Jewish Culture

There are many more places in Tarnów which in one way or another are connected with the local Jewish community. A detailed description is contained in the book *Tarnowskie Judaika* (The Judaica of Tarnów) by Adam Bartosz. Those worth a particular mention are the following: the old people's home and hospital (ul. Matki Boskiej Fatimskiej 25); the Bund headquarters, the B. Michalewicz Workers' House (ul. Ochronek 22) and the former Krzak and Szpiller suitcase factory situated next door; the orphanage (ul. Mostowa 14, now a kindergarten): the Talmud Torah (ul. Sienna 5, now a school for nurses); the Henryk Szancer steam mill dating from 1846 (ul. Sienna); the baron Hirsch Foundation Public School, now the fine arts school; the empty site of the Tempel Reform synagogue and the neighbouring school of the Safa Berura Society (ul. św. Anny 1, now a boarding school). In ul. Lwowska there are a few old houses which once belonged to wealthy Chasids.

In 1991 the original wrought-iron gate was taken to the recently established Holocaust Memorial Museum in Washington and replaced with a modern replica.

The crossroads of ul. Słoneczna and ul. Szpitalna, entrance from ul. Szpitalna. The key is available in the house opposite the gate. If no one is there, the key can also be obtained from the doorman at the District Museum at Rynek 21 (available 24 hours a day, knock on the window; a 15 zł deposit is required).

DĄBROWA TARNOWSKA

The synagogue in Dąbrowa Tarnowska, though half-ruined, is still very impressive. It was designed by Abraham Goldstein. Funds for the construction were provided by Ayzik Stern. In 1937 a major overhaul of the building took place under the supervision of Dorota Mertz from Tarnów. This is when an amazing three-storied gallery was added. The synagogue functioned in this unusual form for no more than two years. At the beginning of the German occupation, the Nazis turned it into a storehouse and the building was used for this purpose until around 1970. Dąbrowa Tarnowska was one of the most important centres of Chasidism in Poland. A large group of eminent *tzaddikim* hailed from here. They were headed by David Unger, dynasty founder and disciple of the Seer of Lublin, and by Cwi Hirsz Rymanower, later *tzaddik* of Rymanów. The graves of the Ungers are in the cemetery situated next to the

The synagogue in Dąbrowa Tarnowska was built in 1865.

synagogue. Attempts were made in 1997 to locate them with the aid of diviners, but their rods failed them when confronted with the power of the cemetery's magnetic field. A small Jewish community somehow managed to survive here throughout the Second World War. They prayed at first in the synagogue's vestibule and then in a private house of prayer. The last of them, Samuel Roth, died in 1995.

Inside the Dąbrowa Tarnowska synagogue, you can see the remains of wall paintings, depicting symbolic animals and views of the Holy Land.

BOBOWA

This sleepy, modest little town was once the private property of two families: the Jaworowskis (who invited Jews to settle here in 1723) and the Długoszewskis. Along with Bełz, Góra Kalwaria, Kozienice and Leżajsk, Bobowa is most probably one of the best-known Polish towns within broad circles of Orthodox Jews. It was never a centre of industry or commerce. It owes its status exclusively to the fact that it was the seat of the court of the Halberstam dynasty, their *yeshivah* and many thousands of their still practising followers known as the Bobowa *Chasidim*. Although the town was a very important centre of Judaism, Jews never formed the majority of its population, constituting a little under 40%.

In 1931, tens of thousands of *Chasidim* went to Bobowa for the wedding of the daughter of the *tzaddik*.

Tourist Attractions

The Church of All Saints from the turn of the 15th century, remodelled in the second half of the 18th century; the late Gothic cemetery church of St Sophie from the second half of the 15th century; the fence surrounding the cemetery with the 17th and 19th-century gates; the remains of mid-17th century fortifications; the country mansion from the 17th century.

The wooden external arcades of the synagogue in Bobowa are particularly eye-catching.

The Synagogue

This original synagogue structure dates from the middle of the 18th century. The main hall is built of stone and the western part of wood. Here you can see the magnificent framework of the *aron ha-kodesh* from 1778, regarded as one of the most precious in Poland. There is little doubt that the white coat of paint on all the walls conceals polychromies known from photographs taken before the Second World War. Under Communist rule the synagogue was used as a workshop for a school of weaving. The *bimah* and the steps by the *aron ha-kodesh* were removed. In 1993 the building was returned to the Cracow Jewish community and is in the process of being renovated.

The number outside the building says: ul. Bobowa 169. The synagogue is situated close to the market square but is easy to miss. Take the street opposite the Urząd Gminy (local government office), which you will easily identify by the sign "fryzjer" outside the hairdresser's, where the key is kept. To obtain it, a donation of 10 zł is required.

The Jewish Cemetery

The leaders of the of the Bobowa *Chasidim* rest in the cemetery on the top of a tall hill on the south-western side of the town. It was tidied up and fenced off a decade or so ago. You can find there the *ohel* of *tzaddik* Halberstam, the remains of approximately 100 *matzevot* and a ditch of what used to be a ritual well.

The Jewish cemetery in Bobowa is situated very high up on a hill.

The Bobowa Chasidim

The Chasidic group which made Bobowa famous the world over owes its existence to Chaim Halberstam, the *tzaddik* from Nowy Sącz. His grandson Shlomo Halberstam (1847–1906), rabbi of Oświęcim and Wisznica, teacher of many well-known rabbis and enemy of state education, settled in Bobowa at the end of the 19th century. He created a court and a *yeshivah*, which quickly gained recognition as one of the leading Jewish colleges in this part of Europe. Lectures followed the teachings of Chaim Halberstam, laying emphasis on Talmudic studies as well the importance of a simple, ascetic lifestyle.

The ancestors of Benzion Miller, one of the most distingushed present-day cantors, also came from the Bobowa *Chasidim*

The Chasidic centre in Bobowa reached its zenith during the time of Ben Cion Halberstam (1874–1941), *tzaddik* Shlomo's successor. Ben Cion Halberstam stood out even among other *tzaddikim*. He worked untiringly in the Małopolska region to establish yet more *yeshivot*, setting up sixteen in all, as well as arranging assistance for Jews escaping from the Third Reich. His musical talent brought him great fame and he composed many songs. The joyous weddings which he gave for his daughters have become a thing of legend. He hid from the Nazis in Lvov but did not manage to elude the Holocaust. He was murdered there together with a group of his followers in July 1941 after Germany attacked the Soviet Union. His son, Shlomo Halberstam (b. 1908) survived and so, as one of the very few, the Bobowa dynasty maintained a historic continuity, moving its headquarters to New York. Today the Bobowa *Chasidim* are one of the largest and most active Chasidic groups in the world. There are Bobowa synagogues in New York (together with the famous Halberstam *yeshivah*), London, Jerusalem, Antwerp, Toronto and Montreal.

Leave Bobowa Miasto train station and go up ul. Zamkowa. From here walk to the right along the main road up towards the Catholic cemetery. Just before it turn into the asphalt road leading eastward and referred to as ul. św. Wawrzyńca (street names are not marked). Follow this road up to the first crossroads and then turn right. Walk up to a farmhouse in a cluster of trees (the gate is painted red). Here you will find another road leading to the right, up the hill and straight to the cemetery. The walk takes 30 minutes. If you want to enter the ohel, you should first telephone the cemetery's caretaker Mr Tomasz Nowak (☎ +18 3515103). It will save you the trouble of walking up and down the adjacent steep hills (Mr Nowak lives way down below the hill, on the other side of the cemetery).

Pilgrims from all over the world travel to Bobowa to the rebuilt *ohel* of Shlomo Halberstam, the founder of the dynasty.

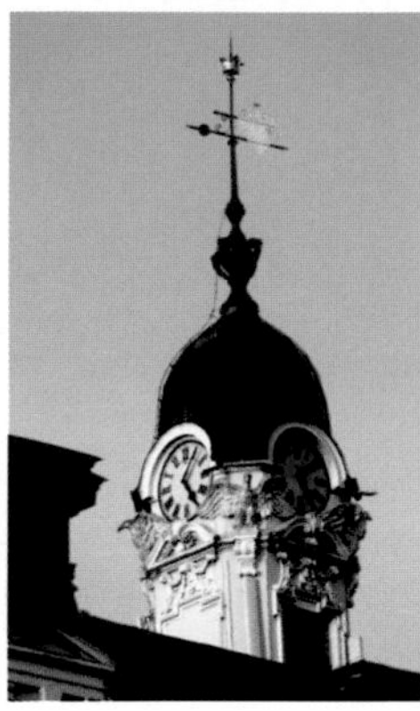

There is a story with a happy ending about a Jewish girl who managed to survive the Second World War by hiding in the mechanisms of the clock in the Town Hall tower.

NOWY SĄCZ | Yiddish: Zantz, Noyzantz

The first accounts of Jewish settlement in Nowy Sącz come from 1469, when the name of a certain Abraham from Sącz appears in the town's documents. Until the middle of the 17th century the city council blocked the influx of Jews and allowed only for the settlement of well-qualified specialists. This situation changed completely in 1673, when in the face of a growing economic crisis King Michael Korybut Wiśniowiecki lifted all existing restrictions. The local Jewish community was mostly involved in the honey, wine, fur, leather and tobacco trades. An ell, the local standard for measuring length, was placed next to the synagogue. The 19th century brought with it the phenomenon of Chasidism. It exploded with great force in Nowy Sącz and made the town one of the main centres of this religious movement. It was due in large part to the charisma of the local *tzaddik* Chaim Halberstam and his *yeshivah*.

Jews constituted approximately 30% of the local population. They lived mostly in the town centre and in Piekło, a part of the Zakamienica district. A large, empty square on the corner of ul. Kazimierza Wielkiego and ul. Bóżnicza is now the only reminder of the Nowy Sącz Jewish quarter.

The Nazi occupation of Nowy Sącz began in September 1939. Jews were forced into slave labour, toiling in quarries or unloading trains. Already poor, they were impoverished still further by the unwarranted contributions which they were required to make. In June 1941 the Nazis marked out the Jewish Housing District, a walled quadrangle situated between the castle and the Market Square. The doors of the houses were bricked up and curtains were to be drawn all the time. The extermination here started at the beginning of 1942. Its main arena was in the Jewish

Tourist Attractions

The medieval urban complex with numerous historical buildings such as: the church of the Nativity of the Most Holy Virgin Mary (now Evengelical) from the second half of the 14th century, with the Lubomirski chapel (1611); the church of the Holy Spirit from the beginning of the 15th century (later remodelled) with the Norbertine cloister (today Jesuit); the collegiate church of St Margaret (from 1446, remodelled in Gothic style in 1970–1973); the Gothic House from 1505, now the District Museum; the ruins of the castle from the 14th century, with a reconstructed tower; the Town Hall (1895–1897). In the Falkowa district there is also the Nowy Sącz Ethnographic Park containing 40 examples of the rural architecture of local Polish highlanders and the Lemko minority and a model of a small town. Nowy Sącz is a good starting point for excursions to the nearby mountains. It is also a good idea to visit Stary Sącz located some 12 km away to see the cloister (1280), the church of the Holy Trinity (1332), a number of 16th and 17th-century buildings, and also the synagogue in ul. Staszica 10, erected in 1906. Today it is used a workshop for the local woodwork school.

The Nowy Sącz Chasidim

In accordance with the teachings of their master, Chaim Halberstam, the *Chasidim* of Nowy Sącz represented an ultra-Orthodox approach which even managed to shock other Chasidic groups, who regarded them as reactionary. Apart from raising asceticism to a point where it became a fundamental principle, they resisted all forms of innovation, including assimilation, Boys were not allowed to attend secular schools; the teaching of Polish language was forbidden; they even condemned the activities of the Agudat Isroel party, which, ideologically speaking, was not that dissimilar in that it forbade participation in politics. The first of many *tzaddikim* was the master, Chaim Halberstam (1793–1876). His successors were as follows: his son Aron (1826–1903), Moshe (d. 1918), Izaak Tobiasz from Głogów Małopolski (d. 1927) and Józef Menachem (d. 1935). The dynasty ended with Mordechai Zeew Halberstam from Grybów (d. 1942), who was murdered by the Nazis in the Tarnów Ghetto. The Nowy Sącz dynasty gave birth to many offshoots and, apart from the most famous of all in Bobowa, there were also dynasties in Cieszanów, Gorlice and Sienawa near Leżajsk.

cemetery in ul. Rybacka, where mass murder and executions by shooting were a regular occurrence. A day which is indelibly marked in the memory is 29 April 1942, when several hundred people were killed in the space of one day. In honour of the victims a memorial was erected at the cemetery. Poles repeatedly tried to help their Jewish neighbours. Despite this, ninety per cent of Nowy Sącz Jews lost their lives. After the Second World War until 1968 a Congregation of the Jewish Faith operated here. The only private Chasidic house of prayer in Poland still functions here today.

The Grodzka Synagogue

This pretty synagogue, once known as Grodzka, was erected in 1780 on the site of the former wooden one. The elaborate Baroque decor was destroyed by fire in 1894, and afterwards the facade was remodelled. The Nazis turned the synagogue into a storehouse. After the war it was returned to the Cracow Jewish community, which donated it to the city in 1974.

The columns of the *bimah* have remained but there is no recess for the *aron ha-kodesh*. The ceiling is new. The interior is filled with the works of local painters. Only the vestibule contains a modest display of Judaica, entitled "They used to be

Since 1974 the Grodzka Synagogue has housed an art gallery. It is a branch of the District Museum.

among us". A plaque commemorating the 25,000 Jewish inhabitants of the city and funded by the Nowy Sącz *Landsmanshaft* can be seen on the wall of the building.

The Dawna Synagoga Art Gallery; the building is marked ul. Berka Joselewicza 12. It is situated on the corner of ul. Berka Joselewicza and ul. Bóżnicza. Open: Wed and Thu 10am–2.30pm, Fri 10am–5.30pm, Sat and Sun 9am–2.30pm.

The Jewish cemetery in Nowy Sącz is a destination for pilgrims coming to visit the *ohel* of *tzaddik* Chaim Halberstam.

The Jewish Cemetery

The Nowy Sącz Jewish cemetery is very close to the Grodzka synagogue and practically on the bank of the River Kamienica. It was laid out at the end of the 19th century and extended in 1926. It is now surrounded by a solid wall and as the grass is cut regularly, one gets an impression that the cemetery is well mantained. Some distance away and surrounded by about 200 *matzevot* (many of them recovered after being used by the Germans as paving stones) you can see the *ohel* of Chaim Halberstam. During the Second World War the cemetery was the site of the gallows and it was here that Jews and Poles (including those who harboured Jews) were hanged. It is commemorated by a memorial, but the inscription: "To the victims of Nazi barbarity and the heroes in the struggle for the freedom of the Polish nation", seems somewhat incomplete and should be modified. Alongside, there is another monument which commemorates the massacre of 29 April 1942.

Chaim Halberstam (1793–1876), founder of a dynasty and referred to as the *Sendzer rebe* (the Teacher from Nowy Sącz) was one of the most distinguished of all *tzaddikim*. He was the representative of an ultra-Orthodox tendency recognising asceticism as the basis for leading a true life. His teachings are contained in the three-part work entitled *Divrei Chaim*, which may be translated in two ways: 'the Words of Chaim' or 'Stories of Life'. The best known fact about the life and teachings of Halberstam is his lengthy dispute with another great *tzaddik*, Izrael Friedmann from Sadogóra near Czerniowce (Chernovitz). Friedmann lived in unusual splendour in a palace, which greatly irritated the leader from Nowy Sącz, who accused him of extravagance and ignorance. In reply to these accusations one of Friedmann's sons, the *tzaddik* Dov Ber from Leow (Moldova), true to the *Haskalah*, stated that the Chasidic belief in the supernatural power of the *tzaddik* was fraudulent. The centre in Sadogóra itself intervened, admitting that Dov Ber was insane. This incident, however, so incensed Halberstam that he put a *cherem* (curse) on the dynasty from Sadogóra, which before long replied in kind. It was the most serious conflict within Judaism at that time.

Ul. Rybacka (left, on the other side of the bridge over the River Kamienica). The keys can be obtained from Ms Barbara Makuch, ul. Rybacka 3/2, ☎ +18 4419381.

Beys Nusn (Natan's House of Prayer)

The only functioning Chasidic synagogue in Poland today, as well as the only private one, was built at the turn of the 20th century by Natan Kriszer, a member of the *Sendzer Chasidim*. During the Second World War it was turned into a storehouse and the wall paintings were destroyed. From 1945 to 1968 it functioned again as a synagogue. It managed to survive until the fall of Communism as it was used once more as a warehouse. In 1992 the synagogue underwent an overhaul. Sabbath services take place on occasion, particularly when groups come to visit. These may include Chasids from Satmar (now the Romanian town of Satu Mare), who have recently joined the group from Bobowa. The matter of the synagogue's affiliation is as yet unsettled. At present it is a private place of worship, but the warden is making efforts to join with the Cracow Jewish community to ensure the prayer hall's continued existence.

Ul. Jagiellońska 12 (in the courtyard). The keys to the synagogue may be obtained from Ms Barbara Makuch, ul. Rybacka 3/2 (opposite the cemetery), ☎ +18 4419381.

The *Beys Nusn* (Natan's house of prayer) has been renovated and reopened thanks to the efforts of Jakub Mueller, one of the very few Jews from Nowy Sącz to have survived the Holocaust.

BIECZ

One of this town's many tourist attractions is the synagogue erected in 1905 and located in the main square at No 20. It is now home to the Town Council, the local administration and a library. The building is easily recognisable by its semi-circular windows and pink elevation. In one of the halls you can still see the recess for the *aron ha-kodesh*. In ul. Tysiąclecia you will find a dozen or so *matzevot* and a number of mass graves from during the war. This is all that remains of the cemetery.

DUKLA

Before the war Jews made up 75% of the population of Dukla. During the occupation many of them were hidden by local Poles. In September 1944 Mieczysław Roj and the five Jews he had been hiding were shot dead by the Nazis. The still visible ruins of the synagogue in ul. Cergowa are worth a look. It was

Fewer than one hundred *matzevot* can still be found in the Old Jewish Cemetery in ul. Kościuszki in Dukla (see below). The new cemetery, the largest in the Podkarpacie region (4 hectares), is situated next to it and contains one hundred and sixty *matzevot*.

Jews first started coming to the spa town of Rymanów in the late 19th century.

built in 1758 and burnt down by the Nazis in 1940. The walls remain, as do the main portal, the *bimah* and the *aron ha-kodesh*. There are also two cemeteries.

RYMANÓW

Rymanów is one of the oldest Jewish centres in the Podkarpacie region. Settlement here was closely linked to the lucrative business of importing wine from Hungary. Local Jews became so involved in their work that in 1594 the Diet of the Four Lands warned them not to drink to excess, or otherwise they would be banned from trading. They must have been effective traders as they were an economic threat to nearby Krosno. This neighbouring town dealt with the competition in a rather original way. In 1700 the councillors of Krosno passed the following resolution: "It is not a punishable offence to rob or kill a Jew from Rymanów".

Rymanów achieved fame as a large centre of Chasidism, chosen as headquarters first by the *tzaddik* Menachem Mendel (d. 1815), disciple of the great Elimelech of Leżajsk, and then by Cwi Hirsz Kohen (d. 1846).

The Synagogue

Accounts vary as to when this historic monument was bulit. Some sources say it was at the turn of the 17th century, others

One of the preserved fragments of the wall paintings in the Rymanów synagogue depicts prayers at the Wailing Wall.

Tourist Attractions

The church of St Lawrence from 1779–1781 (with the interior Renaissance tomb of the Siemieński family, ca 1580); the country mansion with a steward's house and a landscape park from the first half of the 19th century. The history of the spa is shown in the Dr J. Bielecki Memorial Chamber.

mention the turn of the 18th century. This structure, built in fluvial stone and now roofless, has lain in ruin since the Second World War. Brick pillars in the middle indicate where the *bimah* once was. One can also see the recess for the *aron ha-kodesh* (with traces of inscriptions in Hebrew) as well as damaged wall-paintings less than a hundred years old, depicting animals, including an eagle and a leopard. There is a rather curious representation of the Palace of David. As Andrzej Potocki suggests in *Podkarpackie Judaica* (Judaica in the Podkarpacie Region): "The artist most probably took the picture from a postcard. He thought that he was painting the Palace of David, whereas in fact it was the Carmelite convent in Jerusalem". The most eye-catching element is the tower which may once have been used as a prison. The Jewish quarter was spread out around the synagogue. Here one could find the palace of rabbis, the *cheder*, the refuge, the hospital and the *mikvah* situated by the river. Everything was destroyed by the Nazis.

From the main square take ul. Kilińskiego. You will see the synagogue about 100 metres down on the left hand side, just behind the marketplace. The synagogue is in such a state of disrepair that visitors are not allowed inside.

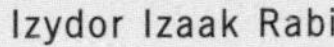

Izydor Izaak Rabi (1898–1988) was born in Rymanów and received the Nobel Prize in physics (1944) for achievements in the field of research into the magnetic properties of atoms. He spent only one year in the place of his birth as in 1899 his parents emigrated to New York. He was one of the creators of the atom bomb, collaborating with Bohr, Pauli, Stern and Heisenberg. Although his whole life was associated with America and Columbia University in New York, he never forgot his roots and visited Rymanów in 1971.

Two hundred *matzevot* remain in the Jewish cemetery in Rymanów.

The Jewish Cemetery

Another of Rymanów's attractions is the cemetery (still referred to here in Old Polish as "the place where the hay is raked up") containing *oholot* raised in the late 1980s, belonging to its two most pious sons, Menachem Mendel and Cwi Hirsz Kohen. Numerous *kvitlech* bear testimony to the fact that these graves are a destination for pilgrims. The cemetery is also the resting-place of *tzaddik* Joseph Ha-Kohen (d. 1913), son of Cwi Hirsz. Here one can also find the graves of two of the rabbis of Rymanów: Hiroch Kohen (d. 1844) and Józef Friedmann. The remains of Hirsz Horowitz, the last rabbi of Rymanów, were exhumed around the year 1960 and taken to Israel. The grave of Austrian soldiers of Mosaic faith who fell during the First World War is also worth a look.

The *oholot* were erected in the late 1980s.

During the Holocaust many Poles in the Podkarpacie Region risked their lives to hide their Jewish neighbours. From among the hundreds of heroes we should spare a special thought for Stanisław Pyrcak from near Sanok. In a cellar at his home he hid twenty Jews who had escaped from the camp at Zastawie. They all survived the war.

On the hill from the Posada Górna side, about 200 metres from the Catholic cemetery. At the end of the Jewish cemetery turn left towards the clearly visible telegraph pole. Just behind it you will see two well-maintained ohelim.

SANOK | Yiddish: Sanuk, Sonik

The Jewish community once constituted half of the population of Sanok and was dominated by *Chasidim*. One could find members of groups from Bobowa, Bełz, Sadogóra as well as ultra-Orthodox *Chasidim* from Nowy Sącz. The Safa Berura school which included classes in secular subjects opened in 1909. A weekly newspaper "Folksfraynd" was published here between 1910 and 1914. The most famous of the Jews from Sanok were: Meir Szapiro, leader of Agudas Isroel and founder of the Lublin Academy of Sages (see page 164); Benzion Katz (1907–1968), Hebrew poet, graduate of the Jagiellonian University in Cracow and rector of the University of Tel Aviv, and Kalman Segal, a modern Polish writer, who died in Israel.

At Rynek 10 (entry through the hallway, you can also go round the frontage onto the square from the right hand side) there is the Chasidic synagogue called Klaus Sadgora, meaning belonging to the *Chasidim* from Sadogóra, followers of the *tzaddik* Izrael Friedmann. Today it is an archive storage and the interior has been completely re-designed. The cemetery, once one of two, is in ul. Kiczury. It contains fifty *matzevot*. All the others form the pavement in ul. Rejtana.

Lesko was the most significant Jewish centre in the south-east reaches of Poland.

LESKO | Yiddish: Linsk, Lisk

The first settlers arrived in Lesko sometime before 1542 and made their living from trade, butchery, goldsmithery, brewing and tailoring. Many travelled with their goods even to distant mountain villages. The *kahal* was formed at the end of the 16th century and assumed a dominant position in the Sanok area. The end of the 18th century saw the rise of Chasidism,

Tourist Attractions

The late Gothic parish church of the Visitation of the Most Holy Virgin Mary (first half of the 16th century), remodelled (the neo-Gothic tower from the end of the 19th century); the Kmita family castle from the 16th century, with a dwelling tower in late Gothic and Renaissance styles; the 16th-century fortifications, now terrace gardens; the houses from the 18th and 19th centuries, including an inn. Lesko is a starting point for trips to the north-east ranges of the Bieszczady and Góry Słone. The Zalew Soliński (an artificial lake on the River Solina) with numerous recreational centres is located 16 km to the north.

which triumphed in Lesko as well. Even *tzaddikim* appeared here, the best known being Samuel Szmelke. Deterioration in the town's economic situation in the 19th century meant that many Jews began moving to neighbouring villlages. In September 1939, Lesko found itself inside the Soviet Union. Jews were persecuted for ideological reasons, although the criterion was not race, as under Nazi occupation, but social standing. They were deported into the depths of Russia. The Germans arrived in Lesko on 24 June 1941. They established a ghetto, which they then liquidated in August 1942, sending all those imprisoned there to death camps.

Up to the German occupation the town had many houses of prayer. They were all in close proximity to the existing synagogue, whether on the other side of the street or where there was a block of dwellings (to the north west of the synagogue). There was the Old Synagogue (built sometime before 1838); the New Synagogue (located in the same building and used as a meeting-place by the communal fraternities); *Sandzer Kloyz* where the followers of the Halberstams from Nowy Sącz gathered (the rabbi of Lesko was a member of this community); and *Sadygorer Kloyz*, for the followers of Izrael Friedmann, opponents of the Nowy Sącz *Chasidim*.

The Synagogue

The synagogue was built sometime between 1626 and 1654, and so the middle of the 17th century is most often cited. The building was not heated, so it functioned only in summer. In winter the main prayer hall was used for Friday night and Saturday morning services only. On all other occasions they were held in two small prayer houses adjacent to the entrance. After several hundred years of peaceful existence the synagogue was seriously damaged by the Germans. Twenty years after the war it was still in a half-destroyed state.

The facade and tower of the only remaining synagogue in Lesko make it one of the most attractive in Poland.

The renovation of the Lesko synagogue began In the 1960s and was later continued in 1981 and 1991.

Erected in stone and rectangular in shape, it has an extension containing a prayer room for women. The inscription on the front wall proclaims: "What fear this place fills us with! There is nothing here but a house of God". The *aron ha-kodesh* is framed by half-columns crowned with a tympanum, similar to that in the famous but no longer existing Golden Rose synagogue in Lvov. The iron doors date from the 19th century. A particular feature is the tower which during post-war repair works was raised even higher. The stone steps and the cellar remain. The tower served as a prison for the Lesko Jewish community which had judicial autonomy. The synagogue now houses the Art Gallery of the Bieszczady House of Culture. Parts of the *bimah*, stolen sometime before 1947, can now be seen in the house in Plac Konstytucji 3 Maja (once an Armenian shrine) where they were used as construction elements for the balcony, as well as in one of the houses in ul. Unii Brzeskiej.

At the crossroads of ul. Berka Joselewicza and ul. Moniuszki.

The Jewish Cemetery

Legend has it that here is the resting-place of the founders of the Lesko Jewish community, some Spanish rabbis driven out of their country in the 16th century. The oldest of the remaining tombstone inscriptions reads as follows (a shortened version): "Here lies the pious man, Eliezer, son of rabbi Meshulam, may the memory of the righteous be blessed. He died on the 9th day of Tishri in the year 309 according to the abbreviated date record". The cemetery is three hectares in size and contains around five hundred *matzevot*.

From the synagogue go down ul. Moniuszki (follow the route marked in blue). At the point where ul. Moniuszki and ul. Źródłowa cross, a little further back on the right there is a gate with stars of David on it. Take the steps behind it and walk up.

The Jewish cemetery in Lesko functioned as early as in 1548.

PRZEMYŚL | Yiddish: Premishla, Premishle

The first confirmed reports of Jews in Przemyśl date from the turn of the 14th century, when they began to settle along the trade route to Lvov. In the Middle Ages Przemyśl Jews were moneylenders and also made their living from handicraft and trade. In 1559 King Sigismund Augustus granted Jews the privilege of legal autonomy. When Przemyśl was part of the Austrian

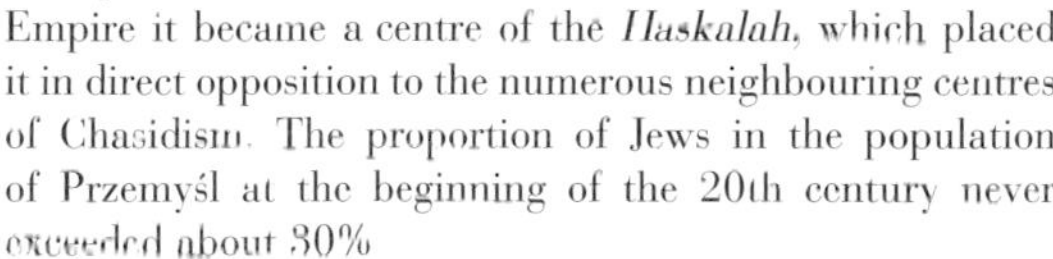

Empire it became a centre of the *Haskalah*, which placed it in direct opposition to the numerous neighbouring centres of Chasidism. The proportion of Jews in the population of Przemyśl at the beginning of the 20th century never exceeded about 30%.

In September 1939, Przemyśl was divided by the German-Soviet border. The town centre found itself in the Soviet Union (in 1940 the Jews were exiled to deepest Russia) while the Zasanie district was now within the borders of the Nazi empire. After Germany attacked the Soviet Union, some of the Jews were deported to Bełżec, while the rest were locked in the ghetto. The ghetto was dissolved in September 1943, although some Jews remained behind as part of a clearing-up brigade. In all 250 Jews survived the war but they all left soon after due to the conflict between Poland and Ukraine, as well as the general geopolitical situation.

Przemyśl is most probably the first town in Poland where Jews settled at the beginning of the 11th century. The question as to why they chose a town so distant from the centre of Europe remains unanswered. One of the hypotheses, purely speculative in character, says that they were not Jews but Judaising Chazars from a fallen state on the southern fringe of eastern Europe.

Tourist Attractions

The city is rich in historical monuments: the Catholic cathedral church of St John the Baptist (initially Gothic, 1460–1571), rebuilt in Baroque style (1724–1744) and partly remodelled (1883–1913); the Franciscan monastery (founded in 1235), with the Baroque church of St Mary-Magdalene (1754–1777), the altar contains sculptures by Piotr Polejowski (1716–1764); the former Jesuit monastery by Jacop Brian (1622); the college building containing the Diocesal Museum with a collection of sacral art; the monastery of Discalced Carmelites (1627–1630) with the Greek-Catholic cathedral (initially the church of St Theresa, functioning as cathedral from 1784 to 1945 and in the 1990s); the Reformed Franciscan Order monastery (founded in 1627) with St Anthony's church (1637–1645); the royal castle built in late Renaissance style (1612–1630), later remodelled, with the remains of a palatium and a pre-Romanesque chapel from the 10th–12th centuries; the remains of city walls; the palace of Greek-Catholic bishops from 1757, now containing the Museum of the Przemyśl Region; the 19th-century Austrian fortifications: the gates, moats and ramparts; the Lubomirski palace in Bakończyce (second half of 19th century); the Benedictine nuns cloister in Zasanie (founded in 1916) with the Holy Trinity church (1768–1777) and the defence wall with loop-holes (second half of 17th century), partly in ruin.

Several hundred 19th and 20th-century gravestones still remain in the Jewish cemetery in Przemyśl.

Local monuments of Jewish culture are collected together in the National Museum of the Przemyśl Region in ul. Czackiego. There is also a Jewish cemetery (on the same side, past the Catholic cemetery in ul. Słowackiego; the gate is open most of the time). As you enter the cemetery you will find graves dating from the 20th century. Further on there are also some much older ones.

The Szajnbach Synagogue erected in 1886–1890 was designed by the local architect Marceli Pilecki.

The Szajnbach Synagogue

The larger and better preserved of the two remaining synagogue buildings is a memorial to the triumph of the *Haskalah* in Przemyśl and this is how it got its former rather colloquial name, the *Tempel*. This place of worship is situated outside the Jewish quarter, to the south east of the old town. In 1960–1961 it was converted into a library. At the same time the wall paintings were obliterated and the stained-glass windows removed. Intermediary ceilings and walls were added, rendering impossible any attempt to give the building a religious feel or to use it for exhibition purposes. Only the exterior decor remains untouched, admirable for its late 19th-century pomposity.

At ul. Słowackiego 15, quite a way down the street near the Słowackiego-Biblioteka bus-stop (buses # 1, 2, 3, 4, 5, 8, 12, 19, 24). The library is open Tuesday to Friday from 9am–7pm. On Saturdays 9am–5pm. Closed on Sundays and Mondays.

The Synagogue in Zasanie

The second of the Przemyśl synagogues also dates from the end of the 19th century. The Society for the Israelite House of Worship in Zasanie originally built the synagogue for the district on the left bank of the River San and it was eventually opened in 1909. It served the faithful for only thirty years, as that part of Przemyśl fell under Nazi control as early as 1939. The occupiers turned it into a temporary power station, adding many ramshackle houses, some of which surround it to this day. After the war the synagogue was used as a garage, first for buses and then for ambulances. In 1994 attempts were made to put an art gallery here. So far, however, the building has remained wrecked, closed and abandoned.

Just past the bridge over the River San in Zasanie, at Plac Unii Brzeskiej 6 (a large square opposite the Statoil filling station), not far from the Orthodox Church

The paintings on the ceiling and walls were removed in the 1960s (photo from 1962).

JAROSŁAW

It is highly probable that Jews first came to Jarosław during the reign of King Casimir the Great, as it is from this period that the oldest tombs in the cemetery date. The first verifiable report is from 1464. Jewish settlers in Jarosław, unlike their counterparts in neighbouring Przemyśl, came up against obstacles set by the rulers of the town. It is enough to quote from a typical document from 1571, the privilege given by Zofia Odrowąż-Kostkowa to the town of Jarosław: "Considering therefore that the numerous Jews living in this town never bring any good on the Christian people, causing rather harm and loss, for it is in their minds to seek Christian misfortune, we resolve and wish to preserve that in our riverside town of Jarosław there should never again be any Jews, only one house or at most two, belonging to those who would never involve themselves in any kind of commerce apart from their own work". Similar acts were also issued in 1614, 1625, and 1676, the last one by King

Before the Second World War the proportion of Jews in the population of Jarosław remained fairly steady at 25–30%.

TOURIST ATTRACTIONS

The town is particular for its rich mixture of nationalities and religions typical of the Polish borderlands before the Second World War. Visit the Baroque church of the Holy Spirit (17th century); the Greek-Catholic church of the Transfiguration (first half of the 18th century); the Orthodox Christian church of the Protection of the Most Holy Virgin Mary (16th century); the cloisters of: the Jesuits, remodelled, with a wall containing sculptures (1582–1594); the Dominicans and the church of God's Mother (1629–1635); the Benedictine nuns and the church of St Michael and St Stanislaus (1622–1624); the Reformed Franciscan Order and the church of St Francis (1710–1716), all designed by Italian architects (J. Bricci, J. Solari, T. Belotti). The market square with late Renaissance arcaded houses (such as the Orsetti) and the Town Hall.

Enormous fairs attracting Jews from all over the country were organised in Jarosław (photo from 1904).

John III Sobieski. However, it was Jarosław which became the centre of Jewish self-government in the time of Commonwealth of Poland, and from 1630 until about 1750 it was the seat of *Vaad Arba Aratzot* (the Diet of the Four Lands).

Jarosław moved into the 19th century as an impoverished town with, as in the entire Małopolska and Podkarpacie regions, a thriving Chasidic movement. The Nazis swept in on 28 September 1939, driving the local Orthodox Jews out beyond the River San to Soviet-occupied territory. Many of those expelled perished there when the Germans invaded in June 1941.

The Great Synagogue

Built in 1811, it remains in extremely good condition. It is an imposing building 25m by 25m. In 1963 it was allocated to the Wyspiański Fine Arts secondary school. The main hall with a vaulting supported on four pillars (it was here that the *bimah* once stood) is used by the school for exhibitions. It no longer has any features of historical importance. The decor was completely destroyed and with it the wall-paintings. The synagogue's favourable appearance is due to repair work carried out in 1990 when a new roof was put on and the prayer room for women was restored.

The dense complex of buildings around the synagogue constitute what used to be the Jewish quarter.

At ul. Opolskiej 12 (actually in pl. Bożnic), ☎ *+16 6211428 (school). The caretakers are not always very helpful.*

The building of the Great Synagogue reflects the look of the earlier one from the first half of the 18th century, which was destroyed by fire in 1809.

The Diet of the Four Lands

Jewish autonomy, in a sense reflecting the traditional Polish communal system of government, was decreed on high. The royal court was in need of a centralised organ to supervise the levying of taxes from Jews. The first initiative was the appointment of a general rabbi for a particular land. Those Jewish communities, under the authority of each rabbi, were made land authorities, of which there were four: Wielkopolska, Małopolska, Ruthenia and Lithuania. The organ charged with assembling these four representations, *Vaad Arba Aratzot* (The Diet of the Four Lands) was set up in 1581, when the Jews took it upon themselves to pay a special duty called the Jewish poll-tax. The official seat of the Diet was Lublin, an important trading centre, but proceedings also took place in other towns, particularly in Jarosław. The Jewish "parliament" had separate legal powers and was the only intermediary between the King of the Two Nations and his Jewish subjects. It was dissolved in 1764 when the Polish parliament came to the conclusion that the *Vaad* was not fulfilling its primary function, that is to say it was not pursuing a fiscal policy. There was also a representation of Jews of the Grand Duchy of Lithuania, known as *Vaad Medinat Lita* (The Diet of the Lands of Lithuania).

The Little Synagogue

The Little Synagogue dates from 1900. "Little" by Jarosław standards once meant enough seats for a thousand worshippers. Its present deformed appearance is a result of extension works carried out between 1969 and 1973. The main prayer hall used to be in the northern part of the building. The vestibule with a prayer room for women situated above it occupied its southern part. All of this was altered during the above-mentioned enlargement. Only a protrusion in the east wall indicates where the *aron ha-kodesh* once was. From the 1970s until recently the building housed the Ateliers for the Preservation of Works of Art. It is now waiting to be let.

At the back of the Great Synagogue, but you will have to go round it. The quickest way is through the entrance hall of the house at ul. Opolskiej 6.

Other Monuments of Jewish Culture

There are traces of one more synagogue in Jarosław. Until 1939 religious services took place in an adapted guild-hall situated upstairs in the building at Rynek 17. We can still see the characteristic high windows deep in the courtyard.

At ul. Tarnowskiego 1 there is a single-storied edifice in the shape of the letter "T". It is the Neo-Classical building of the Jewish Society Yad Charuzim, designed by S. Korman.

The building of the Jewish Society Yad Charuzim now houses a library and a ballet school.

Elimelech of Leżajsk (1717–1787) was the originator of the concept of tzaddikism, fundamental to the existence of Chasidism, and he became the very first *tzaddik* in Jewish history. He came into contact with Dov-Ber of Międzyrzec, disciple of the Baal Shem Tov, the founder of Chasidism. After many years of living as a wandering preacher, in 1772 Elimelech settled in Leżajsk, where he finally formulated the concept of the Chasidic movement in which a group of followers gathered around a leader and teacher. He groomed a number of great *tzaddikim*, including the Seer of Lublin and Menachem Mendel of Rymanów. He recorded his teachings in the work *Noam Elimelech* (The Gentleness of Elimelech) which was published in 1787. His son Elazar (d. 1806) and grandson Naftali (d. 1844) were also *tzaddikim* in Leżajsk.

Sieniawa

On your way from Jarosław to Leżajsk along road 870, you can visit the Jewish cemetery in Sieniawa with the *ohel* of Ezechiel Shraga (1811–1898), the great *tzaddik* of the Halberstam dynasty and son of Chaim of Nowy Sącz. The cemetery is in ul. Zielona. You should drive out of Sieniawa along the local road to Leżajsk, officially named ul. Witosa (the locals call it "na Pigany"). You will see the *ohel* and find the entrance between buildings 44 and 46. The keys can be collected from the house in ul. Kopernika 2. Starting from the summer of 2002 the caretaker will live in a house on the premises of the cemetery.

LEŻAJSK | Yiddish: Lizhansk, Lezhansk

Leżajsk is still a vibrant centre of Chasidism in Poland. Jews first came here in 1521 and their number quickly increased. The privilege granted by King Ladislaus IV in 1635 gave them the right to brew and sell beer and mead. Jews were also the leaseholders of cells and toll-houses. At the end of the 18th century, *tzaddik* Elimelech, a great local figure, turned Leżajsk into one of the largest centres of Chasidism in Poland. The life of the town centred around the local brewery. In the 20th century, until the outbreak of the Second World War, the proportion of Jews among the inhabitants remained constant at 30%. In October 1939 the Germans drove some of the Jews out into the Soviet-occupied zone, the others they locked in the ghetto. A few hundred of those who ended up in the Soviet Union were the only ones to survive the war.

Apart from the cemetery, Jewish memorials in Leżajsk include a part of the former synagogue (now the Bank for the Protection of the Environment) and the *yeshivah* next door. The building of the former *cheder*, situated by the entrance to the cemetery, is now a restaurant. On the site of the pre-war ritual bath there is also a new *mikvah*, opened in 1990 and located at ul. Studzienna 2 (go down the little street to the right of the cemetery).

Alongside his official biographical details, the figure of Elimelech carries with him an aura of wonder to this very

Tourist Attractions

The Renaissance church of the Holy Trinity (1610–1619) with wall paintings; the Greek-Catholic church of The Dormition of The Most Holy Virgin Mary (first half of the 19th century); the famous fortified Bernardine monastery with the church of the Annunciation of the Most Holy Virgin Mary, founded by the Opaliński family in 1618–1628. The church contains a magnificent organ (1688–1693) and stalls (1650). There are also the ramparts (first half of the 17th century), the town hall (18th century), the inn (second half of the 18th century), the cloister of the Servant Sisters (turn of the 19th century) and orphanage, as well as the palace (second half of the 18th century), the wooden mansion house (17th century), and the Bernardine Province Museum at the Bernardine monastery.

day. Apart from the events described below there are many folk tales, both Jewish and Polish, which exist about Elimelech of Leżajsk and his brother *reb* Zusye of Annapol (d. 1800) as well as legends about the supernatural power of the tomb of the *tzaddik*. Elimelech is said to have been able to alter divine judgments and cure fatal diseases. People would ask him to grant them a quick death, a pleasant old age, money, love and fertility. He also possessed the power to drive out demons and to predict the future. A cure for gambling was another of his specialities. He talked to animals. In his soul there was a particle of the soul of Moses. He was one of the 36 people in every generation who, thanks to their virtues and piety, sustain the existence of the world. One is not supposed to speak of him as one of the dead, as his soul was set before the Throne of Glory and there it stands with God. During the war the Germans opened his tomb, looking for gold. People say that before long they all met with terrible suffering and death.

The rule passed down among the pilgrims who have visited the grave of Elimelech of Leżajsk for the past 200 years states the following: "The *tzaddik* will listen to the requests of those who do not want too much".

The Ohel of Elimelech of Leżajsk

Tzaddik Elimelech's tomb from 1776 is the only historical monument of its kind in Poland. To this day things considered miraculous occur here. It is enough to recall the curing of the young girl suffering from bone decay, who was brought to Leżajsk from the United States in 1963, not to mention the cases of the photographic films that became over-exposed or the television cameras that did not work. Local Catholics also testify to these miracles. Some of them even pray here unofficially, comparing the *tzaddik* to St Francis. This place is not lifeless, in fact one can go as far as to say that in recent years the the *ohel* of Elimelech has become tho focus of even greater religious interest.

The number of visitors to the *ohel* of Elimelech increases each year. In 2001 over 10,000 pilgrims came to Leżajsk on the anniversary of his death.

On the anniversary of Elimelech's death on the 21st day of the month of Adar (end of February, beginning of March) the part of the town

The Jewish cemetery in Leżajsk is today the most important centre for *Chasidim* in Poland.

near to the Jewish cemetery is full of announcements in Yiddish, containing practical advice, such as the way to the telephone, the lavatory and the *mikvah*. Pilgrims from Israel, The United States, Hungary, Canada, Belarus and Lithuania pray throughout the night, singing psalms, after which they place *kvitlech* on Elimelech's tomb. A canteen serving *kosher* meals is organised for the pilgrims. During these festivals decorum is called for and strict rules are to be observed. Women are forbidden to enter the main hall of the canteen, the room containing the *ohel* and the men's half of the cemetery. Males are required to cover their heads.

The present edifice around the *ohel* was built in 1960, paid for by donations from American Jews. The building next to it, with a separate entrance, is a prayer room for women.

In ul. Górna. The key is with Ms Krystyna Kiersnowska (ul. Górna 12, ☎ +17 2421265).

Lelów

Similar pilgrimages, but on a much smaller scale (200–300 people), are made to the *ohel* of David Biedermann (1746–1814) in Lelów (the most convenient route from Cracow is through Skała and Wolbrom). The first impression is one of shock as the *ohel* is in a converted storage space which was once part of a shop in ul. Ogrodowa (the key is available from Mr Roman Filewski who lives at ul. Ogrodowa 7). The synagogue, which during the Communist era was turned into a workshop for the co-operative of the disabled, these days performs religious services, although only on certain occasions. It is situated on the other side of the *ohel* at ul. Ogrodowa 3; the key is with Ms Wójcik, ul. Nadrzeczna, ☎ +17 3550109. The anniversary of the death of David of Lelów falls on the 7th day of Shevat. All of the furnishings necessary for conducting prayer are then brought to the synagogue and removed after the service.

ŁAŃCUT

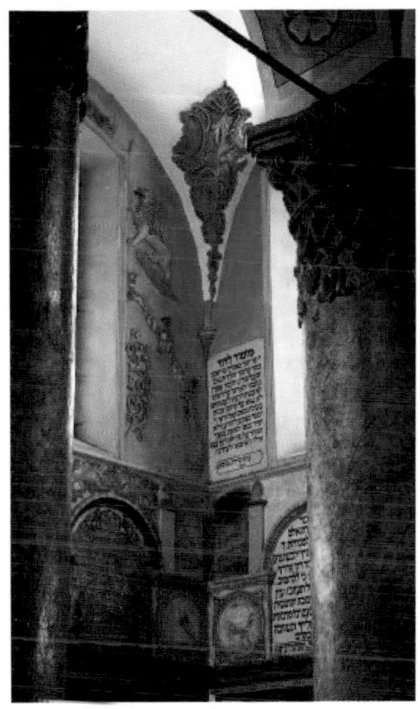

On account of the remaining magnificent stuccos and wall paintings the Łańcut synagogue is regarded as one of the most beautiful in Poland.

Jews arrived here sometime before 1567 and within a hundred years there was a fully functioning community with a synagogue and a cemetery. In Łańcut it was possible to encounter two somewhat rare professions: glaziery and wood-carving. The attitude of the owners of Łańcut evolved from initial mistrust (in 1613 Jews were forbidden to trade in the town, although this was revoked soon after) to approval, particularly among the Lubomirski family who realised that the Jews had the ability to drive the economy. The 19th century saw the rise of Chasidism and the development of the town. Łańcut, however, did not share the fate of many of the small towns in Galicia. The railway passed through it, and the town's next owners, the Potocki family, invested heavily, setting up factories which produced liqueurs, vodka, sugar and eau de cologne. Prosperity was not short-lived and consequently attracted many Jews to the town. Some three thousand lived here, which represented 40% of the local population.

During the inter-war period Łańcut was noted for the strength of its Zionist groups. Several different types of school were to be found there, including Zionist, Hebrew (belonging to the Tarbut network) and Beys Yakov, a traditional school for girls. In September 1939 the Jews of Łańcut were expelled to the zone occupied by the Soviets. About a thousand people remained behind and on 1 August 1942 they were deported to the camp at Pełkinia. There the Nazis murdered children, the elderly and the sick. Those adults who were fit enough to work were sent to the camp at Bełżec, where they later perished.

The Synagogue

The synagogue was built in 1761 and financed by Stanisław Lubomirski, the owner of the town and protector of the Jews. He was probably reasoning in a similar fashion to the founders

Tourist Attractions

The castle, once the seat of the Lubomirski and Potocki families, is an early Baroque building (1629–1641) designed by M. Trapoli. It contains stucco decorations by J.B. Falconi and spires by Tylman of Gameren. Later extended by P. Aigner who added a second floor and another wing. The palace complex includes historical monuments: the orangery (1800), the romantic little castle (1800), the bastions (1629–1641), the landscape park (18th–20th centuries). In 1944 the furnishings were sent abroad by the palace's last proprietor Alfred Potocki. It is a venue for the festival *The Music in the Łańcut Castle*. Outside the palace complex: the church of St Stanislaus (15th century), the Dominican monastery (15th century) and the cloister of the Sisters of Mercy of St Borromeo (18th century).

The synagogue in Łańcut is square in shape. The four pillars framing the *bimah* also support the vaulting. The floor of the main prayer hall is lower than the level of the street, thanks to which the interior gains in height.

The wall paintings depict symbolic animals and other typical motifs.

of the synagogue in Sejny and erected such an impressive building to encourage more Orthodox Jews to settle in Łańcut.

The synagogue's rich decorations are its main attraction. The oldest of these, from the 18th century, is a band of stuccoes at the top of the walls and to the base of the arches of the vaulting. The wall paintings with shallow arcades filled with prayer texts come from the 18th and 19th centuries. The synagogue avoided destruction during the Second World War thanks to Alfred Potocki, the owner of the castle, who forced the Germans to extinguish the fire they had started, and only those parts made of wood, such as the second gallery for women, were destroyed. From 1983 to 1990 the synagogue underwent a major overhaul. It is quite amazing that its adornments, thanks to which we are able to study the motifs of Jewish decorative art, have survived to this day. As there is no heating, the synagogue is open during the summer months only.

In the entrance hall there is a collection of *matzevot* retrieved from the two local cemeteries, both destroyed by the Nazis. On the right there is the smaller of the prayer halls, known as the Lublin Hall, once used for meetings of the *kahal* and the rabbinical court. The name derives from the Seer of Lublin (see page 163), who, before settling by the River Bystrzyca, lived for a while with his disciples in Łańcut. In this very hall an even greater figure, Elimelech of Leżajsk, the Seer's teacher (see page 246), also used to pray. The interior is decorated with wall-paintings from 1912.

In the main hall pride of place is taken by the *bimah*. Its fundamental features are four thick columns with richly sculpted tops. The space above the arches is taken up by symbolic representations, such as deer or *menorot*. The vault of the small dome inside the *bimah* is worth a closer look. Here we can see an image of a serpent swallowing its own tail. It is a symbol of eternity and immortality, and also a portant of messianic times. Above the *bimah*, dating from 1906, are paintings of the following biblical scenes: the temptation of Adam in the Garden of Eden, the sacrifice of Cain and Abel, Noah's ark and the sacrifice of Isaac. Another important place is the *aron ha-kodesh* and the recess for the *Torah* scrolls, covered by a *parochet* and situated on the eastern wall. The most beautiful and crowning feature of the recess is a hand bestowing a blessing, the symbol of the ministry, created in stucco, colourfully painted and adorned with a crown and an ornament bearing representations of plants.

At the top of the *aron ha-kodesh*, there are the Decalogue Tablets which are the only wooden elements to survive the fire of 1939. At the end of the 20th century the tablets underwent thorough restoration bringing out wood carvings and painted ornaments.

The upper band of the walls to the base of the arches of the vaulting is created in stucco dating from the second half of the 18th century. The wealth of examples of plants and shells (rocailles typical of Rococo style) is quite eye-catching. Figures of animals are hidden in a confusion of deliberately twisted lines. Apart from the signs of the zodiac there are also images of different festivals, arranged in such a way as to blend in with the star signs. The delightful green landscape above Gemini signifies *Shavuot*, the Feast of Weeks (on this holiday, corresponding to Polish Whitsun, synagogues are decorated with leaves and flowers); the view of the synagogue and Jerusalem refers to the festival of *Chanukah*. The signs of the zodiac in the shape of medallions form a circle around the prayer area. What is noticeable is the lack of representation of the human form. A thick Syrian cornice, one of the oldest decorative motifs found in synagogues, runs around the lower part of the walls. Moulded and coloured, it goes up to just above the door and the recess for the *aron ha-kodesh*. Above the cornice are the arcades in each of which there is a prayer text, the first being written here in the 18th century and the last shortly before the Second World War. In the synagogue you can view large-scale

Aside from the signs of the zodiac on the western wall there are four symbolic animals: the leopard signifying rapidity of movement, the eagle denoting spiritual lightness, the deer representing swiftness, and the lion symbolising power.

One of the *oholot* (interior shown above) preserved in the Jewish cemetery in Łańcut belongs to Naftali Cwi Horowitz of Ropczyce, who died in 1827. The other belongs to Eliezer of Łańcut (d. 1865).

A large collection of Judaica has been assembled by the District Museum in Rzeszów, ul. 3 Maja 19, ☎ +17 8629516, Tuesdays and Fridays 10am–5pm, Wednesdays and Thursdays 10am–3 pm, Sundays 9am–2pm.

illustrations depicting the history of the Łańcut Jewish community as well as many items used in religious ceremonies. These include a *Torah* scroll and its adornments such as a *yad* (pointer for reading), a *menorah*, spice-boxes, *Seder* plates, *Chanukah* lamps and a *tallit*.

At the intersection of ul. Zamkowa and ul. 3 Maja. The synagogue is administered by Muzeum-Zamek (the castle museum) open daily 9am– 3pm, ☎ +17 2252008. Owing to heating problems the synagogue is open to visitors during the months of July and August only.

The Jewish Cemetery

The Łańcut Jewish cemetery is in fact just an empty field with a fence round it, containing the remains of a number of *matzevot* and two *oholot*. It is usually visited by people travelling from the local synagogue to the cemetery in Leżajsk.

From the castle go towards the House of Culture. Turn left into ul. Moniuszki. First take the key from Ms Helen Kuźniar at ul. Jagiellońska 17, ☎ +17 2252142 (turn right at the crossroads before you get to the cemetery, fourth house on the right, deep in the garden).

RZESZÓW | Yiddish: Rayshe, Reyshe

Jokers from Galicia called Rzeszów "Mojżeszów", which translates from Polish as Mosestown. It was known by this name for a long time, even though the proportion of Jews dropped from more than half at the end of the 19th century to 37% in 1910. The reason for this was the incorporation of the suburbs inhabited by Christians into the town. Even so, it was the Orthodox Jews who took the lead in Rzeszów. In 1886 the ban on working on Sundays and holidays was lifted. Jewish festivals, especially *Pesach*, were celebrated with great pomp. An entry in the *Galician Encyclopaedia* reads as follows: "These holidays gave the town its own particular Jewish character, arousing a lot of interest among the Christian population". Mutual barriers to understanding, however, could not be overcome. In 1902 the assesor Wilhelm Hochfeld twice fought duels having been refused admittance to a Polish clubhouse.

Tourist Attractions

The Church of St Stanislaus and St Adalbert (first half of the 15th century), remodelled in Baroque style; the Bernardine monastery (1624–1629) with sculptures of the Ligęza family members inside the church; the Piarist monastery (1642–1649) containing the District Museum; the remains of the castle; the garrison church from 1709; the 18th-century Town Hall (remodelled 1895–1898); the palace referred to as the Summer Theatre, once the property of the Lubomirski family (18th century); the public buildings from the period of Galician autonomy; the town park in the extended former gardens of the monastery (first half of the 18th century). There is also an underground tourist route open to visitors.

Jews had settled in Rzeszów as early as the middle of the 16th century. They made their living from tailoring, haberdashery (producing trimmings for uniforms and curtains), embroidering, soap-boiling, dispensing medicine and distilling alcohol. They were also known locally for their skills as goldsmiths and makers of seals. Its trading position meant that Rzeszów was even called "Galician Jerusalem". The New Town, marked out in the 17th century, was the traditional Jewish quarter. A rapid growth in the number of Jews accompanied the construction of the railway line to Lvov, Cracow and Jasło. At the outbreak of the Second World War, Jews made up 47% of the local population. They had their own hospital, refuge and schools. Some 75% of the Orthodox Jews in Rzeszów belonged to the Chasidic movement and set the tone for religious life. They were divided into the antagonistic dynastics from Sadogóra and Nowy Sącz and a political grouping, the Zionists, who had 30% of the seats on the city council. The penultimate rabbi of Rzeszów Natan Lewin was a member of the Polish parliament for the Agudas Isroel party.

The Staromiejska Synagogue houses The Centre for Research into Jewish History. It concentrates mainly on archive searches and has created two data bases: "Judaica" containing a register of the Jews of Rzeszów, and "Dębżydzi", a list of Dębica Jews murdered by the Nazis during the Second World War. Address: ul. Bóżnicza 2, Rzeszów; ☎ +17 8532684, 8532670, e-mail: osrodek@rzeszow.ap.gov.pl. A film is shown at the centre for groups of 10–12 people.

During the occupation the Germans created a ghetto for 25,000 people. By the end of September 1943 it had been liquidated. The majority of those imprisoned there were deported to the death camps at Bełżec, Auschwitz and Płaszów. Several thousand were shot in a forest near Rudna.

The Staromiejska or Small Synagogue

The Staromiejska (Old Town) Synagogue caught fire on three separate occasions: in 1660, 1739 and 1842. After the last of these fires it was given a new appearance. In old photographs, it had two annexes, of which only the western one remains. It burned down again in 1944. It was rebuilt from 1953 to 1963 (in 1959 the remains of the scratch-work were removed) and converted into an archive bureau. The present owner is the Cracow Jewish Community which leases it to the archive authority. On the building you will find a memorial plaque containing the following verse: "Day and night I could weep for those killed, the daughters of my people" (Jeremiah 8:23).

At ul. Bóżnicza 4. The bureau is strictly guarded and closed to visitors.

The rectangular building of the Staromiejska Synagogue (15m by 20m) was probably erected at the turn of the 17th century (this being noted in a mention from 1617). Other sources cite the years 1705–1710.

The New Town Synagogue, destroyed in 1944, was rebuilt in 1965 with a complete change of interior.

The Nowomiejska or Great Synagogue

The Nowomiejska (New Town) Synagogue was erected in 1686 and is rectangular in shape, measuring 20m by 30m. It was destroyed in 1944 and rebuilt in 1965 with a totally different interior. Of the key original features the recess for the *aron ha-kodesh* is still there, although hidden behind a screen. An additional storey was also added, the saddle-roof being replaced by an extra floor.

Ul. Sobieskiego 17, ten or so metres from the Staromiejska Synagogue. At present it houses the Offices for Exhibitions of Works of Art. The exhibition hall is open 10am–5pm.

The New Cemetery

The Jewish cemetery, known as the New One, was established in 1849. Burials took place here from 1851 up to the Second World War. Of those interred here, the best known was Natan Lewin, a member of the Polish parliament and the last but one rabbi of Rzeszów, serving until 1926. There are two memorials to Jewish martyrdom during the German occupation. The dedication on the first one, erected in 1947, reads: "To the martyred victims of the bloodthirsty Nazi criminals – from the Jews of Rzeszów who remained alive". The second was funded by the family of Beniamin Gross who, together with 18 comrades, was executed on 4 March 1944. Through the fence one can see many *matzevot*. Unfortunately, the cemetery is tightly locked. A dozen or more tombstones from the Old Cemetery are preserved in pl. Zwycięstwa.

At the crossroads of ul. Rejtana and ul. Dolowa. Bus stop "Rejtana Mostek", bus lines # OA, 17, 19, 29.

The former Jewish quarter, once referred to as the Jewish Acropolis, is spread around both synagogues. It contains the following streets: ul. Bóżnicza, ul. Sobieskiego, ul. Gałęzowskigo, ul. Nowe Miasto and their surroundings.

Wrocław

•

The Epilogue: Needershlezye

•

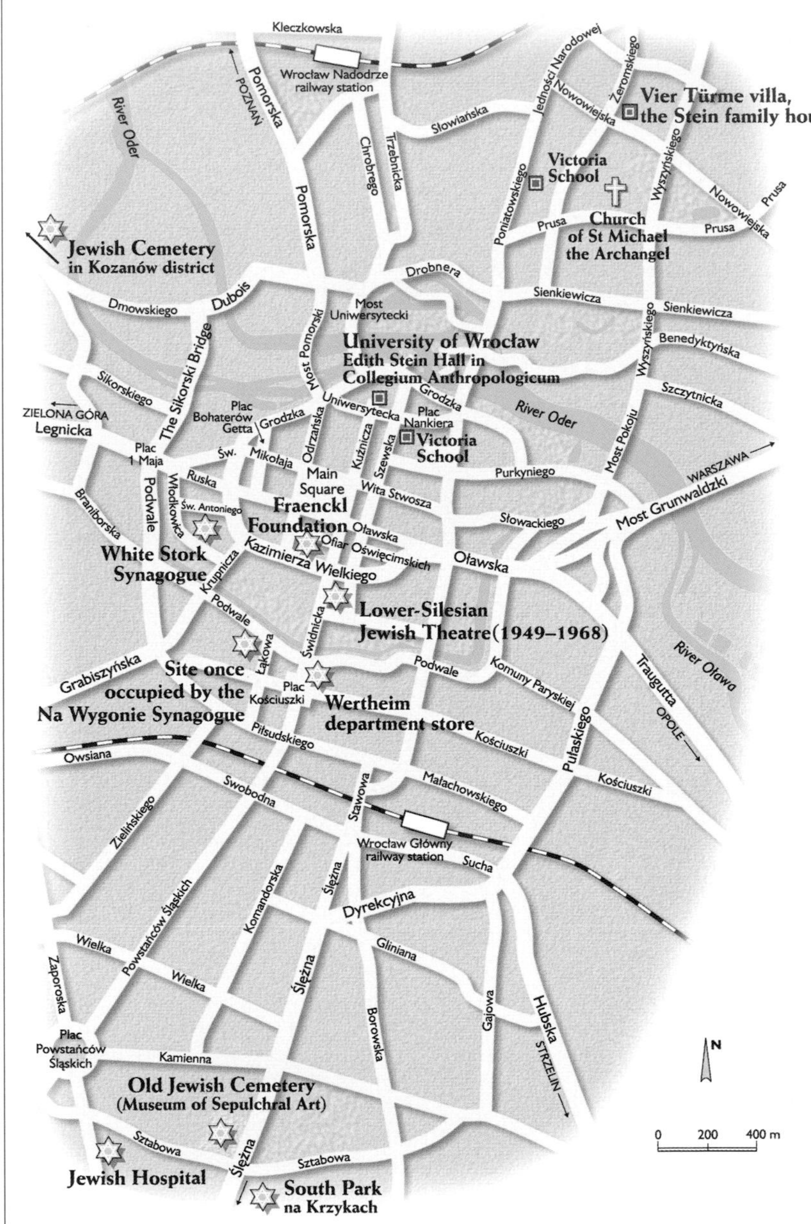

For practical information see page 306

Alongside Przemyśl, Wrocław takes pride in having the oldest Jewish community within the present territory of Poland. Jews lived here from the beginning of the 13th century until the time of the Nazis (with an interval of 200 years). For wealth and level of intellect, local Jewish society was counted among the most important in Europe.

Jews came here again after 1945, this time from *Kresy*, the former eastern borderlands of Poland, thus writing a rather specific epilogue to the history of Jewish society in the pre war Polish Republic.

The earliest accounts of Jews in Wrocław date from the years 1180–1208. The medieval Jewish community numbered around 70 families and had several synagogues. On 30 January 1455, the Czech king Ladislav Posthumous granted the town the writ of rights *privilegia de non tolerandis Judaeis*, which was in force for 200 years. Jews were marked with a round yellow patch on their clothing and allowed into the town only during fairs, and even then it was only those who were involved in the wholesale trade. The year 1657 marked the beginning of their return. This is when Zachary Lazarus from Nahod became leaseholder of the Wrocław mint. He is regarded as the founder of the modern Jewish community in Wrocław. Its core was formed by those arriving from the Commonwealth of Poland. The Jewish quarter

Suggested Route

The White Stork Synagogue → the Site Once Occupied by the Na Wygonie Synagogue → the Old Jewish Cemetery – the Museum of Sepulchral Art

Places Connected with Edith Stein

Jews in Lower Silesia
After the Second World War, Lower Silesia played an important part in the history of Polish Jews. In 1946 those Jews who had managed to survive the war by being in the Soviet Union were given the chance to settle here. The Regional Jewish Committee was established and the main influx of settlers was directed to the town of Dzierżoniów. As a result of waves of emigration in 1946, 1949–1950 and 1968 this idea eventually collapsed. All that remains are a few small Jewish communities in Dzierżoniów, Legnica, Wałbrzych and Żary. According to local people's recollections, Legnica was the last town in Poland where it was still possible to hear Yiddish spoken as recently as 1968.

Recommendations

Visit the **White Stork Synagogue** and the **Old Jewish Cemetery**.

The Wrocław Jewish community has branches in Dzierżoniów, Wałbrzych and Żary, to name but three. It is today one of the largest and most active Jewish communities in Poland (below: the gate leading to the head office of the Jewish community at ul. Włodkowica 9).

occupied a closely-knit district confined to what is now Plac Bohaterów Getta and streets such as ul. Włodkowica, ul. św. Antoniego, ul. Ruska. ul. Złotego Koła and ul. Krupnicza. In the middle of the 18th century, the borders were still delineated by the present Plac Bohaterów Getta, ul. Włodkowica, ul. św. Mikołaja, ul. Kazimierza Wielkiego (where the River Oławka once used to flow), ul. Krupnicza and the town moat.

In the second half of the 18th century, the influence of the *Haskalah* reached Wrocław. Many of the city's most distinguished Jews joined this new movement, including the teachers of the Wilhelm School, a progressive educational institution for Jewish youth, which had been opened towards the end of the 18th century. Supporters of the trend towards enlightenment quickly became assimilated into German society. At the same time a division into two groups, progressive and Orthodox, occurred in Jewish society (although the community remained as one). At the beginning of the 19th century, the progressives were led by Rabbi Abraham Geiger (1810–1874), the forefather of the Reform movement in the entire world of Judaism. Their opponents followed the rabbis from the Tiktin family. As a consequence, two parallel rabbinical offices operated in Wrocław until the Second World War.

After the introduction of equal rights (11 March 1812) as well as a curial voting system, the proportion of Jews in the Wrocław electorate reached 20%. Until the time of the Weimar Republic all of the chairmen of the town council were Jews.

The proportion of Jews here peaked in 1861, when it reached 7.5%. By 1910 it had fallen to around 4%. Relations with the rest of the population were not always harmonious. In 1855, Gustav Freytag published his novel *Soll und Haben* (Debit and Credit). It depicted Wrocław as a place infiltrated by *Ostjuden* who brought with them dishonesty and deception. Between 1855 and 1922 this book was reprinted 113 times.

Ferdinand Lasalle

Many distinguished figures have their roots in Jewish Wrocław. The most famous of them was the brilliant physicist, **Max Born** (1882–1970). Others include: the philosopher and nun **St Edith Stein** (1891–1942, canonised in 1987), the socialist **Ferdinand Lasalle** (1825-1864), the biologist and physician **Leopold Auerbach** (1828–1897) who discovered the part of the nervous system known as the *Auerbach nervenplexus*, the physicist **Leo Graetz** (1856–1941), inventor of the rectifier, referred to as the Graetz system; the chemist **Fritz Haber** (1868-1934), inventor of ammonia synthesis and Nobel prize winner in 1918 and the great dermatologist **Albert Neisser** (1855–1916). The discoverer of the planet Neptune **Gottfried Galle** (1812–1910) is buried in the local German cemetery.

At the turn of the 20th century Jewish activity here was at its height. Jews were members of the Silesian Society of Native Culture, the Cosmos Masonic Lodge, the Wrocław School of Poetry and the Humboldt Society for the Education of the People. There were also associations strictly Jewish in character: the Society of Friends, bringing together the supporters of the *Haskalah* and the Lessing Lodge, which organised cultural events. Large-scale charitable work, including the running of a well-known hospital, was possible thanks to foundations set up by Jonas Fraenckel. The Jewish Theological Seminary in ul. Włodkowica, also operated at that time (the building was pulled down in the 1970s).

In the inter-war period, the largest problem was the dramatic growth in anti-Semitism. Attempts were made to boycott Jewish doctors and discriminate against school children. However, amid the worsening situation, a significant event took place, after lengthy preparations, the pioneering Jewish Museum was opened in Wrocław.

Rabbi Gedalje Tiktin (1818–1886) was leader of the Orthodox faction in the Wrocław Jewish community.

Tourist Attractions

The most important monuments in Wrocław are on the former island called **Ostrów Tumski**: the Gothic cathedral of St John the Baptist (1244–1272); the collegiate church of the Holy Cross (1280–1350); the church of St Idzi (1280–1350); the church of St. Martin (from the 13th century, remodelled in the 16th century), the church of St Peter and St Paul (15th century). **Away from Ostrów Tumski** there is the church of the Most Holy Virgin Mary in Piasek (1334–1390); the church of St Mary Magdalene (1342–1360, a Romanesque portal from the end of the 12th century); the church of St Vincent (1723–1727) as well as many other historical buildings. Monuments of the highest class also include: the Aula Leopoldina (1726–1732, in the Jesuit college, founded by Leopold I, at present a part of Wrocław University); the Gothic town hall from the second half of the 13th century (extended 1471–1504); the houses in the main square (14th and 15th centuries, remodelled in the 17th and 18th centuries); the palaces, the Baroque and Classicist houses; the opera house (1837–1841); Wrocław Świebodzki railway station (1842, extended in 1873); the People's Hall (1912–1913); the rotunda containing the *Panorama of the Battle of Racławice* by J. Styka and W. Kossak (Lvov, 1894).

On *Kristallnacht* (the Night of Broken Glass) on 9/10 November 1938 the synagogue in the Na Wygonie district was destroyed. One of those behind this act was general Erich von dem Bach-Zelewski, later the oppressor of Warsaw.

The hell on earth calling itself the "Thousand-Year Reich" meant that Jews were forced into a "cultural ghetto". 1 April 1933 was Boycott Day. The windows of shops owned by Jews were daubed with the word "Jude". The implementation of the Nuremberg laws in September 1935 meant that Jews became total outcasts from society. In November 1935, Jews were deprived of German citizenship and in 1938 they were forbidden to drive and required to return their licences. Between September 1941 and January 1945, the extermination of the Wrocław Jews was carried out and 7,985 people were either murdered right away or deported to death camps. The Orthodox rabbi Bernard Hamburger was taken to Auschwitz-Birkenau concentration and extermination camp, and the Reform rabbi Reinhold Lewin to another Nazi camp in Poland.

The end of the war opened an unexpected new chapter as 15,000 prisoners of the Gross-Rosen concentration camp, Jews from the pre-war eastern territories of Poland, arrived in Wrocław. They met the thirty remaining local German Jews who had miraculously survived the Holocaust. However, a conflict soon ensued, after which the former inhabitants departed (this is why there is no continuity within the Wrocław community). In February 1946 there were 14,992 Jews in Wrocław. Four synagogues functioned; two at ul. Włodkowica 9, and the other two at ul. Żeromskiego 24 and ul. Oleśnicka 11. There were also *kosher* meat stalls, a *kosher* canteen, a *mikvah*, a *Talmud-Torah* school, the Needershlezye publishing house, and two cemeteries, in ul. Ślężna and in Kozanów.

The Jewish population of Wrocław soon shrank in size, as many members of the community left. In the mid-1950s it numbered no more than 3,800. There was the Sholem Aleichem Primary School and High School No 7, closely linked with each other. In those days Wrocław was also the main centre for the making of *matzah*, mass production of which began in 1962.

Nobel Prize Laureates – University of Wrocław Graduates and Lecturers

One of the greatest achievements of the Jews of Silesia was a whole galaxy of distinguished scientists headed by Nobel Prize winners.

Max Born

Philipp Lenard – physics 1905
Eduard Buchner – chemistry 1907
Paul Ehrlich – medicine 1908
Fritz Haber – chemistry 1918
Friedrich Bergius – chemistry 1931
Otto Stern – physics 1943
Max Born – physics 1954
Konrad Bloch – medicine 1964

The next wave of departures, after which only about 500 Jews remained, took place in 1968. The later years of the communist Polish People's Republic brought about a decline in activity in Jewish society. In 1974, the White Stork Synagogue was taken away from the community by the authorities.

The recovery began in 1986, when Jerzy Kichler arrived from Cracow and set about reviving the community. In the early 1990s charitable organisations resumed their work. The tide of young people leaving the community was stemmed. In 1994 the synagogue was returned and the Ronald S. Lauder *Etz-Chaim* school was set up. There is also a kindergarten as well as Poland's only synagogue choir. In Wrocław at present there are most probably between 150 and 200 Jewish families. The community has over 200 members and covers Lower Silesia (excluding Legnica), the southern part of the Wielkopolska region, the southern part of the Lubuskie region and the Opole area.

The former Lower-Silesian Jewish Theatre (1949–1968), now the Chamber Theatre, in ul. Świdnicka was famous for the performances of Ida Kamińska.

In Wrocław there is no clearly defined former Jewish quarter. The monuments of Jewish heritage are scattered all over the centre. Those worth a mention are: the building in ul. Świdnicka, which houses the Renoma department store, formerly part of the Wertheim chain; the headquarters of Kredyt Bank at ul. Ofiar Oświęcimskich 19, once the Fraenckel Foundation; the railway hospital, the former Jewish hospital; and finally Park Południowy (South Park) in the Krzyki district, founded by Julius Schoettlander.

Zum Weissen Storch (The White Stork Synagogue)

The White Stork Synagogue derives its name from the inn which once occupied the same spot.

The only remaining synagogue in Wrocław today is the vibrant centre of the local Jewish community. The Prussian authorities coerced the Jews into building it in an attempt to close smaller houses of prayer and to concentrate all of the worshippers in one building. The synagogue, designed by Carl Ferdinand Langhans Jr, was opened on the 10 April 1829. The painter Raphael Biow and his son were responsible for the interior decor. The building is rectangular in shape and inside there is a main prayer hall, surrounded on three sides by galleries for

The purpose of the reconstruction works is to restore the synagogue to its original appearance.

The *aron ha-kodesh* is covered by a *parochet* (embroidered curtain).

women. Its original layout was typical of that of a Reform synagogue, where the *bimah* was next to the *aron ha-kodesh*. Between 1838 and 1864, the rabbi here was Abraham Geiger, the famous reformer, and from 1844 to 1874 the position of cantor was filled by the distinguished singer Moritz Deutsch.

In 1872 another synagogue was built in the Na Wygonie district and the White Stork Synagogue became a centre for Orthodox members of the community. In 1925 they moved the *bimah* to the central point of the main prayer hall. Thanks to its location, the synagogue was spared on *Kristallnacht* (the Night of Broken Glass), as the Nazis were afraid the flames might spread to neighbouring buildings. The wooden frame of the *aron ha-kodesh* (now in the local Museum of History) and the damaged tablets bearing the Ten Commandments are the only remnants of the original features.

The synagogue functioned until 1974 when the authorities took it away from the community and gave it to the University of Wrocław as a library. Fortunately, there was not enough money for the conversion of the building, but the new owners did manage to ransack the place and knock a hole in the wall where the *aron ha-kodesh* had been. In the late 1980s, the ravaged synagogue was taken over by the Musical Academy, whose rector sold it to a private individual. A low point was reached when people started haggling over the synagogue building. Finally, in 1994, thanks to the support of Cardinal Gulbinowicz, the Metropolitan Archbishop of Wrocław, it was returned to the Jewish community. Renovation saved the building from falling down completely. In 1998, a remembrance service for the victims of the Night of Broken Glass was held there, attended by the Prime Minister of Poland and the ambassadors of Germany and the United States.

Ul. Włodkowica 7, the key is available at the offices of the Jewish Community at ul. Włodkowica 9 (☎ +71 3436401); opening hours: Monday–Friday 11am–1pm. Before asking for the key, check if the synagogue is not already open.
Prayers and services take place every Sabbath and on all holidays in the community prayer hall at ul. Włodkowica 9. Kindling of Sabbath candles, every Friday at dusk, shachrit *on Saturdays and holidays at 9.30.*

A memorial to the victims of *Kristallnacht* was unveiled in 1998 on the site once occupied by the Na Wygonie Synagogue.

The Site Once Occupied by the Na Wygonie Synagogue

The synagogue in the Na Wygonie district was the centre of the liberal faction of the Wrocław community. Built between 1865 and 1872, it was designed by Edwin Oppler as the largest of any Austrian and German synagogues. Crowned with a dome and 73 metres high, it could accommodate 1,900 worshippers. It was officially opened on 29 September 1872, with both the liberal and Orthodox rabbis taking part in the ceremony. The Nazis set fire to it

The cemetery in Wrocław is one of the most important Jewish landmarks in Poland.

The tomb of botanist Ferdinand Julius Cohn (1828–1898), the first person to classify bacteria as plants (section X).

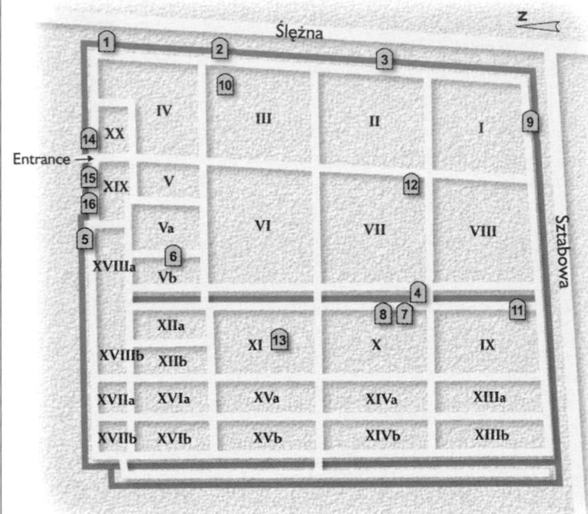

1. Salomon Kauffmann
2. Moritz Caro and Robert Caro
3. Ferdinand Lasalle
4. Julius Schoettlander
5. Isidor and Neander Alexander
6. Hermann Cohn
7. Ferdinand Julius Cohn
8. Heinrich Graetz
9. Frederike Kempner
10. Abraham Levy
11. Henryk Toeplitz
12. Auguste Stein
13. Siegfried Stein

14–16. The oldest *matzevot*

The oldest complete *matzevah* in Poland, that of cantor David (1203), is at present on display in the Wrocław Archaeological Museum at the Arsenal.

on the Night of Broken Glass, on 9/10 November 1938. The following day they blew it up and scrupulously removed all trace of it.

The Old Jewish Cemetery (the Museum of Sepulchral Art)

This cemetery was established when in 1853 the existing one in ul. Gwarna (next to the railway station) ran out of space. The Funeral Society then made attempts to build a new one. A special tax was levied on members of the community. The amount of 21,600 thaler raised in this way was used for the purchase of several plots of land (an area of 4.6 hectares) in what was then *Lohestrasse*. The first burial took place on 18 November 1856. In 1912 a preburial house (which no longer exists) was erected here together with an administrative building. The cemetery functioned until August 1942. During the

Communist era it was deliberately desecrated by the ZOMO (riot control police) stationed nearby. It was registered as a listed monument as late as 1975 and tided up in 1984. It has been open to visitors since 1988.

The most convenient way to start your visit is from the pavilion on the left of the gate. It houses an interesting exhibition displaying images of distinguished figures and the most important buildings of the Jewish quarter in Wrocław. On both sides of the gate you will find the remains of the oldest *matzevot* in Poland, dating from the 13th and 14th centuries. They are the most ancient testimony to the presence of Jews within the present Polish borders. These gravestones come from cemeteries which have not existed since the Middle Ages, among them the one at the Brama Oławska. They were found during excavation works and put here in the inter-war period. They date from 1343 and 1345. The oldest completely preserved headstone is today on display at the Archaeological Museum. It bears the date 4 August 1203 and the inscription: "This stone is a stele on the tomb of Master David of pleasant voice, son of Master Sar Shalom, who died on the 25th day of the month of Av in the year 4963 after the creation of the world. May his soul be bound in the bundle of life". The *matzevah* was unearthed in 1917, during excavation works in Wrocław cathedral.

One is struck by the artistic and historical value of the gravestones. There are tombs in the form of chapels, arches, canopies and portals as well as memorials in the shape of stelae, obelisks, columns and tree-trunks in stone.

You will find here many examples of Art Nouveau and Modernism.

A special railway was laid to faciliate the construction of the vault of Julius Schoettlander.

The cemetery has a regular network of sections, a main avenue and internal walls with family vaults on both sides. Most of the gravestones are from the second half of the 19th century and the beginning of the 20th. The people buried here were of significance not only for the local Jewish community or the town but in several cases for the whole of Europe.

Start your visit by turning left behind the gate and taking the path which runs along the wall. In the corner you will find the vault of the Kauffmann family, the textile industry magnates. Salomon Kauffmann was a personal acquaintance of Liszt, Wagner and Brahms. Further along on the same side there is a vault leaning against the wall, the resting place of Moritz Caro (1792–1860) and Robert Caro (1819–1875), founders of a dynasty of industrialists whose property included shares in the Linke-Hoffman-Busch Werke company, now Adtranz-Pafawag Wrocław, a manufacturer of rolling stock. Some fifty or so paces further on, also by the wall, lies Ferdinand Lasalle (1825–1864), one of the key ideologists of socialism and founder of the first German workers' party.

From here you should go on a little further, then turn right and follow a straight lane running across and leading to a huge structure next to the internal wall. It is the vault of Julius Schoettlander (1835–1911) and the

Julius Schoettlander's life is an example of the stunning success that could be achieved in the second half of the 19th century by a person with drive and ambition. The Schoettlanders came from the little provincial town of Biała Prudnicka. At the age of fifteen Julius started trading in grain and wool. In 1859 he moved to Wrocław. In 1864 the town leased him the Central Mill which brought him huge profits after it had been modernised. From 1869 he supplied rations to the Prussian army, a deal which turned out to be a perfect move in the light of its victory in the war with France. In no time at all he became owner of 2,000 hectares of land. In 1877 he pulled off an amazing feat. He bought a large area of the prestigious Kleinburg housing estate and, having surrounded it with his own property, he donated it to the town authorities as a park (now South Park). Numerous housing estates were then built around the park, of course on the land already owned by Schoettlander. He used part of his fortune to set up charitable foundations, for example the Centre for Care of the Elderly and the House for Jewish Nurses.

members of his family. It is second only in size to the chapel tomb of Izrael Poznański in the Jewish cemetery in Łódź. Other graves worth looking at are those of the brothers Isidor and Neander Alexander (by the northern wall, to the right of the gate), as well as those of Hermann Cohn (1838–1906), the famous oculist also known as "Augencohn" (section Vb); Heinrich Graetz (1817–1891), a distinguished historian and author of *History of the Jews* (section X); Frederike Kempner (1828–1904), a poetess known as the "Silesian Swan" (section I); Abraham Levy (1817–1872), father of Jewish numismatics (section III); Henryk Toeplitz (1822–1891) from a famous Warsaw family, founder of Bank Handlowy (the Trade Bank), friend and patron of the famous Polish composer Stanisław Moniuszko (section IX). You will also find here the graves of Edith Stein's parents: her mother Auguste Stein (1849–1936) in section VII and her father Siegfried Stein (1844–1897) in section XI. It has not been possible to locate the grave of Gustav Born (1851–1900), professor of anatomy, creator of the theory of the evolution of physiology, father of the brilliant physicist Max Born and great-grandfather of the singer Olivia Newton-John, nor that of Clara Sachs (1862–1921), impressionist painter.

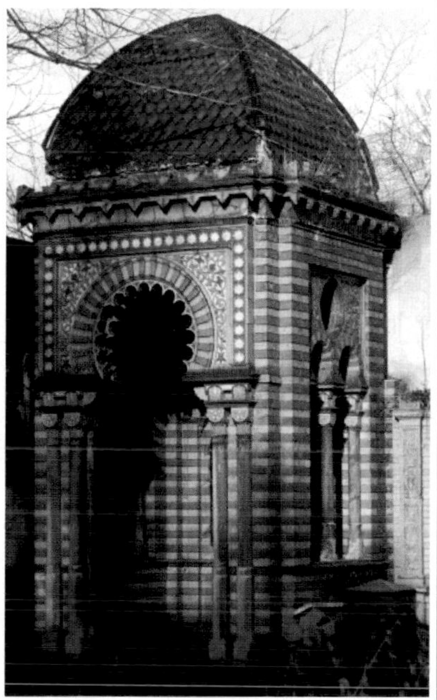

The oriental style of the Kauffmann family vault is particularly eye catching.

The Museum of Sepulchral Art, ul. Ślężna, ☎ +71 7915903. Open daily 9am–6pm. Guided tours on Sundays at noon. Tickets cost 3 and 5 zł. The present-day Jewish cemetery in Wrocław is located in the Kozanów district at ul. Lotnicza 57, ☎ +71 3532501, open on Sundays 9am–1pm. The cemetery, designed by P. Ehrlich, was established in the period from 1898 to 1902. Here you can see the memorial to the Jews who fought in the German army during the First World War as well as the funeral chapel.

Edith Stein

Edith Stein was born to a wealthy family of timber merchants. From childhood she showed extraordinary intelligence. While studying philosophy in Goettingen she became part of the group centred around Edmund Husserl, who offered her the position of assistant. In 1922 she converted to Catholicism and in 1933 she

Along with Max Born, Edith Stein is today one of the best known figures of pre-war Wrocław.

In 1991 an Edith Stein chapel was consecrated in the church of St Michael the Archangel at ul. Prusa 78.

entered a nunnery in Cologne. After taking holy orders she became Theresa Benedicta of the Cross. Her spiritual transformation did not hinder her career as an intellectual.

She was the author of numerous publications, including the translation of the works of St Thomas Aquinas. From the beginning of 1939 she lived in a nunnery in Echt (Dutch Limburgia). On 2 August 1942 she was arrested by the Germans and taken to Auschwitz-Birkenau. A week later she died in a gas chamber together with her sister Rose (baptised in 1936). Edith Stein was canonised on 1 May 1987.

In Wrocław there are many places connected with the life of this saint. Among them are: the Vier Tuerme villa, the Stein family home at ul. Nowowiejska 38 in which she lived for 23 years; the above-mentioned graves of her parents in the Old Jewish Cemetery; the two branches of the Victoria School which she attended, at Plac Nankera 1 and at ul. Ks. Poniatowskiego 9, as well as the Edith Stein Hall in Collegium Anthropologicum of the University of Wrocław, at ul. Kuźnicza 35.

The house where Edith Stein once lived is today the home of the society bearing her name.

RECOMMENDED READING

There are two shops worth mentioning in connection with the purchase of literature about Judaism and the history and culture of Jews in Poland: the bookshop in the foyer of the Jewish Historical Institute in Warsaw (ul. Tłomackie 3/5, above the Ratusz metro station) and the extremely well-stocked Jarden bookshop in the Kazimierz district of Cracow's (ul. Szeroka 2).

Michael Borwicz, **1000 Years of Jewish Life in Poland**. Paris: Centre d'Etudes Historiques, 1995

One of the most interesting syntheses of the history of Jews in Poland, conceived as a memorial to a decimated community. Published in several languages. It contains a rich set of illustrations, fascinatingly organised.

Lucjan Dobroszycki and Barbara Kirshenblatt-Gimblett, **Image Before My Eyes: A Photographic History of Jewish Life in Poland, 1864–1939**. New York: Shocken, 1977

Excellent short texts about the most significant events in the lives of Jews in Poland during an unusually important 75 years. Meticulously illustrated with photographs from the YIVO collection – the world's most important Jewish research institute – taken by the best photographers. This is, in some sense, the canonical work.

Ruth Ellen Gruber, **Jewish Heritage Travel. A Guide to East-Central Europe**. Northvale, New Jersey, Jerusalem: Jason Aronson Inc., 1999

A guide to the countries of the former Communist bloc, written by an American. After many journeys, Gruber communicates her experience and knowledge of the history and remaining traces of the lives of Jews in this part of the world before the Holocaust, as well as the current renaissance of local Jewish communities.

Yisrael Gutman, ed. **Encyclopedia of the Holocaust**. 4 vols. New York: Macmillan, 1990

One of the most important works about the Holocaust, containing texts, photographs, and specially created maps and tables.

Gershon Daivid Hundert, **The Jews in a Polish Private Town: The Case of Opatow in the Eighteenth Century**. Baltimore: John Hopkins University Press, 1992

An excellent analysis of the factors conditioning the lives of Jews in the legal situation in which most of that society existed in Poland before the Partitions.

Jan Jagielski and Robert Pasieczny, **A Guide to Jewish Warsaw**, Warsaw, 1994

Currently the only contemporary guide to the Jewish areas of Warsaw.

Contains routes and descriptions of monuments.

Monika Krajewska, **A Tribe of Stones: Jewish cemeteries in Poland**. Warsaw: Polish Scientific Publishers, Ltd., 1993

A beautiful album. Descriptions of the symbolism appearing on Jewish graves and headstones.

Carol Herselle Krinsky, **Synagogues of Europe. Architecture, History, Meaning**. New York: Architectural History Foundation, 1985

A thorough analysis of the organisation of space in selected synagogues, presented in the context of the history of the local Jewish communities. It enables one to compare synagogues constructed in Poland with those built in other parts of Europe.

Jack Kugelmass and Jonathan Boyarin, From a Ruined Garden: **The Memorial Books of Polish Jewry**. New York: Schocken, 1983. Reprint: New York: Columbia University Press, 1997

A presentation of one of the most interesting events in the life of Jewish society in Poland since the Holocaust: the commemoration of former Jewish communities and their murdered inhabitants through the publication of Memorial Books. The volume contains many extracts from these Books, translated into English from the original Yiddish and Hebrew.

Jerzy Maleńczyk, **A Guide to Jewish Lodz**. Warsaw, 1994

The only relatively current guide to Jewish Łódź. Routes, maps, and descriptions of monuments – unfortunately only 50 pages long.

Maria and Kazimierz Piechotka, **Wooden Synagogues**. Warsaw: Arkady, 1959

Not one of these buildings has been preserved, all were destroyed during the Second World War. This book makes one aware of the scale of the loss to the culture of Polish Jewry.

Antony Polonsky, **The Jews in Old Poland**, 1000–1795. London: Tauris, 1993

A scrupulous selection of texts, chosen by one of the world's greatest experts on the history of Polish Jews.

Jarosław Tambor and Jerzy Znojek, **Społeczeństwo żydowskie w Pińczowie – Jews in the life of Pińczów**. Pińczów, 1999

A short brochure about the Jewish community in Pińczów, published in two languages. Illustrated. Obtainable from the Regional Museum in Pińczów.

Golda Tencer, **And I Still See Their Faces: Images of Polish Jews**. Warsaw: Shalom Foundation, 1996

The excellent catalogue to an excellent exhibition of photography, mainly from the inter-war period.

Alan Unterman, **Jews, Their Religious Beliefs and Practices**. London: Routledge and Kegan Paul, 1981; Alan Unterman, **Dictionary of Jewish Lore and Legend**. London: Thames and Hudson Ltd., 1991

A compendium of information concerning the 3.5 thousand year history of Judaism. A wide-ranging review of knowledge connected with the tradition, spiritual culture and daily life of the Jews.

Miriam Weiner, **Jewish Roots in Poland**. Secaucus, NJ-New York: The Miriam Weiner Routes to Roots Foundation, Inc. and YIVO Institute for Jewish Research, 1997

It is from this book that you can, and should, start researching your family's past if it originated in Poland. It contains a rich variety of illustrations connected with the history of the Jews in many towns and cities, as well as an excellent selection of literature.

Polin. Studies in Polish Jewry. Vols. 1–14. Ed. By Antony Polonsky. Published by The Institute for Polish-Jewish Studies and the American Association for Polish-Jewish Studies. Oxford. Portland, Oregon: The Littman Library of Jewish Civilization

Published annually since 1986. In every volume there is a range of articles about the history of the Jews in Poland. Certain volumes are in the form of monographs.

PRACTICALITIES

•

•

Currency Exchange Rates (January 2004)

$1 = 3.80 zł

1 zł = $0.26

€1 = 4.70 zł

1 zł = €0.21

International Dialling Code: 0048

Emergency Services

997 – Police

998 – Fire Brigade

999 – Ambulance

Travelling around Poland

Regarding public transport, the most convenient means are intercity buses or express or InterCity trains (particularly on the Warsaw–Cracow line). Local buses and trains are fairly slow. Poland has little in the way of motorways, but many trunk roads make travelling by car a sensible option. There is no need to be concerned about the availability of fuel or breakdown services. The only difficulties may result from the deficient state of the surface of some roads, chiefly minor ones. Hitch-hiking is possible, but relatively rare.

Tourist Information

In all the major towns and cities there are tourist information offices and specialised information points. The staff in the majority of these agencies speak some English, and illustrated materials and maps are also available.

Money

Traveller's cheques are rarely used. Banknotes may be exchanged at special places called Kantors, and also in banks. Credit cards are accepted in most places, with the exception of smaller shops. In all the larger towns and cities it is easy to find cash machines accepting international credit cards.

Electronic Communication

All public phones can dial to any country in the world. Mobile phone networks cover 94% of the country (Poland has the eighth best coverage in Europe). Internet cafes function in the larger towns and cities.

Health

There are no problems connected with the level of hospital services. There is no need for any special injections or vaccinations. As in many countries, however, it is wiser to drink bottled water.

Accommodation and Restaurants

All kinds of accommodation are available in Poland, from the renowned hotels of the global chains to youth hostels and campsites. Also, the choice of cuisines available in restaurants is ever greater.

Safety

Anti-Semitism does not appear in an active form in Poland, with the exception of isolated cases. Rather, it is a collection of stereotypes and insulting comparisons which are, in any case, dying out. It is possible, however, to come across xenophobic behaviour or impolite curiosity, and therefore it would be wise for those maintaining a traditional appearance not to stray too far from groups or the main streets, particularly in the provinces. The Anti-Semitic iconography which can be seen painted on the walls in certain cities, particularly Łódź, is chiefly the work of the local football fans and as such is not, paradoxically, directed against Jews.

Polish pronunciation

ą – nasalised 'on'	*drz, dż, dź* – joke	*ł* – walk	*u, ó* – put
c – hats	*ę* – nasalised 'en'	*ń* – onion	*y* – sit
ć, cz – change	*i* – eat	*rz* – pleasure	*w* – vast
ch – hope	*j* – yes	*ś, sz* – shop	*ż, ź* – pleasure

ACCOMODATION PRICE CODES (FOR THE CHEAPEST DOUBLE ROOM)

① below 50 zł
② 51–80 zł
③ 81–120 zł
④ 121–150 zł
⑤ 150–300 zł
⑥ over 300 zł

SYMBOLS

 Jewish food

recommended by Pascal

WARSAW see p. 59

TOURIST INFORMATION

• **Travel agencies** catering to Jewish tourists: Our Roots, Twarda 6, ☎ +22 6200556; Shalom Travel, Twarda 6, ☎ +22 6522802.

• **Centrum Informacji Turystycznej**, pl. Zamkowy 1/13, ☎ +22 6351881.

Stołeczne Biuro Informacji Turystycznej, main hall of the Central Railway Station, ☎ +22 6351881. Recommended as a source of information, with a good choice of maps and guidebooks.

• **Web sites of Warsaw-based Jewish organizations** (all at ul. Twarda 6 and pl. Grzybowski 12/16): religious community and "Jidele" magazine, Polish Union of Jewish Students, Social and Cultural Association of Jews in Poland, Union of Jewish Religious Communities, Association of Jewish War Veterans and Victims of Prosecutions during World War Two, Association of Hidden Children of Holocaust in Poland – all are linked with www.jewish.org.pl; Lauder Foundation: www.lauder.pl; "Midrasz" Jewish Monthly: www.midrasz.home.pl.

RESTAURANTS

With several hundred restaurants in Warsaw, it is obviously impossible to name them all. Also, remember that many hotels may have more than one good restaurant.

• **Amigos**, Aleje Jerozolimskie 119, ☎ +22 6293969; noon–midnight; an American restaurant specializing in steaks (42–97 zł).

• **Arkadia**, Rynek Starego Miasta 18/20, ☎ +22 6359214; 9am–midnight; traditional Polish cuisine, main courses below 50 zł include duck á la Gdańsk and beef fillet á la Madame Walewska.

• **Bazyliszek**, Rynek Starego Miasta 3/9, ☎ +22 8311841; from noon until the last guest leaves; traditional Polish dishes including duck and lamb.

• **Belvedere**, Agrykoli 1, ☎ +22 8414806; from noon until the last guest leaves; very posh, main courses from 55 to 200 zł.

Cafe Ejlat, al. Jerozolimskie 47, ☎ +22 6285472; from noon until the last guest leaves; Jewish cuisine of average quality; speciality is Able's Lamb in blueberry sauce (34 zł). After a meal you can have a walk at the Łazienki Park.

* **Cafe Kredens**, Przemysłowa 36, ☎ +22 6251578; from 11am until the last guest leaves; an atmospheric restaurant in a less touristy, quiet and pleasant neighbourhood. Serves good Italian food and imaginative Polish dishes (stewed salmon in wine, 35 zł).

• **Casa Valdemar**, Piękna 7/9, ☎ +22 6288140; from noon until the last guest leaves; a pricey and elegant Spanish restaurant; try their roasted salmon (46 zł) and paellas (50 zł).

• **Cesarski Pałac**, Senatorska 27, ☎ +22 8288915; noon–11pm; sophisticated Chinese food with main course prices ranging from 22 to 130 zł.

• **Chianti**, Foksal 17, ☎ +22 8280222; noon–11pm; an Italian trattoria with moderate prices – 39 zł for sealoppine con formaggio (its speciality).

• **Cristal Budapest**, Marszałkowska 21/25, ☎ +22 8254733; 11am–3am; a Hungarian restaurant notable for its Transylvanian wooden plate (40 zł); also Polish cuisine.

• **Dom Restauracyjny Gessler**, Rynek Starego Miasta 21/21a, ☎ +22 8314427; from 11pm until the last guest leaves; an expensive place named after a well-known local restaurant-owner; French cuisine – main courses around 70 zł.

• **Dom Restauracyjny Landa**, Waliców 6, ☎+22 6548899; from noon until the last guest leaves. The place consists of three parts: Rodizio El Toro (Brasilian cuisine), Złota Perła (European cuisine) and American night-club South Beach Café.

* **El Popo**, Senatorska 27, ☎ +22 8272340; noon–midnight; outstanding Mexican food, live music in the evening. Be ready to wait for a table. Main courses from 15 to 75 zł.

• **Fisherman**, Jezuicka 1/3, ☎ +22 6353769; 9am–midnight; specializes in fish dishes. Rather pricey; main courses from 35 to 40 zł.

• **Fret @ Porter**, Freta 37, ☎ +22 6353754; noon–midnight; restaurant-gallery specializing in international cuisine (Polish sirloin steak 44 zł).

• **Grand Kredens**, al. Jerozolimskie 111, ☎ +22 6298008; 11am–midnight; European food at moderate prices; good lasagne with spinach (28 zł).

• **Hawełka-Wiejska**, Wiejska 4/6/8, ☎ +22 6941918; 11am–10pm; recommended for those who wish to enjoy their "traditional Polish food" in the company of MPs, senators, presidents etc.

• **Inaba**, Nowogrodzka 84/86, ☎ +22 6225955; noon–11pm; an upmarket Japanese establishment with sushi (in sets from 75 to 150 zł).

• **La Cedre**, al. Solidarności 61, ☎ +22 6701166; 11am–11pm; one of very few good restaurants in this area (Praga); Lebanese dishes á la carte. Try their roasted lamb with rice (33 zł).

• **London Steak House**, al. Jerozolimskie 42, ☎ +22 8270020; 11am–midnight; steaks from 50 zł.

• **Maharaja Tajska**, Szeroki Dunaj 13, ☎ +22 6352501; 12.30pm–11pm; enjoy your affordable Tom Yum soup (20 zł) at the site of the first synagogue in medieval Warsaw.

• **Manufaktura Creperie**, Bednarska 28/30,☎ +22 8288861; 11am–10pm; 36 kinds of crèpes for 20 zł each.

✡ **Menora**, pl. Grzybowski 2, ☎ +22 6203754; top, long--established representative of Jewish culinary art. Menu includes Jewish-style carp, gefilte fish, Jewish caviar, herrings with various tastes, stuffed goose and duck necks, goose with red cabbage, duck with apples, latkes. Plus delicious kosher wines from Israel. Main courses around 30 zł.

• **Montmatre**, Nowy Świat 7, ☎ +22 6286315; 10am–midnight; French dishes – also from Nice and Marsailles. Main courses 35–55 zł.

• **Nowy Świat**, Nowy Świat 63, ☎ +22 8265803; 9am–10pm, a yestoryear star of Warsaw's food scene, now serving "international" staples. Main courses around 40 zł.

✡ **Pod Samsonem**, Freta 3/5, ☎ +22 8311788; 10am–11pm; perhaps slightly too informal, but it's cheap and the chef is a true artist; Jewish dishes include delicious carp (for 12 zł!). Ideal for spending a few hours with friends and beer, though the waiters may sometimes strain your patience.

• **Polska**, Nowy Świat 21, ☎ +22 8263877; noon–midnight or until the last guest leaves; Polish cuisine at its best – żurek with boletuses and a buttered potato (19 zł), pierogi with veal and hot cracklings (23 zł), lettuce with cottage cheese and radishes (19 zł); and if you really want to splurge, order the best wine for 7900 zł a bottle.

• **Prohibicja**, Podwale 1, ☎ +22 6356211; noon–midnight or until the last guest leaves; a swanky piano bar, but you may like it; the menu includes vegetarian penne Putanesca (15 zł).

Qchnia Artystyczna, al. Ujazdowskie 6 (Zamek Ujazdowski), ☎ +22 6257627; noon–midnight; a cultish place with many imaginative dishes (15–45 zł), perfect for a date; lots of imaginative dishes (15–45 zł), excellent avocado and grilled chicken salad in balmy sauce (17 zł). You can sit here for hours, occasionally popping out to the exhibition halls of the Contemporary Art Centre upstairs.

• **San Marzano**, Świętokrzyska 18, ☎ +22 8271976; Mon–Thu 9am–11pm, Fri 9am–midnight, sat 11am–midnight, 11am–11pm; a local variety of the Pizza Express chain; for the masses, yet elegant – though the decor with books cut to shelf depth may be not to your taste. Good pizza quatro formaggi and attractive prices.

• **Tandoor Palace**, Marszałkowska 21/25, ☎ +22 8252375; noon–11pm; dishes from the Indian subcontinent, with Mango Lussi yoghurt (15 zł) as the speciality. Well-priced.

• **Tsarina**, Jezuicka 3, ☎ +22 6357474; noon–11pm; Russian cuisine (Siberian pielmieni 38 zł, with sturgeon – 70 zł). Plush and on the expensive side.

• **Tsubame**, Foksal 16, ☎ +22 8265127; noon–midnight, Sun till 10pm; Japanese dishes at exorbitant prices (sukiyaki 150 zł).

• **U Fukiera**, Rynek Starego Miasta 27, ☎ +22 8311013; from noon until the last guest leaves; one of the best known and certainly the oldest restaurant in Warsaw, with centuries-long traditions. Praised for dainty Polish food (white borsch with boletuses, 30 zł) and a wide selection of wines. Expensive.

✡ **Warszawa–Jerozolima**, Smocza 27, ☎ +22 8383217; noon–midnight; perfect location when you compare it with the topography of the pre-war Jewish Warsaw. Among others good Israeli cuisine. One quibble is slow service. Try their Jewish-style red herring or baked trout with garlic butter and herbs. This is also a place for genuine tsimmes. Main courses priced at 25–80 zł.

Accommodation

There are over 70 hotels in Warsaw. Those listed below are either centrally located or good value. If you want to stay out of the city centre, enquire at tourist information.

• **Belwederski**, Sułkiewicza 11, ☎ +22 8404011, 87 beds; an upmarket hotel offering suites and rooms with bath, phone, Sat TV, radio, fridge; some rooms also with a kitchenette; breakfast included; safe deposit, restaurant, café, bar. ⑥

✱ **Bristol**, Krakowskie Przedmieście 42/44, ☎ +22 6252525, 5511000, bristol@it.com.pl; 376 beds; a legendary hotel now owned by the exclusive Le Royal Meridien chain. Warsaw's symbol, like the Old Town or Łazienki Park. All celebrities who visited the city stayed here, from Marlena Dietrich to the Rolling Stones. Predictably, luxury comes at a price: a night here will cost you at least 1000 zł; suites and rooms with bath, phone, Sat TV, radio, air-conditioning, minibar; breakfast included; safe deposit, restaurants, café, bar, bureau de change, sauna, gym, solarium, swimming pool; unguarded car park. ⑥

• **Dom Literatury**, Krakowskie Przedmieście 87/89, ☎ +22 6350404, 8277428; 25 beds; facing the Column of Sigismund III; one suite, rooms with bath, some rooms with TV, fridge and kitchenette; breakfast included; safe deposit, restaurant, café, guarded car park. ⑤

• **Europejski**, Krakowskie Przedmieście 13, ☎ +22 8265051, europej@orbis.pl; 339 beds; one of the most renowned hotels in Warsaw; suites and rooms with bath, phone, Sat TV, radio, minibar; breakfast included; safe deposit, restaurant, café, bureau de change, casino; guarded car park. ⑥

• **Grand**, Krucza 28, ☎ +22 5832100, 6221652, wagrand@orbis.pl; 564 beds; suites and rooms with bath, phone, Sat TV, radio, some rooms with a fridge; breakfast included; safe deposit, restaurant, café, bar, bureau de change, hairdresser, beauty parlour; guarded car park. ⑥

• **Gromada**, pl. Powstańców Warszawy 2, ☎ +22 582900, 8274943, gromadch@box43.onet.pl; 392 beds; suites and rooms with bath, phone, Sat TV, radio, some rooms with a minibar; breakfast included; safe deposit, restaurant, bar, bureau de change, hairdresser; guarded car park. ⑥

• **Harenda**, Krakowskie Przedmieście 4/6, ☎ +22 8260071–3, info@harenda.pl; 50 beds; close to the Copernicus Monument and the University; suites and rooms with bath, phone, Sat TV, some rooms with a radio and fridge; breakfast included; safe deposit, restaurant, café, bar; guarded car park. ⑥

• **Hera**, Belwederska 26/30, ☎ +22 5531000; 110 beds; university hotel with excellent location near one of the Łazienki Park gates; suites and rooms with bath, phone, Sat TV, radio, some rooms with a fridge; breakfast included; safe deposit, restaurant, café, bar, hairdresser; guarded car park. ⑤

• **Holiday Inn**, Złota 48/54, ☎ +22 6973877, 6973999, holiday@orbis.pl; 622 beds; right at the heart of the city centre, it's a result of the investment boom following the downfall of communism; suites and rooms with bath, phone, Sat TV, air-conditioning, minibar; safe deposit, restaurant, café, bar, bureau de change, hairdresser, beauty parlour, car rental, sauna, gym, solarium; guarded car park, garage. ⑥

• **Jan III Sobieski**, pl. Zawiszy 1, ☎ +22 5791000, hotel@sobieski.com.pl; 787 beds; extravagantly painted, but it's one of Warsaw's landmarks; suites and rooms with bath, phone, Sat TV, air-conditioning, minibar; breakfast included; safe deposit, restaurant, café, bar, bureau de change, hairdresser, fitness club, massage parlour, solarium; garage. ⑥

✱ **Marriot**, al. Jerozolimskie 65/79, ☎ +22 6306306, marriot@it.com.pl; the high-rise opposite the Central Railway Station; symbol of Warsaw's aspirations to the status of a European metropolis. 523 rooms and suites will satisfy all tastes – the most expensive suite is just 2000 € a night, one-day use of their garage – 130 zł; suites and rooms with bath, phone, Sat TV, radio, Internet access, air-conditioning; breakfast included; safe deposit, restaurant, café, bureau de change, hairdresser, beauty parlour, health centre, car rental, sauna, gym, solarium, bank, casino; garage. ⑥

• **Mazowiecki**, Mazowiecka 10, ☎ +22 6879117, 8272365; 103 beds; convenient location almost not far from of the city centre, close to the University and Academy of Fine Arts; rooms with bath, colour TV, radio, some rooms with a phone and fridge; breakfast included; safe deposit, restaurant; unguarded car park. ⑤

• **MDM**, pl. Konstytucji 1, ☎ +22 6216211, 6282526, hotel.mdm@syrena.com.pl; 211 beds for all lovers of monumental, totalitarian architecture; excellent location, close to trams and the underground; suites and rooms with bath, phone, Sat TV, some rooms with a fridge; breakfast included; safe deposit, restaurant, bureau de change, hairdresser, beauty parlour; unguarded car park. ⑥

• **Mercure Fryderyk Chopin**, Jana Pawła II 22, ☎ +22 6200201, mercure@perytnet.pl; 351 beds; in pre-war Warsaw, Mercure would have stood in the centre of the Jewish quarter – today its only remnant is the house at ul. Jana Pawła 38 (Solna 16/18 before the war); suites and rooms with bath, phone, Sat TV, air-conditioning, radio, some rooms with a minibar; breakfast included; safe deposit, restaurant, café, bar, sauna, gym, massage parlour and jacuzzi; garage. ⑥

• **Metropol**, Marszałkowska 99a, ☎ +22 6294001, hotel.metropol@syrena.com.pl; 256 beds; suites and rooms with bath, phone, Sat TV, radio, some rooms with a fridge; breakfast included; safe deposit, restaurant, bar, bureau de change, beauty parlour; guarded car park. ⑥

• **Novotel Warszawa Centrum Hotel**, Nowogrodzka 24/26, ☎ +22 8230364, 6210271, 1289 beds; towering over the city's main street junction; suites and rooms with bath, phone, Sat TV, radio, air-conditioning, some rooms with a minibar; breakfast included; safe deposit, restaurant, café, bureau de change, hairdresser, beauty parlour, car rental; guarded car park. ⑥

• **Praski**, al. Solidarności 61, ☎ +22 8184989, phthot@polbox.com; 71 beds; the best hotel on the right bank, only a two-minute walk from the historical Jewish Praga; rooms with bath, Sat TV, radio; breakfast included; safe deposit, restaurant, café, bar; guarded car park. ⑤

• **Sheraton**, Prusa 2, ☎ +22 6576100, res201@sheraton.com; 496 beds; "hotel & towers", Warsaw's representative of the chain, conveniently located in Plac Trzech Krzyży; suites and rooms with bath, phone, Sat TV, radio, air-conditioning, minibar; breakfast included; safe deposit, restaurants, café, bar, sauna, gym, hairdresser; garage. ⑥

• **Sofitel Victoria**, Królewska 11, ☎ +22 6578011, warsaw@interconti.com; 477 beds; interesting for all Judaica seekers as it stands on the site of the Kronenberg Palace; suites and rooms with bath (also business rooms with fax etc.), phone, Sat TV, radio, air-conditioning, minibar, some rooms with a kitchenette; breakfast included; safe deposit, restaurant, café, bar, bureau de change, beauty parlour, sauna, massage parlour, solarium; guarded car park, garage. ⑥

• **Solec**, Zagórna 1, ☎ +22 6254400, rez.solec@orbis.pl; 274 beds; one suite, rooms with bath, phone, Sat TV, radio; breakfast included; safe deposit, restaurant, café, bar, bureau de change, solarium, hairdresser, beauty parlour; guarded car park. ⑤

• **Szkolne Schronisko Młodzieżowe**, Smolna 30, ☎ +22 8278952; the most convenient of Warsaw's youth hostels, off Nowy Świat, opposite the National Museum. ③

Events

With so many regular events in Warsaw, it's impossible to list them all. You can check what's going on in a listings paper like "Informator Kulturalny Stolicy" or "Warszawski Informator Kulturalny". Information in English (the "Warsaw Voice" weekly and other newspapers) is available in the Central Railway Station hall. Major Jewish events include Dni Książki Żydowskiej (Jewish Book Days, in September), organized by the "Midrasz" magazine and Lauder Foundation. The event is more than its name may suggest – apart from meeting Jewish writers you can also see films, take part in discussions, learn to cook Jewish dishes and sing in Yiddish or (for children) draw and paint. Latest information can be found at www.jewish.org.pl.

Podlasie | see p. 89

Tourist information

Białystok

• **Punkt Informacji Turystycznej**, Sienkiewicza 3, ☎ +85 6537950.

Sejny

• **Fundacja Pogranicze – Ośrodek "Pogranicze – Sztuk, Kultur, Narodów"**, Piłsudskiego 37, ☎ +87 5162765, 5162189, fundacja@pogranicze.sejny.pl.

Tykocin

• **Tykocin Museum – Branch of Białystok's Muzeum Podlaskie**, Kozia 2, ☎ +85 7181626.

Restaurants

Białystok

• **Ananda**, Warszawska 30, ☎ +85 7413336; noon–10pm, Sat–Sun 1pm–11pm; Indian and vegetarian cuisine.

• **Arsenał**, Mickiewicza 2, ☎ +85 7428565; noon–11pm, Sat noon–3am; European cuisine, fish.

• **Astoria**, Sienkiewicza 4, ☎ +85 7435624; 11am–9pm, Sun 1pm–9pm; traditional Polish food.

• **Grodno**, Sienkiewicza 28, ☎ +85 7435240; 10am–1am; Belorussian cuisine.

• **Oaza**, Świętojańska 4, ☎ +85 7328020; 10am–10pm, Sun noon–10pm; Arab and vegetarian cuisine.

• **Sabatino**, Sienkiewicza 3, ☎ +85 7435823; noon–11.30pm; Italian and Mediterranean cuisine.

Ulice Świata, Warszawska 30b, ☎ 85 7404161; 1pm–1am, at weekends until the last guest leaves; the menu includes traditional Polish and international dishes.

• **Vip**, Malmeda 5, ☎ +85 7446447; noon–3am, Sat–Sun 1pm–4am; Polish cuisine.

Sejny

Litewska, 22 Lipca 9, ☎ +87 5162908; noon–8pm; in the same building as the Lithuanian consulate; recommended as one of few places in Poland where you can savour genuine Lithuanian dishes; there are staples like blini and zeppelins, but also very interesting soczewiak (pierogi with lentils – 8.50 zł).

Tykocin

Tejsza, Kozia 2, ☎ +85 7187750; 10am–8pm. Cellar of the local *beit hamidrash* (entrance at the back). Jewish dishes include festive tsimmes (beef stew with carrots, nuts, dried fruit and honey; 13 zł); kugel (potato cake with chicken sausage and onions; 6 zł); kreplach (noodles with chopped beef; 11 zł); veal rissole (9 zł); also served in honey sauce with raisins: chicken stew (8 zł); liver (7 zł) and fish (7 zł). The menu has also Jewish-style herring (5.50 zł) and Jewish gingerbread (2.50 zł).

Accommodation

Białystok

• **Biały**, Łąkowa 9/2, ☎ +85 7322893; 44 beds; shared showers, Sat TV in some rooms, restaurant, bar, guarded car park. ②

• **Cristal**, Lipowa 3, ☎ +85 7425061, cristal@cristal.com.pl; 196 beds; suites, rooms with bath; breakfast included; excellent restaurant, bar, travel agency, bureau de change, safe, newsagent, gym, fitness club, sauna, fitness club, beauty parlour, hairdresser, horses, horse-cabs, sleigh rides, guarded car park. ⑤

• **Diadem**, Kawaleryjska 38, ☎ +85 7443274; 22 beds; one suite, rooms with bath, Sat TV and radio in some rooms; breakfast included; restaurant, bar, café, safe deposit, guarded car park. ③

• **Gołębiewski**, Pałacowa 7, ☎ +85 7435435, bialystok@golebiewski.pl; 376 beds; suites and rooms with bath, Sat TV; breakfast included; good restaurant, café, bar, bureau de change, safe deposit, sauna, gym, indoor swimming pool, billiards, bowling alley, amusement arcade, bike rental, shopping centre, guarded car park. ⑥

• **Gromada**, Jana Pawła II 77, ☎ +85 6511641, lesny@gromada.pl; 82 beds; suites, rooms with bath; breakfast included; safe deposit, restaurant, café, volleyball court, guarded car park. ⑤

• **MOSiR**, Wołodyjowskiego 5, ☎ +85 7422629; 93 beds; suites, rooms with bath or shared showers, Sat TV, radio, fridge and minibar (in some rooms); breakfast included; safe deposit, restaurant, sauna, fitness club, sports stadium, skating rink, unguarded car park. ④

• **Pastel**, Waszyngtona 24a, ☎ +85 7486060; 40 beds; one suite, rooms with bath; breakfast included; restaurant, bar, café, gym, sauna, guarded car park. ④

• **Trzy Sosny**, Leśna 20, ☎ +85 6631311; 100 beds; suites, rooms with bath, radio in some rooms; breakfast included; café, safe deposit, food shop, unguarded car park, garage. ②

• **Turkus**, Jana Pawła II 54, ☎ +85 6513278, 6511211; 99 beds; rooms with bath; breakfast included; restaurant, café, bar, bureau de change, safe deposit, guarded car park. ④

Krynki

• **Agrotourist farm**, Mr Marek Marszałek, Łapicze 27, ☎ +50 2575330; 4 beds; food, forest, pond, bikes, tent sites, hunting; the proprietor speaks German. ②

Sejny

• **Skarpa**, Piłsudskiego 13, ☎ +87 5162065; 48 beds; rooms with bath, Sat TV and radio in some rooms, restaurant, bar, jeweller, billiards, guarded car park. ②

Tykocin

• **Dom pod Czarnym Bocianem**, Poświętna 16, ☎ +85 7187408, www.czarnybocian.prv.pl, jotas6@kki.net.pl; 10 beds; doubles with bath, bikes and canoes included, unguarded car park. ②

Events

Sejny

• **Camera Pro Minoritate**, an international film festival recently held in October; films on the small nations, minorities and ethnic groups from Central and East Europe. The festival is followed by an international seminar on the presence of local communities in modern electronic media. Organized by Fundacja Pogranicze – Ośrodek

"Pogranicze – Sztuk, Kultur, Narodów", Piłsudskiego 37, ☎ +87 5162765, 5162189, fundacja@pogranicze.sejny.pl.

Tykocin

• **Jewish festivals**: the Great Synagogue museum holds meetings on holidays; the schedule for Sukkot includes a lecture on "The Sukkot Tradition" and dinner in a sukkot. Organized by the Tykocin Museum – Branch of Białystok's Muzeum Podlaskie, Kozia 2, ☎ +85 7181626.

ŁÓDŹ

see p. 113

Tourist information

• **Fundacja Monumentum Iudaicum**, Zielona 8/10; established by the municipality, the foundation takes care of Jewish monuments in Łódź, notably the New Cemetery.

• **Wojewódzki Ośrodek Informacji Turystycznej**, Traugutta 18, ☎ +42 6337169

Restaurants

The best restaurants are in ul. Piotrkowska, but these do not serve Jewish dishes.

• **Dworek**, Rogowska 24, ☎ +42 6597640; noon–11pm; Polish cuisine, including sirloin stuffed with bacon (35 zł).

• **Esplanada**, Piotrkowska 100, ☎ +42 6305989; 11am–midnight, at weekends 11am–1am; international cuisine; rather plush.

• **Figaro**, Piotrkowska 92, ☎ +42 6302008; noon–11pm; Polish cuisine, but also good Italian and French dishes including mussels in garlic sauce (46 zł).

• **Ha Long**, Piotrkowska 152, ☎ +42 6362369; 11am–11pm; Chinese and Vietnamese cuisine; goat in red wine for those who like experiments (16 zł).

• **Klub Spadkobierców**, Piotrkowska 77, ☎ +42 6337401; 1pm–11pm; international cuisine, large selection ranging from turkey medallion with croutons and cranberries (35 zł) to delicious pike perch (38 zł).

• **Quo Vadis**, Piotrkowska 64, ☎ +42 6325063; from 10am until the last guest leaves; wine bar with "international" dishes including Sicilian roasted duck. Inexpensive.

• **U Chochoła**, Piotrkowska 200, ☎ +42 6370919; noon–midnight; an inn specializing in traditional Polish cuisine.

• **Złota Kaczka**, Piotrkowska 79, ☎ +42 7126403; 12.30pm–11pm; an upmarket Chinese restaurant with very wallet-friendly prices.

Accommodation

• **Ambasador**, Kosynierów Gdyńskich 8, ☎ +42 6464268; 170 beds; suites and rooms with bath, phone, Sat TV, radio, some rooms with air-conditioning and fridge; breakfast included; safe, restaurant, bar, swimming pool; guarded car park. ⑤

• **Boss**, Tatrzańska 11, ☎ +42 6724889, 6763113, hotelboss@poczta.wp.pl; 184 beds; suites and rooms with bath, phone, radio, some rooms with Sat TV and fridge; safe deposit, restaurant; guarded car park. ④

• **Centrum**, Kilińskiego 59/63, ☎ +42 6328640, centrum@hotelspt.com.pl; 262 beds; luxury hotel with rooms starting at 170 zł per night; suites and rooms with bath, phone, Sat TV, radio, some rooms are air-conditioned; breakfast included; safe, restaurant, bar, bureau de change, food shop, post-office, bank, hairdresser, car rental, sauna, gym, casino; guarded car park. ⑤

• **Eskulap**, Paradna 46, ☎ +42 6457688; 74 beds; suites and rooms with bath, phone, Sat TV, radio, some rooms are air-conditioned and with minibars; breakfast included; restaurant, bar, hairdresser, canoe rental, sauna, gym; guarded car park. ④

• **Fantazja**, Kolumny 296, ☎ +42 6499491; 38 beds; suites and rooms with bath, phone, Sat TV, radio; breakfast included; restaurant; guarded car park. ③

• **Flora**, Szczecińska 111, ☎ +42 6520535; 30 beds; a motel offering one suite and rooms with bath, phone, Sat TV, radio; breakfast included; restaurant, café, bar; guarded car park. ⑤

• **Garnizonowy-Reymont**, Legionów 81, ☎ +42 6338023; 52 beds; centrally located; suites and rooms with bath, phone, TV, radio, some rooms with a fridge; breakfast included; safe, restaurant, café, bar. ⑤

• **Grand**, Piotrkowska 72, ☎ +42 6339920, logrand@orbis.pl; 266 beds in a historic building; suites and rooms with bath, phone, Sat TV, radio, minibar, some rooms with safes and stationary bikes; breakfast included; safe deposit, restaurant, café, night club, casino, bureau de change, guides; guarded car park. ⑤

• **Ibis**, Piłsudskiego 1/11, ☎ +42 6386700; 418 beds; a luxury hotel offering only doubles with bath; phone, Sat TV, air-conditioning; breakfast included; safe deposit, restaurant, café, bar, bowling alley, cinema, disco; guarded car park. ⑤

• **Mazowiecki**, 28 Pułku Strzelców Kaniowskich 53/57, ☎ +42 6374333, hotelspt@hotelspt.com.pl; 148 beds; suites and rooms with bath, one room for disabled tourists; phone, Sat TV, radio, some rooms with fridges; breakfast included; safe, restaurant, café, hairdresser, beauty parlour, sauna, gym; guarded car park. ⑤

• **Polonia**, Narutowicza 38, ☎ +42 6328773, hotelspt@hotelspt.com.pl; 179 beds; rooms with bath, phone, Sat TV, radio, some rooms with fridges; breakfast included; safe, restaurant, café, hairdresser, solarium; guarded car park. ④

• **RAFF**, Milionowa 25, ☎ +42 6847510; 123 beds with private bath or shared showers, radio, some with colour TV and fridge; safe deposit, bar; unguarded car park. ①

• **Savoy**, Traugutta 5, ☎ +42 6329360, hotelspt@hotelspt.com.pl; 125 beds; rooms with bath, phone,

Sat TV, radio, some with a fridge; breakfast included; safe, restaurant, bar, hairdresser. ⑤

• **Syrena**, Zachodnia 56, ☎ +42 6333869; 37 beds; rooms at 40–70 zł per night; shared showers; safe deposit, sauna, solarium; unguarded car park. ②

• **Światowit**, Kościuszki 68, ☎ +42 6363637, swiatowit@hotelspt.com.pl; 283 beds; suites and rooms with bath, phone, Sat TV, radio, some rooms with a fridge; breakfast included; safe, restaurant, café, hairdresser, cake shop, solarium, casino; guarded car park. ⑤

The Kielce Region | see p. 133

Tourist information

Busko Zdrój

• **Biuro Informacji turystycznej**, ☎+41 3784211

Kielce

• **Miejski Ośrodek Informacji Turystycznej**, ☎ +41 3676436, 3676011, fax 3458681.

• Also at the following hotels described below: Bristol, Elita, Stella.

Pińczów

• **Biuro Informacji Turystycznej**, pl. Wolności 22; ☎+41 3575404, fax 3572645.

Sandomierz

• **PTTK**, Rynek 25, ☎ +15 8322305

• **Web-site**: www.sandomierz.pl.

Restaurants

Busko Zdrój

• **Corleone**, Mickiewicza 9, ☎ +41 3781925; 11am–10pm, Sun noon–10pm; a pizza parlour.

Chęciny

• **Pod Zamkiem**, Armii Krajowej, ☎ +41 3151033; Tue–Sun 11am–9pm; Polish cuisine.

Kielce

• **Jodłowa**, Paderewskiego 3/5, ☎ +41 3610487; noon–9.30pm; Polish cuisine, though you can also try a main course named oddly “Oj! Co za cymes”.

• **Winnica**, Winnicka 4, ☎ +41 3444576; 11am–11pm, Sun & Mon 11am–8pm; Polish and Ukrainian cuisine with dishes like *żarkoje* (25 zł).

Pińczów

• **Manhattan**, Krótka 3, ☎ +41 3575389; from 9am until the last guest leaves; Polish cuisine.

• **Tawerna**, Piłsudskiego 8, ☎ +41 3574100; 11am–11pm; Polish and Chinese food.

Sandomierz

• **Ha Noi**, Sokolnickiego 8, ☎ +15 8332522; 11am–10pm; vietnamese cuisine.

• **Królowej Jadwigi**, Krakowska 24, ☎ +15 8322988; open 24hr; Polish food.

• **Oriana**, Mariacka 5, ☎ +15 8322724; 8am–10pm; traditional Polish cuisine.

• **Pod Ciżemką**, Rynek 27, ☎ +15 8320550; noon–11pm; Polish and Italian dishes, cocktail bar.

• **Retro**, Rynek 5, ☎ +15 8322859; 10am–10pm; Polish cuisine.

Accommodation

Busko Zdrój

• **Gromada**, Waryńskiego 10, ☎ +41 3783001–4, radek@gromada.pl; 72 beds; suites, rooms with bath, colour TV, radio, fridge in some rooms; breakfast included; restaurant, café, bar, restaurant, tourist information, unguarded car park. ⑤

• **Marconi**, Park Zdrojowy, ☎/fax +41 3782058, dyrekcja@uzdrowisko-busko-zdroj.com.pl; 159 beds; a sanatorium offering some rooms with bath, Sat TV; café, canteen, sports hall, gym, centre of natural medicine, medical care, concerts, tourist information, unguarded car park. ③

• **Pod Świerkiem**, Waryńskiego 38, ☎ +41 3782854, hotelura@polbox.com; 31 beds; one suite, rooms with bath, Sat TV, radio; restaurant, tourist information, guarded car park, garage. ③

• **Sanato**, 1 Maja 29, ☎ +41 3781951; 42 beds; suites, rooms with bath, colour TV, radio, fridge (in some rooms); breakfast included; safe deposit, cocktail bar, hairdresser, beauty parlour, solarium, massage parlour, sports hall, unguarded car park. ②

• **Willa Słowacki**, 1 Maja 31, ☎ +41 3787879; 55 beds; rooms with baths or shared showers, radio, TV rental, restaurant, hairdresser, beauty parlour, massage parlour, solarium, unguarded car park. ③

Chęciny

• **Raj**, Dobrzączka, ☎ +41 3465127; an inn with 26 beds; one suite, rooms with bath; safe deposit, restaurant, café, bar, unguarded car park, garage. ④

Kielce

• **Arkadia**, Urzędnicza 13, ☎ +41 3455150; 423 beds; rooms with baths or shared showers, some rooms with Sat TV; unguarded car park. ②

• **Bristol**, Sienkiewicza 21, ☎ +41 3682460, 3682466; 45 beds; suites and rooms with bath, phone, Sat TV, radio, fridge; breakfast included; safe deposit, restaurant, café, guarded car park, garage. ⑤

• **Elita**, Równa 4a, ☎ +41 3442230, 3443215, hotelelita@jandb.com.pl; 19 beds; suites and rooms with bath, phone, Sat TV, radio, fridge; breakfast included, safe deposit, bar, tourist office, guarded car park. ⑤

✱ **Exbud**, Manifestu Lipcowego 34, ☎ +41 3326360, 3326393, eb@exbud.com.pl; 105 beds; suites and rooms with bath, phone, Sat TV, radio, fridge, kitchenette; some rooms with a minibar and jacuzzi; breakfast included, safe deposit, restaurant, bar, bureau de change, bookshop, car wash, hairdresser, beauty parlour, sauna, gym and solarium; guarded car park, garage. ⑥

• **Iskra**, Krakowska 72, ☎ +41 3660032; 44 beds; shared showers, some rooms with radio and fridge; restaurant, café, sauna, gym, sports grounds, tennis court; guarded car park. ③

• **Karczówka**, Karczówkowska 64, ☎ +41 3456606, 3662626; 35 beds; rooms with baths or shared showers, phone, Sat TV, radio, fridge (in some rooms); restaurant, café, guarded car park. ⑤

• **Łysogóry**, Sienkiewicza 78, ☎ +41 3662511, 3662594; 201 beds; suites and rooms with bath, phone, Sat TV, radio, fridge, some rooms with a minibar, sauna and jacuzzi; breakfast included; safe deposit, restaurant, café, bar, bureau de change, beauty parlour, hairdresser, newsagent, guarded car park. ⑤

• **Nowiny**, Zgórsko 25a, ☎ +41 3465257; 15 beds; rooms with bath or shared showers, some rooms with colour TV and radio; restaurant, unguarded car park. ③

• **Stadion**, Ściegiennego 8, ☎ +41 3687715; 50 beds; rooms with bath, colour TV, radio; safe deposit, restaurant, cocktail bar, sauna, gym, sports grounds, tennis court; unguarded car park. ④

• **Stella**, Krakowska 374, ☎ +41 3465164, 3465448; 92 beds; rooms with bath; some rooms with Sat TV, phone and radio; bar, sauna, gym; unguarded car park. ③

Pińczów

• **MOSiR**, Pałęki 26, ☎ +41 3572044; 51 beds; guest rooms in a very attractive spot at the Nida reservoir; shared showers, some rooms with colour TV; restaurant, café, tennis court, horses, swimming, water sports, unguarded car park. ②

Sandomierz

• **Agro**, Mokoszyńska 3, ☎ +15 8333106; 30 beds; rooms with baths or shared showers, colour TV (in some rooms), radio; safe deposit, unguarded car park. ③

✱ **Królowej Jadwigi**, Krakowska 24, ☎ +15 8322988; 43 beds; a highly recommended motel, run with dedication and enthusiasm; the proprietor intends to open a small exhibition of local Judaica; rooms with baths or shared showers, Sat TV (in some rooms), safe deposit, restaurant, guarded car park. ④

• **Oscar**, Mickiewicza 17a, ☎ +15 8321144; 16 beds; rooms with bath, Sat TV, radio; restaurant, café, solarium, beauty parlour, unguarded car park. ③

• **Pod Ciżemką**, Rynek 27, ☎ +15 8320550; 20 beds; the most expensive hotel in town, in a historic building in the market square; rooms with bath, phone, Sat TV; restaurant, café, guarded car park. ⑤

• **Winnica**, Mały Rynek 2, ☎ +15 8323130; 44 beds; a pension perfectly located in the heart of the Old Town, thus enormously popular with tourists; shared showers, radio, safe deposit, restaurant, unguarded car park. ②

• **Zacisze**, Portowa 3a, ☎ +15 8321905; an inn with 16 beds; rooms with bath, phone, Sat TV; restaurant, garage. ③

THE LUBLIN REGION | see p. 153

TOURIST INFORMATION

Kazimierz Dolny

• **Biuro Obsługi Ruchu Turystycznego PTTK**, Rynek 27, ☎ +81 8810046, pttk_kazimierz_dolny@poczta.onet.pl, www.kazimierz-dolny.pl.
This very useful office will reserve you a room, restaurant table or guide. Also sells maps, operates boat cruises

down the Vistula River and hires coaches.

Lublin

- **Lubelski Ośrodek Informacji Turystycznej**, Jezuicka1/3, with a bookshop at Brama Krakowska (on the market square side), ☎ +81 5324412; perfectly run, with lots of indispensable materials, including Andrzej Trzciński's guidebook to the monuments of Jewish culture in the Lublin region. Open Mon–Fri 10am–6pm, Sat 10am–5pm, Sun 10am–3pm.
- **Agencja Promocji Artystycznej**, Lipińskiego 8a/19, ☎ +81 7430227, related to the Szeroka 28 restaurant; organizes concerts of klezmer music as well as guided (and translated) tours around Lublin and its vicinity, also offers assistance in genealogical search.

Zamość

- **PTTK – guiding services**, Staszica 31, ☎ +84 6385687.
- **Zamojski Ośrodek Informacji Turystycznej**, Rynek Wielki 13 (Town Hall), ☎ +84 6392292, 6270813.

Restaurants

Kazimierz Dolny

- **Grill**, Nadrzeczna 24, ☎ +81 8810579; from noon until the last guest leaves.
- **Pod Wietrzną Górą**, Krakowska 1, ☎ +81 8810640, www.kazimierz-dolny.pl/wietrzna.html; 9am–10pm; traditional Polish cuisine.

✱ **Staropolska**, Nadrzeczna 14, ☎ +81 8810236; noon–10pm; traditional Polish cuisine, fish.

✱ **U Fryzjera**, Witkiewicza 2, ☎ +81 8810426, www.kazimierz-dolny.pl/fryzjer.html; 9.30am–midnight, Fri–Sat 9.30am–2.00am; the food is Jewish-like rather than genuine Jewish, but the choice is quite interesting. Appetizers (5–8 zł) include: eierzwiebels – chopped hard-boiled eggs with onion and goose fat; tsimmes – carrot stew with prunes and honey, spiced with cinnamon; Jewish caviar – boiled and minced poultry livers with onion and hard-boiled eggs. Soups: sweetish Jerusalem soup, fish soup with almonds and raisins, or with steamed noodles and onion (farfels). Main courses: ox tongues in horseradish sauce (19 zł), poultry livers (19 zł), veal escalopes (22 zł), trout with almonds (23 zł), goose with cabbage (23 zł). Also vegetarian fryser, or goat cheese in walnut crumbs and cranberry sauce.

✱ **Zielona Tawerna**, Nadwiślańska 4, ☎ +81 8810308; 10am–9pm; Polish food; great for pierogi (15 zł).

Kraśnik

- **Musicaffe**, Krasińskiego 11f, ☎ +81 8256804; 11am–1am; Italian cuisine.

Lubartów

- **Max**, Rynek II, ☎ +81 8551782; 9am–midnight; Polish cuisine.

Lublin

- **Duch**, Rynek 17, ☎ +81 5323617, arek@mc-club.com.pl; Sun–Thu 11am–11pm, Fri–Sat 11am–midnight; Polish and Italian cuisine.
- **Hades**, Peowiaków 12, ☎ +81 5328761, hades@platon.man.lublin.pl; noon–midnight; Polish cuisine; a big restaurant known for Sunday piano concerts.

• **Old Pub**, Grodzka 8, ☎ +81 7437127; 11am–11pm; a varied menu including some Tex-Mex dishes.

• **Piwnica**, Skłodowskiej-Curie 12, ☎ +81 5343919; noon–11pm; Mediterranean cuisine.

Piwnica pod Fortuną, Rynek 8, ☎ +81 5340334; noon–midnight; traditional and modern Polish cuisine.

• **Piwnica Rycerska**, Krakowskie Przedmieście 19, ☎ +81 5340595, rezerwacje@piwnica-rycerska.pl; traditional Polish cuisine; 11am–10pm.

• **Resursa**, Krakowskie Przedmieście 68, ☎ +81 5342991; Mon–Fri 10am–10pm, Sat 1pm–11pm, Sun 1pm–11pm; fish.

Szeroka 28, Grodzka 21 (next to the Grodzka Gate), ☎ +81 5346109, www.szeroka28.of.pl; 11am–11pm, Sat–Sun longer hours. Szeroka 28 is the pre-war address of a house belonging to the legendary tsadik known as the Seer of Lublin. The vestibule is styled on an old "Christian" lane with hanging signs, lanterns and cobble stones, while the lower level looks like a Jewish lane, complete with an entrance to a tailor's house. Onion soup 4.90 zł; golden soup with matza balls 5.90 zł; stuffed goose necks 8.90 zł; Jewish-style herring from 5 zł (portion) to 25 zł (dish); ox tongue with raisins and rice 29.90 zł; speciality – Bajnisia goose with hallah 99.99 zł (must be ordered a day earlier). Wide range of alcohols, including Passover Slivovitz. Large terrace; staff speak English.

• **Złoty Osioł**, Grodzka 5a, ☎ +81 5329042; Sun–Thu noon–midnight, Fri–Sat noon–1am; traditional Polish cuisine; an "arty inn" with poetry singing and folk music.

Włodawa

• **Prima**, Partyzantów 12a, ☎ +82 5724576; noon–9pm; Polish cuisine.

Zamość

• **Green**, Staszica 2, ☎ +84 6270336; Mon–Thu 1pm–10pm, Fri 1pm–midnight, Sat 4pm–3am, Sun 1pm–10pm; a pub with a Polish menu.

Muzealna, Ormiańska 30, ☎ +84 6387300; from noon–until the last guest leaves; Polish cuisine.

• **Padwa**, Staszica 23, ☎ +84 6386256; 9am–11pm; traditional Polish, Hungarian and Chinese food.

• **Patio**, Kilińskiego 11, ☎ +84 6389810; 11am–10pm; Polish and Italian cuisine.

• **Ratuszowa**, Rynek Wielki 13, ☎ +84 6271557; from 9am until the last guest leaves; Polish cuisine.

• **Wiatrak**, Lwowska 55, ☎ +84 6385922; Mon–Fri 10am–10pm, Sat–Sun 10am–2am; Polish cuisine.

Accommodation

Kazimierz Dolny

• **Arkadia**, Czerniawy 1, ☎ +81 8810074; 60 beds; suites, rooms with bath, TV; safe deposit, café, dining room, swimming pool (included), table tennis, unguarded car park. ④

• **Dwa Księżyce**, Sadowa 15, ☎ +81 8810833; 38 beds; suites, doubles with bath, breakfast included; Sat TV, restaurant (live music), sauna, solarium, guarded car park. ⑤

• **Góralski Dom**, Krakowska 47, ☎ +81 8810263; 22 beds; doubles, triples and quads, shared showers, unguarded car park. ②

• **Murka**, Krakowska 59/61, ☎ +81 8810036; 30 beds; suites, rooms with bath, Sat TV; safe deposit, café, sauna, gym, water-massage parlour, night club, guarded car park. ⑤

• **Piastowski**, Słoneczna 3, ☎ +81 8810346, 8810351; 107 beds; suites, rooms with bath, Sat TV, safe deposit, restaurant, sauna, gym, horses, billiards, volleyball court, swimming pool, bike rental (included), night club, guarded car park. ③

• **SDP**, Małachowskiego 17, ☎ +81 8810162,ddsdp@lublin.top.pl; 130 beds; suites, rooms with bath; breakfast included; safe deposit, restaurant, café, gym and indoor swimming pool (included), table tennis, children's playroom, dancing. ④

• **Spichlerz**, Krakowska 59/61, ☎ +81 8810036; 50 beds; suites, rooms with or without bath, Sat TV, safe deposit, restaurant, sauna, gym, night club, guarded car park. ⑤

• **Wenus**, Tyszkiewicza 25a, ☎ +81 8820400; 27 beds; suites, rooms with bath, Sat TV, bar, unguarded car park. ⑤

Kraśnik

• **Chemo-Protex**, Lubelska 2, ☎ +81 8840200; a motel with 33 beds; rooms with or without bath, Sat TV, safe deposit, restaurant, food shop, petrol station, car wash, guarded car park. ③

• **Pracowniczy**, Wyszyńskiego 5, ☎ +81 8256169; 50 beds; rooms with or without bath, Sat TV (in some rooms), unguarded car park. ①

Lublin

• **Bystrzyca**, Aleje Zygmuntowskie 4a, ☎ +81 5323003; 50 beds; one suite, rooms with bath or shared showers, safe deposit, bar, billiards club, unguarded car park. ③

• **Dom Nauczyciela**, Akademicka 4, ☎ +81 5338285; 74 beds; rooms with bath or shared showers, extra beds may be added, restaurant, café, disco, cinema, unguarded car park. ③

• **Dom Studenta Zaocznego**, Sowińskiego 17, ☎ +81 5375661; 166 beds; suites, shared showers, restaurant, food shop, guarded car park. ②

• **Huzar**, Spadochroniarzy 7, ☎ +81 5330536; 131 beds; suites, rooms with bath, safe deposit, restaurant, bar, guarded car park. ⑤

• **Mercure Unia Hotel**, Aleje Racławickie 12, ☎ +81 5332061, unia@orbis.pl; 161 beds; suites, rooms with bath, restaurant, cocktail bar, bureau de change, newsagent, perfume shop, car rental, business centre, casino, massage parlour, tourist information, guarded car park. ⑥

• **Piast**, Pocztowa 2a, ☎ +81 5322516; 50 beds; guest rooms, shared showers, bar, guarded car park. ②

• **Pod Kasztanami**, Krężnicka 94a, ☎ +81 7500390; 52 beds; suites, rooms with bath, restaurant, café, sauna, gym, solarium, massage parlour, children's playroom, angling, water sports, guarded car park. ⑤

• **Polonia**, Pogodna 36, ☎/fax +81 7448631; 295 beds; one suite, rooms with bath or shared showers, phones in some rooms, restaurant, bureau de change, newsagent, hairdresser, guarded car park. ⑤

• **PZMot**, Prusa 8, ☎ +81 5334232; a motel with 107 beds; suites, rooms with bath, safe deposit, restaurant, café, car repair shop, dancing, guarded car park. ⑤

• **Victoria**, Narutowicza 58/60, ☎ +81 5327011, fax 5329026; victoria@lublin.top.pl; 219 beds; suites, rooms with bath, safe deposit, restaurant, café, bureau de change, travel agency, newsagent, guarded car park. ⑤

Włodawa

• **Czar Polesia**, Sokołowa 4, ☎ +82 5724574; 24 beds; comfortable and conveniently located; suites, doubles with bath, Sat TV in some rooms, restaurant, café, bar, guarded car park. ②

• **OSiR**, Szkolna 4, ☎ +82 5722584; 36 beds; rooms with bath, food kiosk, gym, playground, wrestling room, tourist information, unguarded car park. ②

Zamość

• **Arkadia**, Rynek Wielki 9a/7, ☎ +84 6386507; 18 beds; rooms with bath, Sat TV, breakfast included, restaurant (also Hungarian and French menu), café, unguarded car park. ④

• **Dom Turysty**, Zamenhofa 11, ☎ +84 6392639; 47 beds; shared showers, extra beds may be added, unguarded car park. ①

• **Jubilat**, Wyszyńskiego 52, ☎ +84 6386401; 90 beds; one suite, rooms with bath, breakfast included; Sat TV, restaurant, pharmacy, health centre, hairdresser, beauty parlour, sauna, gym, solarium, casino, guarded car park, garage. ⑤

• **Junior**, Sikorskiego 6, ☎ +84 6386615, 6386369; 62 beds; suites, rooms with bath, Sat TV, radio, café, bar, guarded car park. ③

• **Korona**, Sikorskiego 7, ☎ +84 6399191; a motel with 45 beds; rooms with bath, Sat TV, bar, guarded car park, garage. ②

• **OSiR**, Królowej Jadwigi 8, ☎ +84 6386011–4; 93 beds; rooms with bath, phone and Sat TV (in some rooms), radio, restaurant, café, sauna, gym, playground, swimming pool, guarded car park. ③

• **Renesans**, Grecka 6, ☎ +84 6392001; 40 beds; suites, rooms with bath, breakfast included; Sat TV, radio, fridge, minibar, safe deposit, restaurant, café, hairdresser, tourist information, guarded car park. ⑤

• **Tani Hotelik**, Śląska 3, ☎ +84 6392189; 26 beds; dorms with shared showers, guarded car park. ①

• **Zamojski**, Kołłątaja 2/4/6, ☎ +84 6392501, 6392516, zamosc@orbis.pl; 106 beds; suites, rooms with bath; breakfast included; Sat TV, radio, minibar, safe deposit, restaurant, bar, hairdresser, beauty parlour, business centre, sauna, gym, solarium, fitness club, guarded car park. ⑤

Events

Lublin

• **Peace Appeals in Majdanek**, July 23 (anniversary of camp liberation; noon at the Monument of Struggle and Martyrdom); September (during Majdanek Days "Truth-Memory-Reconciliation"); November 3 (anniversary of the biggest execution of Jews in the history of death camps, in 1943; noon near the execution ditches).

• **Majdanek Days**, September, celebrations held by the Majdanek

State Museum; include Peace Appeals and Day of Five Prayers. Current information: www.majdanek.pl

• **Day of Five Prayers**, during Majdanek Days in September. Priests of five denominations and religions (Catholic, Muslim, Orthodox, Protestant, Jewish) pray in different places around the camp. Participants impress their fingerprints in clay tablets. Other tablets have prisoners' numbers, chosen at random.
The tablets with fingerprints will be used in an artistic installation, while those with the numbers are presented to the participants.
In this way, the memory of the victims is symbolically passed on; when you take a tablet, you may inquire at the Majdanek archives about the person who had this particular number. Current information: www.tnn.lublin.pl.

Włodawa

• **Festival of Three Cultures**, October. Numerous exhibitions, concerts, theatre productions and contests showing the multicultural tradition of the Włodawa region. Information: ☎ +82 5722178.

The Małopolska Region

see p. 193

Tourist information

Cracow

• **Centrum Informacji Turystycznej**, Pawia 8, ☎ +12 4226091.

• **Fundacja Judaica – Centrum Kultury Żydowskiej**, Meiselsa 17, ☎ +12 4306449; housed in the former B'nei Emuna, an important centre of Jewish culture in Cracow. Aims to protect and promote the cultural heritage of Polish Jews; also to educate and – widely speaking – regain Memory.

• **Lauder Foundation**, Kupa 18, ☎ 12 4293657.

• **Małopolskie Centrum Informacji Turystycznej**, Rynek Główny 1/3, ☎ +12 4217706.

Krosno

• **Tourist information**, Kazimierza Pużaka 49, ☎ +13 4327707.

Łańcut

• **Tourist information**, Dominikańska 1, ☎ +17 2252052.

Nowy Sącz

• **Tourist information**, Piotra Skargi 2, ☎ +18 4435597.

Oświęcim

• **Centrum Żydowskie w Oświęcimiu**, pl. ks. Skarbka 5, ☎ +33 8447002, info@ajcf.pl; summer daily 8.30am–8pm, winter daily 8.30am–5pm.

• **Państwowe Muzeum Oświęcim-Brzezinka**, Więźniów Oświęcimia 20, ☎ +33 8432022, 8432077.
Daily 8am–3pm (Dec 16–Feb 29), 8am–4pm (Mar 1–Mar 31, Nov 1–Dec 15), 8am–5pm (Apr 1–Apr 30, Oct 1–Oct 31), 8am–6pm (May 1–May 31, Sep 1–Sep 30), 8am–7pm (June 1–Aug 31). Information desks in KL Auschwitz: at the beginning of

the tour, in the former reception building; in KL Birkenau: also at the beginning of the tour, in the death gate (main SS guardhouse).

Przemyśl

- **Tourist information**, Władycze 3, ☎ +16 6751664.

Rzeszów

- **Ośrodek Badań Historii Żydowskiej**, archive searches. Contact: Grzegorz Zamoyski, PhD, Bożnicza 2; ☎ +17 8501099, fax 8538304; osrodek@rzeszow.ap.gov.pl, www.rzeszow.ap.gov.pl.

Sanok

- **Tourist information**, 3 Maja 2, ☎ +13 4630938.

Tarnów

- **Regionalne Centrum Informacji Turystycznej**, Rynek 7, ☎ +14 6278735, 6278735, fax 6283440, rezerwacja@it.tarnow.pl.

Restaurants

Biecz

Centennial, Rynek 6, ☎ +13 4470110, fax 4471576; noon–10pm or until the last guest leaves; international menu with Polish, French and Spanish dishes; dancing, disco.

- **Grodzka**, Kazimierza Wielkiego 35, ☎ +13 4471121; 8am–10pm; Polish cuisine.
- **U Becza**, Rynek 2, ☎ +13 4471801; 10am–11pm; Polish food with many game dishes including wild boar roasted á la Judge Potocki and mouthwatering wild boar cutlet.

Bochnia

- **Kasztelania**, Regis 8, ☎ +14 6124642; 10am–10pm; traditional Polish cuisine.
- **Syrenka**, Gazaris 3, ☎ +14 6125005; from 6pm until the last guest leaves; Polish cuisine.

Brzesko

- **Galicyjska**, Kościuszki 61, ☎ +14 6631489; 9am–9pm; traditional Polish cuisine, try their caraway soup.

Cracow

- **Á la Carte**, Izaaka 7, ☎ +12 4306550; noon–11pm. A small establishment with a great menu: dishes prepared by a French chef Olivier Boudon; desserts include goat cheese with peanuts and acacia honey (around 20 zł). As the name says: everything is ordered á la carte

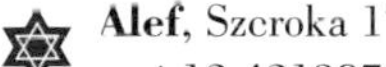

Alef, Szeroka 17, ☎ +12 4213870; 9am–until the last guest leaves. Decor imitating pre-war Jewish restaurants. Menu includes Jewish-style carp, duck with apples, Jewish-style caviar, cholent, chicken soup with matza balls; vegetarian mix. From 8pm klezmer bands: Max Klezmer Band, Yaro Klezmer Group and Iasha Liberman Trio. Occasionally drama evenings, poetry readings, actor's benefits and recitals.

Ariel, Szeroka 18, ☎ +12 4217920; 10am–until the last guest leaves; probably the best known Jewish restaurant in Kazimierz. Impressive choice of 28 main courses, including excellent Sephardi-style carp (22 zł). From 8pm klezmers: Kroke, Ira&Klezmer, The Cracow Klezmer Band.

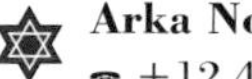

Arka Noego, Szeroka 2, ☎ +12 4291528; 10am–midnight; Jewish menu with many vegetarian dishes. Home-like decor: old furniture, table cloths. Specialities include Jewish barley soup (7.50 zł) and turkey in tsimmes (35 zł). As for desserts, try their baklava, a caramel cake with nuts and dried fruit. Often live Jewish music, usually from 8pm.

• **Bohema**, Gołębia 2, ☎ +12 4302683; noon–11pm; Polish cuisine, folk concerts.

• **Bombaj Tandori**, Mikołajska 11, ☎ +12 4223797; Sun–Thu noon–11pm, Fri–Sat noon–midnight; Indian cuisine.

• **Cherubino**, św. Tomasza 15, ☎ +12 4294007; noon–midnight; traditional Polish cuisine and interesting Italian dishes (also vegetarian).

• **Chimera**, św. Anny 3, ☎ +12 2921212; 9am–10pm; Polish cuisine, speciality: Jewish-style roasted lamb .

• **Chłopskie Jadło**, św. Agnieszki 1, ☎ +12 4218520; Sun–Thu noon–10pm, Fri–Sat noon–midnight; Polish cuisine and a selection of fish.

• **C.K. Browar**, Podwale 6–7, ☎ +12 4292505; 9am–2am; Polish and Viennese food, reviving century-old traditions.

• **C.K. Dezerter**, Bracka 6, ☎ +12 4227931; Mon–Thu 9am–11pm, Fri–Sat 9am–midnight, Sun 10am–11pm; a traditional inn with Polish food (pierogi etc.).

Cyrano de Bergerac, Sławkowska 26, ☎ +12 4295420; noon–midnight, closed on Sun; a classy restaurant with French dishes like duck foie gras with cognac and lamb cutlets with rosemary and garlic served on eggplant. Live music.

• **Da Pietro**, Rynek Główny 17, ☎ +12 4223279; 12.30pm–midnight; Italian cuisine.

• **Dong Yang**, Straszewskiego 16, ☎ +12 4224893; 11am–11pm; Far East delicacies, including Korean food, rare in Poland (pulgogi, Sinsollo – 35 zł).

Eden, Ciemna 15, ☎ +12 4306565; 7am–11pm; kosher Jewish food served to order only.

• **El Paso**, św. Krzyża 13, ☎ +12 4213296; Mon–Thu noon–midnight; Mexican cuisine.

• **Europejska**, Rynek Główny 35, ☎ +12 4293493; 8am–midnight; European food.

• **Gospoda u Zdzicha**, Rynek Główny 24, ☎ +12 4302643; 9am–10pm; Polish and Mediterranean cuisine.

• **Guliwer**, Bracka 6, ☎ +12 4302466; 11am–11pm; French cuisine.

Hawełka, Rynek Główny 34, ☎ +12 4220631; Hawełka proper 11am–11pm, Hawełka Tetmajerowska 1.30pm–11pm; one of Cracow's most renowned restaurants. European cuisine; Hawełka Tetmajerowska serves traditional and modern Polish dishes.

• **Jarema**, pl. Matejki 5, ☎ +12 4293669; from noon until the last guest leaves; old and modern Polish cuisine (including faramuszka, beer soup around 15 zł).

• **Kajzer**, Limanowskiego 12, ☎ +12 6563526; 11am–midnight or until the last guest leaves; a pub serving Polish and French food.

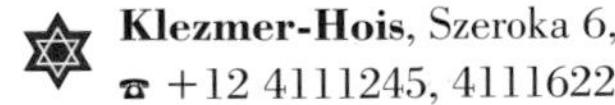

Klezmer-Hois, Szeroka 6, ☎ +12 4111245, 4111622; 7am–11pm; Jewish cuisine; great for stuffed goose necks (15 zł); menu includes also Jankiel soup and Shabbat cholent; large selection of wines. Daily at 8pm live klezmer music played by Kuzmir or Yaro Band (admission 20 zł).

• **La Fontaine**, Sławkowska 1, ☎ +12 4310930; noon–11pm; French cuisine including snails prepared in four ways.

• **Mesa Kapitana Cooka**, Zamojskiego 52, ☎ +12 6560893; noon–10pm; fish.

• **Morskie Oko**, pl. Szczepański 8, ☎ +12 4312423; noon–midnight; mountaineers' dishes with some Polish staples.

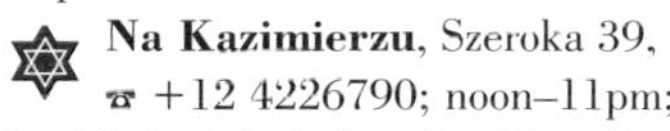

Na Kazimierzu, Szeroka 39, ☎ +12 4226790; noon–11pm; Jewish food including Jewish-style carp (17 zł) and black pudding with tarfles (9 zł); also vegetarian dishes.

• **Na Wawelu**, Wzgórze Wawelskie 9, ☎ +12 4211915; noon–8pm or until the last guest leaves; Polish cuisine, including pork loin with prunes.

• **Orient Express**, Poselska 22, ☎ +12 4226672; 11am–11pm; European food including sole with shrimps.

• **Osorya**, Jagiellońska 5, ☎ +12 2928020; noon–midnight; classic Polish cuisine.

• **Paese**, Poselska 24, ☎ +12 4216273; noon–11pm; French cuisine.

• **Piwnica pod Ogródkiem**, Jagiellońska 6, ☎ +12 2920763; 11am–midnight; Breton cuisine.

• **Pod Aniołami**, Grodzka 35, ☎ +12 4213999; 1pm–midnight; traditional Polish cuisine.

• **Pod Blachą**, Piastowska 22, ☎ +12 6383737; 11am–10pm; an inn serving Polish food and fish.

• **Pod Gruszką**, Szczepańska 1, ☎ +12 4228896; 1pm until the last guest leaves; old and modern Polish cuisine, vegetarian dishes; specialities include Piast food (four meats served in a loaf of bread – 45 zł) and duck with pears (journalist style).

• **Pod Osłoną Nieba**, pl. Dominikański 6, ☎ +12 4225227; 10am–midnight; international cuisine e.g. Tunesian.

• **Pod Słońcem**, Rynek Główny 43, ☎ +12 4229378; noon–midnight; traditional Polish cuisine, also Mediterranean dishes.

• **Pod Złotą Pipą**, Floriańska 30, ☎ +12 4219466; noon–midnight; Polish cuisine.

• **Redolfi**, Rynek Główny 38, ☎ +12 4230579; 9am–midnight; French cuisine.

• **Skarbowa**, Rzemieślnicza 5, ☎ +12 2691565; 7.00–10pm; Polish cuisine.

• **Smak Ukraiński**, Kanonicza 15, ☎ +12 4219294; 11am–9pm; excellent Ukrainian restaurant at the equally interesting Fundacja św. Włodzimierza.

• **Sphinx**, Rynek Główny 26, ☎ +12 4231140; 11am–11pm; Egyptian and Arab cuisine.

• **Srebrna Góra**, Księcia Józefa 120, ☎ +12 4297123; 9am–10pm; old and modern Polish cuisine.

• **Staropolska Gospoda**, Długa 41, ☎ +12 2926131; noon–10pm; traditional Polish food, including mower's lunch (vegetarian).

• **Taco Casa Sosana**, Rynek Główny 19, ☎ +12 4295299; noon–midnight; a Mexican restaurant, fine for burrito.

• **Trattoria**, Brzozowa 18, ☎ +12 2923317, trattoria@poczta.onet.pl; 10am–10pm; Italian cuisine, good lasagne.

• **Trattoria Soprano**, św. Anny 7, ☎ +12 4225195; 9am–midnight; Italian cuisine (a great selection of pasta).

• **U Szkota**, Mikołajska 4, ☎ +12 4221570; noon–midnight; a Scottish restaurant (serving haggis! – 30 zł); rarity in Poland.

• **U Ziyada**, Jodłowa 13, ☎ +12 4297105; noon–10.30pm; Kurdish cuisine.

• **Vega**, Krupnicza 22, ☎ +12 4300836; 9am–11pm; an atmospheric restaurant in the heart of Kazimierz serving only vegetarian food.

• **Villa Decius**, 28 Lipca 1943r. 17a, ☎ +12 4253390; 1pm–10pm; French cuisine.

✱ **Wierzynek**, Rynek Główny 15, ☎ +12 2921088; noon–midnight; Polish cuisine, also some vegetarian dishes. Deserves at least a look inside as it's not easy to find a restaurant that once held a monarchs' meeting.

• **Wiśniowy Sad**, Grodzka 33, ☎ +12 4302111; Mon–Thu 10am–10pm, Fri–Sun 10am–midnight; more of a café than a restaurant, but á la maniere russe (including Siberian pelmieni – 17 zł).

Krosno

• **Piwnica Wójtowska**, Rynek 7, ☎ +13 4321532; 11am–9pm; Polish dishes include papal fillet of beef.

• **Podkarpacka**, Lwowska 21, ☎ +13 4366212; 1pm–midnight; a rather expensive and smart restaurant serving Polish food (like titbits á la Fredro).

Lesko

• **Roma**, pl. Konstytucji 3 Maja 17, ☎ +13 4696566; 10am–11pm; pizza parlour.

• **U Kmity**, Postołów, ☎ +13 4698176; 8am–10pm; Polish cuisine.

Leżajsk

• **71**, Mickiewicza 80, ☎ +17 2428098; 10am–10pm; Polish cuisine including soup á la Leżajsk.

• **U Braci Zygmuntów**, Klasztorna 2e, ☎ +17 2420472; noon–10.30pm; "continental" cuisine including sweet roast pork loin á la Leżajsk with sauerkraut and potatoes.

Łańcut

• **Pałacyk**, Paderewskiego 18, ☎ +17 2252043; 10am–11pm; Polish cuisine.

• Vena, Królowej Elżbiety 4, ☎ +17 2253020; 10am–10pm; traditional Polish cuisine.

Nowy Sącz

• **Bona**, Rynek 28, ☎ +18 4421102; 9am–10pm; Polish and Italian cuisine including canelloni.

✱ **Kupiecka**, Rynek 10, ☎ +18 4420831; noon–midnight; "international" cuisine, including steak with lemon, mushroom sauce and cherry; vegetarians can order mushrooms au gratin.

• **Ratuszowa**, Rynek 1, ☎ +18 4435615; 10am–11pm; Polish specialities: pig's knuckle roasted in beer and mead.

Oświęcim

• **Europa**, Śniadeckiego 20, ☎ +33 8422532; 10am–11pm or until the last guest leaves; traditional Polish and European cuisine; vegetarians may order broccoli with almonds.

• **Skorpion**, Powstańców Śląskich 29, ☎ +33 8432547; 11am–midnight; traditional and modern Polish dishes, also European cuisine.

• **Targowa**, Żwirki i Wigury 31, ☎ +33 8440352; 9am–10pm; Polish cuisine (de volaille is the speciality).

• **Teatralna**, Śniadeckiego 39, ☎ +33 8423306; 11am–7pm or until the last guest leaves; mainly French and Hungarian cuisine, but their speciality is boiled pig's knuckle á la Beskidy.

Przemyśl

• **Eger**, Grunwaldzka 72, ☎ +16 6709283; 10am–11pm; a Hungarian restaurant.

• **Karpacka**, Kościuszki 5, ☎ +16 6786488; 10am–10pm; Hungarian cuisine and fish.

• **Margherita**, Rynek 4, ☎ +16 6789898; 11am–11pm; a pizza parlour serving also other Italian dishes.

• **Trójka**, Lwowska 20, ☎ +16 6787988; 10am–10pm; traditional Polish cuisine.

• **Wyrwigrosz**, Rynek 20, ☎ +16 6785858; 11am–11pm, Fri & Sat 11am–midnight; Polish and Chinese food

Rymanów

• **Zacisze**, Ogrodowa 28, ☎ +13 4357217; 8am–9pm; Polish cuisine.

Rzeszów

• **Akademia**, Piłsudskiego 34, ☎ +17 8503330; 11am–7pm; traditional Polish and Chinese cuisine.

• **Bohema**, Okrzei 7, ☎ +17 8537032; Mon–Thu noon–midnight, Fri & Sat noon–2am; traditional Polish and Hungarian food.

• **Czarny Kot**, Mickiewicza 4, ☎ +17 8523179; 12.30pm–midnight; Polish cuisine including spicy crayfish necks a la Knight Radocha (24 zł).

• **Galicja**, Hetmańska 44, ☎ +17 8549684; noon–midnight; a Polish restaurant serving dishes from Lvov.

• **Ksania**, Rynek 4, ☎ +17 8522840; noon–11pm; international cuisine; cheese tarts with mushrooms for vegetarians.

• **Prohibicja**, Rynek 5, ☎ +17 8527980; 11am–midnight; European cuisine.

• **Rudy Lis**, Okulickiego 15, ☎ +17 8633460; 10am–midnight; Polish menu including zawijaniec bieszczadzki.

• **Sabatini**, Piłsudskiego 17, ☎ +17 8625067; 11am–10pm; Polish food; speciality: forbidden fruit.

• **Wspólnota**, Rynek 19, ☎ +17 8629229; noon–11pm; Polish cuisine.

Sanok

• **Pod Arkadami**, Grzegorza z Sanoka 2, ☎ +13 4644454; 10am–2am; traditional Polish and Hungarian cuisine.

• **Wenecja**, 3 Maja 16, ☎ +13 4637524; 11am–10.30pm; pizzas.

Tarnów

• **Aida**, Wałowa 4, ☎ +14 6274264; 11am–10pm; Italian cuisine.

• **Bristol**, Krakowska 9, ☎ +14 6212279; Mon 11am–9pm, Tue–Sun till 11pm; traditional Polish cuisine.

• **Gospoda Rycerska**, Wekslarska 1, ☎ +14 6275980; noon–midnight; Polish food; despite the name ("Knights' Inn"), their speciality is peasant's bowl.

• **Podzamcze**, al. Tarnowskich, ☎ +14 6277115; noon–midnight; Hungarian menu including Transylvanian dish (37 zł, for 2 persons).

Accommodation

Biecz

✱ **Centennial**, Rynek 6, ☎ +13 4470110, fax 4471576; 20 beds; surprisingly classy hotel right at the Market Square; suites, rooms with bath, Sat TV, minibar, some with a kitchenette; breakfast included; restaurant, guarded car park, garage. ⑤

• **Grodzka**, Kazimierza Wielkiego 35, ☎ +13 4471121; 22 beds; rooms with baths or shared showers, restaurant, unguarded car park. ②

Bobowa

• **Bobowianka**, Rynek 139, ☎ +18 3514023; 30 beds; shared showers, phone, Sat TV, radio; restaurant, café and bar; sauna, gym, solarium; guarded car park. ①

Bochnia

• **Florian**, Galasa 4, ☎ +14 6122229; 140 beds; rooms with baths or shared showers, Sat TV, safe deposit, restaurant, café, bar, sports playgrounds; guarded car park. ②

• **Relaks**, Brzeska 85, ☎ +14 6112621; a motel with 23 beds; shared showers, radio, café, bar; unguarded car park. ①

Brzesko

• **Dom Nauczyciela**, pl. Kazimierza Wielkiego 4, ☎ +14 6863335; only three guest rooms, shared showers, TV, café; unguarded car park. ①

Cracow

• **Alef**, Szeroka 17, ☎ +12 4213870, 4226781, alef@cracow.pl; 12 beds. A few steps from the Remu synagogue. Luxury suites with bath, phone, radio; old furniture, two friendly cats; free modem use; breakfast included, restaurant, café, unguarded car park. ⑥

• **Alf**, Klimeckiego 24, ☎ +12 6561942, fax 6561355, pbinternational@pbhotels.polbox.pl; 200 beds; rooms with bath or shared showers, colour TV, radio; safe deposit, restaurant, bar, guarded car park. ③

• **City SM**, Gajowa 16, ☎ +12 2666021, hotelcity@cracow.pl; 72 beds; rooms with bath, Sat TV, some with a kitchenette; breakfast included; restaurant, café, grill bar, sauna, solarium, swimming pool, fitness club, guarded car park. ⑤

• **Cracovia**, al. Focha 1, ☎ +12 4228666, cracovia@orbis.pl; 509 beds; suites and rooms with bath, Sat TV, radio, some with a fridge; breakfast included; safe deposit, restaurant, café, bar, travel agency, bank, hairdresser, guarded car park. ⑥

• **Czyżyny**, Centralna 32, ☎ +12 6446700, fax 6436566; 300 beds; rooms with shared showers, colour TV, radio, some rooms with a fridge; safe deposit, restaurant, café, bar, gym, health centre; unguarded car park, garage. ②

• **Demel**, Głowackiego 22, ☎ +12 6361600, hotel@demel.com.pl; 124 beds; air-conditioned suites and rooms with bath, Sat TV, radio, fridge, minibar, Internet access; breakfast included; safe deposit, restaurant with Austro-Hungarian cuisine, bar, bureau de change, car rental, travel agency, sauna, gym, guarded car park. ⑤

• **Dwór Orchidea**, Podedworze 30, ☎ +12 2622776, www.orchidea.krakow.pl; 86 beds; rooms with bath or shared showers, radio, some rooms with colour TV; dining room, guarded car park. ③

 **Eden**, Ciemna 15, ☎ +12 4306565, eden@hoteleden.pl; 70 beds in a 15th-century town house; suites and rooms with bath, phone, Sat TV, fridge, minibar; breakfast included; restaurant, café, bar, sauna, Jewish bath, unguarded car park. ⑥

• **Ester**, Szeroka 20, ☎ +12 4291188, biuro@hotel-ester.krakow.pl; 75 beds; rooms with bath (some air-conditioned), phone, Sat TV, radio, fridge, minibar; breakfast included; safe deposit, restaurant, bar, café, guarded car park. ⑤

• **Europejski**, Lubicz 5, ☎ +12 4232510, he@pp.net.pl; 101 beds; suites and rooms with bath, phone, Sat TV, radio, fridge; breakfast included; Noblesse restaurant, café, bar; guarded car park. ⑤

• **Felix**, os. Złotej Jesieni 15b, ☎ +12 6484867; 278 beds; rooms with bath, phone, Sat TV, radio, fridge, some rooms with a minibar and kitchenette; breakfast included; safe deposit, restaurant, guarded car park. ⑤

• **Floryan**, Floriańska 38, ☎/fax +12 4312385, floryan@floryan.com.pl; 42 beds; air-conditioned suites and rooms with bath, phone, colour TV, radio, fridge, minibar; breakfast included; restaurant, café, bar; guarded car park. ⑥

• **Fortuna**, Czapskich 5, ☎ +12 4110806, info@hotel-fortuna.com.pl; 57 beds; suites and rooms with bath, phone, colour TV, radio; breakfast included; safe deposit, restaurant, bar; unguarded car park. ⑥

• **Fortuna Bis**, Piłsudskiego 25, ☎ +12 4301025, 4301039, info@hotel-fortuna.com.pl; 45 beds; suites and rooms with bath, phone, Sat TV, radio, some rooms with a minibar and fridge; breakfast included; safe deposit, Kassumay restaurant (African), café, bar; unguarded car park. ⑥

• **Francuski**, Pijarska 13, ☎ +12 4225122, francuski@orbis.pl; 77 beds; air-conditioned suites and rooms with bath, Sat TV, radio, phone, fridge, minibar; breakfast included; French restaurant, bar, bureau de change. ⑥

• **Galicya**, Rzemieślnicza 4, ☎ +12 2690772, info@hotels.com.pl; 154 beds; rooms with bath (also for the disabled), Sat TV, phone, radio; breakfast included; safe deposit, restaurant, bar, guarded car park. ⑥

Grand, Sławkowska 5/7, ☎ +12 4217255; 104 beds; air-conditioned suites and rooms with bath, Sat TV, phone, radio, fridge, minibar; breakfast included; safe deposit, restaurant, café, guarded car park. ⑥

• **Hotel Polski pod Białym Orłem**, Pijarska 17, ☎ +12 4221144, 4291810, hotel.polski@podorlem.com.pl; 84 beds; suites and rooms with bath, Sat TV, radio, phone; breakfast included; safe deposit, hairdresser. ⑥

• **Ibis**, Przy Rondzie 2, ☎ +12 4218188, ibiskrk@kr.onet.pl; 434 beds; suites and rooms with bath, Sat TV, phone; breakfast included; restaurant, bar, safe deposit, bureau de change, gym, solarium, hairdresser, beauty parlour, massage parlour, newsagent, unguarded car park. ⑤

• **Justyna**, Jana Pawła II 70, ☎ +12 6498000; 123 beds; rooms with bath, Sat TV, phone; breakfast included; safe deposit, restaurant, café, bureau de change, guarded car park. ⑥

• **Kazimierz**, Miodowa 16, ☎ +12 4216629, hot.kazimierz@interia.pl; 32 beds; rooms with bath, Sat TV, phone, radio, fridge; breakfast included. ⑥

• **Klezmer-Hois**, Szeroka 6, ☎ +12 4111622; 26 beds; suites, rooms with bath, Sat TV, phone, radio, fridge; breakfast included; live Jewish music. ⑤

• **Korona**, Kalwaryjska 9–15, ☎ +12 6561780, 6561566; 70 beds; rooms with bath, but also shared showers, some rooms with a colour TV, phone, radio; breakfast included; Perfetto restaurant (Mediterranean), sauna, indoor swimming pool, gym, climbing wall, guarded car park. ④

• **Krak**, Radzikowskiego 99, ☎ +12 6372122; a motel with 130 beds; rooms with bath, colour TV, phone, radio; breakfast included; safe deposit, restaurant, café, children's playroom, garage. ④

• **Krakowiak**, Armii Krajowej 9, ☎ +12 6377304, 6379585; 280 beds; doubles with bath, radio, minibar; Sat TV room, bar, guarded car park. ④

• **Krakowianka**, Żywiecka 2, ☎ +12 2681135, 2681417; 69 beds; shared showers, some rooms with colour TV, radio; breakfast included; café, bar, swimming pool; guarded car park. ②

• **Krakus**, Nowohucka 35, ☎ +12 6520208; 213 beds; suites, rooms with bath, Sat TV, phone, radio; breakfast included; restaurant, café, bar, guarded car park. ②

• **Logos**, Szujskiego 5, ☎ +12 6323333, 6316200; 100 beds; rooms with bath, Sat TV, phone, radio, some rooms with a fridge and minibar; breakfast included; safe deposit, restaurant, cocktail bar, bureau de change, massage parlour, sauna, solarium, beauty parlour, guarded car park, garage. ⑤

• **Mistia**, Szlak 73a, ☎ +12 6332926; 46 beds; rooms with bath, also shared showers, radio; breakfast included; safe deposit, unguarded car park. ④

• **Monopol**, św. Gertrudy 6, ☎ +12 4227666; 64 beds; rooms with bath, but also shared showers; some rooms with colour TV, phone, radio; breakfast included; restaurant, café, bar, guarded car park. ⑥

• **Novotel Bronowice**, Armii Krajowej 11, ☎ +12 6375044, 6387622, continen@cracow.pl; 608 beds; rooms with bath, Sat TV, radio, some with a fridge, minibar, safe, Internet access; breakfast included; restaurant, café, grill bar, sauna, solarium, swimming pool, fitness club, guarded car park. ⑥

• **Orient**, Sołtysowska 25a, ☎ +12 6469100; 120 beds; luxury air-conditioned rooms with bath, Sat TV, phone, radio, fridge, minibar; breakfast included; restaurant, café, swimming pool, jacuzzi, fitness, massage parlour, sauna, business center, guarded car park, garage. ⑥

• **Petrus**, Pietrusińskiego 12, ☎ +12 2692946, hotel@petrus.net.pl; 42 beds; rooms with bath, Sat TV, phone; breakfast included; safe deposit, restaurant, café, sauna, gym, guarded car park. ⑤

• **Piast**, Radzikowskiego 109, ☎ +12 6364600, wimos@kr.onet.pl; 320 beds; rooms with bath, Sat TV, phone, radio, minibar, fridge;

breakfast included; restaurant, café, bar, guarded car park, garage. ⑥

• **Pod Różą**, Floriańską 14, ☎ +12 4243300, pod-roza@hotel.com.pl; 106 beds; rooms with bath, Sat TV, phone, minibar, fridge; breakfast included; safe deposit, two restaurants (including the Italian Amarone), bar, unguarded car park. ⑥

• **Pollera**, Szpitalna 30, ☎ +12 4221044, rezerwac@pollera.com.pl; 86 beds; rooms with bath (some air-conditioned), colour TV, phone, radio, minibar, fridge; breakfast included; safe deposit, restaurant, café. ⑥

• **Polonia**, Basztowa 25, ☎ +12 4221233, polonia@bci.krakow.pl; 123 beds; rooms with bath, Sat TV, phone, radio, some with air-conditioning and fridge; restaurant, bar, guarded car park, garage. ⑥

• **Regent**, Bożego Ciała 19, ☎ +12 4306234, info@rhotels.com.pl; 78 beds; rooms with bath, Sat TV, phone, radio; breakfast included; safe deposit, Oriental restaurant. ⑥

• **Retro**, Barska 59, ☎ +12 2660708; 51 beds; rooms with bath, colour TV, radio and kitchenette (in some rooms); breakfast included; restaurant, café, bar, bike rental, unguarded car park. ④

• **Rezydent**, Grodzka 9, ☎ +12 4295410, info@rhotels.com.pl; 111 beds; suites, rooms with bath, Sat TV, phone, fridge; safe deposit, restaurant, café, bar. ⑥

• **ROKK**, Rzemieślnicza 5, ☎ +12 2691566, hotelrokk@pro.onet.pl; 57 beds; rooms with bath, Sat TV, phone, radio; breakfast included; safe deposit, restaurant, café, bar, guarded car park. ⑤

• **Royal**, św. Gertrudy 26, ☎ +12 4213500; 76 beds; suites and rooms with bath, Sat TV, phone, radio, fridge (in some rooms), Internet access; breakfast included; safe deposit, restaurant, café, bar, bureau de change. ⑤

• **Saski**, Sławkowska 3, ☎ +12 4214222; 123 beds; suites and rooms with bath, Sat TV, fridge (in some rooms); breakfast included; restaurant. ⑥

 **Start**, Kapelanka 60, ☎ +12 2660880, hotel_start@krakow.mtl.pl; 150 beds; a good hotel, one of few budget hotels in Cracow; rooms with bath or shared showers, colour TV, radio and minibar (in some rooms); bar, fitness club, 24hr supermarket nearby, guarded car park. ③

• **Wanda**, al. Armii Krajowej 15, ☎ +12 6371677, wanda@orbis.pl; 155 beds; rooms with bath, Sat TV, phone, radio; breakfast included; restaurant, bar, grill bar, bureau de change, guarded car park. ⑥

• **Warszawski**, Pawia 4–6, ☎ +12 4242100; 70 beds; suites, rooms with bath, Sat TV, phone, radio, fridge (in some rooms); breakfast included; safe deposit, cocktail bar, guarded car park. ⑥

• **Wawel Tourist**, Poselska 22, ☎ +12 4241300; 47 beds; rooms with bath, Sat TV, phone, radio (in some rooms); breakfast included; safe deposit, café. ⑤

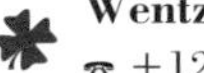 **Wentzl**, Rynek Główny 19, ☎ +12 4302664, hotel@wentzl.pl; 25 beds; top-class air-conditioned rooms with bath, Sat TV, phone, minibar, fridge; breakfast included; safe deposit, restaurant with French cuisine. ⑥

• **Wisła**, Reymonta 22, ☎ +12 6151535, 6334922; 78 beds; rooms with bath, Sat TV, radio; safe deposit, restaurant, café, bar, sauna, gym, car service and rental, unguarded car park. ⑤

• **Wit Stwosz**, Mikołajska 28, ☎ +12 4296026, 4296042, wit.stwosz@hotel.krakow.pl; 44 beds; rooms with bath, Sat TV, phone, radio, some with a minibar and fridge; breakfast included; safe deposit, restaurant. ⑥

• **Wyspiański**, Westerplatte 15, ☎ +12 4229566, www.domturysty.cracow.pl; 303 beds; rooms with bath, Sat TV (in some rooms), phone; breakfast included; safe deposit, restaurant, bar, guarded car park. ⑤

• **Youth hostel**, Oleandry 4, ☎ +12 6338822; 398 beds; rooms ranging from doubles to 16-person dorms, shared showers; restaurant, bar, unguarded car park. ②

• **Youth hostel**, Szablowskiego 1c, ☎ +12 6372441; 160 beds; quads, shared showers, café, unguarded car park. ①

Dukla

• **Galicja**, Trakt Węgierski, ☎ +13 4331455; an inn with 20 beds; rooms with bath, colour TV (in some rooms); restaurant, bar, food shop, unguarded car park. ②

• **Rysieńka**, Lipowica 82, ☎ +13 4330149; an inn with 15 beds; rooms with bath, colour TV, Sat TV, radio, restaurant, guarded car park. ②

Jarosław

• **Asticus**, Rynek 25, ☎ +16 6231344; 15 beds; rooms with bath, Sat TV; café, bar; guarded car park. ④

• **Hetman**, Hetmana Jana Tarnowskiego 18, ☎ +16 6214395; 30 beds; suites and rooms with bath, phone, Sat TV, radio; breakfast included; safe deposit, restaurant, café, bar; guarded car park. ④

• **Pegaz**, 3 Maja 94c, ☎ +16 6217995; a motel with 14 beds; one suite and rooms with bath, phone, Sat TV; restaurant, bar; guarded car park. ③

• **Turkus**, Sikorskiego 5a, ☎ +16 6212640; 99 beds; rooms with baths or shared showers, colour TV (in some rooms); safe deposit, bar, sauna, gym; unguarded car park. ②

Krosno

• **Bengol**, Długa 15d, ☎ +13 4360478; 15 beds; suites and rooms with bath, phone, Sat TV; breakfast included; restaurant; guarded car park. ⑤

• **Elenai**, Łukasiewicza 3, ☎ +13 4364334; 28 beds; one suite and rooms with bath, phone, colour TV, Sat TV, radio; breakfast included; restaurant, café, bar; guarded car park, garage. ③

• **Krosno Nafta**, Lwowska 21, ☎ +13 4366212, hotel@hotel.nafta.pl; 82 beds; suites and rooms with bath, phone, minibar, Sat TV, radio; breakfast included; safe deposit, restaurant, café, bar, night club; sauna, gym, solarium, hairdresser; guarded car park. ⑥

• **Reshotel**, Okulickiego 13a, ☎ +13 4321954; 50 beds; shared showers, TV (in some rooms), radio, fridge; unguarded car park. ①

• **Skorpion**, Podkarpacka 38, ☎ +13 4362174; 14 beds; a motel offering rooms with bath and Sat TV; breakfast included; bar, food shop, petrol station, car wash; unguarded car park. ③

Lesko

• **Zamek**, Piłsudskiego 7, ☎ +13 4696268; 94 beds; rooms with bath, colour TV, radio; café, gym, bike rental, fitness club; unguarded car park. ④

• **U Kmity**, Postołów, ☎ +13 4698176, zajazdukmity@interia.pl; 21 beds; rooms with bath, Sat TV, radio; restaurant, café, bar, gym; unguarded car park. ②

Leżajsk

• **71**, Mickiewicza 80, ☎ +17 2428098; 40 beds; rooms with bath, phone, Sat TV, some with air-conditioning and fridge; restaurant, café, shopping centre, pharmacy, petrol station, tennis courts, garage. ③

• **U Braci Zygmuntów**, Klasztorna 2e, ☎ +17 2420472; 28 beds; suites and rooms with bath, phone; breakfast included; restaurant, café, bar, gym, unguarded car park. ③

Łańcut

• **Bogdanka**, Armii Krajowej 82, ☎ +17 2257159; 20 beds; a motel offering rooms with bath and Sat TV; breakfast included; restaurant, café; guarded car park. ③

• **Pałacyk**, Paderewskiego 18, ☎ +17 2252043; 16 beds; one suite and rooms with bath, phone, Sat TV, fridge; safe deposit, restaurant, café; guarded car park. ③

• **PTTK**, Dominikańska 1, ☎ +17 2254512; 45 beds; mainly for groups; shared showers, radio (in some rooms); safe deposit, Zabytkowa restaurant, café; unguarded car park. ①

• **Szwadron**, Mickiewicza 16, ☎ +17 2256042; 18 beds; rooms with bath, phone, Sat TV; breakfast included; restaurant, café; car rental, garage. ④

• **Zamkowy**, Zamkowa 1, ☎ +17 2252671; 45 beds; rooms with baths or shared showers, phone, colour TV; restaurant, café; unguarded car park. ②

Nowy Sącz

• **Beskid**, Limanowskiego 1, ☎ +18 4435770, beskid@orbis.pl; 141 beds; suites and rooms with bath; breakfast included; phone, Sat TV, fridge and minibar (in some rooms); private safe (in some rooms), safe deposit, restaurant, bureau de change, hairdresser, beauty parlour, solarium, newsagent, dancing; guarded car park. ⑤

• **Max**, Graniczna 95, ☎ +18 4439715; a motel with 27 beds; one suite and rooms with bath, phone, colour TV, radio; restaurant, café, bar; guarded car park. ②

• **Panorama**, Romanowskiego 4a, ☎ +18 4337110; 50 beds, rooms with bath, phone, Sat TV, radio; breakfast included; safe deposit, restaurant; unguarded car park. ⑤

• **PTTK**, Jamnicka 2, ☎ +18 4415012; 55 beds; rooms with baths or shared showers, colour TV (in some rooms), radio; café, hairdresser, guides; guarded car park. ②

• **Sądecki**, Królowej Jadwigi 67, ☎ +18 4436717; an inn with 22 beds; rooms with bath, colour TV, radio; restaurant, café; guarded car park. ②

Oświęcim

• **Glob**, Powstańców Śląskich 16, ☎ +33 8430632, dus@pkp-dus.com.pl; 120 beds; suites and rooms with bath, phone, Sat TV, radio; breakfast included, safe deposit, restaurant, café, bureau de change, guarded car park. ④

• **Kamieniec**, Zajazdowa 2, ☎ +33 8432564; 39 beds; rooms with bath, radio, colour TV, safe deposit, restaurant, café, garage. ③

• **Międzynarodowy Dom Spotkań Młodzieży**, Legionów 11, ☎ +33 8432107, 8431211, mdsmijbs@oswiecim.petex.com.pl; 98 beds; rooms with bath and radio, café, bar, bookshop, unguarded car park. ③

• **Olimpijski**, Chemików 2a, ☎ +33 8423841–2; 56 beds; suites and rooms with bath, phone, colour TV (in some rooms), radio; breakfast included; restaurant, café, sauna, gym, solarium, indoor swimming pool, massage parlour, bureau de change, guarded car park. ⑤

Przemyśl

• **Albatros**, Ofiar Katynia 26, ☎ +16 6780870; 156 beds; suites and rooms with bath, phone and Sat TV (in some rooms); breakfast included; safe deposit, restaurant, café, bar, gym, solarium; guarded car park. ③

• **Facpol**, Armii Krajowej 16b, ☎ +16 6709105; 49 beds; rooms with bath, phone, Sat TV; safe deposit, restaurant, bar; guarded car park. ③

• **Gromada**, Piłsudskiego 4, ☎ +16 6761111; 210 beds; suites and rooms with bath, phone, Sat TV, fridge and minibar (in some rooms); breakfast included; safe deposit, restaurant, café, bureau de change, hairdresser, beauty parlour, solarium; garage. ⑤

• **Krokus**, Mickiewicza 47–49, ☎ +16 6785127; 54 beds; rooms with bath, colour TV, radio; guarded car park. ③

• **Marko Exim**, Lwowska 40, ☎ +16 6789272; 35 beds; one suite and rooms with bath, phone, Sat TV, radio, fridge (in some rooms); breakfast included; safe deposit, restaurant, café, bar; guarded car park. ⑤

• **Pod Białym Orłem**, Sanocka 13, ☎ +16 6786107; 35 beds; rooms with bath; breakfast included; phone, Sat TV, radio (in some rooms); restaurant; guarded car park. ③

• **Podzamcze**, Waygarta 3, ☎ +16 6785374, pttk.przem@poczta.onet.pl; 44 beds; run by PTTK and mainly for groups; shared showers, tourist information; guarded car park. ①

Rymanów

• **Zacisze**, Ogrodowa 28, ☎ +13 4357217; 48 beds; rooms with bath, colour TV (in some rooms); restaurant; unguarded car park. ①

Rzeszów

• **Classic**, Armii Krajowej 32, ☎ +17 8577747; 20 beds; a motel with suites and rooms with bath, Sat TV, radio, air-conditioning; breakfast included; food/off-licence shop; guarded car park. ⑤

• **Eden**, Krakowska 150, ☎ +17 8525683; 64 beds; rooms with baths or shared showers, Sat TV; bar; unguarded car park. ②

• **Etap**, Trembeckiego 7, ☎ +17 8529424; 65 beds; shared showers, Sat TV (in some rooms); gym; unguarded car park. ②

• **Iskra**, Dąbrowskiego 75, ☎ +17 8549740; 94 beds; one suite, rooms with bath, Sat TV, radio; restaurant, bar; unguarded car park. ③

• **Pod Ratuszem**, Matejki 8, ☎ +17 8529780; 22 beds; suites, rooms with bath; breakfast included; phone, Sat TV; Deja'Vu restaurant, café; unguarded car park. ⑤

• **Polonia**, Grottgera 16, ☎ +17 8520312; 73 beds; rooms with baths or shared showers, phone, Sat TV, radio; bar; guarded car park. ④

• **Prezydencki**, Podwisłocze 48, ☎ +17 8626835, prezydencki@hotelesemako.com.pl; 110 beds; suites, rooms with bath, phone, Sat TV, fridge, minibar; breakfast included; safe deposit, restaurant (menu includes pigeon with grapes), bureau de change, sauna, solarium, hairdresser, beauty parlour; guarded car park. ⑥

• **Reshotel**, Okulickiego 2, ☎ +17 8535968; 146 beds; rooms with baths or shared showers, colour TV (in some rooms); breakfast included; restaurant, café, petrol station; guarded car park, garage. ③

• **Rzeszów**, Cieplińskiego 2, ☎ +17 8750000, rzeszow@hotelesemako.com.pl; 400 beds; suites, rooms with bath, phone, Sat TV, fridge (in some rooms); breakfast included; safe deposit, restaurant, café, bureau de change, hairdresser, casino; guarded car park. ⑤

Sanok

• **Autosan-Sanlux**, Lipińskiego 116, ☎ +13 4650640; 55 beds; one suite, rooms with bath, Sat TV, phone, radio; restaurant, guarded car park. ③

• **Błonie**, Królowej Bony 4, ☎ +13 4630257; 76 beds; rooms with bath, colour TV and fridge (in some rooms); safe deposit, sauna, sports equipment rental, garage. ②

• **Dom Turysty PTTK**, Mickiewicza 29, ☎ +13 4631013; 149 beds; rooms with bath; colour TV, phone and radio in some; safe deposit, restaurant, café, guarded car park. ②

• **Jagielloński**, Jagiellońska 49, ☎ +13 4641294; 42 beds; suites, rooms with bath, Sat TV, phone; safe deposit, restaurant, guarded car park. ③

• **Pod Trzema Różami**, Jagiellońska 13, ☎ +13 4630922; 52 beds; suites, rooms with bath, colour TV, phone, radio; breakfast included, safe deposit, restaurant, café, bar, guarded car park. ③

Tarnów

• **Chemik**, Traugutta 5, ☎ +14 6330485, fax 6331227, hotel@hotel-chemik.com.pl; 161 beds; suites and rooms with bath; breakfast included; phone, Sat TV, some with a kitchenette and fridge; safe deposit, restaurant, café, sauna, gym, solarium, fitness club, sports hall; guarded car park. ⑤

• **Hotel Ochrony Zdrowia**, Lwowska 178, ☎ +14 6269855; 40 beds; one suite and rooms with bath, some with phone, colour TV and fridge; food shop, gym; guarded car park. ③

• **Pod Dębem**, Marusarza 9b, ☎ +14 6269620; an inn with 49 beds; rooms with bath, phone, colour TV; children up to seven for free; restaurant; guarded car park. ③

• **Pod Murami**, Żydowska 16, ☎ +14 6216229; 25 beds; run by PTTK and mainly for groups; café, shop, ski instructor; unguarded car park. ②

• **Tarnovia**, Kościuszki 10, ☎ +14 6212671, recepcja@hotel.tarnovia.com.pl; 242 beds; suites and rooms with bath, phone, some with a fridge and minibar; breakfast included; safe deposit, restaurant, cocktail bar, bureau de change, hairdresser, beauty parlour, fitness club, sauna, gym, solarium; guarded car park, garage. ⑤

Events

Cracow

 **Jewish Festival**, early summer; contact and details: ☎ +12 4311517, 4311535; office@jewishfestival.pl, www.jewishfestival.pl, also WAP: wap.jewishfestival.pl. Poland's biggest festival of Jewish culture (for more information see p. 206).

• **Month of Meetings with Jewish Culture "Bajit Chadasz" (New House)**, in the first month of the Jewish calendar. Held by Fundacja Judaica (Centrum Kultury Żydowskiej Kraków, ul. Meiselsa 17), it combines a series of Jewish festivals (New Year – Rosh Hashanah, Yom Kippur, Sukkot, Simhat Torah) with various cultural events. Organized since 1996; every year focuses on one Jewish celebrity; so far they have been Kafka, Zweig, Schulz, Singer and Gebirtig. There are also lectures, meetings, film shows (International TV Festival of Films and Ethnic Programs), exhibitions, concerts, postcard and book auctions.

Oświęcim

• **March of the Living** is the biggest event commemorating the Holocaust victims. It is organized every year on Yom Hashoah (Holocaust Memorial Day, the 27th day of Nisan – variable date: in 2002 – April 5, in 2003 – April 29, in 2004 – April 18; for more information see p. 217).

Wrocław | see p. 255

Tourist information

• **Gmina Wyznaniowa Żydowska (Jewish Religious Community)**, Włodkowica 9, ☎ +71 3436401; open Mon–Fri 11am–1pm.

• **Punkt Informacji Turystycznej**, Rynek 14, ☎ +71 3443111, 3441109.

• **Web sites**: www.wroclaw.pl, www.wroclaw.com, www.um.wroc.pl, www.uwoj.wroc.pl, www.wroclaw.plan.pl.

Restaurants

• **Academia Brasserie**, Kuźnicza 65/66, ☎ +71 3434529; Mon–Fri 10am–11pm, Sat–Sun 11am–11pm; European cuisine; fine for pancakes with camembert cheese, ham, nuts, etc.

• **Akropolis**, pl. Solny 19, ☎ +71 3431413; 11am–midnight; Greek cuisine.

• **Armine**, Bogusławskiego 83, ☎ +71 3671531; 1pm–midnight; Armenian food.

• **Casa Patio**, Odrzańska 2, ☎ +71 3417101; from 1pm until the last guest leaves; Mediterranean cuisine.

• **Casablanca**, Włodkowica 8a, ☎ +71 3447817; from 12.30pm until the last guest leaves; international cuisine including Humphrey Bogart's pancakes with fruit and vanilla ice-cream sprinkled with Amaretto.

• **DaLat**, Piłsudskiego 74, ☎ +71 3443930; 11am–11pm; Chinese and Vietnamese food.

• **Dwór Polski – Karczma Piastów**, Kiełbaśnicza 6, ☎ +71 3724896–8, www.wroclaw.com/dworpol.htm; 11am–11pm; traditional and modern Polish cuisine.
• **Dwór Polski – Sala Czwartkowa**, Rynek 5, ☎ +71 3724896–8, www.wroclaw.com/dworpol.htm; 10am–10pm; European cuisine.
• **Dwór Polski – Sala Królewska**, Rynek 5, ☎ +71 3724896–8, www.wroclaw.com/dworpol.htm; from 1pm until the last guest leaves; not only Polish dishes.
• **Familia**, Średzka 19, ☎ +71 3492139; 11am–11pm; Polish cuisine.
• **Gospoda Wrocławska**, Sukiennice 7, ☎ +71 3427456; from noon until the last guest leaves; traditional Polish cuisine.
• **Guinness**, pl. Solny 5, ☎ +71 3446015; noon–midnight; a pub with Irish/Polish food and live music.
• **Kosher dining room (Jewish Religious Community)**, Włodkowica 9, ☎ +71 3436401. For religious Jews, open on weekdays 11.30am–12.30pm and on Sat after the morning service.
• **La Scala**, Rynek 38, ☎ +71 3725394–5; 10am–11pm, Sun 11am–11pm; an Italian establishment.
• **Los Locos**, Kiełbaśnicza 13, ☎ +71 3426820; from 1pm until the last guest leaves; Latin American food.
Lwowska, Rynek 4, ☎ +71 3439887; from 11am until the last guest leaves; mainly dishes from Lvov, including roast veal á la Dzieduszycki; some Jewish specialities from Lvov like Jewish salad (6.50 zł).
• **Magistracka**, Szewska 59, ☎ +71 3417570; from 1pm until the last guest leaves; European cuisine.
• **Mexico**, Rzeźnicza 34, ☎ +71 3460292; noon–11pm, Fri–Sun noon–midnight; a Mexican restaurant.
• **Palazzo**, Rynek 20/21, ☎ +71 3435617; from 10am until the last guest leaves; a cafeteria serving Italian food.
 **Panorama**, Drobnera 11/13, ☎ +71 3208450, hpwroclaw@beph.pl; 6.30am–midnight; until May 2001 this restaurant at the HP Park Plaza Hotel was the only one in Wrocław to serve Jewish dishes. The new menu doesn't include them any more, but if you ask in advance, the chef can prepare such delicacies as Jewish-style carp (15 zł) poultry-liver mousse (12 zł), Berdyczow soup (8 zł), broad-bean soup with farfels (8 zł), main courses like haliszki (cabbage leaves stuffed with minced meat in raisin sauce; 20 zł) and poultry necks stuffed with meat and mushrooms (25 zł) andhoney cake for a dessert (with sesame-nut filling; 8 zł).
• **Piramida**, Igielna 30, ☎ +71 3447070; 11am–11pm, Fri–Sun noon–midnight; a bar with Arab food.
• **Pod Szczęśliwym Kupcem**, Rynek 46/47, ☎ +71 3432746; from 10am until the last guest leaves; an inn serving Polish dishes.
• **Ragtime**, pl. Solny 17, ☎ +71 3433701; 10am–midnight; European cuisine, good vegetarian dishes.
• **Royal Ginseng**, pl. Hirszfelda 16/17, ☎ +71 3615211, www.royalginseng.com.pl; noon–10pm; a Chinese restaurant.

• **Sankt Petersburg**, Igielna 14/13, ☎ +71 3418084; from noon until the last guest leaves; Russian food, including Astrachan caviar (65 zł).

✱ **Spiż**, Rynek-Ratusz 9, ☎ +71 3445267; noon–midnight; mainly meat dishes, including ribs with spicy sauces.

• **Splendido**, Świdnicka 53, ☎ +71 3447777; from 1pm until the last guest leaves; Polish and Mediterranean cuisine.

• **Szwejk**, Odrzańska 17, ☎ +71 3427071; from noon until the last guest leaves; Hungarian and Czech cuisine.

• **Tequilla**, pl. Solny 11, ☎ +71 3410114; noon–mignight; a Mexican restaurant.

✱ **Vega**, Sukiennice 1/2, ☎ +71 3443934; 8am–7pm; a bar and restaurant with what must be the biggest selection of vegetarian dishes in Poland.

• **Vincent**, Ruska 39, ☎ +71 3410520, www.vincent.wroclaw.pl; noon–11pm; Mediterranean menu.

• **Wall Street**, Podwale 62, ☎ +71 3460809; Mon–Fri 10am–9pm; European cuisine.

• **Żak**, Rynek-Ratusz 7/9, ☎ +71 3408149; from 9am until the last guest leaves.

Accommodation

• **Agro**, Zwycięska 12/b4, ☎ +71 3398021–2, 3398185–6; 101 beds; suites, rooms with bath, colour TV and radio; breakfast included; bar, guarded car park. ③

✱ **Art**, Kiełbaśnicza 20, ☎ +71 7877100, fax 3423929, www.arthotel.wroc.pl, info@arthotel.wroc.pl; 150 beds; excellent though very expensive (33–50% weekend discounts) suites and rooms with bath, phone, Sat TV, fridge and minibar; breakfast included; safe deposit, good restaurant, café, bar, bureau de change, garage, unguarded car park. ⑥

• **Bacero**, Ołtaszyńska 107, ☎ +71 3397550; 60 beds; one suite, rooms with bath, colour TV, radio, kitchenette; unguarded car park. ⑤

• **Best Western Hotel Prima**, Kiełbaśnicza 16–19, ☎ +71 7825555, www.bestwestern.com, bestwestern@prima.multinet.pl; 146 beds; a good and pricey hotel offering suites, rooms with bath, phone; breakfast included, so is the sauna and gym; Sir William restaurant, café, bar, fitness club, jacuzzi, guarded car park. ⑥

• **Dwór Polski**, Kiełbaśnicza 2, ☎ +71 3725829, 3723415, www.wroclaw.com/dworpol.htm; 56 beds; a posh hotel offering suites, rooms with bath, phone, Sat TV, radio; breakfast included; safe deposit, restaurant, café, bureau de change, sauna (included), billiards, casino, guarded car park. ⑤

• **Europejski**, Piłsudskiego 88, ☎ +71 3431071–7, www.dialcom.com.pl/odra-tourist; 108 beds; suites, rooms with bath, phone, Sat TV (in some rooms), radio, fridge, minibar; restaurant, café, bureau de change, hairdresser, beauty parlour, billiards, guarded car park. ⑤

• **Exbud Duet**, św. Mikołaja 47–48, ☎ +71 7855100–2; 92 beds; rooms with bath, phone, Sat TV and minibar; breakfast included; restaurant, tourist information, guarded car park. ⑤

• **GEM**, Baudouina de Courtenay 16, ☎ +71 3729213, hotel@hotelgem.com.pl; 80 beds; luxury suites and rooms with bath, phone, Sat TV, fridge and minibar; breakfast included; safe deposit, restaurant, bar, beauty parlour, sauna, gym (included), solarium, football playground, basketball court, tennis court, children's playroom. ⑤

• **HP Park Plaza**, Drobnera 11–13, ☎ +71 3208400, www.beph.pl, hpwroclaw@beph.pl; 354 beds; a very exclusive hotel, probably the most expensive in Wrocław (parking places at 400 zł a day); suites, doubles with bath, phone, Sat TV and pay-per-view channels, minibar and fridge (in some rooms); Panorama restaurant, café, newsagent, sauna (included), water-massage parlour and fitness club (included), casino, guarded car park, garage. ⑥

• **Inter**, Wejherowska 2, ☎ +71 3501020, www.interhotel.com.pl, recepcja@interhotel.com.pl; 42 beds; suites, rooms with bath, phone, Sat TV and radio; breakfast included, safe deposit, restaurant, skating rink, unguarded car park. ④

• **Maria Magdalena**, św. Marii Magdaleny 2, ☎ +71 3410898, www.hotel-mm.com.pl, hotel@hotel-mm.com.pl; 134 beds; plush and pricey; suites, rooms with bath, phone, Sat TV, minibar and fridge; breakfast included; safe deposit, restaurant, hairdresser, beauty parlour, manicure, sauna and gym (included), solarium and swimming pool (included), guarded car park. ⑥

• **Mars**, Żelazna 46, ☎ +71 3626333, 3652000; 114 beds; suites, rooms with bath, phone, Sat TV (in some rooms), radio, fridge (in some rooms); safe deposit, restaurant, café, dancing, disco, unguarded car park. ③

• **Monopol**, Modrzejewskiej 2, ☎ +71 3437041, monopol@orbis.pl; 100 beds; suites, rooms with bath, phone, Sat TV, fridge (in some rooms), safe deposit, restaurant, bureau de change, hairdresser, beauty parlour, solarium, guarded car park. ⑤

• **Motel Orbis**, Lotnicza 151, ☎ +71 3518153, mwroclaw@orbis.pl; 152 beds; doubles with bath, phone, Sat TV, fridge (in some rooms); safe deposit, restaurant, bureau de change, children's playroom, guarded car park. ④

• **Nauczycielski**, Nauczycielska 2, ☎ +71 3229268–9; 60 beds; suites, rooms with baths or shared showers, colour TV (in some rooms), radio; unguarded car park. ③

• **Novotel**, Wyścigowa 35, ☎ +71 3398515, 3398051, nwroclaw@orbis.pl; 290 beds; doubles with bath, phone, Sat TV; safe deposit, restaurant, bar, swimming pool (included), guarded car park. ⑤

• **Olimpia**, Paderewskiego 35, ☎ +71 3483618, 3486960; 36 beds; a small but classy hotel with suites, all with bath, phone, Sat TV, fridge, minibar; safe deposit, restaurant, café, guarded car park. ⑤

• **Piast**, Piłsudskiego 98, ☎ +71 3430033; 144 beds; mainly for groups; shared showers, colour TV room, bar. ③

• **Podkowa**, Wojszycka 8, ☎ +71 3398360; 32 beds; suites, rooms with bath, phone, Sat TV; breakfast included; restaurant, garage. ④

• **Podróżnik**, Sucha 1, ☎ +71 3732845; 41 beds; rooms with baths or shared showers, colour TV, radio; breakfast included; guarded car park. ④
• **Polonia**, Piłsudskiego 66, ☎ +71 3431021–9; 250 beds; suites, rooms with bath, phone, Sat TV, fridge, minibar, safe deposit, restaurant, bar, bureau de change, hairdresser, casino, guarded car park. ⑤
• **Relax**, Bystrzycka 22, ☎ +71 3510827; 35 beds; suites, rooms with bath or shared showers, phone, colour TV, radio, fridge, minibar; unguarded car park. ③
• **Rezydent**, Różyckiego 7, ☎ +71 3483405; 37 beds; one suite, rooms with bath, phone, Sat TV, fridge, minibar; breakfast included; safe deposit, restaurant, café, guarded car park. ⑤
• **Saigon**, Wita Stwosza 22/23, ☎ +71 3442881–5; 81 beds; suites, rooms with bath, phone, Sat TV, fridge, minibar; breakfast included; restaurant, bar, bureau de change, hairdresser, sauna, solarium, unguarded car park. ⑤
• **Savoy**, pl. Kościuszki 19, ☎ +71 3403219, 3443071; 41 beds; suites, rooms with bath, phone, Sat TV; safe deposit, restaurant, pharmacy, unguarded car park. ③
• **Śląsk**, Oporowska 62, ☎ +71 3612061–4; 232 beds; suites, rooms with bath, phone, radio; restaurant, bureau de change, guarded car park. ③
• **Techma**, Boya-Żeleńskiego 76, ☎ +71 3272208, fax 3254946; 18 beds; rooms with bath, phone, Sat TV, radio; breakfast included; restaurant, bureau de change, guarded car park, garage. ⑤
• **Tumski**, Wyspa Słodowa 10, ☎ +71 3226099, 3226088, www.hotel-tumski.com.pl, hotel@hotel-tumski.com.pl; 102 beds; one suite, rooms with baths or shared showers, phone, Sat TV, breakfast included, minibar, Karczma Młyńska restaurant, children's playground, unguarded car park. ⑤
• **Vega**, Grabiszyńska 241, ☎ +71 3390367–9; a motel with 46 beds; suites, rooms with baths or shared showers, phone, colour TV; breakfast included; safe deposit, restaurant, café, sauna (included), children's playroom, unguarded car park. ⑤
• **Wieniawa**, Gajowicka 130, ☎ +71 3653303; 283 beds; suites, rooms with bath, phone, Sat TV; restaurant, café, bureau de change, hairdresser, guarded car park. ⑤
• **Wodnik**, Na Grobli 28, ☎ +71 3433667, 3429343, wodnik@dozamet.com.pl; 30 beds; suites, rooms with bath (weekends and holidays – 30% off), phone, Sat TV, minibar (in some rooms); breakfast included; safe deposit, restaurant, café, sauna, solarium, billiards, children's playroom, guarded car park, garage. ⑤
• **Wrocław**, Powstańców Śląskich 5/7, ☎ +71 3614651, hwroclaw@orbis.pl; 584 beds; a comfortable giant; suites, rooms with bath, phone, Sat TV, minibar and fridge, breakfast included, safe deposit, restaurant, café, bar, bureau de change, health centre, hairdresser, sauna (included), solarium, massage parlour, indoor swimming pool, guarded car park. ⑥

Glossary
Photographs and Illustrations
Index

GLOSSARY

Alefbet – the Hebrew alphabet, taking its name from the first two letters. Hebrew is written from right to left. In all there are 22 letters. The Hebrew alphabet is also used for **Yiddish** and **Ladino**.

Aravit – see **Maariv**.

Aron ha-kodesh – the "Holy Ark" in which the **Torah** scrolls are kept. Situated on the eastern wall of the synagogue, symbolically indicating the direction of Jerusalem.

Ashkenazim (in Hebrew Ashkenaz means Germany); Jews from the Central European diaspora who initially settled in Germany. They developed the Germanic language called **Yiddish**.

Bar mitzvah – "Son of the Commandment"; the ceremony in which a thirteen-year-old boy reaches manhood, with all the rights and obligations that this entails. He may now take full part in synagogue services by being one of the ten adult males needed to make up a **minyan**.

Beit ha-Midrash – "House of Learning"; a place where every Jew could study the Law.

Besamim – "spice-box"; a decorated container, often in the shape of a tower, to be filled with cinnamon, cloves or any sweet-smelling spices, the scent of which is inhaled to recall the Sabbath.

Bimah – "Platform"; raised dais, usually found in the centre of the synagogue: it is from here that the reading of the Law takes place.

Cantor – person whose function it is to sing parts of the prayer service.

Chanukah – the "Feast of Lights"; festival lasting eight days which commemorates the victory of the Maccabees over the armies of Syria and the return to the Temple. Celebrated by the lighting of candles or lamps.

Chasidism – (in Hebrew "Chasid" means "pious", plural: Chasidim) moral and religious movement, originating in the Podole region of Poland. Ultra-Orthodox in religious matters, traditional in moral matters.

Chazan – see **cantor**.

Cheder (plural: chadarim) – "room"; a religious school for boys aged between 4 and 13.

Chulent – dish made of peas, potatoes, buckwheat, onion and pieces of meat, eaten for **Sabbath** lunch.

Circumcision – ritual removal of the foreskin, a commandment in Judaism performed by a **mohel** when a male child is eight days old.

Dayan – "judge"; leader or member of a religious court.

Gefilte Fish – fish stuffed with **matzah** and vegetables, served cold in jelly, with almonds and raisins.

Gemara – the commentary on the **Mishnah**; together they form the **Talmud**.

Ghetto – "district"; a legally separate area in which Jews lived.

Halachah – "way"; the rules of religious law contained in the **Talmud** and other legal codes.

Haskalah – "enlightenment"; the 18th-century religious and moral movement originating in Germany; it stipulated equal rights for Jews, changes in the liturgy, a secular education, the broadening of professional horizons and the rejection of traditional attire and the **Yiddish** language. Noted in Poland in large cities only.

Havdalah – "separation"; the Saturday evening ceremony which ends the **Sabbath**.

Holocaust – the genocide of the Jews during the Second World War, planned and executed by Nazi Germany and leading to the extermination of some 6 million Jews in death camps between the years 1933–1945. The term "Holocaust" literally means "a completely burned sacrifice". The word **Shoah**, originally a Biblical term meaning "widespread disaster", is the Modern Hebrew equivalent.

Israel – 1. biblical name of the Jewish people; 2. the Jewish State, created in 1948.

Judaism – religion closely related to Jewish tradition and culture. Its most important elements are: the belief in one God, the tradition of the Patriarchs, ethical conduct and the fundamental importance of the Bible (**Torah**) and the **Talmud**, a related commentary.

Kabbalah – "received tradition"; the body of classical Jewish mystical teachings, the central text of which is the **Zohar**.

Kaddish – (in Aramaic "holy"); the prayer for the departed. For a period of eleven months following the death of a parent and on **yortsait** a Jew is required to recite Kaddish in memory of the departed soul.

Kahal, kehilla (plural: kehillot) – the Jewish community council with powers in the following: religion, taxation, legislation, education, charity and welfare. It organised funerals, maintained the cemetery, schools and the **mikvah**, as well as supervising the ritual slaughter and sale of meat.

Kapote – long black coat worn by men.

Kapporet – decoration of the upper part of the Holy Ark.

Kippah – (Hebrew for **Yarmulkeh**); skull-cap.

Kashrut – Jewish dietary laws (see also **kosher**)

Keter Torah – silver adornment in the shape of a crown used to decorate the scrolls of the **Torah**.

Kiddush – "sanctification"; prayer said over a cup of wine at the commencement of the Sabbath and festivals.

Klezmer – musician, playing in a Jewish band made up of instruments such as violin, double-bass, trumpet, drum and dulcimer.

Kloyz – simple wooden, house of prayer used by **Chasidim**. In larger cities it often occupied a room or one floor of a house.

Kosher – "suitable"; food fit for consumption according to religious law. If it does not conform it is **trayf**, and if it does not fall into either category then it is **parve** (neutral). Food may not contain any trace of blood. Only meat from certain animals, ritually slaughtered, may be considered **kosher**. Dairy dishes may not be mixed with meat dishes. Plants are parve.

Kugel – casserole of potato, or rice or pasta, served as a side dish to meat or as a dessert, with fruit, honey and nuts.

Kvitlech – small pieces of paper containing requests, placed by pilgrims at the tombs of great **rabbis** and **tzaddikim**. It is hoped that the deceased will forward these messages to God.

Ladino – Jewish language, related to Spanish, used by **Sephardim**.

Lag B'Omer – joyous festival commemorating the anniversary of the death of Shimon bar Yochai, the alleged author of the Kabbalistic book **Zohar**.

Landsmanshaft – regional community re-created ouside Poland after the Holocaust

Maariv – the evening service.

Matzah (plural: matzot) – "unleavened bread"; eaten instead of ordinary bread throughout the festival of **Pesach**.

Matzevah (plural: matzevot) – "gravestone"; the symbols engraved on them are of particular significance.

Melamed – teacher in a **cheder**.

Menorah (plural: menorot) – seven-branched candelabrum used in religious rituals; also the national symbol of **Israel**.

Mezzuzah (plural: mezzuzot) – small oblong case containing a tiny parchment scroll on which the words of the Shema, one of the most important Jewish prayers, are written. It is placed on the doorframe of a Jewish home, as a constant reminder of God's presence.

Mikvah (plural: mikvaot) – "the gathering of waters"; ritual bath, used for purifying of a person by immersion in spring or rainwater.

Minchah – the afternoon service.

Minyan – "number"; ten adult Jews over the age of **bar mitzvah**. At least this number must be present for a synagogue service to take place.

Mishnah – "repetition" or "study"; name given to the oldest postbiblical codification of Jewish Oral Law. Together with the **Gemara** (later commentaries on the **Mishnah** itself), it forms the **Talmud**.

Mitzvah (plural: mitzvot) – "commandment"; any one of the 613 commandments that a religious Jew is required to observe. May also refer to a religious obligation or a good deed.

Mohel – see **circumcision**.

Ner tamid – the eternal light burning in front of, above or beside the **aron ha-kodesh**.

Ohel (plural: oholot) – "house" or "tent"; a tomb in the shape of a closed chapel. It contains the grave of great **rabbi** or **tzaddik**.

Parochet – the curtain of the **aron ha-kodesh**.

Parve – see **kosher**.

Payes – side-curls worn by Chasidic male Jews.

Pesach – "Passover"; eight-day festival, which commemorates the deliverance of the Children of Israel from Egypt. The last day is the anniversary of the crossing of the Red Sea.

Phylacteries – see **Tefillin**.

Privilegia de non tolerandis... – writ of privileges, usually bestowed by the monarch, regulating where Jews and Christians were allowed to settle. As a rule, it was *de non tolerandis Judaeis*, forbidding Jews to live in a certain place; occasionally it was *de non tolerandis Christianis*, forbidding settlement by Christians, for example, in the Kazimierz district of Cracow.

Purim – popular joyous festival which celebrates the miraculous deliverance of the Jews from the hands of the wicked Haman.

Rabbi – minister and teacher of religion authorised to make decisions regarding issues of Jewish Law.

Rosh Chodesh – the "New Moon"; festival to celebrate the beginning of each new month. (The Jewish year is based on a lunar calendar).

Rosh Hashanah: the Jewish New Year, falling on the 1st and 2nd of Tishri.

Shabbat / Shabbes – (from Shin-Bet-Tav, "to cease, to end, or to rest"); the Sabbath, a day of relaxation and spiritual enrichment to commemorate the rest that the Lord took after creating the world. Shabbat starts just before sunset on Friday and lasts until after sunset on Saturday.

Sephardim – Jews from Spain, Portugal, North Africa and the Middle East and their descendants. They developed several dialects of a language called **Ladino**.

Shacharit – (Hebrew for "dawn"); the morning prayer service.

Shavuot – "weeks"; the Day of Pentecost, receiving of the **Torah**, and the beginning of the wheat harvest. Also, it represents the betrothal between **Israel** and the Lord.

Shalom – "peace"; everyday Hebrew greeting, corresponding to "hello" and "good bye".

Shammes – caretaker of a synagogue, in pre-war Poland also responsible for summoning people to prayer and making sure that shops closed at the appropriate time.

Shoah – see **Holocaust**

Shofar – trumpet made from a ram's horn.

Shtetl (plural: shtetlech) – small Jewish town or village, typical for Poland. It was the social and spiritual centre for a local Jewish community.

Shtibl (plural: shtiblech) – "small room"; prayer room, usually a converted flat, favoured mainly by **Chasidim** for its intimate atmosphere.

Shtreiml – fur hat once worn by male East European Jews, still part of the attire of **Chasidim**.

Shul – (**Yiddish** for "synagogue"), "school"; the word emphasises the importance of the educational function of a house of prayer.

Simchat Torah – "Rejoicing of the Law"; festival closing the annual cycle of the reading of the **Torah**. During the service, all of the **Torah** scrolls are removed from the **aron ha-kodesh** and carried around the synagogue seven times.

Sofer – scribe specially trained to write documents and religious texts such as **Torah** scrolls and **mezzuzot**.

Sukkah (plural: sukkot) – booth, with an opening in the roof through which the sky is visible, erected in the yard or on the balcony of a house during the festival of **Sukkot**.

Sukkot – (Hebrew for tabernacles); festival which commemorates the Israelites' wanderings in the desert after leaving Egypt. It begins on the 15th day of Tishri and lasts seven days.

Synagogue – centre of the Jewish religious community; a place of religious worship, study and education, charitable work, as well as social activities.

Tallit – prayer shawl with symbolic fringes on four corners, worn by men.

Talmud – "Study"; the collection of the most important interpretations of the **Torah**, containing two parts: **Mishnah** and **Gemara**.

Talmud-Torah – school, especially for poor children, continuing the religious education begun in **cheder**.

Tefillin – "phylacteries"; leather boxes containing small scrolls of **Torah** passages, worn at weekday morning services by adult male worshippers. One box is bound to the left forearm and one to the forehead. Like the **mezzuzah**, **tefillin** are meant to remind Jews of God's commandments.

Tempel – Reform synagogue.

Tishah B'Av – "the ninth day of the month of Av"; a day of mourning for the destruction of the ancient Temple in Jerusalem.

Torah – the first five books of the Bible: Genesis, Exodus, Leviticus, Numbers and Deuteronomy, sometimes called the Pentateuch. In a broad sense, the Torah is the entire body of Jewish teachings.

Trayf – see **kosher**.

Tzaddik (plural: tzaddikim) – "Righteous Man"; Chasidic spiritual leader; link between the Lord and those who believe in Him. Tzaddikim created their own "courts", by surrounding themselves with groups of followers. The position of tzaddik was hereditary, and in this way dynasties were formed.

Tzimmes – casserole of cooked carrot, apples and dried fruit, sprinkled with sugar and cinnamon.

Vaad Arba Aratzot – the Diet of the Four Lands; from 1581 the main body of Jewish autonomy in the Polish Commonwealth. The sessions were held twice a year, mostly in Lublin and Jarosław.

Yad – "hand"; decorated pointer with a tiny sculpted hand at the end used when reading from the **Torah**.

Yarmulkeh – "skull-cap"; traditional head covering for Jewish males.

Yeshivah (plural: yeshivot) -"meeting"; religious school for the study of the **Talmud**.

Yiddish – language closely related to German, once the everyday language of the majority of European Jews.

Yizkor – "May He Remember"; prayers for the departed, recited on **Yom Kippur**, Shemini Atzeret, the last day of **Pesach**, the second day of **Shavuot**.

Yom Kippur – "Day of Atonement"; the most important festival in the Jewish calendar. It commemorates the day when Moses come down from Mount Sinai and gave the Ten Commandments to the Children of Israel. A strict fast is observed.

Yortsait – anniversary of a relative's death.

Zionism – ideology formulated by Theodor Herzl at the end of the 19th century in his treatise The Jewish State. It advocated the creation of a Jewish homeland in the historic land of **Israel**.

Zohar – see **Kabbalah**.

Biblical texts are taken from the New King James Bible and the New International Bible.

Photographs and Illustrations

t – top of the page, m – middle of the page, b – bottom of the page
JHI – Jewish Historical Institute

Anna Olej/Krzysztof Kobus:
3, 3m (from the collection of the Old Synagogue in Cracow), 4t1t2 (from the collection of the JHI Museum), 4mb, 5t1 (from the collection of the JHI Museum), 5t2, 5mb (from the collection of the JHI Museum), 6t1 (from the collection of the JHI Museum), 6, 7t (from the collection of the Old Synagogue in Cracow), 7m, 7b (from the collection of the JHI Museum), 9 (from the collection of the JHI Museum), 17b (from the collection of the JHI Museum), 18, 19 (from the collection of the JHI Museum), 20t (from the collection of the JHI Museum), 22b, 24t (from the collection of the JHI Museum), 25b, 26t (from the collection of the Old Synagogue in Cracow), 27 (from the collection of the JHI Museum), 28 (from the collection of the JHI Museum), 30t, 31, 32, 36b, 37, 38 (from the collection of the JHI Museum), 39 (from the collection of the JHI Museum), 41t (from the collection of the Old Synagogue in Cracow), 41b (from the collection of the JHI Museum), 42 (from the collection of the JHI Museum), 43b (from the collection of the JHI), 44t, 44b (from the collection of the JHI Museum), 46t (from the collection of the JHI), 47 (from the collection of the JHI Museum), 48b, 49 (from the collection of the Old Synagogue in Cracow), 51 (from the collection of the JHI Museum), 59, 61, 62, 68, 70, 71t, 72, 74mb (from the collection of the JHI Museum), 75t, 75mb (from the collection of the JHI Museum), 76t, 78, 79, 81t, 82t, 85, 86, 87b, 88, 89, 91, 94b, 95t, 97b, 98b, 99, 100t, 101, 102, 103, 104, 105, 106t, 107b, 108b, 109, 110, 111, 112, 113, 115, 118t (from the collection of the JHI Museum), 119, 120t, 122t, 123b, 124b, 125, 126b, 127, 128t, 129t, 130b, 131, 132, 133, 135, 138, 139b, 140, 141, 142, 143, 145, 146, 147b, 149, 150, 152, 153, 155, 156, 157, 159b, 160, 162, 164t, 166, 167, 169, 170b, 171, 173, 174, 175, 176t, 176b (from the collection of the Pojezierze Łęczyńsko-Włodawskie Museum), 177, 178t, 178b (from the collection of the Pojezierze Łęczyńsko-Włodawskie Museum), 179t (from the collection of the Pojezierze Łęczyńsko-Włodawskie Museum), 179b, 180t, 181, 182, 183b, 184, 185, 186 (from the collection of the Nadwiślańskie Museum), 187, 188, 189, 190b, 192, 193, 196, 197, 199, 200t (from the collection of the Old Synagogue in Cracow), 200b, 201, 202b, 204, 205, 208, 209, 210t, 211, 213, 214, 215, 221b, 222, 224t, 225, 226, 227b, 228, 229t, 230, 231b, 232, 233, 234, 235, 236b, 237m, 237b, 239, 240, 242, 244b, 245, 247, 248, 249, 250, 251, 252, 253, 254, 255, 257, 258, 261b, 262, 263, 264t, 265, 266, 267t, 268, 269, 311 (from the collection of the JHI Museum)

Anna Olej and Krzysztof Kobus wish to thank Andrzej Lechowski, director of the Podlasie Museum in Białystok; Andrzej Szczygieł, director of the Historical Museum in Cracow;

Wit Karol Wojnowicz, director of the Łańcut Castle Museum; Ryszard Czubaczyński, director of the Museum of the History of Łódź; Jerzy Wróblewski, director of the Auschwitz-Birkenau State Museum; the Jewish Community in Cracow; the Jewish Community in Łódź; the Jewish Community in Wrocław; the Jewish Community in Warsaw and the Jewish Historical Institute in Warsaw.

From the collection of the Archive of Audio Visual Records: 63
Jacek Barcz: 52, 71b
From the collection of the State Film Library in Warsaw: 54b
From the collection of the Judaica Foundation – Centre for Jewish Culture: 212b
From the collection of the Shalom Foundation: 16, 25t, 43t, 64, 82b, 92, 95b, 108t, 144, 147t, 165, 180b, 183t, 198, 236t, 243b
From the collection of the Institute of art in Warsaw (H. Poddębski): 148t, 158
From the collection of Ninel Kameraz-Kos: 46b
Grzegorz Kozakiewicz: 10t, 20b, 195, 207b
Bogdan Krężel: 10b, 33, 48t, 50b, 206, 207t, 207m, 231t, 273
Jarosław Kubalski/Agencja Gazeta: 151
From the collection of the Museum of the History of Łódź: 121t (photographer M. Machay)
From the collection of the City Museum in Wrocław: 264b
From the collection of the National Museum in Cracow: 13, 14, 30b, 212t
From the collection of the National Museum in Warsaw: 12t (photographer P. Ligier), 40 (photographer T. Żółtowska-Huszcza), 65t (photographer T. Żółtowska-Huszcza), 172b (photographer T. Żółtowska-Huszcza)
From the collection of the Museum of Art in Łódź: 120b, 121b, 122b
From the collection of the Jewish Historical Institute Museum: 15
Leon Myszkowski: 53t, 191b
Jakub Ostałowski: 217
From the collection of the E.R. Kamińska State Jewish Theatre in Warsaw: 261t
Suren Vardanian: 24b (from the book *Bóżnice Białostocczyzny* by T. Wiśniewski, Białystok 1992)
From the collection of Edward Edwin Śmiłek: 11, 12b, 21t, 26b, 29, 34, 35t, 36t, 45, 53b, 54t, 98t, 106b, 117t, 124t, 128b, 159t, 163, 170t, 172t, 190t, 191t, 202t, 210b, 221g, 237t, 259b, 260, 267b
From the collection of the Local Government Office in Klimontów: 148b
From the collection of Tomasz Wiśniewski: 66, 73b, 94t, 96, 97t, 107t, 116, 123t, 126t, 137, 139g, 161, 168, 227g, 229b, 238, 241, 244g
From the collection of the Jewish Historical Institute: 17g, 21b, 22g, 35b, 50g, 55, 56, 57, 65b, 67, 73g, 74g, 81b, 84, 87g, 93, 100b, 117b, 118b, 129b, 130g, 137, 164b, 224b, 243g, 259g
From private collections: 76b

INDEX

Page numbers referring to the chapter *Practicalities* are marked with italics.

THE "SHALOM" FOUNDATION

"SHALOM" FOUNDATION

The "Shalom" Foundation operates in Poland, but the board members are spread far and wide throughout the world. They were once pupils and friends at the Y. L. Peretz Jewish School in Łódź. Today they live in the United States, Israel and Sweden. They are linked not only by personal friendship but also a feeling of love for, and a duty towards, the Jewish people and their tradition, history, culture and language. This is why as adults they have created this foundation whose symbolic aim may be best expressed in this way: to rescue from oblivion. The voices of the past will then not be only those of sages and writers but also of ordinary people passing the word "Shalom" – "Peace" from generation to generation.

Everything that the "Shalom" Foundation does is directed towards retrieving the past, a fundamental part of which is the history of the Jews of Poland.

The Foundation publishes books of poems and prose by Jewish writers in bi-lingual (Polish-Yiddish) and tri-lingual (Polish-Yiddish-Hebrew) versions. It organises art exhibitions, Jewish song contests, as well as competitions called "The History and Culture of Polish Jews", each one exciting more and more interest, with the number of participants running into thousands.

One of the Foundation's greatest achievements is the exhibition (and accompanying photo album) entitled "And I Still See Their Faces", which for years now has been staged at some of the world's largest galleries. Both the album and the exhibition were made possible thanks to Polish Jews and their neighbours now living all over the world, who had responded to an appeal for pre-war photos and mementos. The organisers hope that this exhibition of exceptional photographs will find a permanent home in the Centre for Yiddish Culture established by the "Shalom" Foundation.

We very much hope that it will become a place in which the whole idea of "Shalom" can best be expressed, by which we mean a vibrant presence of the art, culture and Yiddish language of the Jews of Poland.

We, the founders of the "Shalom" Foundation, have never accepted that the world created by Polish Jews is lost forever. We are determined to save its image not just for sentimental reasons but also out of the conviction that preserving this memory is a task for the future and the accomplishment of the final wishes of generations of Polish Jews dreaming of a Europe and a world free of prejudice, intolerance and xenophobia.

All those of you who wish to participate in the building of this home on the foundations of the past are invited to join us. Let us make sure that the windows open out onto the future.

Gołda Tencer
General Director
of the "Shalom" Foundation

Our address:
Pl. Grzybowski 12/16
00-104 Warsaw, Poland
Tel. +48 22 6203036, 6203037
Fax +48 22 6200559
shalom@shalom.org.pl
jidysz@shalom.org.pl